C3

Karl B Radewald
507 Sixth St
Niles
Mich.

HOYLE'S GAMES

America's Complete Hand-book of Games

CONTAINING ALL THE CARD GAMES PLAYED IN THE UNITED STATES, WITH THEIR RULES, REGULATIONS, TECHNICALITIES, ETC., ADAPTED TO THE AMERICAN MODE OF PLAYING, FROM THE TEXT OF

HOYLE, AND THE BEST MODERN AUTHORITIES

ALSO COMPRISING

BACKGAMMON, CHESS, CHECKERS, BILLIARDS, POOL, BAGATELLE, BOWLS, ETC., WITH NUMEROUS DIAGRAMS AND ENGRAVINGS

COMPLETE EDITION

REVISED, CORRECTED AND ENLARGED

CHICAGO
M. A. DONOHUE & COMPANY

CONTENTS.

CONTENTS.

CONTENTS.

CONTENTS.

HOYLE'S GAMES.

EUCHRE.

The game of Euchre is played with thirty-two cards; all below the denomination of Seven-spot being rejected. Four persons constitute the complement for the game, and partners are determined by dealing and turning up one card to each; those receiving the two lowest cards, and *vice versa*, being associated together.

The value of the cards in Euchre is the same as in All-Fours, and other games, excepting that the Knave of the suit corresponding with the trump is called the *Right Bower*, and is the highest card of the hand; and the other Knave of the same color is called the *Left Bower*, and is the card of second importance. For example: if Hearts should be turned Trump, the Knave of Hearts is the highest card, the Knave of Diamonds second in value, and the Ace, King, Queen, &c., of Hearts then come in their regular order, as at All-Fours. When the Knaves are of the opposite color from the trump card, they rank no higher than at All-Fours.

The players usually cut for deal, and he who cuts the lowest card is entitled to the deal, and that is accomplished by giving the eldest hand, or the first person to the left of the dealer, two cards, and so on all around, and then dealing an additional three cards to each player, in the same order. Regularity should be observed in dealing, and no party should be allowed to receive from the dealer, in any round, more than the number of cards given to the eldest hand. For instance, if the dealer begins by giving the left-hand player two cards, he cannot be allowed to vary, so as to give another three, and then two again, but must continue as he began. The proper manner of dealing is as we pointed out at the outset, and should be rigidly observed.

The advantage which accrues to the dealer is manifest. From the manner in which cards are played in all games, those of a corresponding suit will necessarily fall together, and therefore the dealer enhances his prospects thirty-three and one-third per cent. for an additional trump by dealing three cards last round, for then he has three immediately preceding the trump, when if he had begun the deal with three cards he would end by having only the two cards preceding the trump.

After five cards have deen dealt to each player, in the order as above, the dealer turns up the top card on the pack or talon, which is called the trump. After the firs hand, the deal passes to each player in rotation.

The game consists of five points—the parties getting that number first being the winners—and the points are indicated by the number of tricks taken by the players. If all the tricks are taken by one side it constitutes what is technically termed a *march*, and entitles the fortunate parties to a count of two; and it is necessary to take three tricks in order to count one, or "make a *point*," as it is called. Taking four tricks counts no more than three.

When the trump is turned, the first person to the left of the dealer looks at his cards, for the purpose of determining what he intends to do, whether to "pass" or "order the trump up;" and this, to a certain extent, will depend upon the strength of his hand. If he holds cards of sufficient value to secure three tricks, he will say, "I order it up," and the dealer is then obliged to take the card turned up, and discard one from his hand; and the card thus taken up becomes the trump. If the eldest hand has enough strength to order it up, he will say, "I pass," and then the partner of the dealer has to determine whether he will "pass" or "assist." If he has enough, with the help of the card his partner has turned, to make three tricks, he will say, "I assist," and the card is taken up as before. If he passes, then it goes to the third hand, who proceeds exactly as the eldest hand. Should all the players pass, it becomes the dealer's privilege to announce what he will do, and if he thinks he can take three tricks, he will say, "I take it up," and immediately discard his weakest card, placing it under the remainder of the pack, and instead of the card thus rejected he takes that turned up, which remains the trump. It is not considered *en regle* for the dealer to remove the trump card until after the first trick has been taken, unless he needs it to play. It is let lay, that every one may see what the trump is. We may as well state that it is always the dealer's privilege to discard any one card in his hand, and take up the trump card; and this holds good whether he is assisted by his partner, is ordered up by his adversaries, or takes it up himself. This gives the parties having the deal an advantage about equal to one trick. Should the dealer not be confident of winning three tricks, he says, "I turn it down," and at the same time places the turn-up card face down on the pack. Should all the players decline to play at the suit turned up, and the dealer turn it down, the eldest hand is then entitled to make trump what he chooses (excepting the suit already turned down). If the eldest hand is not strong enough in any suit, and does not wish to make the trump, he can pass again, and so it will go on in rotation, each one having an opportunity to make the trump in his regular turn, to the dealer. If all the players, including the dealer, decline the making of the trump the deal is forfeited to the eldest hand. The eldest hand, after the dealer has discarded, opens the game, and leads any card he chooses. The person playing the highest card takes the trick, and he in his turn is obliged to lead. In this manner the game proceeds, until the five cards in each hand are exhausted. Players are required, under penalty of the loss of two points, to follow suit. If, however, they cannot, they may then throw away a small card or trump at their pleasure.

The Three and Four are used in marking game. The face of the Three being up, and the face of the Four down on it, counts *one*, whether one, two or three pips are exposed, the face of the Four being up, and the Three over it, face down, counts *two*, whether one, two, three, or four of the pips are shown; the face of the Three uppermost counts *three*; and the face of the Four uppermost counts *four*. The Two and Three are now rarely used as counters, being more liable to mistakes.

It may be laid down as one of the general rules of Euchre, that whatever is undertaken by a player must be accomplished, in order to make the point. For instance, if I adopt, or order up the trump, and fail in securing three tricks, it is called being "Euchred," and entitles the opponents to a count of two; or if I make the trump after the original one has been turned down, and do not secure three tricks, I am also "Euchred," and it counts as before. Therefore it will be perceived, that in order to play the game properly one should have, in addition to the ordinary rules, a thorough knowledge of the theory of chances as they apply to this game, and exercise it judiciously.

TECHNICAL TERMS USED IN EUCHRE.

Adopting—Synonyme.—"Taking it up." This is the privilege of the dealer, after the others have passed, to discard an inferior card, and use instead the trump card turned up. The words used are, "I take it up."

Alone.—Playing without the assistance of your partner, when you have a hand which it is probable would take five tricks. The words are, "I play alone," or "Alone." or "Cards away," or "I try it."

Assist.—If, when your partner deals, and the eldest hand passes, you know by your hand alone, or by comparing it with the deck-head, that you can make three tricks, you may say to him, "I assist." This is equivalent to ordering up the trump into his hand, for he thereupon discards his poorest card, and the trump card is his to play when he needs it.

Bower.—The Jack or Knave of the trump suit, and of the suit of the same color.

Bridge.—This is where one side has scored four and the other one or two. When your opponents have one or two and you have four, if you are eldest hand, unless you have one trick certainly in your hand—that is, the right bower, or the left bower guarded—you will order it up whether you have a trump or not, to prevent them going alone, and making four points.

Call.—The right to demand an adversary to play an exposed card.

Coat-Cards.—The Bower, King and Queen, from the fact that they are coated, or dressed.

Court-Cards.—The same as coat-cards.

Cross the Suit.—To make a trump of a different color from the card turned up by the dealer.

Cut.—To separate the shuffled pack into two parts, a right possessed by the right hand opponent.

Deal.—To distribute the cards to which each player is entitled. You give each player five cards, in two rounds, commencing with your left hand opponent. You begin by dealing two cards to each, and then three, or *vice versa*.

Discard.—Putting a card out of the dealer's hand, face down, under pack when he "takes it up" in lieu of the trump card on the deck.

Dutch It.—To make a trump of the color that is turned down.

Eldest Hand.—The left hand adversary of the dealer, so called because he is the first to play.

Euchre.—The failure of that side which makes, orders up, or takes up a trump, to take three tricks; this failure scoring two points to their adversaries.

Face-Cards.—The coat-cards.

Finesse.—This is where a player holding the best and third best trump, plays the latter first, taking the risk that his opponents do not hold the second best trump, or that his partner does. In either case he wins the two tricks.

Force.—To lead a suit of which your opponents hold none, thus obliging them to trump or lose the trick.

Go Alone.—Synonymous with "play alone."

Intimation.—Anything passing from one partner to another, by which the latter knows how to play.

Lay-Card.—Any card other than trump.

Lay-Suit.—Any suit not a trump.

Left Bowsr.—The Knave of the same color as the trump suit.

Left Bower Guarded.—The Left Bower protected by another trump.

Lone Hand.—A hand so strong in trumps alone, or in trumps guarded by high cards of a lay suit, that it will probably win five tricks if its holder plays alone.

Lone Player.—The one playing without his partner.

Lone Game.—Scoring five points to your adversary's none.

Making the Trump.—Naming a new suit for trump after the dealer has turned the trump card down.

March.—Where all the tricks are made by one side.

Next in Suit.—The same as Dutch It.

Numkrical Cards.—Those neither ace nor face.

Ordering Up.—Requiring the dealer and his partner to play the trump as it has been turned.

Partner.—The one joined with you in playing against your adversary. The penalty of the misconduct of one partner falls on both.

Pass.—To decline to play at the trump turned up.

Pass Again.—To decline the privilege of making a new trump after the first has been turned down.

Play Alone.—To play a hand without one's partner.

Point.—One of the five required for the game.

Rank.—The relative power of the cards, commencing and going in trump, as follows: Right Bower, Left Bower, Ace, King, Queen, Ten, Nine, Eight, Seven; but in the Lay Suits the Jacks take place between the Queens and Tens.

Responsible.—The party who orders up a trump, assist, make a trump or take it up.

Revoke.—Playing a card of a different suit from that demanded. This is sometimes vulgarly called renig.

Right Bower.—The Jack of trumps.

Right Bower Followed.—The Right Bower with another trump behind.

Ruffing.—Another term for trumping a suit other than trumps.

Score.—The points gained in a game or rubber.

Sequence.—The numerical succession of cards of the same color.

Side Cards.—Lay Cards.

Slam.—Love game, vulgarly called "a skunk."

Taking it Up.—Indorsing the trump by the dealer, and discarding another card for it, after the rest have passed.

Tenace.—Where the last player holds in his hand the highest and third best of the cards out.

Throw Away.—To play a worthless card when you cannot follow suit and do not desire to trump, as for instance, where it is your partner's trick.

Trump.—The suit turned up, or made the commanding suit.

Trump Card.—The card which is turned up by the dealer after the hands have been dealt around.

Turn Down.—The trump card which is turned face downward on the talon by the dealer after all have passed.

Underplaying.—Following suit and winning with a low card, when you have one in your hand superior to your adversary's.

THE LAWS OF EUCHRE.

SCORING.

1. A game consists of five points. If the side who adopt, make or order up a trump, take—

I. Five tricks, they score two points.
II. Three tricks, they score one point.
III. Four tricks count no more than three.
IV. If they fail to take three tricks they are euchred, and the opposing party score two points.

2. When a player who plays alone takes—

I. Five tricks, he scores four points.
II. Three tricks he scores one point.
III. If he fail to take three tricks he is euchred, and the opposing party score two points.

3, The penalty for a revoke takes precedence of all other scores.

4. An error in count can be rectified at any time before the next deal is completed.

SHUFFLING AND CUTTING.

5. At the outset of the game each player cuts for deal, and the lowest cut deals. If there be a tie, the parties tied cut again. The players cutting the two highest cards play against those cutting the two lowest.

6. In cutting the Ace is lowest, and the other cards rank as at Whist.

7. Should a player expose more than one card, he must cut again.

8. The cards may be shuffled by any player who demands that privilege, but the dealer has always the right to shuffle last.

9. The cards must be cut by the right hand opponent before they are dealt.

10. A cut must not be less than four cards removed from the top, nor must it be made so as to leave less than four cards at the bottom; and the pack must be put on the table for the cut.

DEALING AND DISCARDING.

11. After the first deal, the right of dealing goes to the left.

12. In dealing, five cards must be distributed to each player by the dealer, who may begin by giving first two, and then three cards to each, or *vice versa*; but whichever course is adopted by him must be strictly adhered to until the deal is completed; he must not begin by dealing two to one, three to the next, and so on. When this rule is violated the adverse side may claim a new deal, provided that they have neither of them seen their own hands.

13. A misdeal forfeits the deal, and the following are misdeals:

I. A card too many or too few given to either player.

II. Dealing the cards when the pack has not been properly cut; the claim for a misdeal in this case must be made prior to the trump card being turned, and before the adversaries look at their cards.

14. Whenever a misdeal is attributed to any interruption by adversaries, the deal will not be forfeited. Hence, if an adversary touch his cards during the deal, and the dealer's partner has not done so, no misdeal can be claimed.

[*Case.* A, having misdealt, claimed exemption on the ground of his opponent having interrupted him, by questioning his title. *Decision.*—Claim allowed.]

15.—If, whilst dealing, a card be exposed by the dealer or partner, should neither of the adversaries have touched their cards, the latter may claim a new deal, but the deal is not lost.

16. If, during the deal, the dealer's partner touch any of his cards, the adversary may do the same without losing their privilege of claiming a new deal shovld chance give them that option.

17. If an opponent displays a card dealt, the dealer may make a new deal, unless he or his partner have examined their own cards.

18. If a deal is made out of turn, it is good, provided it be not discovered before the dealer has discarded, and the eldest hand has led.

19. If a card is faced in dealing, unless it be a trump card, a new deal may be demanded, but the right to deal is not lost.

20. If the pack is discovered to be defective, by reason of having more or less than thirty-two cards, the deal is void; but all the points before made are good.

21. The dealer, unlsss he turn down the trump, must discard one card from his hand and take up the trump card.

22. The discard is not complete until the dealer has placed the card under the pack; and if the eldest hand makes a lead before the discard is complete, he cannot take back the card thus led, but must let it remain. The dealer, however, may change the card he intended to discard and substitute another, or he may play alone, notwithsranding a card has been led. After the dealer has quitted the discard card, he cannot take it in hand again under any circumstances.

23. After the discard has been made the dealer must let the trump card remain upon the talon until it is necessary to play it on a trick. After the trump card has been taken in hand, no player has a right to demand its denomination,

but he may ask for the trump suit and the dealer must inform him.

24. Should a player play with more than five cards, or the dealer forget to discard and omit to declare the fact before three tricks have been turned, the party so offending is debarred from counting any points made in that deal, and the deal is lost. Under the above circumstances, should the adverse side win, they score all the points they make.

PLAYING OUT OF TURN, AND EXPOSED CARDS.

25. All exposed cards may be called, and the offending party compelled to lead or play the expossed card or cards when he can legally do so, but in no case can a card be called if a revoke is thereby caused. See Law 39. The following are exposed cards:

I. Two or more cards played at once.

II. Should a player indicate that he holds a certain card in his hand.

III. Any card dropped with its face upwards.

IV. All cards exposed, whether by accident or otherwise, so that an opponent can distinguish and name them.

26. If any player lead out of turn, his adversaries may demand of him to withdraw his card, and the lead may be compelled from the right player, and the card improperly led be treated as an exposed card, and called at any time during that deal; provided that no revoke is thereby caused.

27. If any player lead out of turn and the mislead is followed by the other three, the trick is completed and stands good; but if only the second, or the second and third, have played to the false lead, their cards, on discovery of their mistake, are taken back, and there is no penalty against any one except the original offender, whose card may be called.

28. If any player play out of turn, his opponents may compel him to withdraw his card, and the card improperly played may be treated as an exposed card, and called at any time during that deal, provided no revoke is thereby caused.

29. If any player trump a card in error, and thereby induce an opponent to play otherwise than he would have done, the latter may take up his card without penalty, and may call upon the offender to play the trump at any period of the hand.

30. If two cards be played, or if the player play twice to the same trick, his opponent can elect which of the two shall remain and belong to the trick. Provided, however, that no revoke be caused.

[But if the trick should happen to be turned with five cards in it, adversaries may claim a fresh deal.]

31. If a player, supposing that he can take every trick or for any other reason, throw down his cards upon the table with their faces exposed, the adverse side may call each and all of the cards so exposed, as they may deem most advantageous to their game, and the delinquent party must play the exposed cards accordingly.

THE REVOKE.

32. When a revoke occurs, the adverse party are entitled to two points to their score.

33. If a suit is led, and any one of the players having a card of the same suit shall play another suit to it—that constitutes a revoke. But if the error be discovered before the trick is quitted or before the party having so played a wrong suit or his partner shall play again, the penalty only amounts to the cards being treated as exposed, and being liable to be called.

34. When the player who has made a revoke corrects his error, his partner, if he has played, cannot change his

card played, but the adversary may withdraw his card, and play another if he objects to do so.

35. When a revoke is claimed against adversaries, if they mix their cards, or throw them up, the revoke is taken for granted, and they lose two points.

36. No party can claim a revoke after cutting for a new deal.

37. A revoke on both sides forfeits to neither; but a new deal must be had.

38. If a player makes a revoke, his side cannot count any points made in that hand.

39. A party refusing to play an exposed card on call, forfeits two to his opponents, as in a revoke.

MAKING THE TRUMP, AND PLAYING ALONE.

40. Any player making a trump cannot change the suit after having once named it; and if he should by error name the suit previously turned down, he forfeits his right to make the trump, and such privilege must pass to the next eldest player,

41. A player may only play alone when he adops, orders up or makes a trump; or when his partner assists, orders up or makes a trump. He cannot, however, play alone with a trump he has passed, or with a trump the making of which he has passed; nor can he play alone after a lead has been made by himself or by his opponents.

42. A player cannot play alone when he or his partner is ordered up by an opponent, or when the opposite side adopts or makes the trump. Only those can play alone who have legally taken the responsibility of the trump and may be euchred; therefore, when one player elects to play alone, neither of his opponents may play alone against him.

43. When a player having the right to play alone elects to do so, his partner cannot supersede him and play alone instead.

[In saying "I go it alone," when it is his turn to settle the game and confirm, or make the trump, as the case may be, the partner binds the adversaries, and consequently binds himself and his partner. It is not a question between the partner, but between the partner and the opposing players. The partner, by confirming the trump and declaring to play alone, has settled the game and cut off the opponents right who is third man. It follows that, as he has been allowed to do this, his action must have at the same time cut off the right of his own partner to change the game. It would be a change for him to substitute himself for the player who has declared to go alone. Whenever this declaration is made by the player who has the "say," it creates an obligation on the other side to play against a lone hand, and on his part to play the lone hand. This obligation his partner cannot be permitted to break.]

44. When a player announces that he will play alone, his partner must place his cards upon the table, face downwards, and should the latter expose the face of any of his cards, either by accident or design, his opponents may compel him to play or not to play with his partner, at their option.

45. A player who goes alone must announce his intention in a clear and audible way and tone, so that no doubt can be entertained of his design. If he expresses his purpose in a vague and ambiguous manner, so that it is not clearly understood by his adversaries, and he or they make a lead, he forfeits his privilege, and must play with his partner.

INTIMATION BETWEEN PARTNERS.

46. If a partner indicates his hand by word or gesture to his partner, directs him how to play, even by telling him to follow the rules of the game, or in any way acts unfairly, the adversary scores one point.

47. If a player, when they are at a bridge, calls the attention of his partner to the fact, so that the latter orders up, the latter forfeits the right to order up, and either of the opponents may play alone, if they choose so to do.

["What are trumps?" "Draw your card." "Can you not follow suit?" "I think there is a revoke?" The above remarks, or those analogous, are the only ones allowed to be used, and they only by the person whose turn it is to play.

48. No player has a right to see any trick but the last one turned.

ON ADOPTING OR TAKING UP THE TRUMP.

As to what constitutes a sufficient force of cards to take the trump up, is a matter of considerable importance to the player. The purpose being to make a point, of course there must be a reasonable probability of taking three tricks, and this probability should be made, to a certain extent, dependent upon the position of the game. If the dealer should be three or four on the score, while the opponents are one or two, the deal might be passed by turning the trump down, and still the chances of gaining the game be not materially reduced; but if the position should be reversed, then the dealer would be warranted in attempting the hazard upon a light hand, as the prospects of defeat with the deal in his favor would be no greater than the percentage of the same against him. Of course any player would know that his success would be beyond peradventure, if holding both Bowers and the Ace. The moment you attempt to point out what anything less would avail, you depart from the scope of argument, predicated upon substantial bases, to the unsubstantial realms of hypothesis. Anything less than both Bowers and the Ace *might* be euchred, and the plodding player who exhausted his time in the search of absolute certainty might be beaten a hundred times by the cards which he had rejected. It is generally accepted as "sound doctrine," that three trumps—two of them being Court cards, backed by a lay ace—is sufficient to attempt a point. The player must note the state of the game, and act accordingly. If the game stand four and four, it is better for him to take up the trump on a small hand than to leave it for his adversaries to make. Suppose the game is three and three, he should be very careful of adopting the trump on a weak hand, because a euchre puts his opponents out.

ON PASSING AND ORDERING UP.

No prudent player will "order" the trump unless he holds enough to render his chances of success beyond reasonable doubt. There are times and positions of the game when, however, there would be no imprudence in ordering up upon a light hand; for instance, supposing the game to stand four and four, the dealer turns the trump, and either the eldest or third hand has an ordinary good show of cards, with nothing better of another suit, there it would be proper to order up, for should the trump be turned down, your chances of success would be lost, and in case you are euchred, it would but give the game to those who would win it anyhow at another suit.

If the position of the player is eldest hand, and a suit should be turned in which he receives both Bowers and another large trump, and he has also two cards of the corresponding suit in color, it would clearly be his policy to pass, for the obvious reason that if the dealer's partner snould assist, he would be enabled to euchre the opposing side, and if the trump were turned down, his hand would be just as good in the next suit; and having the first opportunity of makig the trump, he could go it alone, with every probability of making the hand and scoring four.

Should the eldest hand hold the Right Bower, Ace or King, and another small trump, and a card of the same color as the trump suit, it would be good play to pass; for if the adversaries adopt the trump, he will, in all probability euchre them; and if they reject it, he can make the trump the next in suit, and the chances of scoring a point are in his favor.

When a player is four ana holds commanding trumps sufficient to make a sure point, he should order up, particularly if he is eldest hand, for then he will take his opponent's deal.

As a general rule the eldest hand should not order up the trump, unless he has good commanding cards, say, Right Bower, King and Ten of trumps, with a lay Ace of a different color, or Left Bowsr, King and two numerical trumps. The player at the right of the dealer should hold a very strong hand to order up the trump, because his partner has evinced weakness by passing, and if the opposing side turn down the trump, his partner has the first say to make a new trump.

ON MAKING THE TRUMP.

If the dealer turns the trump down, the eldest hand has the privilege of making it what he pleases, and the rule to be generally followed is, if possible, to Dutch it, *i. e.*, to make it next in suit, or the same color of the trump turned. The reason for this is very evident. If Diamonds should be the trump turned, and the dealer refuse to take it up, it would be a reasonable supposition that neither of the Bowers were in the hands of the opponents; for if the dealer's partner had held one of them, he would in all probability have assisted; and the fact of its being turned down by the dealer also, raises the presumption that he had neither of them. Then, in the absence of either Bower, an oth rwise weak hand could make the point in the same color. For reverse reasons, the partner of the dealer would cross the suit, and make it Clubs or Spades; as his partner had evidenced weakness in the red suit by turning a red card down, it would be but fair to presume that his strength was in the black.

Be careful how you make the point when your adversaries have scored three points, and, as a general rule, do not make or order up a trump unless you are eldest hand or the dealer's partner.

ON ASSISTING.

"Assisting" is where your partner is the dealer, and, with the help of the card he has turned trump, you deem your hand sufficient to take three tricks. In other words, suppose the Ace of Hearts to be turned, and you hold the Left Bower and King; you say to your partner, "I assist," and then he is obliged to take up the Ace turned and discard, the same as though he had taken it up voluntarily. Two Court-cards are considered a good assisting hand; but where the game is very close, of course it is advisable to assist, even upon a lighter hand; for if the game stands four and four, the first hand will order up if the card turned is the best in his hand, and therefore the fact of his passing would be an evidence of weakness.

When assisted by your partner, and you hold a card next in denomination to the card turned up (whether higher or lower), play it as opportunity offers. For instance, if you turn up the Ace, and hold either the Left Bower or King, when a chance occurs play the Bower or King, and thus inform your partner that you have the Ace remaining. The same policy should be adopted when your partner assists and you have a sequence of three trumps, the trump card being the smallest of the three, in such a situation inveriably play the highest card of the sequence, this will inform your partner that you hold the balance of the sequence, and with this knowledge he can shape his play to suit circumstances. Supposing the King is turned up and you hold the Queen and Ten Spot, when an occasion presents itself play the Queen, and if pour partner is *au fait* at the game he will know you have the Ten Spot in your hand.

As a general rule, always assist when you can take two tricks.

ON THE LONE HAND.

There is still another privilege allowed the nolder of a good hand, and that is to play it alone. If from the fullness of your hand there is a reasonably possibility that you can secure all the tricks, you play it alone, or without the assistance of your partner, and if successful, you are entitled to a score of four points,

In order to avail yourself of the privilege of going alone, it is necessary that you should assume the responsibility of the trump; that is, you must adopt, order up, or make the trump; or your partner must assist, order up, or make the trump; but you cannot play alone with a trump you have passed, or with a trump the making of which you have passed. Having complied with the above requirements, there is no abridgement to the right to play alone, except when the attempt has been anticipated by your adversay ordering up the trump, which a prudent player will always do in certain positions of the game. (See "the Bridge.") Should your partner announce that he will play alone, you cannot supersede him and play alone yourself, but must place your cards upon the table, face downwards, no matter how strong your hand may be. You must also bear in mind, that order to avail yourself of the privilege of playing alone, it is necessary to declare your intention of doing so distinctly and in plain terms, thus: "I play alone;" if you fail to do this and the adverse side make a lead, you forfeit all claim to the privilege. You must also be careful and make the announcement, in good season; if you neglect to do so, and the adverse side make a lead, or if you lead yourself before declaring your intention of playing alone, you lose the the right, and your opponents may compel you to play with your partner.

Some players mey have an absurd notion that one side may play alone against the other, and in case of the failure of the original player to take three tricks, that the adverse side may score four points. This is, however, directly opposed to the axiom in euchre, that only those can play alone that take the responsibility of the trump, and incur the chance of being euchred.

In playing a lone hand it is always a great advantage to have the lead. The next advantage is to have the last play on the first trick, therefore the eldest hand and the dealer may assume the responsibility of playing alone on a weaker hand than either of the other players.

When your opponent is playing alone, and trumps a suit you or your partner leads, be sure and throw away all cards of that suit upon his subsequent leads, provided you do not have to follow suit.

When opposing a lone hand and your partner throws away high cards of any particular suit, you may be sure he holds good cards in some other suit; you should therefore retain to the last the highest card of the suit he throws away (if you have one) in preference to any other card, unless it be an ace of some suit.

THE BRIDGE.

If one side has scored four and the other one, such position is called a "bridge," and the following rule should be observed:

To make the theory perfectly plain, we will suppose A and B to be playing against C and D, the former being four in the game and the latter but one. C having dealt, B first looks at his hand, and finds he has but one or two small trumps; in other words a light hand at this stage of the game it would be his policy to order up the trump, and submit to being euchred, in order to remove the possibility of C or D playing it alone; for if they should by good fortune happen to succeed, the score of four would give them the game; when, if it were ordered up, the most that could be done would be to get the euchre, and that giving but a score of two, the next deal, with its percentage, would in all probability give A and B enough to make their remaining point and go out. If, however, B should have enough to prevent a lone hand, he can pass as usual, and await the result. The Right Bower or Left Bower guarded is sufficient. to block a lone hand.

The eldest hand is the only one who should order up at the bridge, for if he passes, his partner may rest assured that he holds commanding cards sufficient to prevent the adversaries making a lone hand. If, however, the eldest hand passes, and his partner is tolerably strong in trumps, the latter may then order up the trump to make a point and go out, for by the passing of the eldest hand his partner is informed that he holds one or more commanding trumps, and may therefore safely play for the point and game.

The eldest hand should always order up at the bridge when not sure of a trick; the weaker his hand, the greater the necessity for doing so.

ON DISCARDING.

When the dealer takes the trump up before the play begins, it is his duty to discard or reject a card from his hand, in lieu of the card taken up. We will suppose the Ten of Hearts to be turned, and the dealer holds the Right Bower, with the Ace and Nine Spot of Clubs and King of Diamonds; the proper card to reject would be the King of Diamonds, for there would be no absolute certainty of its taking a trick. The Ace might be held by the opponents, and by retaining the Ace and Nine spot of of Clubs, the whole suit of Clubs might be exhausted by the Ace, and then the Nine Spot would be good; or, if the trump should be one of the red suits, and the dealer held three trumps and a Seven of Spades and a Seven of Hearts, it would be better to discard the Spade, for, as the dealer's strength was in the red suit, the probabilities would be that the other side would be correspondingly weak, and and therefore the Heart would be better than the Spade. Where you have two of one suit and one of another to discard from, always discard the suit in which you have one card, for then you may have an opportunity to "ruff."

THE LEAD.

We have seen that the game is opened by the eldest hand leading, and much depends upon this feature of the game.

Where a dealer has been assisted, it is a common practice to lead through the assisting hand, and frequently results favorably; for, in the event of the dealer having but the trump turned, a single lead of trump exhausts his strength, and places him at the mercy of a strong suit of lay cards. It is not, however, always advisable to lead a trump, for if the eldest hand holds a tenace, his duty is to maneuvre so as to secure two tricks; but this is only an exceptional case. The proper method of determining the nature of the lead is indicated by the quality of the hand and the purpose to be accomplished. The eldest hand, holding two Aces and a King with two small trumps, of course would lead trump through an assisting hand, for the reason that the only hope of securing a euchre would be dependent upon the success of the lay suits, and they only can be made available after the trumps have been exhausted.

Where the dealer takes the trump voluntarily, the eldest hand is of course upon the defensive, and to lead trump under such circumstances would be disastrous.

Should your partner have the Right Bower turned, lead a small trump; by so dong you will be sure to weaken your adversary's hand.

When your partner makes the trump or orders it up, lead him the *best* trump you hold. Do this in any case.

When you hold the commanding cards they should be led to make the *march;* but if you are only strong enough to secure your point, side cards should be used; put the lowest on your partner's lead, if it be a commanding card; the highest on your adversary's.

When opposed to a lone hand, always lead the best card you have of a lay suit, so that the possibility of your partner's retaining a card of the same suit with yourself may be averted; particularly if it is a card of opposite color from the trump, for if a red card should be trump and an opponent played it alone, there would be more probability of his not having five red cards than of his holding that number, and the further chance that if he did hold five red cards, it would, in like proportion, reduce the probability of your partuer having one of the same suit, and give him an opportunity to weaken your opponent's hand by trumping it.

The exception to the abov rule is, when you hold two or three cards of a suit, including Ace or King, and two small cards in other suits; in this case your best play would be to lead one of the latter and save your strong snit, for the reason that your partner may hold commanding cards in your weak suits, and thus you give him a chance to make a trick with them, and if this does not occur, you have your own strong suit in reserve, and may secure a trick with it.

When playing to make a lone hand, always lead your commanding trump cards first, reserve your numerical trumps and lay suit for the closing leads. When you have exhausted your commanding trumps, having secured two tricks, and retain in your hand a numerical trump and two cards of a lay suit, lead the highest of the lay suit to make the third trick, then your trump. For instance, suppose Hearts are trumps, and you hold the Right and Left Bowers and Ten of Trumps, and Ace and Nine of Spades, lead your Bowers, then the Ace of Spades, following with the Ten of Trumps and your lay Nine. The reason for playing thus is obvious. You *may not* exhaust your adversaries' trumps by the first two leads, and if either of them were to retain a trump card superior to your Ten, by leading the latter you would, in all probability, suffer the mortification of being euchred on a lone hand. For example—we will suppose one of your opponents holds the Queen, Seven and Eight of trumps, with a small Diamond and Club, or two of either suit; he would play the small trumps on your Bowers, and if you led the Ten of trumps he would capture it with his Queen, and lead you a suit you could not take. Your chance of escape from such a dilemma would be very small. On the other hand, if on your third lead you were to lead the lay Ace, you would force your adversary to play his remaining trump, and allow you to win the point.

When you hold three small trumps and good lay cards and desire to euchre your opponents, lead a trump, for when trumps are exhausted you may possibly make your commanding lay cards win.

When you make the trump next in suit, always lead a trump, unless you hold the tenace of Right Bower and Ace, and even then it would be good policy to lead the Bower, if you hold strong lay cards.

When you hold two trumps, two lay cards of the same suit, and a single lay card, lead one of the two lay cards, for you may win a trick by trumping the suit of which you hold none, and then, by leading your second lay card, you may force your opponents to trump, and thus weaken them. With such a hand it would not be good play to lead the single lay card, for you might have the good fortune to throw away on your partner's trick, and ruff the same suit when led by your opponents.

When your partner has made or adopted the trump, it is bad play to win the lead, unless you are the fortunate possessor of a hand sufficiently strong to play for a march.

If your partner assists you and has played a trump, and you have won a trick and the lead, do not lead him a trump unless you hold commanding cards, and are pretty certain of making the old trick or a march, for your partner may have assisted on two trumps only, in which case such a lead would draw his remaining trump, and, in all probability, prove fatal to his most cherished plans.

When you have lost the first two tricks and secured the third, if you hold a trump and a lay card, play the former, for in this position of the game it is your only chance to make or save a euchre. There are only two exceptions to this rule, viz: when you have assisted your partner, or when he has adopted the trump and still retains the trump card in his hand. In the former instance you should lead the lay card, trusting to your partner to trump it; in the latter case, you should also lead the lay card, unless your trump is superior to your partner's and your lay card is an Ace or a King, in which case you should play trump, and trust to the lay card to win the fifth trick. The reason for this play is very manifest: if your opponents hold a better trump than you, it is impossible to prevent them winning the odd trick, and therefore, the euchre or point; but if they hold a smaller trump, your lead ex hausts it, and you may win the last trick with your lay card. This position frequently occurs in the game, and we recommend it to the attention of the novice.

TRUMPS.

In the game of euchre, nothing is more important than the judicious employment of trumps, and the successful issue of the game is, perhaps, more dependent upon a thorough knowledge of their power and use than all other points of the game combined. In the course of this article we have already had much to say about trumps, particularly in that portion which treats of the lead, but if our readers will permit, we propose to briefly notice one subject which has remained untouched—that of trumping, or ruffing, as it is technically termed; and if our ideas on the subject will prove of any service to the tyro in the game, we shall have accomplished all we designed, both by this and other portions of the present article.

If your partner adopts or makes the trump, and you hold the Right or Left Bower alone, ruff with it as soon as you get the opportunity.

When playing second, be careful how you ruff a card of a small denomination the first time round, for it is an even chance that your partner will take the trick if you let it pass. When such a chance presents itself, throw away any single card lower than an Ace, so that you may ruff the suit you throw away when it is led.

When your partner assists and you hold a card next higher to the turn-up card, ruff with it when an opportunity occurs, for by so doing you convey valuable information to your partner.

When you are in the position of third player, ruff with high or medium trumps. This line of play forces the high trumps of the dealer, as at the game of whist, and thereby you weaken your adversaries.

When your partner leads a lay Ace, and you have none of the suit, do not trump it, but if you have a single card, throw it away upon it.

CONCLUDING HINTS.

Never lose sight of the state of the game. When you are four and four, adopt or make the trump upon a weak hand.

When the game stands three to three, hesitate before

adversary may pass again or make a trump (which, as a general rule, should be next in suit); if he pass a second time, the dealer has the right to make a trump or again pass, in which case the cards are to be bunched, and the deal passed to the original non-dealer.

If the dealer takes up the trump and plays the hand, he must win three tricks to make a point; or should he take the five tricks, he make makes a "march," which entitles him to score two points. Should he fail to make three tricks he is euchred, and his adversary counts two points. The same rules apply to the party ordering up or making the trump.

In passing or ordering up, much will depend upon the state of the game, and what the player desires to accomplish; he may pass upon a good hand, when he has reason to believe that by so doing he will euchre his adversary, should he play the hand. In this case, too, he should have good reason to suppose that his adversary will take up the trump, or else have cards to make the trump himself.

The player, remembering that he has but a single hand to contend against, may play or order up, if he has reasonable hope of making three tricks.

Lead your strongest trumps first, until you have won two tricks, and then, having a trump left, lead some other card, so that if your adversary takes it, you may have a chance to trump the card he leads, and thus make your point. Having won two tricks, and your adversary being without a trump, play for a *march* by leading trumps or your highest cards.

The deal is considered equal to a point, therefore never pass the deal unless to save a euchre.

Having discarded, you have no right to take the card back and discard another, even though you have made a mistake. Your opponent must profit by your mistakes, as well as by your bad play or weak hand.

you adopt or make a trump upon a weak hand, for euchre will put your adversaries out.

When you are one and your opponents have scored four, you can afford to try and make it alone upon a weaker hand than if the score was more favorable to you.

When you are eldest hand and the score stands four for you and one for your opponents, do not fail to order up the trump, to prevent them from going alone. Of course you need not do this if you hold the Right Bower, or the Left Bower guarded.

Be very careful how you finesse or underplay; skilful players may attemp this in critical positions, but as a general rule the tyro should take a trick when he can.

Never trump your partner's winning cards, but throw your losing and single cards upon them.

When second hand, if compelled to follow suit, head the trick if possible; this greatly strengthens your partners' game.

EUCHRE WITH THE JOKER.

A euchre pack is usually accompanied by a specimen blank card, which has given rise to this amusing variety of the game of euchre. It is called "the Joker," or highest trump card, and ranks above the Right Bower. If this "Joker" should happen to be turned for trump, the dealer has the privilege of naming any suit he pleases for trump. In all other particulars the game is played in the same manner as the regular game of euchre.

TWO-HANDED EUCHRE.

In this, as in the four-handed game, the deal being made, the non-dealer may pass or order up; should he pass, the dealer, at his option, may pass or discard and take up the trump, when the game begins by the lead of the non-dealer; but should the dealer think his hand not strong enough to risk a play, he too will pass, when his

The rules of the four-handed game apply equally to two handed euchre.

THREE-HANDED EUCHRE.

This game, as its name indicates, is played by three persons, and as each one plays for himself, and is therefore opposed by two adversaries, the game requires closer attention. and the exercise of more judgment than any of the other euchre games.

This variety of the game of euchre is, of course, in almost all points, identical with the four-handed game; although the object of the players each being opposed to the other two become greatly modified by circumstances. The only point of difference is in the *march*, which gives the successful player three points following the analogy of the four-handed game, where a lone hand counts four—and the two-handed game, where a march counts two, one for each player.

In two-handed euchre the player may stand upon a slight hand, but not so in this game; to stand or order up he must have a good hand, inasmuch as he has two hands combined against him, and should he be euchred, both adversaries count two.

Another important feature of the game is, that the play varies according to the stage of the game; for example—at the beginning of the game each player strives to make all he ean for himself; at the first play the dealer makes a *march*, and counts three; the next dealer makes one point, and the third dealer one; the first dealer again deals and turns down the trump, No. 2 passes and No. 3 makes the trump and a point; the game now stands thus:

Dealer No. 1, ...	3 points.
" " 2, ...	1 point.
" " 3, ...	2 points.

No. 2 now has the deal, and should he be euchred, No. 1 wins the game; therefore, while No. 1 plays to win the game by a euchre, No. 3 plays to let the dealer make a point, which would make the game stand thus:

No. 1,	. . . .	3 points.
" 2,	. . . .	2 points.
" 3,	. . . .	2 points.

The deal is now with No. 3, and he will play to make a a march and go out; No. 1 will oppose, and if possible, euchre No. 3, which would of course put him out. It is, however, evidently the policy of No. 2 to prevent the euchre, and allow No. 3 to gain a point, that each may have another chance to win the game. No. 1 and No. 3 are now both three and No. 1 deals, but not having a strong hand and fearing a euchre, he turns down the trump. No. 2 *makes* the trump and a point, his adversaries playing to prevent him making a march. Each player is now three. and No. 2 deals; but as all are anxious to win the game without dividing the honor or profit, the dealer is permitted to make a point, but not a march, if his opponents can prevent it.

No. 3 next strives to win by a march, but, as in the last case, his adversaries play to prevent him making more than one point, and the same strife occurs when No. 1 deals.

Now, as each player is four, the game must terminate with the next deal, so that the dealer must either make his point or be euchred, in which case both his adversaries win, and therefore on the last deal both non-dealers play the strength of their combined game against the common enemy, and thus beat him if they can. The dealer, however, has a remedy against a defeat, which is in this: if, upon examining his hand, he believes he cannot make a point, he can pass, and thus throw the deal elsewhere, thus having one more chance to win, and the same policy may be pursued by each player, until the game is played out. If two players go out together in consequence of a euchre, the elder hand of the two wins.

SET-BACK EUCHRE.

This game may be played by two or more persons, and is governed by the same rules as ordinary euchre, except in the manner of counting, as hereinafter explained. It is quite amusing and exciting, especially when played for money.

Suppose four persons sit down to play, and agree that the pool shall be one dollar; each one contributes twenty-five cents. At the beginning of the game each player is five, and now the struggle commences to wipe out these scores and thus win the game. Each player plays for himself, and all are combined against him who orders up or plays the hand. Should any one not win a single trick, he has one point added to his score, and whoever is euchred is obliged to put another quarter into the pool, and has two points added to his score.

The player who thinks he cannot take a trick has the right to throw up his hand, and thus save himself from being *set back.* The player who is the first to reduce his score to nothing wins the game and the pool.

A *march* counts from two to six points, corresponding with the whole number of players in the game.

The above is the game of set-back euchre pure and simple, but various modifications are frequently introduced. The following are the most popular of these:

After a trump is made, ordered up, or taken up, should any player deem himself possessed of a sufficient force of trumps to make a march, he will say, "I declare,"—which signifies he will play to make all the tricks—and if he is successful in making the march, he wins the game and pool, no matter how many points are scored against him. Should he, however, be unsuccessful in the undertaking, he forfeits double the number of points against him, and in addition must pay in the pool the penalty of a euchre. For instance, if a player stands with seven points to go, and *declares* without making the march, he must be "set back" to fourteen points, and pay a quarter to the pool. The player who declares to make a march has the privilege of the lead, aud becomes eldest hand, unless he be the dealer; but if the dealer declares, he does not have that privilege. In some circles it is customary for the unsuccessful players to pay the winner of the pool a certain sum (previously agreed upon) for each point they have to go when the game is concluded; this is not however considered a rule to be strictly followed, but may be left to the option of the players.

Another variety of this game is played as follows: When the party adopting, making, or ordering up the trump is euchred, he is set back two points, while his adversary scores two, as in the ordinary game.

SIXTY-SIX.

This is a German game, but has gained much fame in the United States, from the fact that it is very scientific, and it may be considered in the first rank among games.

Twenty-four cards are used, viz: The Ace, Ten, King, Queen, Jack and Nine of each suit. The cards are valued as in the order named above, trumps of course being the superior suit.

In cutting for deal, Ace is high and the Ten next, and so on in accordance with their value in the game.

The cards are shuffled by the dealer and cut by the

eldest hand. Six cards are then dealt, three at a time, and the trump turned as in Euchre. Misdeals are dealt over again by the same dealer. A peculiar feature of the game is that the player who holds the nine of trumps may exchange it at any time (after he has taken a trick), at his option, for the trump card turned up.

The eldest hand leads first, but afterwards the winner of the trick has the lead. After each trick, each player takes a card from the top of the pack, in rotation, the winner taking the first card and the loser the next; this continues until the pack is exhausted or one of the players closes or shuts down, as it is sometimes called. (See terms used in Sixty-Six.)

The game is seven points, and they are made in the following manner: The player scoring sixty-six first is entitled to one point, but if he should score sixty-six before the other players have scored thirty-three, then he is entitled to two points, or if his opponents should not take a trick, then he is allowed three points.

The cards count as follows: Each Ace, eleven; each Ten, ten; each King, four; each Queen, three; each Jack, two.

If at any time after he has taken a trick, the player has a King and Queen in the same suit in his hand, he may declare them by leading one of them out and showing the other, this enitles him to twenty points. If they are the King and Queen of trumps, they count forty.

The player who obtains sixty-six first announces the fact, and that closes the round; but if he should claim sixty-six and his cards do not show that number, he forfeits two points to his opponent.

THE RULES OF SIXTY-SIX.

1. After the game is closed or shut down, no more cards can be drawn from the pack. and if the player who shut

down fails to make sixty-six, his opponent scores two points.

2. If a player should shut down before his opponent has taken a trick, and then fails to make sixty-six, his opponent is entitled to three points.

3. Before the game is shut down and the pack is exhausted, neither player is compelled to follow suit, but is at liberty to play any card he pleases, but after the shut-down, each player must not only follow suit but is compelled to take each trick that he can, no throw-offs being allowed, and if he cannot follow suit must trump. Any failure to observe this rule forfeits the count on that hand and adds two points to his opponents score.

4. Players may examine the last trick taken, but no others.

5. When sixty-six is declared, all unemployed cards are void, and the round is ended.

6. If at the end of a round, each player counts sixty-five points, neither score; but the one who wins the next round is allowed one point in addition to what he may then make.

7. If a player should have dealt to nim the Ace, Ten, King and Queen of trumps he may lay down his hand and claim three points, as these cards count sixty-eight.

8. The discarding of the nine of trumps for any other card must be done before the last card in the pack is drawn.

9. If the trump be turned down, the exchange must be made before another card is played.

10, Marriages can be announced only when it is the announcers lead.

11. Marriages can be announced after the shut-down or after the pack is exhausted.

FORTY-FIVE.

Forty-Five can be played by two or four persons, with a pack of fifty-two cards. Five cards are dealt to each player, by twos and threes, or *vice versa*, and the next card is turned for trump, as at euchre. The deal passes to the left, each player in rotation.

The following tables will show the rank of the cards when trumps, or when not:

THE RANK OF THE CARDS WHEN TRUMPS.

Clubs and Spades.	*Diamonds.*	*Hearts.*
Five,	Five,	Five,
Knave,	Knave,	Knave,
Ace of Hearts,	Ace of Hearts,	Ace,
Ace,	Ace,	King,
King,	King,	Queen,
Queen,	Queen,	Ten,
Two,	Ten,	Nine,
Three,	Nine,	Eight,
Four,	Eight,	Seven,
Six,	Seven,	Six,
Seven,	Six,	Four,
Eight,	Four,	Three,
Nine,	Three,	Two. 13 in all
Ten. 14 in all,	Two. 14 in all.	

THE RANK OF THE CARDS WHEN NOT TRUMPS.

Clubs and Spades.	*Diamonds.*	*Hearts.*
King,	King,	King,
Queen,	Queen,	Queen,
Knave,	Knave,	Knave,
Ace,	Ten,	Ten,

Two,	Nine,	Nine,
Three,	Eight,	Eight,
Four,	Seven,	Seven,
Five,	Six,	Six,
Six,	Five,	Five,
Seven,	Four,	Four,
Eight,	Three,	Three,
Nine,	Two,	Two. 12 in all.
Ten. 13 in all	Ace. 13 in all.	

From these tables it will be observed that the Five is first and the Jack second in rank when trumps, and that the Ace of Hearts is always trump, and ranks as the third best card. The holder of the Five or Knave has the privilege of revoking when it suits him to do so; that is, he may retain the Five or Knave of trumps in hand, although trump be led, and the holder of the Ace of Hearts has also the privilege of revoking from any trump card but the Five or Knave; but in all other cases the players must follow suit when trumps are lead, under penalty of forfeiting the game. The largest trump always forces the smaller, as in the game of *Spoilt Five;* thus the Knave of trumps unguarded *must* be played upon the Five of trumps. The Ace of Diamonds, which is fourth in order when that suit is trumps, is the lowest when not trumps. The usual rank of the inferior card is reversed in the black suits, the the Two being above the Three, the three above the Four, and so on, the Ten ranking lowest, whether trumps or not.

When a lay suit is led, the players must follow suit or trump.

The King or Ace, when turned up by the dealer, counts five. Any person holding the King of trumps must, when it comes to his turn to play, lay out a card for it; and if the Ace should not be in play, the trump turned up is his. Should the Ace be out, the turned up trump belongs to its holder, and he who holds the King takes up the card he laid out. This is called "robbing the trump." The lead commences at the eldest hand, and each trick taken counts five. The game consists of forty-five, and the player or players (if partners) first scoring that number, win the stakes.

ROUNCE.

Rounce, as played in the United States, is taken from the German game of *Ramsch*, and in its principles features resembles Division Loo.

Rounce is played with fifty-two cards, which rank as at Whist. The deal is determined by cutting, and the player who cuts the lowest card is entitled to the deal. In cutting the Ace is low. Five cards are dealt to each player by two's and three's, as in the game of euchre, and an extra hand of six cards is dealt in the centre of the table which is called *dumby*.

The dumby must be dealt before the dealer takes the full complement of cards himself, and should be filled immediately preceding his own hand. When the cards have been dealt in the manner described, the dealer turns up the top card on the pack, which is the trump. After the first hand, the deal passes to the left. The game consists of fifteen points, which number is scored with three crosses, in the following manner: X X X. Each cross represents five points. When a player makes one point, he rubs out the centre of the cross, thus: X, and when he makes another point he rubs out one of the remaining portions of the cross, and so on until all are wiped out.

After the ceremony of the deal has been concluded, the dealer asks each player in regular succession, beginning with the eldest hand—*i. e.*, the player immediately to the left of the dealer—what he will do, whether he will stand his hand, take dumby, or decline playing for that round. The eldest hand has first privilege of taking dumby, and if he elects to do so, he must place his hand in the centre of the table, face down, and discard one card from his new hand. If he declines to take dumby then the option passes to the next player, and so in succession to the dealer.

Whoever takes dumby must play it. Any player who thinks he cannot take a trick may decline to play his hand. When all refuse to play then the player at the *right* of the dealer must play his hand, take dumby, or in default of doing either, give the dealer five points. The dealer may discard any card in his hand and take in hand the card turned up for trump.

Each trick taken in play counts one point, and if a player fail to take a trick after entering to play his hand, he is *Rounced*, that is sent up five points, which adds a X to his score.

In this game suit must be followed: but if this is not possible, a player may trump or not, at his option. The winner of a trick must lead a trump, if he can; if however, he holds no trump, he may lead any card he chooses. If the dealer make a misdeal, he is rounced, and loses his deal. A player is also rounced if he fail to follow suit when he can, or to lead a trump after taking a trick, when it is possible for him to do so.

The German game *Ramsch*, differs from Rounce in the following particulars:—*1st.* The game is played with a pack of thirty-two cards, the same as euchre. *2d.* A player is not compelled to lead trumps if he has already done so twice. *3d.* If a player holds no trumps, and elects to play his hand, trusting to make a trick in good cards of other suits, he may, in his proper turn, play his poorest card *face down*, which card represents a trump, and such a lead calls for a trump from every player who holds one. In all other particulars, Ramsch is identical with the American game of Rounce.

PEDRO SANCHO.

The game of Pedro Sancho is played the same as Commercial Pitch or Auction All-Fours; with the following exceptions:

I.—The Five of trumps is called *Pedro*, and counts five in the score.

II.—The Nine of trumps is called *Sancho*, and counts nine in the score.

III.—It is possible to hold eighteen points in one hand, and the points score and take precedence in the following order, viz:—1st, High; 2d, Low; 3d, Jack; 4th, Game; one point each. 5th, Pedro, five points; 6th, Sancho, nine points.

IV.—Pedro and Sancho, like Jack and Game, are not sure cards; they may be respectively captured by any trump of a higher denomination, and count in the score of the winner of the trick containing them.

V.—The *dealer* sells the trump; not the eldest hand, as in Auction All-Fours.

VI.—The bids may pass around the board one or more times, until all the players are satisfied. For instance: after all the players (once around) have bid or refused, they may *again*, in turn, supersede their former bids; and this process may be repeated until the highest possible bid that can be obtained has been made, and accepted or rejected by the dealer.

VII.—The game is won by the player who first scores fifty points.

In scoring, each player commences with fifty points (or more, if previously agreed). All points made are deducted from the player's score; any accepted bid not accomplished is added to his score. The player whose score is first reduced to nothing wins the game.

The game is usually kept by a scorer, chosen by mutual agreement. It his business to see that the points claimed by any player are in accordance with the cards held by him; he must also declare the state of the game, when requested to do so by any of the players.

A player whose bid has been accepted, is permitted to score not only the amount of his bid, when he has made it, but also any points he may succeed in making in excess of his bid.

If the dealer refuses to entertain the highest bid, he is entitled to score all the points he makes; but if he fails to make as much as the highest bid offered, he is set back just that number of points.

The first object for a player to attain in this game is, of course, to make points for his own score; but, if he finds that he is not able to succeed, his next endeavor should be to do all in his power to set back the player who is striving to secure the amount of his bid; in doing this, however, strict attention must be paid to the state of the score, and the play regulated in accordance with it. Thus, it is good policy, when a player holds points which he finds he cannot make, to play them, if possible, into the hands of the one whose score is lowest. It is even better to let these points go to the bidder, if his score is low, than to permit them to fall to another player whose score already stands high.

If two players have already reduced their score to two, and one of them has made High, Game, Pedro and Sancho, the other player could go out before him with Low and Jack.

The foregoing is the method usually adopted for playing the game of Pedro Sancho. There are, however, a few modifications which find favor in some localities. These are as follows:

1. When four play, the four Threes may be discarded from the pack, and twelve cards dealt to each player, so that all the cards are in play. For eight players, six cards to each will produce the same result. When less than four play, nine or twelve cards may be dealt to each, as agreed upon, to increase the chances of counting-cards being out.

2. The Deuce only is *low*, and is not a sure card, as in the regular game, but counts for the taker instead of the holder. If the Deuce of trumps has not been dealt, no point can be scordd for *low*.

3. Game is represented solely by the Ten of trumps, which can be captured by any higher trump. If the Ten has not been dealt, no one can score the one point for game.

4. The Joker is sometimes introduced; it scores fifteen, is captured by any trump card, it being the lowest trump, and is *low*. In scoring, the Joker, or *Dom*, counts after Pedro. In this case thirty-three points may be scored. The game thus played is "Dom Pedro."

5. The player who has the pitch can only, if successful, score the amount of his bid. The other players scoring at the close of the round any points each has made.

6. The game is also played without Sancho, making the score only nine points, and game twenty-one points. This variety is generally known as "Pedro."

PENUCHLE.

TWO-HANDED PEUCHLE. SO PLAYED WITH A PACK OF THIRTY-TWO CARDS.

When the game is played by two only, it is commenced by cutting for deal; or by one of them dealing the cards alternately, one at a time, face upwards—the player to whom the first *Ace* falls winning the first deal. In cutting, the highest card wins the deal, *Ace* being high, the other cards following their rank in the game, which is as follows. *Ace, Ten, King, Queen, Knave, Nine, Eight* and *Seven.* The face value of the cards is the same as in Sixty-Six.

The dealer, after shuffling and cutting, deals each player eight cards, commencing with the eldest hand, by two and three at a time; the next or seventeenth card being turned up for trump, and laid on the table face upwards. If the trump card be a *Seven*, the dealer scores ten points for it *at once.*

The eldest hand leads first, after which the lead belongs to the winner of the previons trick. Suit may or may not be followed, at discretion. After each trick, each player draws a card from the top of the talon, the winner of the previous trick first, continuing the drawing after each trick, until the talon is exhausted.

An announcement can only be made and scored by the winner of the previous trick, and before drawing from the talon: and only one announcement can be declared at a time. When the talon is exhausted, no more announcements can be made, and suit *must* be followed; if, however, a player cannot follow suit, he *must* play a trump, if he has one.

At the end of each round each player counts the face

va e or the cards in the tricks he has won, these points are added to the value of the announcements he has made, and the whole placed to his score; the winner of the last trick counting ten points additional.

The announcements are based on the cards held in hand at the time of announcing.

The five highest trumps count	150
Four *Aces*	100
Four *Kings*	80
Four *Queens*	60
Four *Knaves*	40
Penuchle, or *Queen of Spades* and *Knave of Diamonds*	40
King and *Queen* of trumps	40
King and *Queen* of any other suit	20

The *Seven* of trumps counts for ten, and is exchangeable, when duly announced, for the turned-up card.

If a player announces 40 trumps (*King* and *Queen*), and subsequently draws the other card necessary to constitute 150 trumps, he may announce these also when he has the proper opportunity. If, however, he first announces 150 trumps, he cannot *afterwards* announce 40 trumps.

Five hundred points usually constitute the game, and as soon as a player knows he has scored the necessary points, he may throw down his hand and claim the game. If he does this, and, on examination, it is is found that he has not sufficient points, he loses the game.

FOUR-HANDED PENUCHLE.

The method of playing this game is the same as laid down for "Four-Handed Sixty-Six." If this trump-card be a *Seven*, he scores ten points. If any other player holds the *Seven*, he exchanges that card for the turned-up trump, and scores ten points. The announcements, if any, are declared by each player immediately after he has played his card to the first trick—no sooner and no later. The score is reckoned at the end of each round, in the same manner as in the two-handed game; the partners in the game combining their points, including the ten points for the last trick.

THREE-HANDED PENUCHLE.

In this game each player scores for himself. The cards are dealt around two or three at a time, giving ten cards to each player, leaving two cards not dealt. The first of these two is turned up for trump, and, if a *Seven*, scores ten points for the dealer *at once.* The player that holds the *Seven* of trumps exchanges his *Seven* for the turn-up, and scores ten points. The *Seven* and the last undealt card belong to the dealer, giving him twelve cards in all, out of which he must discard two before any play or any announcement is made. The two discarded cards belong to and are counted in with the tricks that the dealer may hereafter take, but they do not count unless he makes a trick.

The announcements are made in the same manner as in the four-handed game, and count *at once* to the score of the announcing player.

The three-handed game is generally played to decide who shall be the loser, and the first player who makes four hundred points retires from the game at the end of the round, leaving the other two players to continue up to five hundred points, in the manner laid down for "Two-Handed Penuchle." Where a stake is played for, the loser pays the winner; the middle, or second man out, neither winning nor losing.

AUCTION PITCH.

Auction Pitch is played with a pack of fifty-two cards, which rank as at Whist, and by any number of persons, from four to eight.

The deal is determined by cutting; the player cutting the highest card deals. Ace is high.

After the deal has been determined, and the cards have been shuffled and cut by the player to the right of the dealer, the dealer delivers six cards to each player, three at a time, in rotation, beginning with the player to his left. No trump is turned. After the first hand has been played, the deal passes in rotation to the left.

After the cards have been dealt, the *eldest hand* (the player to the left of the dealer) proceeds to sell the privilege of pitching the trump.

Each player in turn has the right to make one bid, but no more.

The bidding proceeds in rotation, beginning with the player to the left of the eldest hand. The eldest hand has the last say, and may either sell to the highest bidder, or decline to sell, and pitch the trump himself.

If the seller decline to entertain the highest bid, and pitch the trump himself, he is entitled, if successful, to score all the points he may make; but if he fail to make as many points as the highest number offered, he must be *set back* just that number of points, and he cannot score anything he may have made during the play of that hand.

A player whose bid has been accepted may score not only the number of points he bid, if he make them, but also any points he may make in excess thereof.

If a player buy the privilege of pitching the trump and fail to make or save the necessary number of points, he must be set back the number of points he bid, and he cannot score anything he may have made during the play of that hand.

The seller, when he accepts a bid, scores the points at once, and before a card is led.

If no bid is made, the seller must pitch the trump himself.

The game is ten points. All points a player may make are deducted from his score. All points a player may be set back are added to his score. The player whose score is first reduced to nothing wins the game.

The points rank and are scored in the following order of precedence:

High (the highest trump out). 2. *Low* (the lowest trump out). 3. *Jack* (the Knave of trumps). 4. *Game.*

Low scores for the player who originally held it. *Jack* may be taken with any superior trump, and scores for the player who makes or saves it.

In the event of a tie in counting game, that point is not scored by either party.

The game is usually scored on a slate in the following manner: Two crosses are made thus, X X. Each cross represents five points. When a player makes one point, he rubs out the centre of the cross thus, —, and when he makes another point he rubs out one of the remaining portions of the cross, and so on until all are wiped out. If a player is set back, the additional points are marked in a similar manner.

PLAYING THE HAND.

After it has been determined who is to pitch the trump, the player having that privilege must lead a card of the suit he makes trump. Each player, beginning with the player to the left of the leader, plays a card to the lead. When all the players have played to the lead, that constitutes trick.

The highest card of the suit led wins the trick, and the winner of the trick has the next lead.

After the first trick it is not compulsory to lead a trump, and a player may lead a card of any suit he chooses.

Each player must follow suit if he can, unless he choose to trump. If he has no card of the suit led, he is not compelled to trump, but may play a card of any suit he chooses.

The playing proceeds in this way until all the cards held by each of the players are played out. After the hand is played the scores are made, and a new deal ensues; this is continued until some player wins the game.

If a player make a revoke he is debarred from scoring any point he may have made in the play of the hand; and in addition, the revoking player must be set back the highest number of points that was bid (in the hand) for the privilege of pitching the trump.

Any loss an innocent player may have sustained by reason of the revoke, if claimed, must be rectified and made good, provided the same can be clearly demonstrated by subsequent examination of the tricks.

In all other particulars this game is governed by the laws of All-Fours.

CALIFORNIA JACK.

This game is another of the numerous progeny of All-Fours. It is usually played by two or four persons, with a pack of fifty-two cards which rank as at Whist.

The deal is determined by cutting the cards; the player cutting the highest card deals. Ace is high; ties cut over.

After the deal has been determined, and the cards cut by the player to the right of the dealer, the dealer delivers six cards to each player, three at a time, in rotation, beginning with the player to his left.

After the cards have been dealt, the dealer turns the remainder of the pack (the stock) face upwards upon the board. The exposed card determines the trump suit. The exposed card is then taken by the dealer and slipped into the stock, as near the centre as possible, and the stock remains face upwards. Sometimes the dealer, instead of placing the trump card in the centre of the stock, shffles the stock back upwards, and then turns it face upwards again. This is done to prevent any possible indication of the whereabouts of the trump card.

The eldest hand, that is the player to the left of the dealer, now leads any card he chooses, and each player, beginning with the player to the left of the leader, plays a card to the lead.

When all the players have played to the lead, that constitutes a trick. The highest card of the suit led wins the trick, and the winner of the trick has the next lead.

Each player must follow suit, if he holds a card of the suit led. If he has no card of the suit led, he is not compelled to trump, but may play a card of any suit he chooses.

After each trick is played, the dealer gives the exposed card on the top of the stock to the winner of the trick, and the next card to the next player, and so on; one card to each player, all face upwards. Each player will thus continue to hold six cards in hand until the stock is exhausted.

The game is usually ten points, and the points score in the following order of precedence: 1. High, the Ace of trumps. 2. Low, the Deuce of trumps. 3. Jack, the Knave of trumps. 4. Game. High is the only sure point. Low, Jack and Game are each scored by the player who wins or saves them in play.

The penalty for revoking is the same as in All-Fours.

DRAW POKER.

Draw Poker is played with a pack of fifty-two cards and by any number of persons from two to six.

DEALING.

Before the dealer begins to deal the cards, the player next to his left who is called the *ante-man* or *age*, must deposit in the pool an *ante* not exceeding one-half the limit previously agreed upon. This is called a blind.

The deal is performed by giving five cards to each player, one at a time, beginning with the player to the left of the dealer.

GOING IN ON THE ORIGINAL HAND.

After the cards have been dealt the players look at their hands, and each player in rotation, beginning with the player to the left of the *age*, determines whether he will *go in* or not. Any player who decides to go in, that is to play for the pool, must put into the pool double the amount of the ante, except the player holding the age, who contributes the same amount as his original ante. This makes the blind good, and all the players interested in that hand will have contributed alike.

Those who decline to play throw their cards, face downward, upon the table in front of the next dealer.

Any player when it is his turn, and after making the ante good, may *raise*, *i. e.*, increase the ante any amount within the limit of the game; the next player, after making good the ante and raise, may then also raise it any amount within the limit; and so on. Each player, as he makes good and equals the other players who are in before him, may thus increase the ante if he chooses, compelling the others to equal that increase, or abandon their share of the pool.

Each player who raises the ante, must do so in rotation, going round to the left, and any player who remains in to play, must put in the pool as much as will make his stake equal to such increase, or abandon all he has already contributed to the pool.

THE STRADDLE.

Another feature that may be introduced when betting upon the *original hand*, is the *straddle*. The straddle is nothing more than a double blind. For example:

A, B, C, D and E play. A deals. B, the player holding the age, antes one chip. C can straddle B's ante by putting in the pool two chips, provided he does so before the cards are cut for the deal. D may double the straddle, *i. e.*, straddle C, and so on up to the age, provided the bets do not exceed the limit. In the above instance, supposing C only to straddle, it would cost D, E and A each four chips to *go in*, and it would cost B three and C two chips. Each straddle costs double the preceding one.

The straddle does not give the player the age, it only gives him the first opportunity to be the last in before the draw; that is, the player to the left of the last straddler, after looking at his hand, and before the draw, must be the first to declare whether he will make good the straddle, and so on, in rotation, up to the player who made the last straddle. After the draw, the player to the left of the age must make the first bet, provided he remains in. A good player very rarely straddles.

FILLING THE HANDS.

When all are in who intend to play, each player has the right to draw any number of cards he chooses, from one to five, or he can retain his cards as originally dealt to him. If a player draws cards, he must discard a like number from his hand previous to drawing, and the rejected cards must be placed face downward upon the table near the next dealer.

The dealer asks each player in rotation, beginning with the holder of the age, how many cards he wants, and when the player has discarded, he gives the number requested from the top of the pack. When the other hands have been helped, the dealer, if he has gone in and wants cards, then helps himself last.

BETTING, RAISING AND CALLING.

When all the hands are filled, the player to the left of the age has the first say, and he must either bet or retire from the game, forfeiting what he has already staked. The same with all the other players, in rotation, up to the age. When a player makes a bet, the next player must either *see him*, *i. e.*, put in the pool an equal amount, or *go better*, *i. e.*, make the previous bet good, and raise it any amount not exceeding the limit; or he must pass out. This continues either until some one player drives all the others out of the game and takes the pool without showing his hand; or until all the other players who remain in see the last raise (no one going better) and *call* the player who made the last raise. In this event, *i. e.*. when a *call* is made, the players remaining in all show their hands, and the strongest hand takes the pool.

The following is an example illustrating the mode of betting before and after the draw; The limit is thirty chips, and A, B, C, D and E are the players. A deals. B, holding the age, antes one chip; C goes in and puts up two chips; D makes good and raises ten chips, putting in twelve chips; E passes out of the game; A makes good, sees D's raise, putting in twelve chips; B makes good, sees D's raise, and goes five chips better, this costs him sixteen chips; C passes out and abandons the two chips he has already put in; D sees B's raise, and bets the limit better, contributing thirty-five chips; A sees D, and deposits thirty-five chips; B also sees D, and puts thirty chips in the pool. A, B and D now each have forty-seven chips in the pool, which, together with the two chips abandoned by C, make a total of one hundred and forty-three chips.

After the hands are filled, B holding the age, and C having passed out, it becomes D's *say*, *i. e.*, D's turn to declare what he will do. D determines to stake five chips; A sees D's bet and goes thirty chips better, and puts up thirty-five chips; B sees A, and deposits thirty-five chips, D makes good, putting up thirty chips, and *calls* A.

Each of the players now have eighty-two chips in the pool, which, including the two chips which C forfeited, make a total of two hundred and forty-eight chips. They show their hands, and A having the best hand, captures the pool.

Suppose that instead of B and D calling A, they had passed out. Then A would have taken the pool without showing his hand.

If all the players pass, up to the age, the latter takes the pool, and the deal ends.

THE OLD-FASHIONED GAME.

The foregoing is a description of what is called modern Draw Poker, and is the game now almost universally played in this country; but some old-fashioned players, who object to a compulsory blind, which the ante of the player holding the age really is, prefer the old game of Draw Poker, which differs from the modern game in the following particulars:

1. The dealer opens the hand by putting up a fixed ante

before dealing, which is not, in the strict sense of the term, a bet or a blind.

2. The age alone has the privilege of going a blind, provided he does so before the cards are cut for the deal, but this is optional, and not compulsory.

3. Previous to the *draw* any player may pass and afterwards come in again, provided no bet or blind has been made before he passes.

4. If, previous to the draw, all the players, including the dealer, pass without making a bet, the hand is ended, and the eldest hand puts up an ante and deals. This contingency is not likely to occur very often.

VALUE OF THE HANDS.

The value of the hands are as follows, commencing with the lowest:

1. *One Pair.*—(Accompanied by three cards of different denominations). If two players each hold a pair, the highest pair wins; if the two are similar, the highest remaining card wins.

2. *Two Pair.*—(Accompanied by a card of another denomination.) If two players each hold two pairs, the highest pair wins. If the two pairs are similar, the player whose remaining card is the highest wins.

3. *Triplets* (that is three cards of the same denomination, not accompanied by a pair). The highest triplets win. Triplets beat two pair.

4. *A Straight* (that is a sequence of five cards not all of the same suit). An Ace may either begin or end a straight. For example: Ace (highest), King, Queen, Knave, Ten, is a straight, and the highest straight. Five, Four, Three, Two, Ace (lowest) is a straight, and the lowest straight. An Ace cannot occupy an intermediate position, thus: King, Queen, Ace, Two, Three, is not a straight. If more than one player hold a straight, the straight headed by the highest card wins. A straight will beat triplets.

Straights are not always played; it should therefore be determined whether they are to be admitted at the commencement of the game. If, however, it has been agreed before commencing to play that straights are to be counted in the game, a straight flush outranks four cards of the same denomination, four Aces, for instance.

5. *A Flush*, (that is five cards of the same suit not in seqence). If more than one player holds a flush, the flush containing the highest card wins; if the highest cards tie, the next highest cards in these two hands win, and so on. A flush will beat a straight, and consequently triplets.

6. *A Full*, (that is three cards of the same denomination and a pair.) If more than one pair holds a full, the highest triplets win. A full will beat a flush.

7. *Fours* (that is four cards of the same denomination, accompanied by any other card). If more than one player holds fours, the highest fours win. When straights are not played, fours beat a straight flush.

8. *A Straight Flush* (that is a sequence of five cards, all of the same suit). If more than one player holds a straight flush, the winning hand is determined in the same manner as the straight, which see. When straights are not played, the straight flush does not rank higher than a common flush, but when straights are played, it is the highest hand that can be held, and beats four of a kind.

When none of the foregoing hands are shown, the highest card wins; if these tie, the next highest in these two hands, and so on.

If upon a *call* for a show of cards, it occurs that two or more parties interested in the call hold hands identical in value, and those hands are the best out, the parties thus tied must divide the pool, share and share alike.

TECHNICAL TERMS USED IN POKER.

Age.—Same as eldest hand.

Ante.—The stake deposited in the pool by the age at the beginning of the game.

Blaze.—This hand consists of five court cards, and when it is played, beats two pairs.

Blind.—The ante deposited by the age previous to the deal. The blind may be doubled by the player to the left of the eldest hand, and the next player to the left may at his option *straddle* this bet; and so on, including the dealer, each player doubling. The player to the left of the age alone has the privilege of the first straddle, and if he decline to straddle, it debars any other player coming after him from doing so (*See note to Rule 17*). To make a blind good costs double the amount of the ante, and to make a straddle good costs four times the amount of the blind. Each succeeding straddle costs double the preceding one.

Call.—When the bet goes round to the last better, a player who remains in, if he does not wish to see and go better, simply sees and calls, and then all those playing show their hands, and the highest hand wins the pool.

Chips.—Ivory or bone tokens, representing a fixed value in money.

Chipping, or to Chip.—Is synonymous with betting. Thus a player instead of saying "I bet," may say "I chip" so much.

Discard.—To take from your hand the number of cards you intend to draw and place them on the table, near the next dealer, face downwards.

Draw.—After discarding one or more cards to receive a corresponding number from the dealer.

Eldest Hand, or Age.—The player immediately at the left of the dealer.

Filling.—To match or strengthen the cards to which you draw.

Foul Hand.—A hand composed of more or less than five cards.

Freeze Out.—In Freeze-out Poker each player exposes an equal amount at the beginning of the game, which cannot be added to from any source other than winnings from other players. No player can retire with any of this stake until the close of the game or the hour fixed for its close. No player can be deprived of a call if he puts up all his money, and no player when his money is exhausted, can borrow or continue in the game on credit under any circumstances.

Going Better.—When *any* player makes a bet it is the privilege of the *next player to the left to raise him*, that is, after making good the amount already bet by his adversary, to make a still higher bet. In such a case it is usual to say, "I see you and go (so much) better," naming the extra sum bet.

Going In.—Making good the ante of the age and the straddles (if any), for the privilege of drawing cards and playing for the pool.

Limit.—A condition made at the beginning of a game, limiting the amount of any single bet or raise.

Making Good.—Depositing in the pool an amount equal to any bet previously made. This is done previous to raising or calling a player, and is sometimes called *seeing* a bet.

Original Hand.—The first five cards dealt to any player.

Pat Hand.—An original hand not likely to be improved by drawing, such as a full, straight, flush, or pairs.

Pass.—"*I pass*" is a term used in Draw Poker to signify that a player throws up his hand and retires from the game.

Jack-Pots—Is a Western modification introduced into the game, and is fully explained at page 63.

Raising a Bet.—The same as *going better.*

Say.—When it is the turn of any player to declare what he will do, whether he will *bet* or *pass* his hand, it is said to be his *say.*

Seeing a Bet.—The same as *making good.*

Straddle.—*See Blind*

Table Stakes.—A table stake simply means that each player places his stake where it may be seen, and that a player cannot be raised more than he has upon the table; but at any time between deals, he may increase his stake from his pocket, or he may put up any article for convenience sake, say a knife, and state that he makes his stake as large as any other player's, and he is then liable to be raised to any amount equal to the stake of any other player, and must make good with cash. When playing table stakes, if a player have no money on the table, he must put up or declare his stake previous to raising his hand, and failing to do this, he must stand out of the game for that hand.

CUTTING AND DEALING.

1. The deal is determined by throwing around one card to each player, and the player who gets the lowest card deals.

2. In throwing for the deal, the Ace is lowest and the King highest. Ties are determined by cutting.

3. The cards must be shuffled above the table; each player has a right to shuffle the cards, the dealer last.

4. The player to the right of the dealer must must cut the cards.

5. The dealer must give each player one card at a time, in rotation, beginning to his left, and in this order he must deliver five cards to each player

6. If the dealer deals without having the pack properly cut, or if a card is faced in the pack, there must be a fresh deal. The cards are re-shuffled and re-cut, and the dealer deals again.

7. If a card be accidentally exposed by the dealer while in the act of dealing, the player to whom such card is dealt *must* accept it as though it had not been exposed. (See Rule 25.) This rule does not apply when a card is faced in the pack.

8. If the dealer give to himself, or either of the other players, *more* or *less* than five cards, and the player receiving such a number of cards discover and announce the fact *before* he raises his hand, it is a misdeal. The cards are re-shuffled and re-cut, and the dealer deals again.

9. If the dealer give to himself, or either of the other players, more or less than five cards, and the player receiving such improper number of cards *lift* his hand before he announces the fact, no misdeal occurs, and he must retire from the game for that hand.

10. After the first hand the deal proceeds in rotation, beginning with the player to the left of the dealer.

DISCARDING AND DRAWING.

11. After the deal has been completed, each player who remains in the game may discard from his hand as many cards as he chooses, or his whole hand, and call upon the dealer to give him a like number from the top of those remaining in the pack. The eldest hand must discard first, and so in regular rotation round to the dealer, who discards last; and the players must discard before any party is helped.

[For the sake of convenience, each player should throw his discarded cards face downwards upon the table near the next dealer.]

12. Any player after having asked for fresh cards, must take the exact number called for; and after cards have once been discarded, they must not again be taken in hand.

13. Any player, previous to raising his hand or making a bet, may demand of the dealer how many cards he drew, and the latter must reply correctly. By raising his hand or making a bet, the player forfeits the right to inquire, and removes the obligation to answer.

14. Should the dealer give any player *more* cards than the latter has demanded, and the player discover and

announce the fact before raising his cards, the dealer must withdraw the superfluous cards and restore them to the pack. But if the player raise the cards before informing the dealer of the mistake, he must retire from the game during that hand.

15. Should the dealer give any player fewer cards than the latter has discarded, and the player discover and announce the fact previous to lifting the cards, the dealer must give the player from the pack sufficient cards to make the whole number correspond with the number originally demanded. If the player raise the cards before making the demand for more, he must retire from the game during that hand.

16. If a player discard and draw fresh cards to his hand, and while serving him the dealer expose one or more of the cards, the dealer must place the exposed cards upon the bottom of the pack, and give the player a corresponding number from the top of the pack. (See Rule 8.)

BETTING, CALLING AND SHOWING.

17. In opening the pool before the cards are dealt, the age makes the first ante, which must not exceed one-half the limit. After the cards are dealt, every player in his proper turn, beginning with the player to the left of the age, must make the ante good by depositing double the amount in the pool, or retire from the game for that hand. [This opening bet of the age is simply a compulsory blind. Many fine poker players consider this objectionable, aad prefer the old-fashioned game, as follows:

1. The dealer antes a fixed sum previous to dealing, which is not a bet or a blind.

2. The age may go a blind, but this is optional, and not compulsory.

3. Previous to the draw, any player may pass and come in again, provided no bet or blind has been made before he passed.]

18. After the cards have been dealt, any player in his proper turn, beginning with the player to the left of the age, after making good the age's ante, may raise the same any amount not exceeding the limit of the game.

19. After the hands are filled, any player who remains in the game may, in his proper turn, beginning with the player to the left of the age, bet or raise the pool any amount not exceeding the limit of the game.

20. After the draw has been made, the eldest hand or age has the privilege of deferring his say until after all the other players have made their bets or passed. The age is the last player to declare whether he will play or pass. If, however, the age pass out of the game *before* the draw, then the next player to his left (in play) after the draw, must make the first bet, or failing to bet, must pass out. The privileges of the age cannot be transferred.

21. If a player in his regular turn bet or raise a bet any amount not exceeding the limit of the game, his adversaries must either call him, go better, or retire from the game for that hand.

When a player makes a bet he must deposit the amount in the pool.

22. If a player makes good or sees a bet, and calls for a show of hands, each player must show his entire hand to the board, the caller last, and the best poker hand wins the pool.

23. If a player bets or raises a bet, and no other player goes better or calls him, he wins the pool, and cannot be compelled to show his hand.

24. Upon a show of hands, if a player miscall his hand. he does not loose the pool for that reason, for every hand shows for itself.

25. If a player pass or throw up his hand, he passes out of the game, and cannot, under any circumstances whatever, participate further in that game.

26. Any player betting with more or less than five cards in his hand, loses the pool, unless his opponents all throw up their hands before discovering the foul hand. If only one player is betting against the foul hand, that player is entitled to the ante and all the money bet; but if there are more than one betting against him, then the best hand among his opponents is entitled to the pool.

27. If a player makes a bet and an adversary raise him, and the player who made the previous bet has not money sufficient to see the raise, he can put up all the funds he may have and call for a show for that amount.

28. None but the eldest hand (age) has the privilege of going a blind. The party next and to the left of the eldest hand may double the blind, and the next player straddle the next double the straddle, and so on, but the amount the straddle, when made good, must not exceed the limit of the game.

29. A player cannot straddle a blind and raise it at the same time, nor can any player raise a blind before the cards are dealt.

30. If the player to the left of the age decline to straddle a blind, he debars any other player from doing so.

JACK-POTS.

The Jack Pot is a modification introduced in the game of Draw Poker, and is played as follows:

When all the players pass up to the blind hand, the latter allows his blind to rmain in the pot, and each of the other player dsposit a similar amount. The blind now deals, and any player, in *his regular turn*, may *open* or *break* the pot, provided he holds a pair of Jacks or better; but a player is not compelled to do so, this being entirely optional.

Each player in turn, commencing with the one at the left of the dealer, declares whether he can or will open the pot; if he decline to open he says: "I pass." If he has the requisite hand, elects to open, he says: "I open."

If no player opens the pot, then each player deposits in the pool the same amount that was previously contributed, and the deal passes to the next player. The same performance ensues until some player holds the necessary cards, and is willing to break the pot.

A player may break the pot for any amount within the limits of the game. and each player in turn must make the bet good, raise it, or pass out.

After all the players who determine to go in have made good the bet of the player who opened the Jack Pot, and the hands have been filled, then the player who opened the pot makes the first bet.

If all pass up to the player who broke the pot, the latter takes the pool and can only be compelled to show the Jacks, or better, necessary to break the pot.

A player who breaks the pot on a pair may split the pair in order to draw to a four flush or straight (if the latter be played); but if he does so, he must lay the discard to one side, separate from any other cards, so that after the result has been determined, he may satisfy the other players that he broke the pot with a legal hand. If this precaution is not observed, and attention called to it, the delinquent is subject to penalty prescribed in the following rule:

When a player breaks the pot without holding the requisite cards to do so, he must deposit in the pool, as penalty, twice the amount of his original bet.

[The amount of penalty for such an error should *preferably* be mutually agreed upon before opening the game. The above penalty seems light enough, considering the injustice that an error of this kind might work on the rest of the players. It has been suggested that ten times the original ante would not be an excessive penalty.]

If no player come in except the one who broke the pot on an insufficient hand, a new hand must be dealt and the penalty added to the pot.

If one or more players participate in the call when such an error as the foregoing occurs, the player holding the best hand outside the delinquent player takes the pool; or if a player drives the original breaker and all others out, then the pool must go to him.

Progressive Jack-Pots is played as follows: When, after a deal, no one opens the game, the players each place another chip in pool, new hands are dealt, etc., as before described, and no player can, under the second deal, open with less than Queens or better. If a third deal becomes necessary, it requires Kings or better to break the pot; and should it come to a fourth deal, it takes Aces or better, and so remains for any subsequent deals, until some player can and will break the pot.

CRIBBAGE.

Cribbage differs from all other games by its immense varieties of chances. It is reckoned useful to young people in the science of calculation. It is played with the whole pack of cards, generally by two persons, sometimes by three, sometimes by four.

There are different modes of playing, with five, six, or eight cards; sixty-one is game.

TERMS USED IN THE GAME.

Crib.—The cards laid out.

Pairs.—Two similar cards, as two aces, count two.

Pairs Royal.—Three similar cards count six.

Double Pairs Royal.—Four similar cards count twelve.

Fifteens.—Every fifteen counts two; made either by two cards, such as five and and a ten, a six and nine, a seven and eight, or by three or more, as two, five, and eight, &c.

Sequences.—Three, four or more successive cards, and count for as many points.

Flush.—Your cards being all of one suit, and counts as many points as cards; for the crib, the card must be of the same suit.

Tenth Card.—King, Queen, Knave, Ten, reckon as ten.

End Hole.—The last player, if he make thirty-one, scores two; if less, one.

LAWS OF THE GAME OF CRIBBAGE.

1. You may score two and call a new deal, if in dealing the dealer discover any of your cards.

2. You may score two and call a fresh deal if the dealer give more cards than he ought, or may draw the extra card from his hand, but you must detect it before taking up your cards.

3. If you have too many cards, your adversary may score four, and call a new deal.

4. The cards are dealt, if you touch them before the turn-up or cut, the other scores two.

5. If you score more than you ought, your adversary may put you back as many and score the same number himself; scoring less incurs no penalty.

6. Either party touching even his own pegs unnecessarily, the adversary may score two.

METHOD OF PLAYING FIVE CARD CRIBBAGE.

The cribbage board must have sixty-one holes.

The parties cut for deal, settled by the lowest cribbage card, the non-dealer scores "three for the last;" these may be marked at any period of the game; the dealer gives a card alternately until each have five.

If two play, each must lay out two of the five cards for crib, which belongs to the dealer. This done, the non-dealer cuts and the dealer turns the uppermost. This is reckoned by each in hand and crib. If a knave, the dealer scores two.

After laying out and cutting, the eldest hand plays; the dealer trys to pair or find a card which, reckoned with the first, will make 15; then the non-dealer plays, trying to make a pair, pair royal, flush where allowed, or 15, if the cards already played do not make that number; when your turn to play, if you cannot produce a card that will make 31, or come in under that number, you say "Go," to your antagonist, who must play any card he has that will make 31, and score two, if under one for the end hole; the last player has often opportunities to make pairs or sequences. The cards that remain are not to be played; score what you make during the play as you go on.

In playing suppose you play a nine, your adversary another nine, it makes a pair, and he scores two; if you play another nine it makes a pair royal, and you score six; if he play the fourth nine it makes a double pair royal.

Again, suppose you play a deuce, the dealer plays an eight, and you then play a five, it makes fifteen, aad you score two; so if you play a nine and the dealer a six, that makes fifteen, and he scores two; and as often as the first fifteen be made in the play by any number of cards.

In playing, if there be a sequence, it matters not which card is thrown first, thus: suppose you play *Ace*, your antagonist *Five*, then you *Three*, he *Four*, you *Deuce*, you score five for a sequence, as 1, 2, 3, 4, 5, so for others.

Having played a card, seppose your antagonist plays one of the same suit, if you play another of that suit it is a flush, and you score three; if he play a fourth of the same suit he scores four for the flush, and so on, as long as the same suit lasts.

The elder hand counts and takes his game first; the dealer next scores his hand and crib; you are to reckon the cards every way they can be possibly varied, always including the turn-up card, and count for every

Fifteen	2	Double Pair Royal	12
Pair	2	Sequences,	according to No.
Pair Royal	6	Flush	according to No.

Nobody of the suit turned up, one; when turned up it cannot be counted again.

MAXIMS FOR PLAYING THE CRIB CARDS.

In laying out crib, consider your hand, also whom the crib belongs to, and the state of the game, because what might be prudent in one situation would be imprudent in another.

If you have a pair royal, lay out the other two cards for either crib, except you hold two fives with it; then it would be injudicious to lay them out for your adversary's crib, unless the cards you retain insure your game, or your adversary so near home that the crib is of no importance.

It is right to flush your cards in hand, it may assist your crib, or baulk your opponent's.

Try to retain a sequence in your hand, particularly if a flush.

Lay out close cards, as three and four, five and six, for your crib, unless it break your hand.

As there is a card more in crib than in hand, pay attention to the crib; the probability of counting more for the crib than hand is five to four.

For your own crib, lay out two cards of the same suit in preference; it gives you the chance of a flush, but not for your adversary's crib.

Try to balk your opponent's crib. The best cards for this are a King and Ace, Six, Seven, Eight, Nine or Ten; or Queen with an Ace, Six, Seven, Eight or Nine, or any card not likely to form a sequence; King is the greater balk, being the highest card, no higher can come to form a sequence.

Never lay out a knave for your adversary's crib, it is only three to one that the card turned up is of the same suit, by which he will count one.

Even though you hold a pair royal, never lay out for your adversary's crib a Two and a Three. a Five and Six, a Seven and Eight, or a Five and any tenth card. When you hold such cards, observe the stage of your game, whether your adversary is within a moderate show; if your deal, retain such cards as will, in playing, prevent your adversary from making pairs or sequences, &c.. and enable you to win the end-hole; this will often prevent your opponent winning the game.

Each player ought to make sixteen in two deals; for each hand, more than four and less than five; for the crib, five; for the play, two for dealer, one for adversary; dealer has the advantage. Attend to this, play accordingly; if not at home, and a good hand, make a push; if your hand be indifferent try to balk your adversary.

THREE OR FOUR HAND CRIBBAGE

Differs from the preceding, as the parties only put out one card each to the crib; when thirty-one, or as near as can be, has been made, the next elder hand leads, the players go on with remaining cards till all are played, before they show

SIX CARD CRIBBAGE

Is similar to five card, except at the beginning, the non-dealer is not to score any for last, and all the cards must be played, scoring for the pairs or fifteens they may form. When last player retains close cards, you may make four points in play.

The dealer is said to have some advantage.

The dealer should make twenty-five by his hand, crib, and next hand; at his second deal, if his peg be in the twenty-fifth hole he has his complement; at his third deal, if within eleven of game.

If the non-dealer make eleven first hand, he has the best of the game, he may make his second deal in the thirty-sixth hole; he will probably win by his hand, crib, and next hand.

If dealer and your adversary has above his complement, play your game accordingly. If you have good cards, make as many as possible by pairing, fifteens, &c. If your cards be indifferent, play off to prevent your adversary scoring.

Eight card cribbage is played like six.

CALCULATIONS FOR BETTING.

FOR DEALER.

Before you bet, ascertain who has the deal.

Each 5 hole is	6 to 4	Each 35 hole is	7 to 6
Each 10 hole is	12 to 11	Each 40 hole is	10 to 9
Each 15 hole is	7 to 4	Each 45 hole is	12 to 8
Each 20 hole is	6 to 4	Each 50 hole is	5 to 2
Each 25 hole is	11 to 10	Each 55 hole is	21 to 20
Each 30 hole is	9 to 5	Each 60 hole is	2 to 1

When the dealer wants 3 and his adverary 4...... 5 to 4
At all points of the game, till within 15 of the end, when the dealer is 5 ahead.................. 3 to 1
But when within 16 of the end.................. 8 to 1
If the dealer wants 6 and the adversary 11........10 to 1
If the dealer is 10 ahead, it is.................... 4 to 1
And near the end of the game....................12 to 1
When the dealer wants 16 and his opponent 11....21 to 26

AGAINST THE DEALER.

When both players are at 56 holes each, is........ 7 to 5
When both players are at 57 holes each, is........ 7 to 4
When both players are at 58 holes each, is........ 3 to 2
When the dealer wants 20 and his opponent 17... 5 to 4
When the dealer is 5 behind previous to turning the top of the board.......................... 6 to 5
When he is 31 and his opponent 36.............. 6 to 4
When he is 16 and his opponent 41.............. 7 to 4

EVEN BETTING.

In all points of the game, till within 20 of the end, when the non-dealer is 3 ahead.

The dealer wanting 14 and his opponent 9.

The dealer wanting 11 and his opponent 7

And when each player is 59 holes.

LOO.

THREE CARD LOO.

The game of Loo is the most interesting and most usually played in the Old World, and justly entitled to the first place among what are called Round Games, in which each individual plays on his own account. It is played with a complete pack of fifty-two cards, and admits any number of persons under seventeen; but from five to eight form a pleasanter party than any larger or smaller number. The cards rank the same as at Whist.

TERMS USED IN LOO.

Paying for the Deal.—At each new deal the dealer puts into the pool three counters, and this is called the price of the deal.

Misdeal is when the dealer gives any of the party more or less than three cards, or deals too many or too few hands, or deals out of regular order, or shows a card in dealing, or turns up the trump card at *Force* before different suits have been played.

Force is when there is only the price of a deal in the pool, in which case all must play, and the trump card is not turned up till different suits have been played.

Pool is the stake to be played for, usually put into a small salver, which lies in the middle of the table.

To Stand.—When a person declares his intention to play, he says, "I stand," or "I play."

Looed.—A person playing is looed when he does not take a trick, or when he breaks any of the laws of the game.

Flush is three cards of the trump suit in one hand.

Miss is the spare hand (when there is a pool), and must be dealt in the regular order of the other hands, either first or last but one, and not according to the dealer's whim

MODE OF PLAYING.

Loo is either limited or unlimited, and the laws and mode of playing both are precisely similar, except that at Limited Loo those who play and do not get a trick pay into the pool only the price of the deal, while at Unlimited Loo they pay the whole amount that happens to be in the pool at the time. But as by the latter mode the pool may accumulate, and by the former it is generally kept very low, a medium between the two extremes may be accomplished by limiting the loo to double or four times the price of the deal; but, of course to be looed in no more than the stake played for, should it be under the amount limited.

The amount to be played for, and whether Limited or Unlimited, being distinctly settled, the parties cut for the deal; which, having been paid for, the cards are shuffled and cut, and the dealer gives three cards, by one at a time, to each player, beginning at the person on his left hand, without turning up a card for trumps, the first hand being always *Force*.

The elder hand now plays, and the rest after him in order, each following suit if he can, and placing his card just before him on the table. If different suits have been played in the first round, the dealer turns up the trump card, and the person who has played the highest trump wins the trick, and becomes elder hand. But if it so happens that no trumps have been played, then the highest card of the suit led wins the trick; or if each of the players has followed suit, the trump card is not to be turned up till the next round is played. The winner of a trick must always lead a trump if he can; and the second and third tricks being played, each trick is entitled to a third of the pool, and those who have not taken tricks pay a loo of three each—that is, the price of the deal.

The cards being again shuffled and cut, and the deal paid for, the dealer, (the person on the left of last dealer) proceeds as before described; but in addition to a hand for each player, he deals a spare hand called *Miss*, and turns up a card for trumps. It is now optional to play or not; and before looking at his own cards, the dealer asks, in the regular order of playing, beginning at the elder and, whether they play their own hand or take *Miss*, or decline playing for that pool. If the elder hand declines to take *Miss*, the next in hand has the option, and so on; but whoever takes it must play it. Each individual must announce his intention before the next is asked, and if he declines playing must give his cards to the dealer to place under the pack, or do so himself. No one can retract after declaring his intention to stand or not, and each should be attentive while the dealer is asking, as it is not permitted to inquire how many are playing. When all including the dealer, have declared their intention, the first in hand of those who play, if he holds two trumps, must lead the highest of them; and each player in succession must "head the trick"—that is play a higher card if he can. The three tricks being played, the contents of the pool are shared in the proportion of a third to each trick; and the losers pay each the whole amount in the pool if the game is Unlimited Loo, or the price of the deal, or such sum as may have been fixed on as the maximum of the loo.

The game goes on in this way till the pool happens to be empty, when the next hand is *Force*, and is dealt and played as first described.

The dealer being last in hand, has the advantage of always knowing how many are to play before he himself decides. It likewise sometimes happens, when a large sum is in the pool, that none of the players holding good cards consider it safe to stand in which place the dealer takes the whole pool.

When any hand is a flush of trumps, it is entitled to the pool, and loose the board besides—that is to say. each of the party is looed in the price of a deal, whether playing or not; but there being no trump at *Force* till a round has been played, a flush does not in that case stand good. In some companies those only who have declared their intention of playing are looed, and pay each the whole amount in the pool, or the maximum, as before stated; but in this case the holder of a flush must not announce it till it be ascertained how many intend to play, otherwise he forfeits his right, and must play his flush as a common hand.

If two flushes occur in one deal, the elder hand has the preference, though he holds inferior cards; but a younger hand likewise holding a flush is exempted from being looed. The effect which a flush is to have, namely, whether to loo the board or only those who play, should be destinctly stated and understood at the commencement of the game.

This is so much a game of chance, that very little skill is required in playing it. It is in general safe to stand if you hold two indifferent trumps, or one good one, though it sometimes happens that a person holding both king and knave is looed. The player must be regulated in some measure by the number of the party; for supposing half of the cards to be dealt, it is an equal chance that ace, king, or any particular card, better than that which he holds, is out. The character of the other players must likewise be taken into account; for a person sometimes boldly declares his intention to play when he holds a very indifferent hand, in the hope of deterring the rest.

LAWS OF THE GAME.

There is no game in which the laws vary so much in different companies as in that of Loo. The following are those observed at the Loo Clubs:

1. The person who misdeals forfeits a loo and loses his deal; but if a card is faced in the pack, he is to deal again; or if any of the company is the cause of showing a card in dealing, that person forfeits a loo, and the cards must be dealt afresh.

2. If the dealer looks at his own hand before he has asked each individual whether they play or not, he forfeits a loo.

3. The hands ought to be lifted in succession from the dealer, and anyone taking up and looking at another's hand forfeits a loo, and the person whose cards have been taken, may inspect both hands and take his choice of the two.

4. The person who announces his intention to play or not, or who throws down his cards, till all those to the right have decided, forfeits a loo.

5. No person is to look at *Miss*, if not taken, before the dealer has decided, under the penalty of a loo, besides being obliged to play *Miss*.

6. Whoever plays a card out of the regular order of play forfeits a loo.

7. A card played by mistake, if seen, must remain; but if it cause revoke, it must be taken up, and may be called as at Whist when it does not oblige the party to revoke: and the person who played it forfeits a loo.

8. The person who neglects to put his loo into the pool before the trump card is turned up, forfeits a loo.

These forfeitures go to the present pool.

9. The elder hand who holds two trumps, and does not lead from them, playing the highest first;—and the person who does not lead a trump, if he can, after taking a trick and the player who revokes, or who does not either follow

suit or trump, provided he can thereby "head the trick," —each forfeit a double loo (or in some companies the whole amount in the pool, or the maximum loo, and loses his share of the stake, which is divided equally among those who play the hand, it being difficult to determine how the cards might have been played had the false play not taken place.

This forfeiture goes to the next pool.

FIVE-CARD LOO.

The principle of this game is the same as that of three-card Loo. It does not admit of so large a party; but for three, four, or five, it is perhaps a more pleasant game.

Instead of three, the dealer (having paid *five* half-pence for his deal) gives five cards to each player, first three and then two, and turns up the upper card of the remainder of the pack for trumps. He then exchanges to each player, from the top of the pack, all or as many of their five cards as the parties choose, in the same order as he dealt. Those who exchange any of their cards must play, and are looed in five if they do not get a trick; but if they do not change they may play without running the risk of being looed. The dealer may also change any or all of his own cards, and he takes the turn up card into his hand likewise, throwing out one in lieu of it. The cards have the same value as at three-card Loo and Whist, except that the knave of clubs, which is called *Pam*, is superior to any trump. If the elder hand holds *Pam*, he must lead it; if not, a small card of trumps if he has it, or any other suit which is considered as trumps; and the holder of *Pam* is expected to play it in the first round. If the winner of the first trick hold a trump, he must play it next; but for the remaining three tricks the players are left to their own discretion. Each trick is entitled to a fifth of the pool. A flush of five trumps or four trumps with *Pam* in one hand, takes the whole pool, and the other players, except the holder of *Pam*, are looed in five each.

The only laws in this game are, that you must follow suit if you can, and that in the first round trumps must be played, though the elder hand, sometimes not holding a trump card may lead from another suit.

It is sometimes played with what is called a *Running Pam*, that is, making the knave of the trump suit the best card, instead of the knave of clubs.

ALL-FOURS.

The game, sometimes called *Old-Sledge* and *Seven-Up*, is played with a full pack of fifty-two cards, which take rank as at Whist—the Ace being the highest and the Deuce the lowest.

DEALING.

The players cut for deal, the highest card having the deal. The dealer then gives six cards to each player, three at a time, and turns up the thirteenth, if there be two players, and the twenty-fifth if there be four. The turn-up is the trump.

BEGGING.

The non-dealer then looks at his hand, and determines whether he will hold it for play, or *beg*. If he is satisfied with his hand, he says, "I stand;" but if he is not satisfied with his cards, he says, "I beg," in which case the dealer must either suffer his adversary to score one point, saying, "Take one," or give each three more cards from the pack, and then turn up the next card, the seventh for trumps; if, however, the trump turned up be of the same suit as the first, the dealer must go on, giving each three cards more, and turning up the seventh, until a chance of suit for trump takes place

PLAYING THE HAND.

After these preliminaries have been settled, the eldest hand leads a card, and the dealer plays a card to it; these two cards constitute a trick.

The player who plays the highest card of the suit led, or trumps, wins the trick, and has the next lead. The play proceeds in this way until all the tricks are played.

SCORING.

The points that may be scored are herewith given in their order of precedence:

High.—The highest trump out; the holder scores one point.

Low.—The lowest trump out; the original holder scores one point, even if it be taken by his adversary.

Jack.—The knave of trumps. The winner of the trick containing it scores one point.

When the Jack is turned up for trump it counts one point for the dealer, and in that case takes precedence of every other point in the score.

Game.—The greatest number that, in the tricks gained, can be shown by either party; reckoning for—

Each Ace..............*four* towards game.
" King..............*three* " "
" Queen.............*two* " "
" Knave.............*one* " "
" Ten...............*ten* " "

The other cards do not count towards game; thus it may happen that a deal may be played without either party having any to score for game, by reason of holding neither court cards nor Tens.

When the players hold equal numbers—ties—the eldest hand scores the point for game.

One card may count all fours: for example, the eldest hand hold only the Knave of the trump suit, and stands his game; the dealer having neither trump, Ten, Ace, nor court card, it will follow that the Knave will be both High, Low, Jack and Game.

The game consists of seven points, and the player who scores that number first wins the game.

FOUR-HANDED ALL-FOURS.

The parties usually who shall be partners by *cutting the cards*, the two highest and the two lowest being partners. The four players divide themselves into two *sets*, each player sitting opposite his partner. The firt deal is decided dy *cutting* the cards, the highest *cut* having the deal, but afterwards it is taken by each player in rotatation.

The *dealer* and the player on his *left only* are permitted to look at their cards previous to the latter deciding upon his hand, and in case he begs, the other parties must not raise their cards until the dealer announces whether he will "give one" or run the cards for another trump.

LAWS OF THE GAME OF ALL-FOURS.

CUTTING AND DEALING.

1. The deal is determined by cutting the cards, and the player cutting the highest card deals. In cutting the Ace is the highest card, and ties cut again.

[In the four-handed game, the two highest play against the two lowest.]

2. Less than four cards is not a cut, and the player cutting must leave at least four cards at the bottom of the pack.

3. If a card be exposed, a new cut may be demanded.

4. The dealer must give each player three cards at a time, alternately, if two are playing, and in rotation, beginning with the player to his left, if four are playing. In this order he must deliver six cards to each player.

5. If the dealer deals without having the cards properly cut; or if a card is faced in the pack; or if the dealer in any way expose any of his adversary's cards, or if he give to either player too few or too many cards, there must be a fresh deal. The cards are re-shuffled and re-cut, and the dealer deals again. If the dealer expose any of his own cards, the deal stands good.

6. After the first hand the players deal alternately, if only two play. If more than two play, the players deal in rotation to the left. When playing for money, the players cut for deal at the commencement of each game.

[The following case may, and frequently does arise in a three-handed game of All-Fours: A, B and C are playing; A deals, and B goes out in that hand. In the regular course, it would be B's deal and C's beg; and B being out of the game, the question arises, must C deal. or can he claim his beg? *Decision.*—In a somewhat analogous position in the game of Pitch, when A dealt and B went out, it was decided that it would be proper for B to deal A and C their hands, and then retire from the game. The decision was made upon the ground that it would be a manifest wrong to deprive C of the great advantage of the pitch, while A's right would not in any way be compromised or interfered with. We concur in this opinion, as far as the game of Pitch is concerned, but such a rule would not be proper in three-handed All-Fours, for the reason that if B were to deal, and A were to beg, the dealer B would have no power to gi , or run the cards, having retired from the game. The deal must, therefore, in a case like this, pass to C.]

THE SCORE.

7. The points score in the following order of precedence 1st, *High*; 2d, *Low*; 3d, *Jack*; and 4th, *Game*.

[Thus it will be seen that if two parties are playing, and the game stands six points each, he who scores High goes out first, as that takes precedence of the other points, unless Jack is *turned up* by the *dealer*. The same is the case when the game stands *five* to *six*; the former goes *out* on *High* and *Low*, although the latter may make *Jack* and *Game* in *play*; but if the former make *High*, *Jack*, the latter will go out on *Low*.]

8. Each Jack turned up by the dealer counts one point for him in the game, unless a misdeal should occur *before* the Jack is turned. If the dealer turns Jack, and a misdeal should occur afterwards, even though it be in the same hand, or if he turn Jack and the cards run out by reason of the same suit being turned, he is not debarred from scoring the point.

9. Should there be a tie for *Game*, the non-dealer scores the point. If three or more are playing, and there is a tie the eldest hand scores game.

THE BEG.

10. If a player beg, it is at the option of the dealer to give him one point or run the cards for a new trump. When playing three-handed, if the dealer give one player, he must give both.

[Running the cards is accomplished in the following manner. The dealer having laid aside the old trump, deals three more cards to each player, and then turns up the next card for the new trump. If, however, the card turned up should be of the same suit as the original trump, the dealer must repeat this operation until the trump suit is changed.]

11. No player may beg more than once in each hand.

[There is nothing to prevent the dealer and the eldest hand from *bunching the cards—i e.*, having a fresh deal, after the latter has begged, and the cards have been run by the former provided they mutually agree to do so; or if the new trump is unsatisfactory to both, they may agree to run them again intead of bunching; but a suit cannot become trump that has once been turned down during the deal; this, however, is more a matter of agreement than of actual law.]

12. Should the same suit be turned until the cards run out, then the cards must be bunched, and dealt anew.

[*Case.*—A, B, C, and D. are playing All. Fours; A having the deal, turns up a Club for trump; B begs; A runs them and again turns up a Club; he still continues, and once more turns up a Club. The question is, can B insist that the dealer turn the last card for trump? *Decision.*—No. If A elect to bunch the cards and deal anew, under these circumstances, he may do so. The dealer *must* give each player three cards *before* turning for a new trump. and continue doing so until a trump is obtained. When he cannot comply with this condition, a new deal ensues.]

13. When playing the four handed game the *dealer* and the player on his *left only* are permitted to look at their cards previous to the latter deciding upon his hand; and in case he begs the other parties must not raise their cards until the dealer annouces whether he will "give one;" or run the cards to another tramp.

THE REVOKE.

14. Each player must follow suit, if he can, unless he chooses to trump, and failing to follow suit, provided he can (unless he trumps), he becomes liable to the following penalty:

I. If the player making the revoke make Jack and Game, he cannot score either point, but his adversary may add both points to his score.

II. If the player making the revoke makes either Jack or Game, when both points are out, he cannot score the point, but his adversary may add two points to his score.

II. If both Jack and Game are out, and the revoking player holds Jack, but does not make it; his adversary may score two points.

IV. If Jack is not out, the adversary scores one point for the revoke.

15. A revoke is established as soon as the trick in which it occurs is turned and quitted; or a card has been led for the next trick.

The regular game of All-Fours has been subjected at various times to important modifications; the principal varieties are known under the names of *Californiu Jack*, *Pitch*, *Commercial Pitch*, *Pedro Sancho*, each of which involves distinctive points of difference in the method of playing them. They will be found fully described under their respective headings.

CATCH THE TEN.

SOMETIMES CALLED SCOTS WHIST.

This is a favorite game in Edinburgh and other parts of Scotland, though we believe it is not much known in the sister kingdom: It may be played by from 2 to 8 persons with 36 cards of each suit, viz: the 2, 3, 4, and 5, being thrown out; and if necessary for an equal division of the cards, one or two of the sizes. If the party consisis of 2, 3, 5, or 7, each plays on his own account.

When two play, three hands are dealt for each player, the first two hands from the top of the pack, then other two, and lastly the third two, the 36 being turned up. The hands are played in the order in which they were dealt. In like manner, when three play, two hands are dealt to each, and played in the same order. If the party consist of 4, A and C are partners against B and D, if 6, A, C, and E. against B, D, and F—or A and D, B and E, C and F, in three partnerships if 8, A, C, E, and G, against B, D, F, and H, or they may form four partnerships—the partners always sitting opposite to each other. with an adversary between each two.

THE MODE OF PLAYING.

Is the same as at whist; the cards being cut, and dealt by one or three at a time, and the last one turned up for trump; they have the same value as at whist, except in the the trump suit. Forty-one is game, and the points are made by counting the cards in, the tricks taken, and the honors of trumps. Each card above the party's share in the tricks taken counts for one. Thus, if four are playing, each person's share of the 36 cards is 9. If two partners take eight tricks, (4 multiplied by 8 are 32) they reckon 14 towards game, that being the number over their joint shares of twice 9, or 18. The knave of trumps is the best, and reckons for 11, ace next, for 4, king for 3, queen for 2, and the Ten for 10. They are not reckoned, as at whist, by the party to whom they are dealt, but to those who take them in the course of playing.

MAXIMS FOR PLAYING.

As the name implies, the grand object in this game is to *Catch* the *Ten* of trumps, or to prevent its being caught by the adversary. The only safe way of saving or *passing* the Ten, is to play it in a round of trumps, when one of your partnerse as played the best trump; or if you happen to be last player, and have none of the suit led, trump with you Ten, if it will take the trick, or if your partner has already taken it. There are very favorable opportunities and do not often occur; so that it is frequently necessary to run some risk to secure so important a card—[illegible]g suit in the second round, though not last player—[illegible]ing to your partner's holding the best trump, &c. If you hold the knave and king, or ace, and king and have the lead, play two rounds of trumps, and you will have a chance of catching the Ten in the second rouud, or enabling your partner to pass it under cover of your best trump. But these rules must vary so considerably according to the greater or smaller number of the party playing, that it is almost impossible, without confusing the learner, to lay down particular rules for every case. Attention to the game, with a little calculation, for the principles laid dow for whist, will soon enable any person of moderate capacity to play this game sufficiently well for the purpose of amusement; and his own interest will quickly render the gambler who understands the principles of the game, an adapt at it.

Note. A revoke is punished by the total loss of the game.

BRAG.

Like most other round games. Brag is variously played in different companies. The simplest mode is called

SINGLE BRAG.

In this game the Nines and Knaves are called "Braggers, from their being the best cards—or "Turners," because they are convertible into cards of any other value, so as to form pairs or pair royal by the highest of which the game is decided. Thus three braggers in one hand cannot be beat, as they form a pair-royal cards, and are better than a natural pair-royal of aces, etc. Two braggers and an ace, etc., are better than one bragger and two aces, etc. In the same manner. a pair formed by the assistance of a bragger is better than a natural pair, or tw cards, of like value. Thus a nine and a king take precedence of two kings, but are inferior to two aces. A knave and a king are better than a nine and a king; and if the pairs in two hands are equal, the higher value of the third card gives the preference; if they are equal in every respect, the elder hand has the preference. The lowest pair-royal that can be formed, as three twos, is better than the highest pair, as two aces, &c.

N. B.—In some companies the knave of clubs and the nine of diamonds only are admitted to be braggers or turners; and it is sometimes agreed that natural pairs of pairs royal are to precede artificial ones of the same value, or those formed by the assistance of the knave of clubs or nine of diamonds; as thus, two kings to be considered better than a king with a nine or knave, but to yield to an ace or a nine or knave.

MODE OF PLAYING.

The cards being shuffled and cut, a certain stake, from a cent to five dollars, is deposited by the dealer, who gives three cards to each of the company. The elder hand, and the others after him, having examined their hands, either "pass," which is signified by laying down their cards, or "brag," in which case the dealer's stake is to be answered by all who brag. On putting down another stake, or bragging a second time, the person doing so, if he holds a pair, but not otherwise, may insist on seeing the next player's hand, saying, "I'll see you," or "I'll sight you." in which case they examine each other's cards, and the person having the worst hand of the two is oblidge to lay it down, or "pass." The players go on in this way till the braggers are reduced to two, who continue bragging against each other (either an equal sum with the dealer's stake, or higher,) till one "sights," the other, and whichever of the two has the best brag hand, wins the whole of the stakes put down.

BRAG AND PAIRS.

To vary the above game, the dealer sometimes deposits *two* separate stakes, one of which is for natural pairs, and the company may brag on either stake they please, or on both. Thus if one of the players has a pair or pair-royal of good cards, such as aces, down to ten or eights, he may answer one or both of the dealer's stakes, according to the chance of success afforded by the cards he holds; and can, if he holds a pair, "sight," those who are bragging on the same end with himself, as described above. Those who put their stakes on the brag-end proceed exactly as as at Single Brag.

THREE STAKE BRAG.

There is another way playing this game, in which three stakes are deposited by the dealer, who gives two cards to each player, and then turns up a third all round. The best whist card turned up takes the first stake, the elder hand having the preference if two equal cards are turned, except in the case of the ace of diamonds, which is always the best at this stage of the game.

The second stake is the brag-stake, and is determined as at Single Brag, each reckoning his turned-up card along with the other two.

The third is gained by the player who holds, or obtains by drawing from the undealt cards, 31, or the highest number under that, the ace reckoning for 11, the pictured cards for 10 each, and the rest according to their pips. The elder hand has the preference in case of equality, and any one drawing above 31, loses of course.

N. B.—The three stakes may be all gained by one person, in which case he is entitled, in some companies, to three more from each player; but this advantage is usually set aside, as savoring too much of gambling.

HOW TO PLAY CASSINO.

The game of Cassino is played by two persons, with a pack of fifty two cards.

DEALING.

The players cut for deal. Lowest deals. At the outset of the game, the dealer gives four cards to each player, and lays out four other cards face upwards upon the table The cards are dealt two or four at a time; the eldest hand first, the laid-out cards next, the dealer last.

After the cards are all played, four more cards are similarly dealt to each player, but none laid out; and this is repeated until all the cards have been dealt. (See Rule 4.)

PLAYING.

After the deal is completed th eldest hand plays first.

The primary object in Cassino is to capture as many cards as possible, and this is done in four different ways; Pairing, Combining, Building, and Calling. A description of each of these will cover all the possible varieties of play that can take place.

It must first be understood that one card *must* be played from the hand every time that it is the player's turn to play; and further, that *only one* card can be played at each turn.

If a card is played, and it cannot be used for pairing, or to take a combination, or to form a build or call it, it must remain on the table.

Pairing.—This consists in capturing one or more cards by means of a similar card played from the hand. Thus, a King (or a Seven) for instance, held in the hand will take all the Kings (or Sevens) that are upon the table. The card played and all the cards it captures becoming the property of the player.

Combining.—A player, when it is his turn to play, may group together two or more cards that are upon the table. Thus, a Two and a Six on the table may be combined to to form an eight; or an Ace, Three, and Five will form a nine. Two or more combinations may be made at the same time, provided each combination produces a similar numerical result. Thus: Suppose there are on the table an Ace, Two, Four, Five, and Six; the Four and five will combine to make a nine; and the Ace, Two, and Six will form another nine. They are all then captured by a Nine played from the hand.

Buildeng.—This consists in playing a card from the hand upon a card or cards on the table, which can then only be captured by a card representing an aggregate of their pips they cannot be captured separately by *pairing*. Thus: Supposing there is a Five on the table, and a player has a Seven and a Two in his hand; when it is his turn, he may play his Two upon the Five, and say "Seven." When his next turn comes to play, he can capture the build with his Seven, unless his adversary has already done so, or has raised the build.

A player cannot raise his own build; but his opponent can, if he hold the card needed to redeem it. Thus, as in the previous instance, A has *built* a seven; he cannot raise his build by playing, say, a Three upon it, to make a ten; but his opponent, B, can. B plays, for instance, a Two upon A's build, and says "Nine"; A, if he have an Ace and a Ten, can then play his Ace on the nine-build, and say "Ten," and then nothing but a Ten would capture it.

Again: Suppose there are a Two and a Four on the table; a player having a Three and Nine in his hand, may combine the Two and Four, play his Three upon them, and say "Nine" (not "Nines."

A player may make another build, or may pair or combine other cards previous to taking in his first build.

Calling.—This consists in grouping together similar cards, builds, or combinations, and then *calling* their denomination. Cards, builds, or combinations thus called cannot be built upon or otherwise interfered with; they can only be captured by a card of the denomination *called*. Thus: Supposing a player has two Nines in hish and, and there is a Nine (or a *build* or a combination of nine) on the table; instead of pairing it or taking the build (or combination), he can play one from his hand upon the Nine, etc., on the the table and say. "Nines"—in the plural number, to distinguished it from a *build*.

Again: A Five, Four and Eight on the table, and an Ace and Nine in the players hand; he can combine the Five and Four, then play his Ace on the Eight, put them all together, and call "Nines." If he had two Nines (instead of one) in his hand, when it is his next turn to play he can play one of the Nines on the same pile, and again call "Nines"; and next turn capture the whole with his remaining Nine, unless his opponent should have forestalled him.

A Sweep.—If a player can capture *all* the cards on the board with one play it is called a sweep, and counts one point for the player.

When a player makes a sweep he turns the *sweep-card* (the card that takes the sweep) face upwards. This is done to keep tally of the number of sweeps made by each player. If the opposing player makes a sweep, these two sweeps cancel each other; and the players turn the canceled sweep-cards down. The difference in the number of sweeps, only, is scored; thus, if A makes three and B makes two sweeps, A deducts B's two sweeps from his own three scores the difference one.

Last-cards.—After *all* the cards are dealt out, the player who who wins the last trick takes all the cards remaining on the table.

VALUE OF THE POINTS, AND SCORING.

The following are the points that may be scored by the player who makes or takes them in play:

Grat Cassino.—The Ten of Diamonds......2 points.

Little Cassino.—The Two of Spades.........1 "

The majority of Cards......................3 points
The Majority of Spades....................1 "
Each Ace...................................1 "
Each Sweep................................1 "

The points gained by each party are counted at the end of the deal, and that party which has the greatest number of points wins the game.

If both players make the same number of points, the game is drawn.

Cassino is sometimes played for a fixed number of points and this method is growing in favor. When thus played it requires several deals to complete it. (*See* Twenty:one Point Cassino.)

RULES OF CASSINO.

CUTTING AND DEALING.

1 The deal is determined by cutting, and the player cutting the lowest card must deal. Ties cut over. In cutting, Ace is low.

2. Each player has a right to shuffle. The dealer has the right of shuffiing last.

3. If, in cutting to the dealer, or in re-uniting the separated packets, a card be exposed, or if there be any confusion of the cards, there must be a fresh cut.

4. The dealer must deal the cards either two or four at a time ; first to his adversary, next for the lay-out, and lastly to himself. The laid-out cards are dealt face upwards. After the first four cards thus dealt are all played four more cards must be similarly dealt to each player, but none laid out ; and this is repeated as fast as each hand of four card has been played, until the pack is exhausted.

5. If the dealer deals witbout having the pack cut, or if he shuffles the pack after it has been cut with his consent, there must be a fresh deal ; provided the opposing side claim it before any cards of the lay out are turned up on the table ; in this case the cards must be re-shuffled and re-cut, and the dealer must deal again.

6. If a card is faced in the pack, or if the dealer, while dealing, expose any of his adversary's cards, previous to turning up any of the cards in the lay-out, there must be a fresh deal, and the dealer must deal again; provided the opposing player demand it. If the card is expposed, or discovered to be faced, after any portion of the lay out has been turned up, the opposing player may keep it or reject it; if he reject it, the dealer must place the rejected card in the middle of the stock, and deal a fresh card from the top of the same.

[If the dealer expose a card in the last round, that is, the round, that exhausts the stock, he should be compelled to take the exposed card, and allow his adversary to draw one of the delinquent's own unexposed cards in exchange for it.]

7. If the dealer give to himself or to the opposing player, too many or too few cards, it is a misdeal and the dealer forfeits the game and all depending on it.

[This penalty is not usually enforced when the misdeal is made in the first hand dealt, and is discovered before the cards are raised from the table. In such an instance the deal is rectified, if rectification is possible and clearly evident; if, however, any doubt exists as to locating the cards property, or if the eldest hand so demands, a fresh deal ensues, and the dealer deals again.]

BUILDING, COMBINING AND CALLING.

8. If a player build one or more cards to a certain denomination, or call a build or combination (*see* Calling, page 15), and it subsequently transpires that he holds no card of a similar denomination with which to redeem the cards thus built or called, the cards which constitute such build or call must be separated, and the opposing player may use them in any legitimate way he chooses.

9. If a player makes a build, his adversary cannot raise

the build by employing for that purpose any card upon the board. The denomination of a build can only be changed by a card played from the hand.

10. Should a player make a build, and his opponent decline to build it up higher, he the first player, may not alter his build, but take it up with a card of the same denomination. He may however, make another build, or he may pair or combine any other cards before taking up his first build ; but he must comply with one of the above conditions before playing a card which will not do either.

11. When a card is played for the purpose of building or calling, the player must declare the denomination of the proposed build or call audibly and distinctly, so that no doubt of his intentions may exist ; and failing to comply with this requirement, his opponent may separate the cards, and employ them in any lawful way he may deem to his advantage.

12. If a player, when taking in a build or any other combination, should take up a card or cards which do not belong to the combination, the delinquent player must not only restore to the lay-out the card or cards thus improperly taken up, but also all the cards that rightly composed the combination. (*See* Note to Rule 13.)

13. Tricks that have been taken must not be examined until all the cards have been played ; nor may any trick but that last won be looked at, as every mistake must be challenged immediately.

[*Note.*—A and B play Cassino. A builds Two on Seven, then builds Ace en Eight, calling "Nine"; subsequently taking in the build by mistake with an Eight. Next plays his Nine. B sees that A took in his build with the wrong card and claims that in consequence, A must restore to the lay-out all the cards taken by mistake, although two plays had been made after the mistake had been made. ***Decision.***—**B saw the mistake too late for his** own advantage, and could not prove that any error had been made, as he was entitled to examine only the last trick won.]

TWENTY-ONE POINT CASSINO.

Cassino is now very generally played for a fixed number of points (usually twenty-one), and the first player who succeeds in scoring the number agreed upon wins the game. No one point takes any precedence over another: the points are scored as soon as made, and a player wins the game the moment he has made the requisite points.

When playing for a given number of points, sweeps are scored as soon as made, and are not turned down as in the single deal game.

If a player claims to have won the game and cannot show the requisite points, the hand is ended and he loses the game.

The deal passes in rotation throughout the game.

It is sometimes agreed to turn down sweeps and defer scoring the points for sweeps (if any) until the end of the hand; so that a sweep will not count a player out *when made*. This is done because when sweeps are turned, a sweep is liable to be canceled in playing out the hand. This method of playing is not recommended, as it is contrary to the spirit of the game. and the occasion of much dispute.

THREE AND FOUR-HANDED CASSINO.

Three-handed Cassino is in all essential particulars identical with the Twenty-one Point game. The dealer delivers the cards to each player in rotation, beginning with the player to his left. The player who first scores the number of points agreed upon wins the game.

The Four-handed game is played with partners for a given number of points, the same as at Whist. The score is reckoned the same as the two-handed game, the partners combining their points.

If a player make a build, the fact that he holds the necessary card to redeem it is sufficient authority for his partner to make a similar build, or to *call* a card upon the build, without having a card of the same denomination in his hand. To avoid disputes, this point should be made the subject of special agreement before beginning the game.

WHIST: FROM THE TEXT OF HOYLE.

Though not the first writer on the game of Whist, Hoyle was undoubtedly the first of any authority. Long before he wrote, there existed certain rules for ordering its economy, as well as for playing it upon system. Like most other samples of "the good old times," Whist, as practised in the days of our forefathers, was no such shining light of the *prisca fides.* We take it up at an epoch in which the game must have attained a certain amount of respectability, namely, in the year 1734, when Richard Seymour, Esquire, published the fifth edition of his "Compleat Gamester, for the use of the Young Princesses." If his record be true, which there is good reason to believe was the case, society in the reign of George the Second was by no means in a state of chivalry as to morals. He shall tell his own tale, and in his own fashion.

Whist, vulgarly called "Whisk."

"This is a very ancient game among us; and is said to be the foundation of all the English games upon the cards.

"Very few persons play correctly at it; though there are many pretenders, who are the easiest to be made, and generally are made, the greatest bubbles.

"Considerable sums of money are played away at this game; which has put sharpers upon inventions to deceive and cheat unwary players, as will be showed in the sequel.

"Formerly it was usual to deal four cards together; but it is demonstrable there is no safety in that method; but now the cards are dealt round one and one at a time, as the securest and best way.

"In playing your cards, you must have recourse altogether to your own judgment; and though you have but mean cards in your hand, yet you may (by observing the course of the cards) play them so suitable to those in your partner's hand, that he may either trump them or play the best of that suit on the board.

"You ought to have a strict eye on what cards are played out, that you may know by that means either what to play, if you lead, or how to trump securely and advantageously. Renouncing, or not following suit when you have it in your hand, is very foul play; and he that doth it ought to forfeit one, or the game upon a game, and he that loseth dealing loseth one, or a trick, as you make it.

"At ruff and honours, by some called slam, you have in the pack all the deuces, and the reason is, because four persons playing have dealt twelve a-piece, there are four left for the stock, the uppermost whereof is turned up, and that is trumps. He who hath ace of trumps ruffs, that is, he takes in those four cards, and lays out four; the four honours are the ace, king, queen, and knave; he who hath three honours in his hand, his partner not having the fourth, sets up eight by cards, that is, two tricks; if he hath all four, then sixteen, that is, four tricks. It is all one if the two partners make them three or four between them, as if one had them. If the honours are equally divided among the gamesters of each side, then they say honours are split. If either side are at eight groats, he hath the benefit of calling, Can ye? If he hath two honours in his hand, and if the other answers one, the game is up, which is ten in all; but if he hath more than two he shows them, which is the same thing; but if he forgets to call, after playing a trick, he loseth the advantage of calling for that deal.

"All cards are of value as they are superior one to another, as a ten wins a nine, if not trumps; so a queen a knave in like manner; but the least trump will win the highest card of any other card: where note, the ace is the highest.

"Some play at two-handed, or three-handed Whist. If three-handed, always two strive to suppress and keep down the rising man. They deal to each twelve a-piece, and the trump is the bottom card. The manner of crafty playing, the number of the game ten, honours and dignity of other cards are all alike; and he that wins most tricks is most forward to win the set.

"He that can by craft overlook his adversary's game, hath a great advantage; for by that means he may partly know what to play securely; or if he can have some petty glimpse of his partner's hand. There is a way by making some sign by the fingers, to discover to their partners what honours they have, or by the wink of one eye, it signifies one honour, shutting both eyes two; placing three fingers or four on the table, three or four honours. For which reasons all nice gamesters play behind curtains.

"Dealing the cards out by one and one round to each person, is the best method of putting it out of the dealer's power to impose on you. But we shall demonstrate that, deal the cards which way you will, a confederacy of two sharpers will beat any two persons in the world, though ever so good players, that are not of the gang, or in the secret; and three poll one is as safe and secure as if the money was in their pockets. All which will appear presently. The first necessary instructions to be observed at Whisk, as principals of the secret, which may be likewise transferred to most other games at cards, are

Breef Cards.
Corner-bend.
Middle-bend (or Kingston-bridge).

"Of breef cards there are two sorts: one is a card longer than the rest; the other is a card broader than the rest.

"The long sort are such as three, four, five, six, seven, eight, and nine; the broad sort are such as aces, kings, queens, and knaves. The use and advantage of each are as follows.

Example.

"When you cut the cards to your adversary, cut them long or end-ways, and he will have a three, four, five, six, seven, eight, or nine at bottom. When your adversary cuts the cards to you, put them broadside to him, and he will naturally cut (without ever suspecting what you do) ace, king, queen, or knave, &c., which is sufficient advantage to secure any game. It is a fine manner, especially in the old bet that the dealer does not score two that deal, since shuffling is of no signification here. And in case you cannot get cards of the proper sizes ready made to mix with others, you may shave them with a razor or penknife from the threes to the nines each side, and from the aces to the knave each end; then put them up in the same case or cover, and if they are done as they ought to be, they will pass upon anybody. As Whisk is a tavern game, the sharpers generally take care to put about the bottle before the game begins, so quick that a bubble cannot be said to see clearly even when he first begins to play.

"The next is the corner-bend, which is four cards turned down finely at one corner, a signal to cut by.

"The other is vulgarly called Kingston-bridge, or the middle-bend: it is done by bending your own or adversary's tricks two different ways, which will cause an opening or arch in the middle, which is of the same use and service as the other two ways, and only practised in its turn to amuse you.

"After a deal or two is formally played, A and B will begin to operate in the following manner:

"When A or B are to deal, they observe (the preceding deal) to take up the tricks thus:

1. A bad card.	2. A good card.
3. A bad card.	4. A good card.

[Meaning the best and worst that fall in that lift.]

"When C or D deals, they must be taken up thus:

1. A good card.	2. A bad card.
3. A good card.	4. A bad card.

"By this rule it is very plain that the best cards fall to A and B every deal. How is it possible, therefore, that C and D should ever win a game without permission? But it would be deemed ill policy, and contrary to the true interest of A and B, to act thus every deal: I will therefore suppose it is practised just when they please, according as bets happen in company; though the rule with gamesters, in low life, is at the first setting out to stupefy you with wine and the loss of your money, that you may never come to a perfect understanding of what you are doing. It may be truly said, that many an honest gentleman has been kept a month in such a condition by the management and contrivance of a set of sharpers.

"Now you may imagine it not in the power of A and B to cause the tricks to be taken up after the manner aforesaid; but there is nothing so easy or so frequently practised, especially at three poll one; for in playing the cards, the confederates will not only take care of their own tricks, but also of yours; for the cards may be so played and shoved together in such a manner, as will even cause you to take them right yourself; and if a trick should lie untowardly upon the table, A or B will pay you the compliment of taking it up for you, and say, Sir, that's yours.

"This operation will the more readily be apprehended by seeing it practised half a score times; when once you are aware of it, it will otherwise (I may safely say) pass upon any person that has not been let into the secret. This being allowed, the next point and difficulty is to shuffle and cut.

"I say, that either A or B are such curious workmen, and can make a sham shuffle with a pack of cards so artfully, that you would believe they were splitting them, when at the same time they will not displace a single card from its order

"Now to cut the cards, a bend is prepared for you to cut to; the middle is best, and it is odds but you unwarily cut to it; if not, Slip is the word; but if you have no opportunity to do that neither, then deal away at all hazards, it is but an equal bet that they come in your favour; if right, proceed; if otherwise, miss a card in its course, and it brings the cards according to your first design; it is but giving two at last where you missed; and if that cannot be conveniently done, you only lose the deal, and there is an end of it.

"But when A or B are to cut, they make it all safe; for then they make the corner-bend, which any one that knows may cut to, a hundred times together.

Piping at Whisk.

"By piping I mean, when one of the company that does not play (which frequently happens) sits down in a convenient place to smoke a pipe, and so look on, pretending to amuse himself that way. Now the disposing of his fingers on the pipe, whilst smoking, discovers the principal cards that are in the person's hand he overlooks; which was always esteemed a sufficient advantage to win a game by another way, viz., Indeed, signifies diamonds; Truly, hearts; Upon my word, clubs; I assure you, spades: but as soon as these methods become known new ones are invented; and it is most certain that two persons may discover to each other what sort of cards they have in hand, and which ought to be first played, many different ways, without speaking a word. Talking is not allowed at Whist; the very word implies, Hold your tongue."

Mr. Seymour's whole book indeed indicates a very truculent social condition at the date of its indicting. "The games," he says, "are always precarious, and betting money that way was thought to be like licking honey off thorns. . . . I have been told of one of these sharpers who caused a box to be made, not as they are usually, screwed within, but smooth, and procured it to be so well painted and shadowed within, that it looked like a screwed box; now this box was but half board, wide at the top and narrow at the bottom, that the dice might stick, and the box being smooth, would come out without tumbling. With this box he went and played at Inn and Inn,* by virtue whereof, and his art of taking up and throwing his dice into the box, he got the first night £1000, and the next night £200 a year, with a coach and six horses. and enjoys the estate to this day with great improvements, and never would handle a dice since, well knowing how many worthy families it hath ruined." Moreover we read, as no doubt "the young princesses" read also, how that at the "Game of Nazarene," the knave of clubs is called Knave-Knocker, and he that hath it challengeth two a piece. If women play among men, it is customary for Knave-Knocker to kiss Queen Nazarene, a practice that would extend of course to a royal lady of any kith or country.

In 1743, was published, as we have already said, the treatise ascribed to Hoyle, the great father of the game. It saw the light when obviously it was much needed. Public taste seems just then to have taken up Whist as a necessary accomplishment, for persons of condition. There is the following passage in "A Lady's Letter," in the "Rambler," of May 8, 1750: "Papa made me drudge at whist till I was tired of it; and Mr. Hoyle, when he had not given me above forty lessons, said I was one of his best scholars." The anonymous "Treatise" may however be spared quotation beyond the advertisement, a curious document, helping us to a view of the period, in relation to such matters as came within compass of its observation.

"As some people in particular may be anxious to know,

* This was one of those gambling contrivances, known in those days as "Games without the Tables." Hazard belonged to this class.

and the public in general may be glad to be informed, by what means the following Treatise came to be ushered into the world in this manner, we think they cannot be better satisfied on this head, than by making public the following letter from a gentleman at Bath to a friend of his, and hope they will not take it amiss if the gentleman's name is concealed, since we are not at liberty to publish it.

"'Dear Sir,

"'In an age where the ignorant and the unwary, as well as the plain downright honest man of sense, are so exposed to the tricks of sharpers of all denominations, from the counter up to the most sacred and respectable offices and institutions, I thought it would be doing no inconsiderable service to many of my countrymen, If I contributed a little to put them upon their guard and preserve their purses, while they are indulging themselves in what is elegantly called killing time. It were indeed to be wished that less time was killed in the manner which has put me upon this undertaking, but as the itch of gaming is likely to prevail as long as we preserve anything of what is now-a-days called polite taste; and as it seems to be an almost necessary evil, which keeps people of a certain disposition from employing their time worse, so I hope I shall deserve the thanks of a great many, for having been instrumental in rescuing them from the snares which they are but too frequently caught in, by being over-matched in these sorts of amusements.

"'I myself, as you very well know, am one of those unfortunate beings, that being possessed of a pretty handsome fortune, and having a great deal of idle time upon their hands, constantly spend a little portion of it in gaming. The game of Whist is that which I take most delight in, and till of late, fancied myself all along a pretty good master of it. But to my vexation, it is not long since I lost a considerable sum of money one night at it, and yet I could not perceive that the cards run extraordinary cross against me; so that I could not but conclude I was beat by superior skill. This put me upon inquiring into the cause, for I was very far from imputing my misfortune to unfair play; and at last I found that there was a treatise on the game of Whist lately dispersed among a few hands at a guinea price. How to come at one of these books I know not; but at length I wrote to an acquaintance of mine in London to purchase it for me by all means, which he accordingly did, with no small difficulty. As soon as I had perused it, I found I had heretofore been but a bungler at this game, and being thoroughly sensible of the advantage which those that are possessed of this book have over the innocent player, I thought I could not oblige my friends better than by printing a few of them to make presents of. Accordingly I applied to a stationer, who offered to make me a present of half a hundred of them, provided I would allow him to print a few more for his own use. This I readily complied with, especially in consideration of the imposition and hardship the public lay under; first, by not being able to get the said book under a guinea, and then by its being reserved only in a few hands, that might make a bad use of it; for though a man of superior skill in these amusements, that takes an advantage of an ignorant player, cannot according to the common acceptation of the word, be deemed a sharper, yet, when he pursues that advantage, after he has found out the weakness of his antagonist, it must be confessed that if he is not a sharper, he is at least very near akin to one.

"'Thus much I have thought fit to acquaint you with, in regard to my conduct in this affair, which I hope will receive the commendations of every honest well-meaning man and fair gamester, and your's in particular, which is the greatest ambition of your sincere friend, and humble servant.'"

We now come to deal with Hoyle in *propria persona*, the professor who took up an art which society had adopted, with all the enthusiasm that fancies it has discovered a specific against *eunui*. He rose a benefactor of his race. Poetry never sung of patience so tried as it has been, and ever will be, at the Whist table

"Sir, I protest, were Job himself at play,
He'd rave to see you throw your cards away:
Not that I care a button, not a pin,
For what I lose—but we have cards to win.

We start with Hoyle at the commencement of the present

century, when the game had assumed most of its principles. A century before, it differed essentially in several respects from the fundamental rules now established, and fifty years ago, recognized. For instance in Swift's time, it went generally by the double title of "Whist" and "Swabbers." These "swabbers" were certain cards, the possession of which entitled the holders to a part of the stakes; in the same way that now a claim is made for the aces at quadrille. In like manner, there was no bar to counting honours, they reckoned at nine, as well as at any other score. It is not clear when the existing custom of their not counting after eight first obtained. M. Deschapelles calls it "a fashionable embellishment." His observations, always most pertinent, will be read with much interest, on this and many other modern innovations. Our text of Hoyle has been carefully collated with the different editions, some of which are faulty. We omit for the present the *mise en scene*, which will be minutely detailed in Part the Third.

HOYLE'S GENERAL RULES FOR BEGINNERS.

When you lead, begin with the best suit in your hand; if you have a sequence of king, queen, and knave, or queen, knave, and ten, they are sure leads, and gain the tenace to yourself and your partner in other suits. Begin with the highest of a sequence, unless you have five in number; in that case play the lowest (except in trumps, when you must always play the highest) in order to get the ace or king out of your partner's or adversary's hand, to make room for your strong suit.

If you have five of the smallest trumps, and not one good card in the other suits, trump out, which will make your partner the last player, and by that means give him the tenace.

If two small trumps only, with ace and king of two other suits, and a deficiency of the fourth suit, make as many tricks as you can immediately; and if your partner refuses either of your suits, do not force him, because that may weaken his game too much.

You need seldom return your partner's lead immediately, if you have good suits of your own to play, unless it be to endeavour to save or win a game; what is meant by good suits is, sequences of king, queen, and knave, or queen, knave, and ten.

If you have each five tricks, and you are assured of getting two tricks in your own hand, win them, in expectation of scoring two that deal; because if you lose the odd trick, it makes two difference, and you play two to one against yourself.

An exception to the foregoing rule is, when you see a probability either of saving your lurch or winning the game; in either of which cases risk the odd trick.

When you have a probability of winning the game, always risk a trick or two, because the share of the stake, which your adversary has by a new deal, will amount to more than the point or two which you risk.

If your adversary is six or seven love, and you are to lead, in that case risk a trick or two, in hopes of putting the game upon an equality; therefore, admitting you have the queen or knave, and one other trump, and no good cards in other suits, play out your queen or knave of trumps; by which means you will strengthen your partner's game, if he is strong in trumps; if weak, you do him no injury.

If you are four of the game, play for an odd trick, because it saves one-half of the stake; and in order to win the odd trick, though you are pretty strong in trumps, be cautious how you trump out. What is meant by strength in trumps, is, 1 honour and 3 trumps.

If you are nine of the game, and though very strong in trumps, yet if you observe your partner to have a chance of trumping any of your adversary's suits; then do not trump out, but give him an opportunity of trumping those suits. If your game is scored one, two, or three, you must play the reverse; and also five, six, or seven; because in these two last recited cases, you play for more than one point.

If you are last player, and find that the third hand cannot put on a good card to his partner's lead, admitting you have no good game of your own to play, return the lead upon the adversary; which gives your partner the tenace in that suit, and often obliges the adversary to change suits, and consequently gives the tenace in that new suit also.

If you have ace, king, and four small trumps, begin with a

small one; because it is an equal wager that your partner has a better trump than the last player; if so, you have three rounds of trumps; if not, you cannot fetch out all the trumps.

If ace, king, knave, and three small trumps, begin with the king, and then play the ace, (except one of the adversaries refuses trumps,) because the odds are in your favour that the queen falls.

If king, queen, and four small trumps, begin with a small one, because the odds are on your side that your partner has an honour.

If king, queen, ten, and three small trumps, begin with the king, because you have a fair chance that the knave falls in the second round, or you may finesse your ten upon the return of trumps from your partner.

If queen, knave, and four small trumps, begin with a small one, because the odds are in your favour that your partner has an honour.

If queen, knave, nine, and three small trumps, begin with the queen, because you have a fair chance that the ten falls in the second round; or you may wait to finesse the nine.

If knave, ten, and four small trumps, begin with a small one.

If knave, ten, eight, and three small trumps, begin with the knave, in order to prevent the nine from making a trick; and the odds are in your favour that the other three honours fall in two rounds.

If six trumps of a lower denomination, begin with the lowest, unless you should have ten, nine, and eight, and an honour turns up against you; in that case, if you are to play through the honour, begin with the ten, which obliges the adversary to play his honour to his disadvantage, or leave it in your partner's option, whether he will pass it or not.

If ace, king, and three small trumps, begin with a small one.

If ace, king, and knave, and two small trumps, begin with the king, which, next to a moral certainty, informs your partner that you have ace and knave remaining; and by putting the lead into your partner's hand, he plays you a trump; upon which you are to finesse the knave, and no ill consequence can attend such play, except the queen lies behind you single.

If king, queen, and three small trumps, begin with a small one.

If the queen, knave, and three small trumps, begin with a small one.

If queen, knave, nine, and two small trumps, begin with the queen.

If knave, ten, and three small trumps, begin with a small one.

If knave, ten, eight, and two small trumps, begin with the knave, because in two rounds of trumps it is odds but that the nine falls; or upon the return of trumps from your partner, you may finesse the eight.

If five trumps of a lower denomination, it is the best play to begin with the lowest, unless you have a sequence of ten, nine, and eight; in that case begin with the highest of the sequence.

If ace, king, and two small trumps, begin with a small one

If ace, king, knave, and one small trump, begin with the king.

If king, queen, and two small trumps, begin with a small one.

If king, queen, ten, and one small trump, begin with the king, and wait for the return of trumps from your partner, when finesse your ten, in order to win the knave.

If queen, knave, nine, and one small trump, begin with the queen, in order to prevent the ten from making a trick.

If knave, ten, and two small trumps, begin with a small one.

If knave, ten, eight, and one small trump, begin with the knave, in order to prevent the nine from making a trick.

If ten, nine, eight, and one small trump, begin with the ten, which leaves it in your partner's discretion whether he will pass it or not.

If ten, and three small trumps, begin with a small one.

SOME PARTICULAR RULES.

If you have ace, king, and four small trumps, with good suit, play three rounds of trumps, otherwise you may have your strong suit trumped.

If king, queen, and four small trumps, with a good suit, trump out with the king, because when you have the lead again, you will have three rounds of trumps.

If king, queen, ten, and two small trumps, begin with the king.

If king, queen, ten, and three small trumps, with a good suit, trump out with the king, in expectation of the knave's falling at the second round; and do not wait to finesse the ten, for fear your strong suit should be trumped.

If queen, knave, and three small trumps, with a good suit, trump out with a small one.

If queen, knave, nine, and two small trumps, with a good suit, trump out with the queen, in expectation of the ten falling at the second round; and do not wait to finesse the nine, but trump out a second time, for the reason assigned above.

If knave, ten, and three small trumps, with a good suit, trump out with a small one.

If knave, ten, eight, and two small trumps, with a good suit, trump out with the knave, in expectation of the nine falling at the second round.

If ten, nine, eight, and one small trump, with a good suit, trump out with the ten.

PARTICULAR GAMES.

Suppose you are elder hand, and that your game consist of king, queen, and knave of one suit; ace, king, queen, and two small cards of another suit; king and queen of the third suit, and three small trumps. You are to begin with the ace of your best suit (or a trump) which informs your partner that you have the command of that suit; but you are not to proceed with the king of the same suit, but play a trump next; and if you find your partner has no strength to support you in trumps, and that your adversary plays to your weak suit, *viz.* the king and queen only, in that case, play the king of the best suit: and if you observe a probability of either your adversaries being likely to trump that suit, proceed then and play the king of the suit of which you have king, queen, and knave. If it should so happen that your adversaries do not play to your weakest suit, in that case, though apparently your partner can give you no assistance in trumps, pursue your scheme of trumping out as often as the lead comes into your hand; by which means, supposing your partner to have but two trumps, and that your adversaries have four each, by three rounds of trumps, there remain only two trumps against you.

ELDER HAND.

Suppose you have ace, king, queen, and one small trump, with a sequence from the king of five in another suit, with four other cards of no value. Begin with the queen of trumps, and pursue the lead with the ace, which demonstrates to your partner that you have the king: and as it would be bad play to pursue trumps the third round, till you have first gained the command of your great suit, by stopping thus, it likewise informs your partner that you have the king, and one trump only remaining; because if you had ace, king, queen, and two trumps more, and trumps went round twice, you could receive no damage by playing the king the third round. When you lead sequence, begin with the lowest, because if your partner has the ace he plays it, which makes room for your suit. And since you have let your partner into the state of your game, as soon as he has the lead, if he has a trump or two remaining, he will play trumps to you, with a moral certainty that your king clears your adversaries' hands of all then trumps.

SECOND PLAYER.

Suppose you have ace, king, and two small trumps, with a quint-major of another suit; in the third suit you have three small cards, and in the fourth suit one. Your adversary on your right hand begins with playing the ace of your weak suit, and then proceeds to play the king: in that case do not trump it, but throw away a losing card; and if he proceeds to play the queen, throw away another losing card; and do the like the fourth time, in hopes your partner may trump it, who will in that case play a trump, or will play to your strong suit. If trumps are played, go on with them two rounds, and then proceed to play your strong suit; by which means, if there happens to be four trumps in one of your adversaries' hands, and two in the other, which is nearly the case, your partner being entitled to have three trumps out of the nine; your strong suit forces their best trumps, and you have a probability of making the odd trick in your own hand only; whereas if you had trumped one of your adversaries' best cards, you had so weakened your hand as probably not to make more than five tricks, without your partner's help.

Suppose you have ace, queen, and three small trumps; ace, queen, ten, and nine of another suit; with two small cards of each of the other suits: your partner leads to your ace, queen, ten, and nine; and as this game requires rather to deceive your adversaries, than to inform your partner, put up the nine, which naturally leads the adversary to play trumps if he wins that card. As soon as trumps are played to you, return them to your adversary, keeping the command in your own hand. If your adversary, who led trumps to you, puts out a trump which your partner cannot win, if he has no good suit of his own to play, he will return your partner's lead imagining that suit lies between his partner and your's: if this finesse of yours should succeed, you will be a great gainer by it, but scarcely possible to be a loser.

Suppose you have ace, king, and three small trumps, with a quart from a king, and two small cards of another suit, and one small card to each of the other suits; your adversary leads a suit of which your partner has a quart-major; your partner puts up the knave, and then proceeds to play the ace; you refuse to that suit by playing your loose card; when your partner plays the king, your right hand adversary trumps it. Suppose with the knave or ten, do not overtrump him, which may probably lose you two or three tricks by weakening your hand: but if he leads to the suit of which you have none, trump it, and then play the lowest of your sequence, in order to get the ace either out of your partner's or adversary's hand; which accomplished, as soon as you get the lead, play two rounds of trumps, and then proceed to play your strong suit. Instead of your adversary playing to your weak suit, if he should play trumps, do you go on with the two rounds, and then proceed to get the command of your strong suit.

GAMES TO BE PLAYED, WITH CERTAIN OBSERVATIONS, WHEREBY YOU ARE ASSURED THAT YOUR PARTNER HAS NO MORE OF THE SUIT PLAYED EITHER BY YOURSELF OR HIM.

Suppose you lead from queen, ten, nine, and two small cards of any suit, the second hand puts on the knave, your partner plays the eight: in this case, you having queen, ten, and nine, it is a demonstration, that he can have no more of that suit. Therefore you may then play your game accordingly, either by forcing him to trump that suit, if you are strong in trumps, or by playing some other suit.

Suppose you have king, queen, and ten of a suit, and you lead your king, your partner plays the knave, this demonstrates he has no more of that suit.

Suppose you have king, queen, and many more of a suit, and you begin with the king, in some cases it is good play in a partner, when he has the ace, and one small card in that suit only, to win his partner's king with his ace; for suppose he is very strong in trumps, by taking his partner's king with the ace, he trumps out, and after he has cleared the board of trumps returns his partner's lead; and having parted with the ace of that suit, has made room for his partner to make that whole suit, which possibly could not have been done if he had kept the command in his hand.

And supposing his partner has no other good card besides that suit, he loses nothing by the ace taking of his king; but if it should so happen that he has a good card to bring in that suit, he gains all the tricks which he makes in that suit, by this method of play. And as your partner has taken your king with the ace, and trumps out upon it, you have reason to judge he has one of that suit, to return you; therefore do not throw away any of that suit, even to keep a king or queen guarded.

PARTICULAR GAMES, BOTH TO ENDEAVOUR TO DECEIVE AND DISTRESS YOUR ADVERSARIES, AND TO DEMONSTRATE YOUR GAME TO YOUR PARTNER.

Suppose I play the ace of a suit of which I have king, and three small ones; the last player does not choose to trump it, having none of the suit; if I am not strong enough in trumps, I must not play out the king, but keep the command of that suit in my hand by playing a small one, in order to weaken his game.

If a suit is led, of which I have none, and a moral certainty that my partner has not the best of that suit, in order to deceive the adversary, I throw away my strong suit; but to clear up doubts to my partner when he has the lead, I throw away my weak suit. This method of play will generally succeed, unless against very good players; and even with them, you will oftener gain than lose by this method.

PARTICULAR GAMES TO BE PLAYED, BY WHICH YOU RUN THE RISK OF LOSING ONE TRICK ONLY TO GAIN THREE.

Suppose clubs to be trumps, a heart is played by your adversary; your partner having none of that suit, throws away a spade; you are then to judge his hand is composed of trumps and diamonds; and suppose you win that trick, and being too weak in trumps, you dare not force him; and suppose you shall have king, knave and one small diamond; and further, suppose your partner to have queen, and five diamonds; in that case, by throwing out your king in your first lead, and your knave in your second, your partner and you may win five tricks in that suit; whereas if you had led a small diamond, and your partner's queen having been won with the ace, the king and knave remaining in your hand obstructs the suit: and though he may have the long trump, yet by playing a small diamond, and his long trump having been forced out of his hand, you lose by this method of play three tricks in that deal.

Suppose, in the like case of the former, you should have queen, ten, and one small card in your partner's strong suit; which is to be discovered by the former example; and suppose your partner to have knave and five small cards in his strong suit; you having the lead are to play your queen, and when you play again, you are to play your ten; and suppose him to have the long trump, by this method he makes four tricks in that suit; but should you play a small one in that suit, his knave being gone, and the queen remaining in your hand in the second round of playing that suit, and the long trump being forced out of his hand, the queen remaining in your hand obstructs the suit, by which method of play you lose three tricks in that deal.

In the former examples you have been supposed to have had the lead, and by that means have had an opportunity of throwing out the best cards in your hand of your partner's strong suit, in order to make room for the whole suit: we will now suppose your partner is to lead, and in the course of play, it appears to you that your partner has one great suit; suppose ace, king, and four small ones, and that you have queen, ten, nine, and a very small one of that suit; when your partner plays the ace, you are to play the nine; when he plays the king, you are to play the ten; by which means you see, in the third round, you make your queen, and having a small one remaining, you do not obstruct your partner's great suit; whereas if you had kept your queen and ten, and the knave had fallen from the adversaries, you had lost two tricks in that deal.

Suppose in the course of play, as in the former case, you find your partner to have one great suit, and that you have king, ten, and a small one of the same; your partner leads the ace; in that case play your ten, and in the second your king: this method is to prevent a possibility of obstructing your partner's great suit.

Suppose your partner has ace, king, and four small cards in his great suit, and that you have queen, ten, and a small card, in that suit; when he plays his ace, do you play your ten, and when he plays his king, you play your queen; by which method of play you only risk one trick to get four.

Now suppose you have five cards of your partner's strong suit; viz. queen, ten, nine, eight, and a small one; and that your partner has ace, king, and four small ones; when your partner plays the ace, do you play your eight; when he plays the king, do you play your nine; and in the third round, nobody having any of that suit, except your partner and you, proceed then to play the queen, and then the ten; and having a small one remaining, and your partner two, you thereby gain a trick.*

PARTICULAR GAMES TO BE PLAYED WHEN EITHER OF YOUR ADVERSARIES TURNS UP AN HONOUR.

Suppose the knave is turned up on your right-hand, and that you have king, queen, and ten; in order to win the knave, begin to play with your king; by which method of play, your partner may suppose you to have a queen and ten remaining, especially if you have a second lead, and that you do not proceed to your queen.

The knave being turned up as before, and that you have ace, queen, and ten, by playing your queen, it answers the like purpose of the former rule.

If the queen is turned up on your right-hand, and that you have ace, king, and knave, by playing your king it answers the like purpose of the former rule.

* These directions imply that the trumps are out.

Suppose an honour is turned up on your left-hand, and you hold no honour, in that case you are to play trumps through that honour; but in case you should hold an honour, (except the ace) you must be cautious how you play trumps, because in case your partner holds no honour, your adversary will play your own game upon you.

A CASE TO DEMONSTRATE THE DANGER OF FORCING YOUR PARTNER.

Suppose A and B partners, and that A has a quint-major in trumps, with a quint-major, and three small cards of another suit, and that A has the lead; and let us suppose the adversaries C and D to have only five trumps in either hand; in this case, A having the lead, wins every trick.

Suppose, on the contrary, C has five small trumps with a quint-major and three small cards of another suit, and that C has the lead, who forces A to trump first, by which means A wins only five tricks.

A CASE TO DEMONSTRATE THE ADVANTAGE BY A SAW.

Suppose A and B partners, and that A has a quart-major in clubs, they being trumps, another quart-major in hearts, another quart-major in diamonds, and the ace of spades. And let us suppese the adversaries C and D to have the following cards: viz. C has four trumps, eight hearts, and one spade; D has five trumps and eight diamonds; C being to lead, plays an heart, D trumps it; D plays a diamond, C trumps it, and thus pursuing the saw, each partner trumps a quart-major of A's, and C being to play at the ninth trick, plays a spade, which D trumps; thus C and D have won the nine first tricks, and leave A with his quart-major in trumps only.

Whenever you can establish a saw, it is your interest to embrace it.

VARIETY OF CASES, INTERMIXED WITH CALCULATIONS, DEMONSTRATING WHEN IT IS PROPER, AT SECOND HAND, TO PUT UP THE KING, QUEEN, KNAVE, OR TEN, WITH ONE SMALL CARD OF ANY SUIT, &C.

Suppose you have four small trumps, in the three other suit.

you have one trick secure in each of them: and suppose your partner has no trump, in that case the remaining nine trumps must be divided between your adversaries; suppose five in one hand, and four in the other; as often as you have the lead, play trumps: and suppose you should have four leads, in that case, your adversaries make only five tricks out of nine trumps; whereas if you had suffered them to make their trumps single, they might possibly have made nine.

This example shows the necessity of taking out two trumps for one upon most occasions.

There is an exception to the foregoing rule; if you find in the course of play, that your adversaries are very strong in any particular suit, and that your partner can give you no assistance in that suit, in such a case you are to examine your own, and also your adversaries' scores; because by keeping one trump in your hand to trump such suit, it may be either a means to save or win a game.

Suppose you have ace, queen, and two small cards of any suit, your right-hand adversary leads that suit; in that case, do not put on your queen, because it is an equal wager that your partner has a better card in that suit than the third hand; if so, you have the command of that suit.

An exception to the foregoing rule is, in case you want the lead, then you are to play your queen.

Never choose to lead from king, knave, and one small card in any suit, because it is two to one that your partner has not the ace, and also thirty-two to twenty-five, or about five to four, that he has ace or queen; and therefore, as you have only about five to four in your favour, and as you must have four cards in some other suit, suppose the ten to be the highest, lead that suit, because it is an equal wager that your partner has a better card in that suit than the last player; and if the ace of the first mentioned suit lies behind you, which is an equal wager it should so happen, in case your partner has it not; in this case, on your adversaries leading this suit, you probably make two tricks in it by this method of play.

Suppose in the course of play it appears to you that your partner and you have four or five trumps remaining, when your adversaries have none, and that you have no winning card in your hand, but that you have reason to judge that your partner has a thirteenth card or some other winning card in his hand; in that case play a small trump, to give him the lead, in order to throw away any losing card in your hand, upon such thirteenth or other good card.

SOME DIRECTIONS FOR PUTTING UP AT SECOND HAND, KING, QUEEN, KNAVE, OR TEN OF ANY SUIT, &C.

Suppose you have the king, and one small card of any suit, and that your right-hand adversary plays that suit; if he is a good player, do not put up the king, unless you want the lead, because a good player seldom leads from a suit of which he has the ace, but keeps it in his hand to bring in his strong suit after the trumps are played out.

Suppose you have a queen, and one small card, or any suit, and that your right-hand adversary leads that suit; do not put on your queen, because, suppose the adversary has led from the ace and knave, in that case, upon the return of that suit, your adversary finesses the knave, which is generally good play, especially if his partner has played the king, you thereby make your queen; but by putting on the queen, it shows your adversary that you have no strength in that suit, and consequently puts him upon finessing upon your partner throughout that whole suit.

In the former examples you have heen informed when it is thought proper to put up the king or queen at second hand; likewise observe, in case you should have the knave or ten of any suit, with a small card of the same, it is generally bad play to put up either of them at second hand, because it is five to two that the third hand has either ace, king, or queen, of the suit led; it therefore follows, that as the odds against you are five to two, and though you should succeed sometimes by this method of play, yet in the main you must be a loser; because it demonstrates to your adversaries, that you are weak in that suit, and consequently they finesse upon your partner throughout that whole suit.

Suppose you have ace, king, and three small cards of any suit that your right-hand adversary leads; upon which you play your ace, and your partner the knave. In case you are strong in trumps, return a small one in that suit, in order to let your partner trump: and this consequence attends such play, viz. you keep the command of that suit in your own hand, and at the same time it gives your partner an intimation that you are strong in trumps; and, therefore, he may play his game accordingly, either in attempting to establish a saw, or by trumping out to you, if he has either strength in trumps, or the command of the other suits.

Suppose A and B's game is scored six, the adversaries C and D is scored 7, and that nine rounds are played out, of which A and B have won seven tricks, and suppose no honours are reckoned in that deal; in this case A and B have won the odd trick, which puts their game upon an equality; and suppose A to have the lead, and that A has two of the smallest trumps remaining with two winning cards of other suits: and suppose C and D have the two best trumps between them, with two other winning cards in their hands. It is eleven to three that C has not the two trumps; and likewise eleven to three that D has them not; the odds being so much in A's favour to win the whole stake, it is his interest to play a trump; for suppose the stake to be £70 depending, A and B win the whole, if he succeeds by this method; but, on the contrary, should he play the close game, by forcing C or D to trump first, he having won the odd trick already, and being sure of winning two more in his own hand. By this method his game will be scored nine to seven, which is about three to two, and, therefore, A's share of the £70 will amount only to £42, and A only secures £7 profit; but in the other case, upon supposition that A and B have eleven to three of the stake depending, as aforesaid, A, by playing his trump, is entitled to £35 out of the £70 depending.

The foregoing case being duly attended to, may be applied to the like purpose in other parts of the game.

DIRECTIONS HOW TO PLAY WHEN AN ACE, KING, OR QUEEN, ARE TURNED UP ON YOUR RIGHT-HAND.

Suppose the ace is turned up on your right-hand, and that you have the ten and nine of trumps only, with ace, king, and queen, of another suit, and eight cards of no value. *Query*, How must this game be played? Begin with the ace of the suit of which you have the ace, king, and queen, which is an information to your partner that you have the command of that suit; then play your ten of trumps, because it is five to two that your partner has king, queen, or knave of trumps;

and though it is about seven to two that your partner has not two honours, yet, should he chance to have them, and they prove to be the king and knave, in that case, as your partner will pass your ten of trumps, and as it is thirteen to twelve against the last player for holding the queen of trumps, upon supposition your partner has it not, in that case, when your partner has the lead, he plays to your strong suit, and upon your having the lead, play the nine of trumps, which puts it in your partner's power to be almost certain of winning the queen if he lies behind it.

The foregoing case shows, that turning up of an ace against you may be made less beneficial to your adversaries.

If the king or queen are turned up on your right-hand, the like method of play may be made use of; but you are always to distinguish the difference of your partner's skill, because a good player will make a proper use of such play, but a bad one seldom.

Suppose the adversary on your right-hand leads the king of trumps, and that you should have the ace and four small trumps, with a good suit; in this case it is your interest to pass the king; and though he should have king, queen, and knave of trumps, with one more if he is a moderate player, he will play the small one, imagining that his partner has the ace: when he plays the small one, you are to pass it, because it is an equal wager that your partner has a better trump than the last player. If so, and that he happens to be a tolerable player, he will judge you have a good reason for this method, and consequently, if he has a third trump remaining, he will play it; if not, he will play his best suit.

A Critical Case to win an Odd Trick.—Suppose A and B partners against C and D, and the game to be nine all, and suppose all the trumps are played out, A being the last player, has the ace and four other small cards of a suit in his hand, and one thirteenth card remaining; B has only two small cards of A's suit; C has queen and two other small cards of that suit; D has king, knave, and one small card of the same suit. A and B have won three tricks, C and D have won four tricks; it therefore follows, that A is to win four tricks out of the six cards in his hand, in order to win the game. C leads this suit, and D puts up the king; A gives him that trick, D returns that suit; A passes it, and C puts up his queen: thus C and D have won six tricks, and C imagining the ace of that suit to be in his partner's hand, returns it; by which means A wins the four last tricks, and consequently the game.

Suppose you should have the king and five small trumps, and that your right-hand adversary plays the queen; in that case do not put on the king, because it is an equal wager that your partner has the ace; and suppose your adversary should have queen, knave, ten, and one small trump, it is also an equal wager that the ace lies single, either in your adversary's hand or partner's; in either of which cases it is bad play to put on your king; but if the queen of trumps is led, and that you should happen to have the king, with only two or three trumps, it is the best play to put on the king, because it is good play to lead from the queen and one small trump only: and in that case should your partner have the knave of trumps, and your left-hand adversary hold the ace, you neglecting to put on the king lose a trick.

THE TEN OR NINE BEING TURNED UP ON YOUR RIGHT-HAND.

Suppose the ten is turned up on your right-hand, and that you should have king, knave, nine, and two small trumps, with eight other cards of no value, and that it is proper for you to lead trumps; in that case, begin with the knave, in order to prevent the ten from making a trick; and though it is but about five to four that your partner holds an honour, yet if that should fail, by finessing the nine on the return of trumps from your partner, you have the ten in your power.

The nine being turned up on your right-hand, and that you should have ten, eight, and two small trumps, by leading the knave it answers the like purpose of the former case.

You are to make a wide difference between a lead of choice, and a forced lead of your partner's; because, in the first case, he is supposed to lead from his best suit, and finding you deficient in that, and not being strong enough in trumps, and not daring to force you, he then plays his next best suit; by which alteration, it is next to a demonstration that he is weak in trumps; but should he persevere, by playing off his first lead, if he is a good player, you are to judge him strong in trumps, and play your game accordingly.

There is nothing more pernicious than to change suits often, because in every new suit you run the risk of giving your adversary the tenace; and, therefore, though you lead from a suit of which you have the queen, ten, and three small ones, and your partner puts on the nine only, in that case, if you should happen to be weak in trumps, and that you have no tolerable suit to lead from, it is your best play to pursue the lead of that suit by playing your queen, which leaves it in your partner's option whether he will trump it or not, in case he has no more of that suit; but in your second lead, in case you should happen to have the queen or knave of any other suit, with one card only of the same suit, it would be better play to lead from your queen or knave of either of these suits, it being five to two that your partner has one honour at least in either of those suits.

When you have ace, king, and one small card of any suit, with four trumps; if your right-hand adversary leads that suit, pass it, because it is an equal wager that your partner has a better card in that suit than the third hand; if so, you gain a trick by it; if otherwise, as you have four trumps, you may not lose, because when trumps are played, you probably will have the long trump.

CAUTIONS NOT TO PART WITH THE COMMAND OF YOUR ADVERSARY'S GREAT SUIT, &c.

In case you are weak in trumps, and it does not appear your partner is very strong in them, be very cautious how you part with the command of your adversary's great suit; for suppose your adversary plays a suit of which you have the king, queen, and one small card only, the adversary leads the ace, and upon playing the same suit again you put on your queen, which makes it almost certain to your partner that you have the king; and suppose your partner refuses to that suit, do not play the king, because if the leader of that suit, or his partner, have the long trump, you risk the losing of three tricks to get one.

Suppose your partner has ten cards remaining, and it appears to you that they consist of trumps and one suit only; and suppose you should have king, ten, and one small card of his strong suit, with queen and two small trumps; in this case, you are to judge he has five cards of each suit, and therefore you ought to play out the king of his strong suit; and if you win that trick, your next play is to throw out the queen of trumps; if that likewise comes home, proceed to play trumps: this method of play may be made use of at any score of the game, except at four and nine.

The Trump turned up to be remembered.—It is so necessary that the trump turned up should be remembered, both by the dealer and his partner, that the dealer should always so place that card, as to be certain of having recourse to it; for suppose it to be only a five, and that the dealer has two more, viz. the six and nine, if his partner trumps out with ace and king, he ought to play his six and nine; because suppose your partner to have ace, king, and four small trumps; in this case, by your partner knowing you have the five remaining, you may win many tricks.

Your right-hand adversary leads a suit of which you have the ten and two small ones; the third hand puts up the knave, your partner wins it with the king; when your adversary leads that suit again, and plays a small one, do you put on your ten, because it may save your partner's ace, upon supposition that your right-hand adversary led from the queen.

Suppose you have the best trump, and that the adversary A has one trump only remaining, and that it appears to you that your adversary B has a great suit; in this case, though you permit A to make his trump, yet by keeping the trump in your hand, you prevent the adversary B from making his great suit; whereas, if you had taken out A's trump, it had made only one trick difference; but by this method you probably save three or four tricks.

The following Case happens frequently:—That you have two trumps remaining when your adversaries have only one, and it appears to you that your partner has one great suit; in this case always play a trump, though you have the worst, because by removing the trump out of your adversary's hand, there can be no obstruction to your partner's suit.

Suppose you should have three trumps when no one else has any, and that you should only have four cards of any certain suit remaining; in this case play a trump, which shows your partner that you have all the trumps, and also gives you a fair chance for one of your adversaries to throw away one card of the aforesaid suit; by which means, supposing that suit to have been once led, and one thrown away, makes five, and four remaining in your hand makes nine, there being only four remaining between three hands, and your partner having an equal chance to hold a better card in that suit than the last player, it therefore follows that you have an equal chance to make three tricks in that suit, which probably could not otherwise have been done.

Suppose you have five trumps, and six small cards of any suit, and are to lead; then lead from the suit of which you have six, because, as you are deficient in two suits, your adversary will probably trump out, which is playing your own game; whereas, had you begun with playing trumps, they would force you, and consequently destroy your game.

THE MANNER OF PLAYING SEQUENCES FURTHER EXPLAINED.

In trumps play the highest of your sequences, unless you should have ace, king, and queen; in that case play the lowest, in order to let your partner into the state of your game.

In suits which are not trumps, if you have sequence of king, queen, and knave, and two small ones; whether you are strong in trumps or not, it is the best play to begin with the knave, because by getting the ace out of any hand, you make room for the whole suit.

And in case you are strong in trumps, supposing you should have sequence of queen, knave, ten, and two small cards of any suit; play the highest of the sequence, because, if either of the adversaries should trump that suit in the second round, you, by being strong in trumps, fetch out their trumps, and consequently make the remainder of that suit.

The like method may be taken in a sequence by knave, ten, nine, and two small cards of any suit.

If you have a sequence of a king, queen, knave, and one small card of any suit, whether you are strong in trumps or otherwise, play your king, and do the like by any inferior sequences, if you have only four in number.

But if you are weak in trumps, always begin with the lowest of the sequence in case you have five in number; for suppose your partner to have the ace of that suit, he then makes it; and if you have the ace and four small cards of any suit, and are weak in trumps, and led from that suit, play the ace; and if you are very strong in trumps, you may play your game as backward as you please; but if you are weak in trumps, you must play the reverse.

Let us explain what is meant by being strong or weak in trumps.

If you have ac king, and three small trumps.

King, queen, and three small trumps.

Queen, knave, and three small trumps.

Queen, ten, and three small trumps.

Knave, ten, and three small trumps.

Queen, and four small trumps.

Knave and four small trumps.

In any of the aforesaid cases, you may be understood to be very strong in trumps, and therefore play by th foregoing rules, being morally assured of having the command.

If you have two or three small trumps only, you are weak in them.

What strength in trumps entitles you to force your partner at any point of the game?

Ace, and three small trumps.

King, and three small trumps.

Queen, and three small trumps.

Knave, and three small trumps.

If, by accident, either you or the adversaries have forced your partner (though you are weak in trumps) if he has had the lead, and does not choose to trump out, force him as often as the lead comes into your hand, unless you have good suits of your own to play.

If you should happen to have only two or three small trumps, and that your right-hand adversary leads a suit of which you have none, trump it, which is an information to your partner that you are weak in trumps.

Suppose you have ace, knave, and one small trump, and that your partner trumps to you, suppose from the king and three small trumps, and suppose your right-hand adversary has three trumps, and that your left-hand adversary has the like number; in this case, by finessing your knave, and playing your ace, if the queen is on your right-hand, you win a trick; but if queen is on your left-hand, and you should play the ace, and then return the knave, admitting your left-hand adversary put on the queen, which he ought to do, it is above two to one that one of the adversaries has the ten and consequently you gain no tricks.

If your partner has led from the ace of trumps, and you have king, knave, and one small trump, by putting on your knave, and returning the king, it answers exactly the like purpose of the former rule.

In other suits practise the like method.

If you are strong in trumps, and have king, queen, and two or three small cards in any other suit, lead a small one, it being five to four that your partner has an honour in that suit, but if you are weak in trumps, you ought to begin with the king.

If your right-hand adversary leads a suit of which you have king, queen, and two or three small cards of the same suit, you being strong in trumps, may pass it, because it is an equal wager that your partner has a better card in that suit than the third hand; if not, by your strength in trumps, you need not fear making that suit

If your right-hand adversary leads a suit of which you have king, queen, and one small card, whether in trumps or not, put on the queen: also, if you have queen, knave, and one small card, put on the knave: and if you have knave, ten, and one small card, put on the ten: by putting up the second best, as aforesaid, your partner has an expectation of your having a better card or cards in the same suit: and by the calculations annexed to this treatise, he may judge what are the odds for or against him.

When you have ace, king, and two small cards in any suit, being strong in trumps; if your right-hand adversary leads that suit, you may pass it, because it is an equal wager that your partner has a better card in that suit than the third hand; if so you gain a trick by it, if otherwise you need not fear to make your ace and king by your strength in trumps.

If you have the ace, nine, eight, and one small trump, and your partner leads the ten; in that case pass it, because, unless the three honours lie behind you, you are sure of making two tricks; do the like, if you should have the king, nine, eight, and one small trump; or the queen, nine, eight, and one small trump.

In order to deceive your adversaries, if your right-hand adversary leads from a suit of which you have ace, king, and queen, or ace, king and knave, put on the ace; because that encourages the adversaries to play that suit again: and though you deceive your partner by this method of play, you also deceive your adversaries, which is of greater consequence in this case; because if you had put on the lowest of the tierce-major, or the knave, your right-hand adversary had made a discovery that the strength of that suit was against him, and consequently would have changed suits.

Suppose you have ace, ten, and one small card, in any suit; also the ace, nine, and one small card of another suit to lead; from the suit of which you have the ace, nine, and one small card; it being an equal wager that your partner has a better card in that suit than the last player; if not, let us then suppose that your right-hand adversary leads from the king or queen of the suit of which you have the ace, ten, and one small card; in that case it is an equal wager that your partner has a better card in that suit than the third hand; if that happens to be the case, upon the return of the suit, you lie tenace, and consequently stand a fair chance for three tricks.

A Case to demonstrate the Tenace.—Let us suppose A and B to play at two-handed whist,* and A to have the ace, queen, ten, eight, six, and four of clubs, which, in case B always leads, are six sure tricks. Let us suppose he has the same hand in spades, which, in case B always leads, are six more sure tricks. We suppose B has the remainder of these two suits

Suppose B to have the same hand in hearts and diamonds as A has in spades and clubs, and that A has the remainder of the hearts and diamonds, which, in case A always leads, are twelve sure tricks to B.

The foregoing case shows that both hands are exactly equal; and therefore let one of them name his trumps, and lead, he wins thirteen tricks only.

But if one names the trumps, and the other leads, he that names the trumps ought to win fourteen tricks.

He who would play whist to perfection, must not be content only with being a master of the calculations contained in this treatise, and also an exact judge of all the general and

* In this example, Hoyle evidently means that the 52 cards should be divided between two players, which would give 26 tricks.

particular cases in the same; but be a very punctual observer of such cards as are thrown away, both by his partner and adversaries, and at what time.

ADDITIONAL CASES.

When it appears to you that the adversaries have three or four trumps remaining, and that neither you nor your partner have any, never attempt to force one hand to trump, and to let the other throw away a losing card, but rather endeavour to find out a suit in your own partner's hand in case you have no suit in your own; by which means you prevent them from making their trumps separate.

Suppose A and B are partners against C and D, and suppose nine cards are played out; and also that eight trumps are played out; and further suppose A to have one trump only, and his partner B to have the ace and queen of trumps, and the adversaries C and D to have the king and knave of trumps between them. A leads his small trump, C plays the knave of trumps. *Query*, Whether B is to play his ace or queen of trumps upon the knave? because D having four cards in his hand remaining, and C only three, consequently it is four to three in B's favour, that the king is in D's hand: if we reduce the number of four cards in hand to three, the odds then is three to two: and if we reduce the number of three cards in a hand to two the odds then is two to one in favour of B's winning another trick, by putting on his ace of trumps. By the like rule you may play all the other suits.

Suppose you have the thirteenth trump, and also the thirteenth card of any suit, and one losing card; play the losing card, because if you play the thirteenth card first, the adversaries knowing you to have one trump remaining, will not pass your losing card, and therefore you play two to one against yourself.

Suppose that you have the ace, king, and three small cards, in any suit which has never been played; and that it appears to you that your partner has the last trump remaining, lead a small card in that suit, because, it is an equal wager that your partner has a better card in it than the last player; if so, and that there are only three cards in that suit in any one hand, it follows that you win five tricks; whereas, if you play the ace and king in that suit, it is two to one that your partner does not hold the queen, and consequently you win only two tricks in that suit. This method may be taken in case all the trumps are played out, provided you have good cards in other suits to bring in this, and you may observe that you reduce the odds of two to one against you to an equal chance by this method of play, and probably gain three tricks by it.

If you choose to have trumps played by the adversaries, and that your partner has led a suit to you of which you have the ace, knave, ten, nine, and eight, or the king, knave, ten, nine, and eight, you are to play the eight; which probably leads the adversary, if he wins that card, to play trumps.

Suppose you have a quart-major in any suit, with one or two more of the same, and that it is necessary to let your partner know that you have the command; in that case throw away the ace upon any suit of which you have none in your hand, to clear up his doubts, because the odds are that neither of the adversaries have more than three in that suit: the like method may be taken if you have a quart to a king, the ace being played out, you may throw away the king; also, if you should have a quart to a queen, the ace and king being played out, you may throw away your queen; all of which lets your partner into the state of your game; and you may play by the like rule in all inferior sequences, having the best of them in your hand.

There is scarcely anything more common amongst moderate players, in case the king is turned up on the left hand, and they have the queen and one small trump only, to play out their queen, in hopes their partner may win the king if it is put on; not considering that it is about two to one that their partner has not the ace, and admitting he has the ace, they do not consider that they play two honours against one, and consequently weaken their game. The necessity only of playing trumps should oblige them to play thus.

A case which frequently happens.—A and B are partners against C and D, and all the trumps are played out except one, which C or D has; A has three or four winning cards in his hand of a suit already played, with an ace and one small card of another suit: it is A's best play to throw away one of his winning cards; because, if his right-hand adversary plays to his ace-suit, he has it in his power to pass it, and consequently his partner B has an equal chance to have a better card in that suit than the third hand; if so, and B has any forcing card, or one of his partner's suit to play to, in order to force out the last trump, A's ace remaining in his hand, brings in his winning cards; whereas, if A had thrown away the small card to his ace-suit, and that his right-hand adversary had led that suit, he had been obliged to put on his ace, and consequently had lost some tricks by that method of play.

Suppose ten cards have been played out, and it appears very probable that your left-hand adversary has three trumps remaining, viz., the best and two small ones; and you have two trumps only, and your partner no trump; and suppose your right-hand adversary plays a thirteenth or some other winning card, in that case pass it, by which means you gain a trick, because the left-hand adversary must trump.

In order to let your partner into the state of your game, suppose you to have a quart-major in trumps (or any other four best trumps) if you are obliged to trump a card, win it with the ace of trumps, and then play the knave, or win it with the highest of any four best trumps, and then play the lowest, which clears up your game to your partner: and may be the means of winning many tricks: practise the like rule so, in all other suits.

If your partner calls at the point of eight before his time you are to trump to him, whether you are strong in trumps or suits, or not; because, as he calls before he is obliged to do so, it is a declaration of his being strong in trumps.

Suppose your right-hand adversary turns up the queen of clubs; and, when he has the lead, plays the knave of clubs; and suppose you have the ace, ten, and one club more, or the king, ten, and one small card; when he leads his knave, you are not to win it, because it is an equal wager, you not having the king, that your partner has it: also it is an equal wager, when he leads his knave, you not having the ace, that your partner has it, and consequently you may gain a trick by passing it; which cannot be done, if you either put on your king or ace of clubs.

A Case for a Slam.—Let us suppose A and B partners against C and D; and C to deal; and let us suppose A to have the king, knave, nine, and seven of clubs, they being trumps; a quart-major in diamonds, a tierce-major in hearts and the ace and king of spades.

B to have nine diamonds, two spades, and two hearts.

Also D to have the ace, queen, ten, and eight of trumps, with nine spades.

And let C have five trumps and eight hearts.

A is to lead a trump, which D is to win, and D is to play a spade, which his partner C is to trump; C is to lead a trump, which his partner D is to win; when D is to lead a spade, which C is to trump; and C is to play a trump which D is to win; and D having the best trump is to play it; which done, D having seven spades in his hand, wins them, and consequently slams A and B.

If your partner leads the king of a suit and that you have none of that suit, pass it, by throwing away a losing card, (unless your right-hand adversary has put on the ace) because, by so doing, you make room for his suit.

Suppose your partner leads the queen of a suit, and your right-hand adversary wins it with the ace, and returns that suit: in case you have none of it, do not trump, but throw away a losing card, which makes room for your partner's suit. An exception to this is, if you play for an odd trick, and are very weak in trumps.

Suppose you have the ace, king, and one small card of a suit, and that your left-hand adversary leads that suit, and suppose you should have four small trumps, and no suit of consequence to lead from; and your right-hand adversary should put on the nine, or any lower card; in this case win it with the ace, and return the lead upon the adversary by playing the small card of that suit; who will have reason to judge that the king lies behind him, and consequently will not put up his queen if he has it; and therefore you have a fair probability of winning a trick by this method of play, at the same time letting your partner into the state of your game.

If your partner forces you to trump a card early in the deal, you are to suppose him strong in trumps, except at the points of four or nine; and, therefore, if you are strong in trumps, play them.

Suppose you call at the point of eight, and your partner has no honour; and suppose you should have the king, queen, and ten; the king, knave, and ten; or the queen, knave, and ten of trumps: when trumps are played, always put on the ten, which demonstrates to your partner that you have two honours remaining, and so he plays his game accordingly.

Suppose your right-hand adversary calls at the point of eight, and his partner has no honour; and you should have the king, nine, and one small trump, or the queen, nine, and two small trumps; when trumps are played by your partner, put on the nine, because it is about two to one that the ten is not behind you.

If you lead a suit of which you have the ace, king, and two or three more, when you play the ace, if your partner plays the ten or knave, and suppose you should have one single card in your hand in any other suit, and two or three small trumps only; in this case lead the single card, in order to establish a saw; and this consequence attends such play, viz. upon leading that suit it gives your partner an equal chance of having a better card in it than the last player; whereas, had he led that to you, which is probable had been his strong suit, the adversaries would discover your attempt to establish a saw, and would trump out.

Suppose you have the ace and deuce of trumps, and strong in the three other suits; if you are to lead, play the ace, and next your deuce of trumps, in order to put the lead into your partner's hand, to take out two trumps for one; and suppose the last player wins that trick, and that he leads a suit of which you have the ace, king, and two or three more, pass it, because it is an equal wager that your partner has a better card in that suit than the third hand; if so, he will then have an opportunity of taking out two trumps to one; when the lead comes into your hand, endeavour to force out one of the two trumps remaining, upon supposition eleven trumps are played out, and the odds are in your favour that your partner has one of the two trumps remaining.

Suppose ten cards are played out, and that you have the king, ten, and one small card of any suit, which has never been led; and suppose you have won six tricks, and your partner leads from that suit, and that there is neither a trump or thirteenth card in any hand; in this case, unless your right-hand adversary puts on so high a card as obliges you to play the king, do not put it on, because upon the return of that suit you make your king, and consequently the odd trick, which makes two difference; if there happens to be only nine cards played out, in the like circumstance, play by the like rule. This method is always to be taken, unless gaining two tricks gives you a chance either to save your lurch or to win or save the game.

Suppose A and B partners against C and D, and B has the two last trumps, also the queen, knave, and nine of another suit; and suppose A has neither the ace, king, or ten of that suit, but A is to lead. B should play the nine, because it is only five to four against him that his left-hand adversary holds the ten; and if he plays either the queen or knave, it is about three to one the ace or king is in his left-hand adversary's hands, and consequently he reduces the odds of three to one against him, to five to four only.

Vary the foregoing case, and put the king, knave, and nine of a suit into B's hand, upon supposition that A has neither ace, queen, or ten; when A leads that suit, it is exactly equal whether B plays his king, knave, or nine.

Suppose you have ace, king, and three or four small cards of a suit not played, and that it appears to you that your partner has the last trump; in this case, if you are to lead, play a small card in that suit, it being an equal wager that your partner has a better card in that than the last player; if so, the probability is in your favour that you make five or six tricks in that suit; but if you should play out ace and king of that suit, it is two to one that your partner has not the queen, and consequently it is two to one that you make only two tricks, by which method, you risk the losing of three or four tricks in that deal to gain one only.

If your partner leads a suit of which he has the ace, queen, knave, and many more, and leads his ace, and then plays his queen; in case you have the king and two small cards in that suit, win his queen with the king; and suppose you are strong in trumps, by clearing the board of trumps, and having a small card of your partner's great suit, you do not obstruct his suit, and consequently win many tricks.

HOW TO PLAY FOR AN ODD TRICK.

Suppose you are elder hand, and that you have the ace, king, and three small trumps, with four small cards of another suit, three small cards of the third suit, and one small card of the fourth suit; lead the single card, which, if it is won by the last player, puts him upon playing trumps, or to play to your weak suit; in which case your partner and you gain the tenace.

THE LIKE CASE FOR AN ODD TRICK, AND THAT YOUR PARTNER IS TO LEAD.

Suppose he plays the ace of the suit, of which you have only one, and proceeds to play the king of the same suit, and that your right-hand adversary trumps it with the queen, knave, or ten; do not overtrump him, but throw away a small card of your weakest suit; because it makes your partner the last player, and gives him the tenace in your weak suits.

THE LIKE CASE, UPON SUPPOSITION YOU WANT FOUR OR FIVE POINTS, AND THAT YOU ARE ELDER HAND.

Play a small trump, and if your partner has a better trump than the last player, and returns the lead, put on the king of trumps, and then proceed to play the suit of which you have four in number.

These examples being duly attended to, on all parts of the game, must be of great consequence to the player; because when he has no good suit to play, his partner being the last player gains the tenace in his weak suits.

A and B are partners against C and D, twelve trumps are played out, and seven cards only remain in each hand, of which A has the last trump, and also the ace, king, and four small cards of a suit.

A ought to play a small card of that suit, because it is an equal wager that his partner has a better card in it than the last player; and in this case, if four cards of that suit should happen to be in either of his adversaries' hands, he will be able to make five tricks in that suit: when if he played off his ace and king, he had made only two tricks. If neither of the adversaries have more than three cards in that suit, A has an equal chance to win six tricks in it.

Suppose A and B are partners against C and D, and that eight trumps are played out, and that A has four of those trumps remaining, C having the best trump, and to lead. C ought not to play his trump to take out one of A's trumps, because he would leave three trumps in A's hand; but in case A's partner has any great suit to make, C, keeping the trump in his own hand, can prevent him from making that suit by trumping it.

A Case of Curiosity.—Suppose three hands of cards, containing three cards in each hand: let A name the trumps, and let B choose which hand he pleases, A having his choice of either of the other two hands, wins two tricks.

Clubs are to be trumps.

First hand, ace, king, and six of hearts.
Second hand, queen, and ten of hearts, and ten of trumps.
Third hand, nine of hearts, and two and three of trumps.
The first hand wins of the second.
The second wins of the third.
And the third wins of the first.

THE LAWS OF WHIST.

OF DEALING.

If a card is turned up in dealing, it is in the option of the adverse party to call a new deal; but if either of them have been the cause of turning up such card, in that case the dealer has his option.

If a card is faced in the deal, there must be a new deal, unless it is the last card.

Every person ought to see that he has thirteen cards dealt; therefore, if any one should happen to have only twelve, and does not find it out till several tricks are played, and that the rest of the players have their right number, the deal stands good; and also the person who plays with 12 cards is to be punished for each revoke, in case he has made any; but if any of the rest of the players should happen to have fourteen cards, in that case the deal is lost.

The dealer ought to leave in view upon the table his trump card, till it is his turn to play; and after he has mixed it with his cards, nobody is entitled to demand what card is turned up, but may ask what is trumps. This consequence attends such a law that the dealer cannot name a wrong card, which otherwise he might have done.

None of the players ought to take up or look at their cards, while any person is dealing; and if the dealer should happen to miss deal, in that case he shall deal again, unless it arises from his partner's fault; and if a card is turned up in dealing, no new deal shall be called, unless the partner has been the cause of it.

If the dealer, instead of turning up the trump, puts the trump card upon the rest of his cards, with the face downwards, he is to lose his deal.

OF PLAYING OUT OF TURN.

If any person plays out of his turn, the card so played may be called at any time in that deal, provided it does not cause a revoke; or either of the adversaries may require of the person who ought to have led, to play the suit the said adversary may choose.

A and B are partners against C and D, A plays the ten of a suit, the adversary C plays the knave of the same suit, B plays a small card of the same suit, but before D plays, his partner C leads another card, the penalty shall be in the option of A or B to oblige D to win the trick if he can.

A and B are partners against C and D; A leads a club, his partner B plays before the adversary C; in this case D has a right to play before his partner C, because B played out of his turn.

If the ace, or any other card of a suit is led, and it should so happen that the last player plays out of his turn, whether his partner has any of the suit led or not, provided you do not make him revoke, he is neither entitled to trump it, nor to win the trick.

OF REVOKING.

If a revoke happens to be made, the adversaries may add three to their scores, or take three tricks from the revoking party, or to take down three from their score; and the revoking party, provided they are up, notwithstanding the penalty, must remain at nine: the revoke takes place of any other score of the game.

If any person revokes, and before the cards are turned dis covers it, the adverse party may call the highest or lowest card of the suit led, or have their option to call the card then played, at any time when it does not cause a revoke.

No revoke to be claimed till the trick is turned and

quitted, or the party who revoked, or his partner have played again.

If any person claims a revoke, the adverse party are not to mix their cards, upon forfeiture of the revoke.

No revoke can be claimed after the cards are cut for a new deal.

OF CALLING HONOURS.

If any person calls at any point of the game, except eight, either of the adverse parties may call a new deal; and they are at liberty to consult each other whether they will have a new deal.

After the trump card is turned up, no person must remind his partner to call, on penalty of losing a point.

If the trump card is turned up, no honours in the preceding deal can be set up, unless they were before claimed.

If any person calls at the point of eight, and his partner answers, and both the opposite parties have thrown down their cards, and it appears that the other side had not two by honours; in this case they may consult with one another about it, and are at liberty to stand the deal or not.

And if any person answers when he has not an honour, the adverse party may consult one another about it, and are at liberty to stand the deal or not.

If any person calls at eight, after he has played, it shall be in the option of the adversaries to call a new deal.

OF SEPARATING AND SHOWING THE CARDS.

If any person separates a card from the rest, the adverse party may call it, provided he names it, and proves the separation; but in case he calls a wrong card, he or his partner are liable for once to have the highest or lowest card called in any suit led during the deal.

If any person throws his cards upon the table with their faces upwards, upon supposition that he has lost the game, the adversaries have it in their power to call any of the cards when they think proper, provided they do not make the party revoke, and he is not to take up his cards again.

If any person is sure of winning every trick, he may show his cards upon the table; but he is then liable to have all his cards called.

OF OMITTING TO PLAY TO A TRICK.

A and B are partners against C and D; A leads a club, C plays the ace of clubs, B plays a club, and D, partner to C, takes up the trick without playing any card; A, and the rest of the players, play on, till it appears D has one card more than the rest: penalty to be in the option of the adversaries to call a new deal.

RESPECTING WHO PLAYED ANY PARTICULAR CARD.

Each person in playing ought to lay his card before him; after he has done so, if either of the adverse parties mix their cards with his, his partner is entitled to demand each person to lay his card before him; but not to enquire who played any particular card.

AN EXPLANATION OF THE TERMS, OR TECHNICAL WORDS, IN THIS TREATISE.

Finessing, means endeavouring to gain an advantage thus: When a card is led, and you have the best and third best of that suit, you put your third best card upon that lead, and run the risk of your adversary having the second best; if he has it not, which is 2 to 1 against him, you are then sure of gaining a trick.

Forcing, means obliging your partner or adversary to trump a suit, of which he has none. The cases mentioned in this Treatise will show when it is proper to force either of them.

Long Trump, means having one or more trumps in your hand, when all the rest are out.

Loose Card, is a card of no value, and, consequently, the properest to throw away.

Points, ten of them make a game; as many as are gained by tricks or honours, so many points are set up to the score.

Quart is a sequence of any four cards immediately following one another in the same suit.—Quart-major is a sequence of ace, king, queen, and knave.

Quint is a sequence of any five cards immediately following one another in the same suit.—Quint-major is a sequence of ace, king, queen, knave, and ten.

Reverse, means only playing the hand in a different manner; that is, if you are strong in trumps, you play one way; if weak in trumps, you play the Reverse, viz. another.

See-saw, is when each partner trumps a suit, and plays those suits to one another to trump.

Score, is the number of points set up, ten of which make a game.

Slam, is when either party win every trick.

Tenace, is having the first and third best cards, and being last player, and, consequently, catching the adversary when that suit is played; as, for instance, in case you have ace and queen of any suit, your adversary leads, you must win those two tricks; and so of any other tenace in inferior cards.

Terce or Tierce, is a sequence of any three cards immediately following one another in the same suit. Terce-major is a sequence of ace, king, and queen.

AN ARTIFICIAL MEMORY, FOR THOSE WHO PLAY AT THE GAME OF WHIST.

Place, of every suit in your hand, the worst to the left hand, and the best (in order) to the right; and the trumps, in the like order, always to the left of all the other suits.

If in the course of play you have the best card remaining in any suit, put the same to the left of your trumps.*

And if you find you are possessed of the second best card of any suit, place it on the right of your trumps.

And if you have the third best card of any suit, place a small card of that suit between the trumps and that third best, to the right of the trumps.

To remember your partner's first lead, place a small card of that suit in the midst of your trumps, and if you have but one trump, on the left of it.

When you deal, put the trump turned up to the right of all your trumps, and keep it as long as you can, that your partner may, knowing that you have that trump left, play accordingly.

TO FIND WHERE OR IN WHAT SUIT YOUR ADVERSARIES REVOKE.

Suppose two suits on the right-hand to represent your

* This conspicuous mode of arrangement is hardly suitable to the present day; players have become too sharpsighted.

adversaries in the order they sit, as to your right and left hand.

When you suspect either of them to have made a revoke, clap a small card of that suit amongst the cards representing that adversary, by which you record not only that there may have been a revoke, but also who made it, and in what suit.

If the suit representing the adversary that made the revoke, happens to be the same he revoked in, change that suit for another, and put a small card of the suit revoked in the middle of that exchanged suit, and if you have not a card remaining of that suit reverse a card of any other you have, (except diamonds) and place it there.

As you have a way to remember your partner's first lead, you may also record in what suit either of your adversaries made their first lead, by putting the suit so led in the place which in your hand represents that adversary; and if other suits were already placed to represent them, then exchange those for the suits in which each of them makes his first lead.

The foregoing method is to be taken when more necessary to record your adversary's first lead, than to endeavour to find out a revoke.

CALCULATIONS WHICH DIRECT WITH MORAL CERTAINTY HOW TO PLAY WELL ANY HAND, BY SHOWING THE CHANCES OF YOUR PARTNER HAVING 1, 2, OR 3, CERTAIN CARDS.

☞ **Read with attention those marked N. B.**

FOR EXAMPLE.

What is the chance of your friend having one certain card?

Answer.	against him		for him
That he has it not, is, N. B.	2	to	1

What is the chance of having two certain cards?

Answer.

That he has one of them only, is	31	to	26
That he has not both of them	17	to	2

	against him	for him
But that he has one or both, is about 5 to 4, or N. B.	25 to	32

What are the chances of having 3 certain cards?

Answer.

That he holds one of them only is 325 for him to 378 against him, or about	6 to	7
That he has not 2 of them only, is 156 for him to 547 against him, or about	2 to	7
That he has not all 3 of them, is 22 for him to 681 against him, or about	1 to	31
But that he has 1 or 2 of them, is 481 for him to 222 against him, or about	13 to	6
And that he has 1, 2, or all 3 of them, is about N. B.	5 to	2

AN EXPLANATION AND APPLICATION OF THE CALCULATIONS NECESSARY TO BE UNDERSTOOD BY THOSE WHO READ THIS TREATISE.

First Calculation

It is 2 to 1 that my partner has not one certain card.

To apply this calculation, suppose the right-hand adversary leads a suit, of which you have the king and one small card only; observe that it is 2 to 1, by putting on your king, that the left-hand adversary cannot win it.

Again, suppose that you have the king and three small cards of any suit, likewise the queen and three small cards of any other suit, lead from the king, because it is 2 to 1 that the ace does not lie behind you; but it is 5 to 4 that the ace or king of any suit lies behind you, and consequently, by leading from your queen suit, you play to a disadvantage.

2nd Calculation. It is 5 to 4, at least, that your partner has one out of any 2 certain cards; the like odds are in favour of your adversaries; therefore, suppose you have two honours of any suit, and knowing it is 5 to 4 that your partner holds one of the other two honours, you do by this play your game to a greater degree of certainty.

Again, suppose that you have the queen and one small card in any suit only, and that your right-hand adversary leads that suit, if you put on your queen, it is 5 to 4 that your left-hand adversary can win it, and therefore you play 5 to 4 to disadvantage.

3*d Calculation.* It is 5 to 2 that your partner has one out of any three certain cards.

Therefore, suppose you have the knave and one small card dealt, and that your right-hand adversary leads from that suit, if you put on the knave, it is 5 to 2 that your left-hand adversary has either ace, king, or queen of the suit lead, and therefore you play 5 to 2 against yourself; besides, by making a discovery to your right-hand adversary, he finesses upon your partner throughout the whole suit.

And, in order to explain the necessity there is of putting on the lowest of sequences in all the suits led, suppose that your adversary led a suit of which you have the king, queen, and knave, or queen, knave, and ten; by putting on your knave of the suit of which you have the king, queen, and knave, it gives your partner an opportunity of calculating the odds for and against him in that suit, and also in all inferior suits of which you have sequences.

A farther use to be made of the foregoing calculation: suppose that you have the ace, king, and two small trumps, with a quint-major or five other winning cards in any other suit, and that you have played trumps two rounds, and each person followed trumps; in this case there are eight trumps out, and two trumps remaining in your hand, which make ten, and three trumps divided between the remaining three players, of which three, the odds are 5 to 2 that your partner has one; and, therefore, out of seven cards in your hand, you are entitled to win five tricks.

SOME COMPUTATIONS FOR LAYING WAGERS.

All with the Deal.

The deal .... is	21 to 20	6	5 to 2
1 love	11 — 10	7	7 — 2
2	5 — 4	8	5 — 1
3	3 — 2	9 is about	9 — 2
4	7 — 4		
5 is 2 to 1 of the game, and 1 of the lurch	2 — 1	2 to 1 .... is	9 to 8
		3 — 1	9 — 7
		4 — 1	9 — 6

5 to 1	9 to 5	5 to 4	is 6 to 5
6 — 1	9 — 4	6 — 4	6 — 4
7 — 1	3 — 1	7 — 4	2 — 1
8 — 1	9 — 2	8 — 4	3 — 1
9 — 1 is about	4 — 1	9 — 4 is about	5 — 2
3 to 2	is 8 to 7	6 to 5	is 5 to 4
4 — 2	4 — 3	7 — 5	5 — 3
5 — 2	8 — 5	8 — 5	5 — 6
6 — 2	2 — 1	9 — 5 is about	2 — 1
7 — 2	8 — 3		
8 — 2	4 — 1	7 to 6	is 4 to 3
9 — 2	7 — 2	8 — 6	2 — 1
		9 — 6 is about	7 — 4
4 to 3	is 7 to 6		
5 — 3	7 — 5	*8 to 7 is above	3 to 2
6 — 3	7 — 4	9 — 7 is about	12 — 8
7 — 3	7 — 3		
8 — 3	7 — 2		
9 — 3 is about	3 — 1		

8 to 9 is about 3 and a half in the hundred, in favour of 8 with the deal; against the deal, the odds are still, though small, in favour of 8.

CALCULATIONS FOR THE WHOLE RUBBER.

Suppose A and B are at play, and that A is 1 game, and 8 love of the second game, with the deal.

Query. What are the odds throughout the whole rubber?

1 Game love and 9 love of the second game (upon supposition of 9 love with the deal) being nearly 6 to 1.

First game and 9 love of the second game is nearly 13 to 1

First game and 8 love of the second game is a little more than the former .... 13 — 1&c.

First game and 7 love of the second is nearly .. 10 — 1

Ditto and 6 love of the second is nearly .... 8 — 1

Ditto and 5 love of the second is nearly .... 6 — 1

Ditto and 4 love of the second is nearly .... 5 — 1

Ditto and 3 love of the second is nearly .... 4½ — 1

Ditto and 2 love of the second is nearly .... 4 — 1

Ditto and 1 love of the second is nearly .... 7 — 2

The above calculations are made with the deal.

AGAINST THE DEAL.

Suppose A and B are at play, and that A is one game, and any number of points in the second deal.

First game and 9 love of the second is nearly ...	11 to 1
Ditto and 8 love of the second game, is a little more	11 —1
Ditto and 7 love of the second game is...........	9 —1
Ditto and 6 love of the second game is...........	7 —1
Ditto and 5 love of the second game is...........	5 —1
Ditto and 4 love of the second game is...........	4½—1
Ditto and 3 love of the second game is...........	4 —1
Ditto and 2 love of the second game is...........	7 —2
First game and 1 love of the second is nearly....	6½—2

The use which is to be made of the foregoing calculations, may be made by dividing the stake, according to the tables herewith set down.

BACKGAMMON.

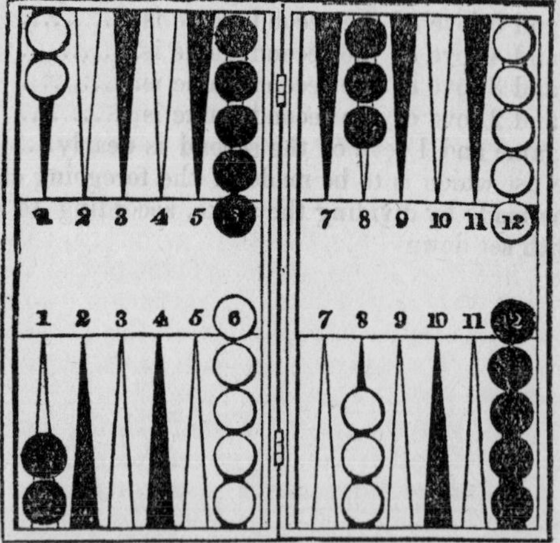

THIS is a mixed game, being a combination of chance and calculation. Its derivation is a vexed question, both as to whence it came and how it acquired its present designation. "La Maison des Jeux Académiques" abandons its origin as a desperate problem, and Dr. Henry claims its name as a Welsh compound, from "bach," little, and "cammon," battle. On the other hand, Bp. Kennett and Strutt derive it from the Anglo-Saxon, viz., from "bac," back, and "gamone," a game, that is to say, a game where players are exposed to be sent back. Perhaps this may satisfy the antiquarian and be accepted as a sufficient offering to the etymologist. It would have been a mere recreation in chronology, to have disputed all the probabilities for assigning Backgammon to the antediluvian age. One portion of its machinery consists of dice—now dice defy chronology. Their types are found in Etruscan tombs and in the hieroglyphics of Egypt; and the historian of Chæronea asserts, that Mercury had a throw of the dice once upon a time with the Goddess Luna.

From Chaucer we gather that the early name of Backgammon, or at all events its synonyme, was "Tables;" at which period it was played with three dice, and all the "men" commenced their action from the adversary's table. Backgammon has always been a particularly respectable instrument of amusement, like the Organ in "She Stoops to conquer." Even Whist has not escaped defilement, but Backgammon "was never a vulgar game, never beloved of lackeys." Shakspeare has used it as a medium for his philosophy, and Bacon has served bail for its good behaviour.

Backgammon is played by two persons, with two boxes and two dice, upon a quadrangular table or board, on which are figured 24 points or *flèches*, of two colours, placed alternately. The board is divided into four compartments, two inner and two outer ones, each containing six of the 24 points (alternate colours.) The players are each furnished with fifteen men or counters, black and white (usually draughts.) These are arranged upon the board, in the following manner. To play into the left hand table, two of your men are placed upon the ace point of your opponent's inner table, five upon the sixth point in his outer table (numbered 12 in our diagram,) three upon the cinque-point in your own outer table numbered 8,) and five upon the sixth point, in your own inner table. The adversary's men are to be placed in corresponding order, in a position directly opposite. All this is shown in the diagram annexed, and to facilitate reference the points or flèches are numbered from 1 to 12 of each colour.

The game consists in moving your men from point to point, so as to bring them round into your own inner table (*i. e.*, that on your left hand,) and then moving or bearing them off the board. The player who first clears off his men wins.

The moves of the men are determined by the throws of the dice, according to the directions for playing, at page 394. It will there be seen that the most advantageous throw at the outset is that of aces, as it blocks the bar or sixth point in your other table (numbered 7,) and secures the cinque-point in your inner table, so that your adversary's two men cannot move if he throw either quatre, cinque, or size. This throw is frequently conceded to inferior players, at the commencement of the game, by way of odds.

As the grand object of the game consists in bringing round your men into your own inner table, all throws that contribute towards that end, and prevent your adversary from doing the same are advantageous, and *vice versâ*. During the progress of the game you should endeavour to block up or detain a part of your adversary's men, in your own tables; and to obstruct his re-entering such of them as you may happen to have taken up, unless all your own men have passed his main body, and are so far advanced to your inner table (which we will here call home) as to possess the best chance, should he seek to win by running away.

At the commencement of the game the players must agree towards which end of the board they will play. Each party plays into one of the tables on his own side; thus, if Black plays into his left-hand table, White plays into his right (*i. e.*, that which is exactly opposite,) and *vice versâ*, their men advancing in contra-position to each other, as in the annexed diagram.

For a right of first play each party throws a single die; he who throws the highest number wins, and may, if he chooses, adopt and play the joint number of the preliminary throw. If he reject, then the first step is made by his throwing both the dice, and moving any one of his men to an open point at the distance indicated by one of the dice, and then moving another man (or the same man farther on, if he think proper,) to another open point indicated by the number of the second die. This completes his move, his adversary then follows in a similar manner, and so on alternately to the end of the game. Thus, double aces (which count as 4) would entitle you (say White) to move two men from 8 w. to 7 w., and two from 6 w. to 5 w., which covers the bar point (No. 7,) and also covers the cinque point in your inner table, and then, should your next throw be 5 and 6, you would play the five from 12 b. to 8 w., and so cover the blot before left; and you would play the six from 12 b. to your bar point. Pairs count double; thus, sixes entitle you to move four men, each six points forward, and you may either move four together, say, from 12 B. to 7 W., or two together, as, say, two from 1 B. to your adversary's bar point (No. 7,) and two from 12 B. to 7 W. (your own bar point,) or singly,—as, say, a single man from 1 B. to 1 W. in your own inner table, presuming that your adversary had ceased to occupy it.

The direction in which your men move is from the adverse inner table over the bar, through the adversary's outer table round into your own outer table, and then over your bar, home.

When during the progress of the game only a single man is left on a point, it is called "a blot," and is exposed to be taken by the adversary, who generally endeavours to "hit" the blot by bringing one of his own men to that point. When a man is thus captured it must be removed, and placed upon the bar (*i. e.*, the division joint of the table,) and the player to whom it belongs cannot move again, until he has "entered his man." This can only be effected by throwing a number which is vacant, or is left a "blot" on the adversary's inner table, playing it as from a point off the board, adjoining to the adversary's ace point. Towards the end of the game, when most of the points in your adversary's inner table are covered (*i. e.*, have two or more men on each,) it becomes difficult to enter, and you must remain on the bar, till you have either thrown the exact number required to suit perhaps a single open point, or till more points are exposed, by your adversary having played some of his men off the table. When all the six points are blocked, it is of course useless your throwing, and your adversary throws alone. "Hitting" a blot frequently adds extreme variety and interest to the game.

When doublets are thrown, four moves are played of the distance indicated by the dice, instead of two, as usual in ordinary throws. For instance, should two quatres be thrown, any of the following moves may be played, either one man may be moved sixteen points; two men each eight points; one man eight, and two men four points; or four men four points each. Should, however, the points indicated by the throw of the dice be covered, the moves are lost. For instance, if double quatres be cast, and the first fourth point from all the player's men be covered by the adversary, the move is lost, although the eighth, twelfth, and sixteenth points be uncovered, as the first fourth point, if occupied, cannot be passed over.

If, during the course of the game, every point upon which a man could be moved is covered by the adversary's men, your men are compelled to remain in *statu quo,* and the adversary takes his turn. If one man only can be played, it must be played.

When a player has brought all his men home, he must begin to "bear them," *i. e.,* to take them off the board. For every number thrown a man is removed from the corresponding point, until the whole are borne off. In doing this, should the adversary be waiting to "enter" any of his men which have been "hit," care should be taken to leave no "blots" or uncovered points. In "bearing off" doublets have the same power as in the moves, four men are removed; if higher numbers are on the dice than on the points, men may be taken from any lower point, thus if double sixes are thrown, and the point has been already stripped, four men may be removed from the cinque point of any lower number. If a low number is thrown, and the corresponding point hold no men, they must be played up from a higher point. Thus, if double aces be thrown, and there are no men upon the ace point two or more men must be played up from the higher points, or a fewer number played up and taken off.

If one player has not borne off his first man before the other has borne off his last, he loses a "gammon," which is equivalent to two games, or "hits." If each player has borne off it is reduced to a "hit," or game of one. If the winner has borne off all his men before the loser has carried his men out of his adversary's table, it is a "back-gammon," and usually held equivalent to three hits or games.

Calculation of the Chances.

As it is necessary for a learner to know how many points he ought to throw upon the two dice, one throw with another; we will take the following method to demonstrate it.

There are thirty-six chances upon two dice, the points of which are as follows:

	Points.
2 aces	4
2 deuces	8
2 trois	12
2 fours	16
2 fives	20
2 sixes	24
6 and 5 twice	22
6 and 4 twice	20
6 and 3 twice	18
6 and 2 twice	16
6 and 1 twice	14
5 and 4 twice	18
5 and 3 twice	16
5 and 2 twice	14
5 and 1 twice	12
4 and 3 twice	14
4 and 2 twice	12
4 and 1 twice	10
3 and 2 twice	10
3 and 1 twice	8
2 and 1 twice	6

Divided by 36 . . { 294 / 288 } 8

6

294 divided by 36, shows that, one throw with another, you may expect to throw 8 upon two dice.

The chances upon two dice are as follows:

	Points.
2 sixes	1
2 fives	1
2 fours	1
2 trois	1
2 deuces	1
*2 aces	1
6 and 5 twice	2
6 and 4 twice	2
Carried over	10

	Points
Brought forward	10
6 and 3 twice	2
6 and 2 twice	2
*6 and 1 twice	2
5 and 4 twice	2
5 and 3 twice	2
5 and 2 twice	2
*5 and 1 twice	2
4 and 3 twice	2
4 and 2 twice	2
*4 and 1 twice	2
3 and 2 twice	2
*3 and 1 twice	2
*2 and 1 twice	2
	35

To find out by this table, what are the odds of being hit, upon a certain, or flat die, look in the table, where thus* marked,

	Points.
*2 aces	1
*6 and 1 twice	2
*5 and 1 twice	2
*4 and 1 twice	2
*5 and 1 twice	2
*2 and 1 twice	2
Total	11
Which deducted from	36
The remainder is	25

By this it appears, that it is twenty-five to eleven against hitting an ace, upon a certain, or flat die.

The like method may be taken with any other flat die, as with the ace.

What are the odds of entering a man upon one, two, three, four, or five points?

	for.	against.		Reduced. for.	against.
A. to enter it upon 1 point is	11	to 25,	or about	4	to 9
upon 2 points	20	" 16,	"	5	" 4
upon 3 points	27	" 9,	"	3	" 1
upon 4 points	32	" 4,	"	8	" 1
upon 5 points	35	" 1,	"	35	" 1

What are the odds of hitting, with any chance, in the reach of a single die?

		for.	against.		Reduced. for.	against.
A. to hit upon 1	is	11	to 25,	or about	4	to 9
upon 2	"	12	" 24,	"	1	" 2
upon 3	"	14	" 22,	"	2	" 3
upon 4	"	15	" 21,	"	5	" 7
upon 5	"	15	" 21,	"	5	" 7
upon 6	"	17	" 19,	"	8½	" 9½

What are the odds of hitting with double dice?

		for.	against.		Reduced. for.	against.
A. To hit upon 7	is	6	to 30,	or about	1	to 5
upon 8	"	6	" 30,	"	1	" 5
upon 9	"	5	" 31,	"	1	" 6
upon 10	"	3	" 33,	"	1	" 11
upon 11	"	2	" 34,	"	1	" 17
upon 12 (or 2 sixes)		1	" 36,	"	1	" 36

To explain farther how to use the table of thirty-six chances, to find the odds of being hit upon any certain or flat die, this second example is added to show how to find by that table the odds of being hit upon a 6.

2 sixes	1
2 trois	1
2 deuces	1
6 and 5 twice	2
6 and 4 twice	2
6 and 3 twice	2
6 and 2 twice	2
Carried over . .	11

Brought forward . .	11
6 and 1 twice	2
5 and 1 twice	2
4 and 2 twice	2
	17
Which deducted from .	36
The remainder is . .	19

So that it is nineteen to seventeen against being hit upon at 6.

The odds of 2 love are about 5 to 2,
and of 2 to 1 are 2 " 1,
and of 1 love is 3 " 2.

General Instructions.

I. If you play three up at Backgammon, your principal view, in the first place, is to secure your own, or your adversary's cinque point, or both; when that is effected, you may play a pushing game, and endeavour to gammon your adversary.

II. The next best point (after you have gained your cinque point) is to make your bar point, thereby preventing your adversary's running out with doublet sixes.

III. After you have proceeded thus far, prefer the making your quatre point in your own table, rather than the quatre point out of it.

IV. Having gained these points, you have a fair chance to gammon your adversary, if he is very forward: For, suppose his tables are broke at home, it will be then your interest to open your bar point, and to oblige him to come out of your tables with a six; and having your men spread, you not only may catch that man which your adversary brings out of your tables, but you will also have a probability of taking up the man left in your tables (upon supposition that he has two men there). If he should have a blot at home, it will then be your interest not to make up your tables; because, if he should enter upon a blot, which you are to make for the purpose, you will have a probability of getting a third man; which, if accomplished, will give you, at least, 4 to 1 of the gammon; whereas, if you have only two of his men up, the odds are that you do not gammon him.

V. If you play for a hit only, 1 or 2 men taken up of your adversary's, makes it surer than a greater number, provided your tables are made up.

Directions how to carry your Men home.

VI. When you carry your men home, in order to lose no point, you are to carry the most distant man to your adversary's bar point, that being the first stage you are to place it on; the next stage is six points further, viz., the place where your adversary's five men are first placed out of his tables; the next stage is upon the six point in your tables. This method is to be pursued till all your men are brought home, except two, when, by losing a point, you may often save your gammon, by putting it in the power of two fives, or two fours to save it.

VII. If you play to win a hit only, endeavour to gain either your own or your adversary's cinque point; and if that fails, by your being hit by your adversary, and you find that he is forwarder than you, you must throw more men into his table. Thus: put a man upon your cinque or bar point, and if your adversary neglects to hit it, you may then gain a forward instead of a back game; but if he hits you, you must play a back game, and then the greater the number of men which are taken up, the better it makes your game, because you by that means preserve your game at home; and you must then always endeavour to gain both your adversary's ace and trois points, or his ace and deuce points, and take care to keep three men upon his ace point, that if you chance to hit him from thence, that point may remain still secure to you.

VIII. At the beginning of a set do not play for a back game, because by so doing you would play to a great disadvantage, running the risk of a gammon to win a single hit.

Directions for Playing at setting out the Thirty-six Chances of Dice, for a Gammon, or for a Single Hit.

I. Two aces (the best of all first throws), to be played two on your cinque point, and two on the bar point for a gammon, or for a hit.

II. Two sixes (the second best throw), should be played

two on your adversary's bar point, and two on your own bar point, for a gammon, or a hit.

III. Two trois, two be played on your cinque point, and the other two on your trois point in your own tables, for a gammon only.

IV. Two deuces to be played on the quatre point in your own tables, and two to be brought over from the five men placed in your adversary's outer tables, for a gammon only.

V. *Two fours, to be brought over from the five men placed in your adversary's outer tables, and to be put upon the cinque point in your own tables, for a gammon only.

VI. Two fives, to be brought over from the five men placed in your adversary's outer tables, and to be put on the trois point in your own tables for a gammon, or a hit.

VII. Size ace, you are to make your bar point, for a gammon, or for a hit.

VIII. Size deuce, a man to be brought from the five men placed in your adversary's outer tables, and to be placed on the cinque point in your own tables, for a gammon, or a hit.

IX. Six and three, a man to be brought from your adversary's ace point, as far as he will go, for a gammon, or a hit.

X. Six and four, a man to be brought from your adversary's ace point, as far as he will go, for a gammon, or a hit.

XI. Six and five, a man to be carried from your adversary's ace point, as far as he can go, for a gammon, or a hit.

XII. Cinque and quatre, a man to be carried from your adversary's ace point, as far as he can go, for a gammon, or a hit.

XIII. Cinque-trois, to make the trois point in your table, for a gammon, or a hit.

XIV. Cinque-deuce, to play two men from the five placed in your adversary's outer tables, for a gammon, or a hit.

XV. Cinque-ace, to bring one man from the five placed in your adversary's outer tables for the cinque, and to play one man down on the cinque point in your own tables for the ace, for a gammon only.

XVI. Quatre-trois, two men to be brought from the five placed in your adversary's outer tables, for a gammon, or a hit.

XVII. Quatre-deuce to make the quatre point in your own tables, for a gammon, or a hit.

XVIII. Quatre-ace, to play a man from the five placed in your adversary's outer tables for the quatre, and for the ace, to play a man down upon the cinque point in your own tables, for a gammon only.

XIX. Trois-deuce, two men to be brought from the five placed in your adversary's tables, for a gammon only.

XX. Trois-ace, to make the cinque point in your own tables, for a gammon, or a hit.

XXI. Deuce-ace, to play one man from the five placed in your adversary's tables for the deuce; and for the ace, to play a man down upon the cinque point in your own tables, for a gammon only.

Directions how to Play the Chances that are marked thus (*) when you are only to Play for a Hit.

I. *Two trois, two of them are to be played on your cinque point in your own tables, and with the other two take the quatre point in your adversary's tables.

II. *Two deuces, two of them are to be played on your quatre point in your own tables, and with the other two take the trois point in your adversary's tables.

The two foregoing cases are to be played in this manner, for this reason, viz., That thereby you avoid being shut up in your adversary's tables, and have the chance of throwing high doublets to win the hit.

III. *Two fours, two of them are to take your adversary's cinque point in his tables; and for the other two, two men are to be brought from the five placed in your adversary's tables.

IV. 1. *Cinque-ace, play the cinque from the five men placed in your adversary's tables, and play the ace from your adversary's ace point.

V. 2. *Quatre-ace, play the quatre from the five men placed in your adversary's tables, and the ace from the men on your adversary's ace point.

VI. 3. *Deuce-ace, play the deuce from the five men placed in your adversary's tables, and the ace from your adversary's ace point.

The three last chances are played in this manner, for, by

laying an ace down in your adversary's tables, you have a probability of throwing deuce ace, trois deuce, quatre trois, or size cinque, in two or three throws; in any of which cases you are to make a point, which gives you the better of the hit.

You may observe, by the directions given in this chapter, that you are to play nine chances out of the thirty-six in a different manner for a single hit, to what you would do when playing for a gammon.

Some Observations, Hints, and Cautions, which are to be attended to.

1. By the directions given to play for a gammon, you are voluntarily to make some blots, the odds being in your favor, that they are not hit; but should it so happen, that any blot is hit, as in this case, you will have three men in your adversary's table, you must then endeavour to secure your adversary's cinque, quatre, or trois point, to prevent a gammon, and must be very cautious how you suffer your adversary to take up a fourth man.

II. Take care not to crowd your game at any time, if possible. What is meant by crowding a game, is the putting many men either upon your trois or deuce point in your own tables; which is, in effect, losing those men, by not having them in play.

Besides, by crowding your game, to attempt to save a gammon, you are often gammoned; because when your adversary finds your game open, by being crowded in your own tables, he may then play his game as he thinks fit.

III. By recourse had to the calculations, you may know what are the Odds of your entering a single man upon any certain number of points, and by that means you may play your game accordingly.

IV. If you are obliged to leave a blot, by recourse to the calculation for hitting it, you will find the chances for and against; and consequently you will be enabled to judge how to play your game to the greatest advantage.

V. You will also find by the calculations, the odds for and

against you, upon being hit by double dice, and consequently you will choose such a method of play as is most to your advantage.

VI. If it is necessary to make a run, in order to win a hit, and you would know to a point which is the forwarder, take the following method:

Begin with reckoning how many points you must have, to bring home to your size point in your own tables, the man that is at the greatest distance from it, and do the like by every other man that is abroad; when the numbers of those absentees are summed up, add to them the following numbers for those already in your own tables, (supposing the men that were abroad as on your size point for bearing) namely, six for every man on the size point, five for every man on the cinque point, four for every man on the quatre point, three for every man on the trois point, two for every man on the deuce point, and one for every man on your ace point. Do the like to your adversary's game, and then you will know which of you is forwardest, and likeliest to win the hit.

Observations and Directions for a Learner who has made some Progress at Back-gammon; particularly Directions for bearing his men.

I. If your adversary be greatly before you, never play a man from your quatre, trois, or deuce points, in order to bear that man from the point where you put it, because nothing but high doublets can give you any chance for the hit; therefore, instead of playing an ace or a deuce from any of the aforesaid points, always play them on from your size or highest point; by which means you will find, that throwing two fives, or two fours, will, upon having eased your size and cinque points, be of great advantage to you: Whereas, had your size point remained loaded, you must, perhaps, be obliged to play at length those fives and fours.

II. Whenever you have taken up two of your adversary's men, and happen to have two, three, or more points made in your own tables, never fail spreading your men, in order either to take a new point in your tables, or to be ready to hit the man your adversary may happen to enter As soon as he enters one of his men, you are to compare his game with your's; and if you find your game equal to his, or better, never fail taking his man up, if you can, because it is 25 to 11 against his hitting you; which chance being so much in your favor, you ought always to run that risk, when you have already two of his men up.

There is this exception to this rule, that if you play for a single hit only, and your playing that throw otherwise gives you a better chance for the hit, you ought not to take up that man.

III. Never be deterred from taking up any one man of your adversary's, by the apprehension of his hitting you with double dice, because the fairest probability your adversary has of hitting you, is 5 to 1 against him.

IV. If you should happen to have five points covered in your tables, and to have taken up one of your adversary's men, and are obliged to leave a blot out of your tables, rather leave it upon doublets, than any other chance, because doublets are 35 to 1 against his hitting you, and any other chance is but 17 to 1 against him.

V. Two of your adversary's men in your tables, are better for a hit, than any greater number, provided your game be forwardest, because his having three or more men in your tables, gives him more chance to hit you, than if he had only two men there.

VI. If you are to leave a blot, upon entering a man in your adversary's tables, or otherwise, and have it in your choice to leave it upon what point you please, always choose that which is the most disadvantageous to him. To illustrate this by an example, let us suppose it his interest to hit you or take you up as soon as you enter, in that case leave the blot upon his lowest point; that is to say upon his deuce, rather than upon his trois point, or upon his trois, preferable to his quatre point; or upon his quatre, preferable to his cinque point; because, (as has been mentioned before) all the men your adversary plays upon his trois, or his deuce points, are deemed as lost, being in a great measure out of play, those men not having it in their power to make his cinque point, and consequently his game will be crowded there, and open elsewhere, whereby you will be able also much to annoy him.

VII. To prevent your adversary from bearing his men to the greatest advantage, when you are running to save your gammon; as, for instance, suppose you should have two men upon his ace point, and several other men abroad, though you should lose one point or two in putting your men into your tables, yet it is your interest to leave a man upon your adversary's ace point, which will have this consequence; that it will prevent his bearing his men to the greatest advantage, and will also give you the chance of his making a bolt, which you may chance to hit. But if, upon a calculation, you find that you have a throw, or a probability of saving your gammon, never wait for a blot, because the odds are greatly against hitting it.

Cases, showing how to calculate the odds of saving or winning a Gammon.

I. Suppose your tables are made up, and that you have taken up one of your adversary's men; and suppose your adversary has so many men abroad as require three throws to put them in his tables.

It is then about an equal wager that you gammon him.

Because, in all probability, you will bear two men before you open your table, and when you bear the third man, you will be obliged to open your size or cinque point: in that case it is probable that your adversary must take two throws before he enters his man in your tables, and two throws more before he puts that man into his own tables, and three throws more to put into his own tables the men which were abroad, which in all, make seven throws; and as you have twelve men to bear, these probably will take seven throws in bearing, because you may twice be obliged to make an ace, or a deuce, before you can bear all your men.

No mention is made of doublets on either side, that event being equal to each party.

The foregoing case shows it is in your power to calculate very nearly the odds of saving or winning a gammon upon most occasions.

II. Suppose I have three men upon my adversary's ace

point, and five points in my tables, and that my adversary has all his men in his tables, three upon each of his five highest points:

What is the probability for his gammoning me, or not?

For his bearing 3 men from his 6 point, is	18
from his 5 point,	15
from his 4 point,	12
from his 3 point,	9
from his 2 point,	6
Total, ——	60
To bring my three men from my adversary's ace point, to my size point in my tables, being for each 18 points, makes in all ——	54
The remainder is	6

And besides the six points in your favor, there is a further consideration to be added for you, which is, that your adversary may make one or two blots in bearing, as is frequently the case. You see by this calculation, that you have greatly the better of the probability of saving your gammon.

This case is supposed upon an equality of throwing.

III. Suppose I leave two blots, neither of which can be hit but by double dice; to hit the one, that cast must be eight, and to hit the other it must be nine; by which means my adversary has only one die to hit either of them.

What are the odds of his hitting either of these bolts?

The chances on two dice are in all, 36.

The chances to hit 8 are,	**6 and 2 twice,**	**2**
	5 and 3 twice,	**2**
	2 deuces,	**1**
	2 fours,	**1**
The chances to hit 9 are,	**6 and 3 twice,**	**2**
	5 and 4 twice,	**2**
	2 trois,	**1**
	Total chances for hitting,	**11**
	Remaining chances for not hitting,	**25**

So that it is 25 to 11 that he will not hit either of those blots.

IV. To give another example, let us suppose that I leave two other blots than the former, which cannot be hit but by double dice, the one must be hit by eight, and the other by seven.

What are the odds of my adversary's hitting either of these blots?

The chances on two dice are in all, 36.

The chances to hit 8 are,	6 and 2 twice, . .	2
	5 and 3 twice, . .	2
	two fours, . . .	1
	two deuces, . .	1
The chances to hit 7 are,	6 and 1 twice, . .	2
	5 and 2 twice, . .	2
	4 and 3 twice, . .	2
	m	—
	Total chances for hitting, . .	12
		—
	Remain chances for not hitting, . .	24
		—

Therefore it is two to one that I am not hit

The like method is to be taken with three, four, or five blots upon double dice; or with blots made upon double and single dice at the same time; you are then only to find out (by the table of 36 chances) how many there are to hit any of those blots, and add all together in one sum, which subtract from the number of 36, which is the whole of the chances upon two dice: so doing resolves any question required.

V. The following cases are to show a way of calculating, which may be called a mechanical way of solving questions of the like nature.

What are the odds of throwing 7 twice, before 10 once?

It is 5 to 4 that 10 is thrown once before 7 is thrown twice, which is demonstrated as follows:

Suppose the stake depending is nine pounds, my first throw entitles me to have one-third part of that money, because 7 has 6 chances for it, and 10 has but 3 chances, and therefore it is two to one.

For the first throw, . . .	£3 0s. 9d.
Having taken 3*l.* out of the 9*l.* for the first throw, the remainder is 6*l.* out of which a third part is to be taken for the second throw	2 0 0
The total is,	5 0 0
Remains,	4 0 0
The whole stake is,	£9 0 0

VI. What are the odds of entering a man upon any certain point in two throws?

Suppose 36 shillings is the whole stake depending, what is my share of that stake, having laid 18 shillings that I enter in two throws? By the calculations in the table of 36 chances, it is found that I have 11 chances out of the 36 for entering the first throw, for which therefore I am entitled to 11 out of the 36 shillings.

The stake is,	0 36 0
For the first throw,	0 11 0
Remains,	£0 25 0
The remainder, being 25 shillings, is to be divided into 36 equal parts, of which I am entitled to eleven of those parts, which makes 7*s.* 7½*d.*, for the second throw . .	0 7 7½
Adding this to the other 11 shillings, makes my share of the stake to be	0 18 7½
Then my adversary's share will be . .	0 17 4½
Total of the stake,	£0 36 0

Therefore it is very nearly 15 to 14 in favor of entering a man upon any certain point in two throws.

Chapter VIII.—*Critical case for a Back-game.*

I. Let us suppose A plays the fore-game, and that all his men are placed in the usual manner:

For B's game, suppose that fourteen of his men are placed upon his adversary's ace point, and one man upon his adversary's deuce point, and that B is to throw.

Which game is likeliest to win the hit?

A's is the best by 21 for, to 20 against; because, if B misses an ace to take his adversary's deuce point, which is 25 to 11 against him, A is, in that case, to take up B's men in his tables, either singly, or to make points; and if B secures either A's deuce or trois point, in that case, A is to lay as many men down as possible, in order to be hit, that thereby he may get a back-game.

When you are pretty well versed in the game of Backgammon, by practising this back-game, you will become a greater proficient in the game than by any other method, because it clearly demonstrates the whole power of the back-game.

Back-game.

II. Let us suppose A to have five men placed upon his size point, five men upon his quatre point, and five men upon his deuce point, all in his own tables:

And suppose B to have three men placed upon A's ace point, three men upon A's trois point, and three men upon A's cinque point; let B also have three men upon his size point in his own tables, and three men placed out of his tables, in the usual manner:

Who has the better of the hit?

It is an equal game; but to play it critically, the difficulty lies upon B, who is in the first place to endeavour to gain his cinque and quatre points in his own tables; and when that is effected, he is to lay two men from A's cinque point, in order to oblige his adversary to blot, by throwing an ace, which, if B hits, he will have the fairest probability of winning the hit.

Back-game.

III. Suppose A has three men upon B's ace point, and three men upon B's deuce point, also three men upon his size point in his own tables, and three men upon his usual point out of his tables, and three men where his five men are usually placed in his adversary's tables:

And let us suppose B has his men placed in the same manner, both in his own and his adversary's tables, with this difference only, viz instead of having three men put upon A's deuce point, let him have three men upon A's trois point:

Q. Who has the best of the hit?

A. A, because the ace and trois points are not so good for a hit, as the ace and deuce points in your adversary's tables, for when you are bearing your men, you have the deuce point in your own tables to play your men upon, which often prevents your making a blot, which must happen otherwise to your adversary; and take care to lay down men to be hit as often as you can, in order to keep your game backward, and for the same reason avoid hitting any blots which your adversary makes.

A Case of Curiosity and Instruction.

IV. Let us suppose A has fifteen men upon B's ace point, B is supposed to have his bar point, also his size, cinque, quatre, and trois points in his own tables:

How many throws is A likely to take to bring his fifteen men into his own tables, and to bear them?

A. You may undertake to do it in seventy-five throws.

It is odds in A's favor that he throws an ace in two throws; it is also odds in A's favor that he throws a six in two throws; when these events happen, A has a probability of not wanting above two or three throws to play till he has got all his fifteen men into his own tables: therefore, by a former rule laid down to bring your men home, and also for bearing your men, you may be able to find out the probability of the number of throws required. Note, B stands still, and does not play.

A Case of Curiosity and Instruction.

V. Where A and B shall play as fast as usual, and yet A shall make the hit last, probably, for many hours.

We will suppose B to have borne thirteen men, and that A has taken up the two remaining men:

And let us suppose that A has fifteen men in B's tables, viz. three men upon his size point, three men upon his cinque point, three upon his quatre point, three upon his trois point, two upon his deuce point, and one upon his ace point:

The method, which A is to take, is this: let him bring his fifteen men home, by always securing six close points, till B has entered his two men, and brought them upon any certain point; as soon as B has gained that point, A must open an ace, deuce, or trois, or all three; which effected, B hits one of them, and A, taking care to have two or three men in B's tables, is ready to hit that man; and also, he being assured of taking up the other man, has it in his power to prolong the hit to almost any length, provided he takes care not to open such points, as two fours, two fives, or two sixes, but always to open the ace, deuce, or trois points, for B to hit him.

VI. To know what are the odds upon two dice, for throwing two sixes, two fives, or two fours, in three throws; by mechanical calculation, it may be found thus:

	s.	d.
A. Supposing 36 shillings to be the stake depending, the thrower will be entitled to have for his first throw,	3	0
which deducted out of 36, remains 33; which divided again into 36 parts, make so many eleven pences, out of which the thrower is to have 3 for his second throw,	2	9
The remainder, 30 shillings and three pence, is again to be divided into 36 parts; dividing the 30 shillings so, make so many ten pences, and the three pence divided into so many parts, make so many thirds of farthings, of which the thrower is to have three parts for his share for his third throw	2	6¼
Total for the thrower .	8	3¼

So that it is 27*s.* 8¾*d.* to 8*s.* 3¼*d.* against the thrower, which reduced into the smallest number, is very nearly as 10 to 3, that two sixes, or two fives, or two fours, are not thrown in two throws.

Back-game.

VII. Suppose A to have two men upon his size point in his own tables, three men upon his usual point in his outer table, two men upon the point where his five men are usually placed in his adversary's tables, five men upon his adversary's ace point, and three men upon his adversary's quatre point:

And suppose B to have two men upon his size point in his own tables, three men upon his usual point in his outer table, two men upon the point where his five men are usually placed in his adversary's tables, five men upon his adversary's ace point, and three men upon his adversary's trois point:

Who has the fairest chance to win the hit?

A has, because he is to play either an ace, or a deuce, from his adversary's ace point, in order to make both these points as occasion offers; and having the quatre point in his adversary's tables, he may more easily bring those men away, if he finds it necessary, and he will also have a resting place by the conveniency of that point, which at all times in the game will give him an opportunity of running for the hit, or staying, if he thinks proper. Whereas B cannot so readily come from the trois point in his adversary's tables.

A Case of Curiosity.

I. Let us suppose A and B place their men in the following manner for a hit:

Suppose A to have three men upon his size point in his own tables, three men upon the usual point in his outer table, and nine men upon his adversary's ace, deuce, and trois points, three men to be placed upon each point; and suppose B's men to be placed in his own, and in his adversary's tables, in the same order and manner.

The result is, that the best player ought to win the hit; and the dice are to be thrown for, the situation being perfectly equal in A's and B's game.

If A throws first, let him endeavour to gain his adversary's cinque point; when that is effected, let him lay as many blots as possible, to tempt B to hit him; for every time that B hits them will be in A's favor, because it puts B backward; and let A take up none of B's men for the same reason.

A is always to endeavour to have three men upon each of his adversary's ace and deuce points; because when B makes a blot, these points will remain secure, and by recourse had to a former case (No. V. in the former chapter) when A has borne five, six, or more men, yet A may secure six close points out of his tables, in order to prevent B from getting his man home; and by recourse had to the calculations, he may easily find out (in case he makes up his tables) who has the better of the hit; and if he finds that B is forwarder, he is then to endeavour to lay such blots to be taken up by his adversary, as may give him a chance for taking up another man, in case B should happen to have a blot at home.

Those who play the foregoing game well, may be ranked in the first form.

A Case of Curiosity.

II. A and B play at Backgammon. A has borne thirteen men, and has two men to bear upon his deuce point, B has thirteen men in his own tables, with two men to enter. B is to throw, and to name the throws both for himself and A, but not to hit a blot on either side:

What throws is B to name for both parties, in order to save his gammon?

B calls for himself two aces, which enter his two men upon A's ace point. B also calls two aces for A, and consequently A cannot either bear a man, nor play one; then B calls for two sixes for himself and carries one man home upon his size point in his own tables, and the other he places upon his adversary's bar point: B also calls size-ace for A, so that A has one man left to bear, and then B calls for himself either two sixes, two fives, or two fours, any of which bear a man, in case he has men in his own tables upon those points, and to save his gammon.

II. The following question is to be attended to, as being critical and instructive:—

Suppose that all the points both on yours and your adversary's tables are covered:

Also that you have one man to carry home, but that he has two men on your barr point to carry home, which lie in wait to catch your man, and that if you pass him you are to win the hit: suppose also that you have it in your choice to run the risk of being hit, by 7, or by 8, both of which are chances upon double dice:—

Which of these chances is it best for you to venture?

That of 7, for the following reasons: First, because that the chances of being hit by 7, or by 8, are equal.

Secondly, If he does not hit 7, you will then have in your favor 23 chances to 13, that by your next throw you either hit him or pass beyond him.

Thirdly, In case your second throw should happen to be

under 7, and that consequently you cannot hit him, yet you may play that cast at home, and consequently leave the blot upon double dice.

Whereas if, on the contrary, you had left the blot upon 8, you would have made a bad choice, for the reasons following:—

First. Because the chances of being hit by 7, or by 8, are only equal.

Secondly. Because if you should escape the being hit by 8, yet you would then have but 17 chances in your favor, against 19 for either hitting him, or passing beyond him by your next throw.

Thirdly. In case your second throw should happen to be size-ace, which is short of him, you would then be obliged to play the man that is out of your tables, not being able to play the 6 at home, and consequently to leave a blot to be hit by a single (or flat) die; which event, upon supposition that you play for 18 shillings a game, would entitle him to 11 shillings of the whole stake depending.

THE LAWS OF BACKGAMMON.

I. If you take a man from any point, that man must be played; the same must be done if two men are taken from it.

II. You are not understood to have played any man, till you have placed him upon a point, and quitted him.

III. If you play with fourteen men only, there is no penalty attending it, because by playing with a lesser number than you are entitled to, you play to a disadvantage, by not having the additional man to make up your tables.

IV. If you bear any number of men, before you have entered a man taken up, and which consequently you were obliged to enter, such men, so borne, must be entered again in your adversary's tables, as well as the man taken up.

V. If you have mistaken your throw, and played, and if your adversary has thrown, it is not in your or his choice to alter it, unless both parties agree.

DRAUGHTS.

THIS interesting and highly scientific game has, by several of the writers upon it, been held to have preceded chess, of which it is supposed to be the root or source. Whether it may claim descent from the Greeks or Scandinavians is a point that may be left to the antiquarian, without any great social loss should he never succeed in settling it. In like manner the attempt to confer upon it any higher character than that of a rational means for the employment of a leisure hour may as conveniently be spared. The utility—in a general sense—of any mere game of science or skill, may be a question for philosophy—but it is one with which those who treat of its practical details have nothing to do—and of which most probably they could make nothing, if they had. Chess, according to Sir William Jones, dates some four thousand years back: if Draughts anticipated it, then, upon the principle that "age is honorable" the recreation we are about to treat of is one of no mean pretensions.*

We do not discover, from any written record, that Draughts was much practised in Europe till the middle of the sixteenth century. In 1668, an elaborate treatise upon it was published in Paris, written by a celebrated professor of mathematics, M. Mallet. Nearly a century later Mr. William Payne, teacher of mathematics, published his celebrated Introduction to the Game of Draughts, London, 1756. Subsequently, in 1767, appeared "a Companion for the Draught-player," by W. Painter, and there are other essays in type, but none that bear any comparison with "The Guide to the Game of Draughts, by Joshua Sturges, printed for the author, in London, 1800." Sturges worked up the whole of his predecessor's treatise in his more extended work, and with so much care and diligence, that half a century has elapsed without disturb-

* In Mr. Angas's "Savage Life and Scenes," it is stated that draughts is played by the savage tribes of the interior of New Zealand, under the name of E'mu, and that it does not seem possible they could have derived their knowledge of it from any other people.

ing the authority of his book. Mr Walker re-edited Sturges in 1835, and this improved edition is here given entire, with some additions by a skilful player of our metropolis, Mr. Martin.

Draughts it should always be remembered is purely a game of calculation, and as such craves wary policy. It is played by two persons upon a board of sixty-four squares, colored alternately Black and White, or any other two opposite colors. The board is placed with an upper white corner on the right hand, which brings the double white square to the lower right-hand corner.

Each player has twelve men; which on beginning the game, are placed on their respective sides, on the first three lines of white squares. The following diagrams represent the board and men in their original position; and also the mode in which the squares are conventionally numbered for the sake of reference.* It will be seen that, throughout this work, the upper half of the board is occupied by the twelve Black men, and the lower half by their antagonists, the White.

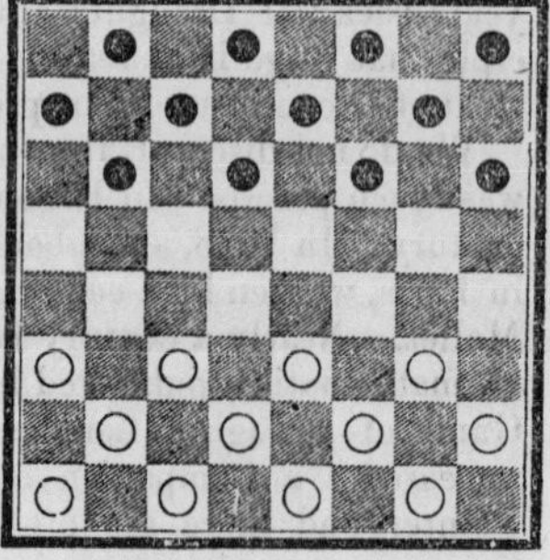

The men being placed, the game is begun by each player moving alternately one of his men, along the white diagonal on which they are first posted. The men can only move forward, either to the right or left, one square at a time, unless they have attained one of the four squares on the extreme line

* Practised players who have studied printed games are generally so familiar with the numerical position of the square that they can read and comprehend a series of intricate moves without even referring to the board.

of the board, on which they become kings, and can move either forward or backward, but still only one square at a time. The men take in the direction they move, by leaping over any hostile piece or pieces that may be immediately contiguous, provided there be a vacant white square behind them. The piece or pieces so taken are then removed from off the board, and the man taking them is placed on the square beyond. If several pieces, on forward diagonals, should be exposed by alternately having open squares behind them, they may all be taken at one capture, and the taking piece is then placed on the square beyond the last piece. To explain the mode of taking by practical illustration, let us begin by placing the draughts in their original position. You will perceive that if Black should move first he can only move one of the men placed on 9, 10, 11, or 12.—Supposing him then to play the man from 11 to 15, and White answering this move by playing his piece from 22 to 18, Black can take White by leaping his man from 15 to 22 and removing the captured piece off the board. Should Black not take in the above position, but move in another direction,—for instance, from 12 to 16, he is liable to be huffed; that is, White may remove the man with which Black should have taken, from the board, as a penalty for not taking; for, at Draughts, you have not the option of refusing to take, as at Chess, but must always take when you can, whatever be the consequence. The player who is in a position to huff his adversary has also the option of insisting on his taking, instead of standing the huff. When one party huffs the other, in preference to compelling the take, he does not replace the piece his adversary moved; but simply removes the man huffed, from off the board, and then plays his own move. Should he, however, insist upon his adversary taking the piece, instead of standing the huff, then the pawn improperly moved must first be replaced.

To give another example of huffing. Suppose a white man to be placed at 28, and three black men, at 24, 15, and 6, or 24, 16, and 8, with unoccupied intervals, he would capture all three men, and make a king, or be huffed for omitting to take them all, and it is not uncommon with novices to take one man, and overlook a second or third, "*en prise*" (*i. e.*, liable to be taken.)

When either of the men reaches one of the extreme squares of the board, he is, as already indicated, made a king, by having another piece put on, which is called crowning him. The king can move or take both forward or backward; keeping, of course, on the white diagonals. Both the king and common man can take any number of pieces at once which may be "*en prise*" at one move, and both are equally liable to be huffed. For instance: if White by reaching one of the back squares on his antagonist's side, say No. 2, had gained a king, he might upon having the move, and the Black pieces (either kings or men) being conveniently posted at No. 7, 16, 24, 23, and 14, with intermediate blanks, take them all at one fell swoop, remaining at square 9. But such a coup could hardly happen in English draughts. One of the great objects of the game, even at its very opening, is to push on for a king; but it is unnecessary to dwell much on the elementary part of the science, as the playing through one of the many games annexed, from the numbers, will do more in the way of teaching the rudiments of Draughts, than the most elaborate theoretical explanation.

The game is won by him who can first succeed in capturing, or blocking up, all his adversary's men, so that he has nothing left to move; but when the pieces are so reduced that each player has but a very small degree of force remaining; and, being equal in numbers, neither can hope to make any decided impression on his antagonist, the game is relinquished as drawn. It is obvious that were this not the case, and both parties had one or two kings, the game might be prolonged day and night, with the same hopeless chance of natural termination, as at the first moment of the pieces being resolved into the position in question. It has already been shown that when a man reaches one of the squares on the extreme line of the board, he is crowned and becomes a king; but there is another point relative to this, which it is necessary to understand. The man, thus reaching one of the extreme squares, finishes the move on being made a king, and cannot take any piece which may be "*en prise.*" He must first await his antagonist's move, and should he omit to remove or fortify an exposed piece it may then be taken. To exemplify this, place a White man on 11, and Black men on 7 and 6:—White, having the move, takes the man and demands that his own man should be crowned; but, he cannot take the man on 6 at the same move; which he could do were his piece a king when it made the first capture. But if the piece be left there after the next move he must take it.

In particular situations, to have the move on your side, is a decisive advantage. This is a matter little understood by ordinary players, but its importance will fully appear by studying the critical situations. To have the move, signifies your occupying that position on the board which will eventually enable you to force your adversary into a confined situation, and which at the end of the game, secures to yourself the last move. It must, however, be observed, that where your men are in a confined state, the move is not only of no use to you, but, for that very reason, may occasion the loss of the game. To know in any particular situation whether you have the move, you must number the men and the squares, and if the men are even and the squares odd, or the squares even and the men odd, you have the move. With even men and even squares, or odd men and odd squares, you have not the move. This will be best explained by an example: Look, then, at the 8th critical situation, where White plays first; there the adverse men are even, two to two; but the White squares, being five in number, are odd. The squares may be thus reckoned—from 26, a White king, to 28, a Black king, are three, viz. 31, 27, and 24—The White squares between 32, a White man, and 19, a Black man, are two, viz. 27 and 23. You may reckon more ways than one, but reckon which way you will, the squares will still be found odd, and therefore, White, so situated, has the move. When you have not the move, you must endeavour to procure it by giving man for man, a mode of play fully and successfully exemplified in this treatise.

There is another mode which will, in less time than reckoning the squares, enable you to see who has the move. For instance, if you wish to know, whether any one man of your's has the move of any one man of your adversary's, examine the situation of both, and if you find a Black square on the right angle, under his man, you have the move:—For example, you are to play first, and your White man is on 30, when your adversary's Black man is on 3. In this situation, you will find the right angle in a black square between 31 and 32, immediately under 3, and therefore you have the move This Rule will apply to any number of men, and holds true in every case.

There is a third mode, more ingenious still, communicated by Mr. Martin, and now published for the first time. Count all the pieces (of both colours) standing on those columns (not diagonals) which have a white square at the bottom, and if the number be odd, and White has to play, he has the move; if the number be even, the move is with Black.

It is a mistake to suppose that any advantage is derived from playing first. It is admitted, that he who plays first has not the move, the men and squares being then both even; but, though he who plays second has the move, it can be of no service to him in that stage of the game. The truth is, that when the combatants continue giving man for man, the move will alternately belong to one and the other. The first player will have it at odd men, at 11, 9, 7, 5, 3, and 1; the second player will have it at even men, at 12, 10, 8, 6, 4, and 2; and therefore some error must be committed, on one side or the other, before the move can be forced out of that direction.

To play over the games in this work, number the White squares on your draught-board from 1 to 32, and remember that in our diagram the Black pieces always occupy the first twelve squares. The abbreviations are so obvious, that they cannot need explanation;—a B. for Black, W. for White, Var. for Variation, &c. Occasionally, stars (asterisks) are introduced, to point out the move causing the loss of the game. The learner begins with the first game, and finding the leading move to be 11. 15 (that is, from 11 to 15), knows that Black begins the game. The second move 22. 18 belongs to White, and the game is thus played out; each party moving alternately. After finishing the game, the player proceeds to examine the variations to which he is referred by the letters and other directions. The numerous variations on some particular games, and the consequent necessity each time of going through the leading moves up to the point at which the variation arises, will, probably, at first, occasion some little fatigue; but this will be soon forgotten in the speedy and decided improvement found to be derived from this course of study. One of the minor advantages resulting from a numerous body of variations is, that, in tracing them out, the leading moves are so frequently repeated that they become indelibly fixed in the mind of the player; who thus remembers which moves are to be shunned as dangerous if not ruinous, and which moves are to be adopted as equally sound and scientific.

As to general advice relative to draught-playing, next to nothing can be learnt from a volume of such instruction The various modes of opening will be seen by reference to the accompanying examples. Among the few general rules that can be given you should bear in mind, that it is generally better to keep your men in the middle of the board, than to play them to the side squares,—as, in the latter case, one-half of their power is curtailed. And when you have once gained an advantage in the number of your pieces you increase the proportion by exchanges; but in forcing them you must take care not to damage your position. If you are a chess-player, you will do well to compare the draughts in their march and mode of manœuvring with the Pawns at Chess; which, as well as the Bishops or other pieces, are seldom so strong on the side squares as in the centre of the board. Accustom yourself to play slow at first, and, if a beginner, prefer playing with those who will agree to allow an unconditional time for the consideration of a difficult position, to those who rigidly exact the observance of the strict law. Never touch a man without moving it, and do not permit the loss of a few games to ruffle your temper, but rather let continued defeat act as an incentive to greater efforts both of study and practice. When one player is decidedly stronger than another, he should give odds to make the game equally interesting to both parties. There must be a great disparity indeed if he can give a man, but it is very common to give one man in a rubber of three games; that is, in one of the three games, the superior player engages to play with only 11 men instead of 12.—Another description of odds consists in giving the drawn games; that is, the superior player allows the weaker party to reckon as won, all games he draws Never play with a better player without offering to take such odds as he may choose to give. If you find yourself, on the other hand, so superior to your adversary, that you feel no amusement in playing even—offer him odds, and should he refuse, cease playing with him unless he will play for a stake; the losing which, for a few games in succession, will soon bring him to his senses, and make him willing to receive the odds you offer. Follow the rules of the game most rigorously, and compel your antagonist to do the same; without which, Draughts are mere child's play. Never touch the squares of the board with your finger, as some do, from the supposition that it assists their powers of calculation, and accustom yourself to play your move off-hand when you have once made up your mind: without hovering with your fingers over the board for a couple of minutes, to the great annoyance of the lookers-on. Finally, bear in mind what may well be termed the three golden rules to be observed in playing games of calculation: —Firstly, to avoid all boasting and loud talking about your skill—Secondly, to lose with good temper—and, Thirdly, to win with silence and modesty.

LAWS OF THE GAME.

1. The first move of each game is to be taken by the players in turn, whether the game be won or drawn. For the move in the first game at each sitting, the players must cast or draw lots, as they must for the men, which are, however, to be changed every game, so that each player shall use the black and white alternately. Whoever gains the choice may either play first, or call upon his adversary to do so.

2. You must not point over the board with your finger, nor do any thing which may interrupt your adversary's full and continued view of the game.

3. At any part of the game you may adjust the men properly on the squares, by previously intimating your intention to your adversary. This in polite society is usually done by saying "J'adoube." But after they are so adjusted, if you touch a man, it being your turn to play, you must play him in one direction or other if practicable; and if you move a man so far as to be in any part visible over the angle of an open square, that move must be completed, although by moving it to a different square you might have taken a piece, for the omission of which you incur huffing. The rule is "touch and move." No penalty, however, is attached to your touching any man which cannot be played.

4. In the case of your standing the huff, it is optional or

he part of your adversary, to take your capturing piece, whether man or king, or to compel you to take the piece or pieces of his, which you omitted by the huff. The necessity of this law is evident, when the young player is shown that it is not unusual to sacrifice two or three men in succession, for the power of making some decisive "*coup.*" Were this law different, the players might take the first man so offered, and on the second's being placed "*en prise,*" might refuse to capture, and thus spoil the beauty of the game, (which consists in the brilliant results arising from scientific calculation,) by quietly standing the huff. It should be observed, however, that on the principle of "touch and move," the option ceases the moment the huffing party has so far made his election as to touch the piece he is entitled to remove.—After a player entitled to huff has moved without taking his adversary, he cannot remedy the omission, unless his adversary should still neglect to take or to change the position of the piece concerned, and so leave the opportunity. It does not matter how long a piece has remained "*en prise,*" it may at any time either be huffed or the adversary be compelled to take it. When several pieces are taken at one move, they must not be removed from the board until the capturing piece has arrived at its destination; the opposite course may lead to disputes, especially in Polish draughts. The act of huffing is not reckoned as a move, a "huff and a move" go together.

5. If, when it is your turn to play, you delay moving above three minutes, your adversary may require you to play; and should you not move within five minutes after being so called upon, you lose the game; which your adversary is adjudged to have won, through your improper delay.

6. When you are in a situation to take on either of two forward diagonals, you may take which way you please; without regard (as in Polish Draughts) to the one capture comprising greater force than the other. For example, if one man is "*en prise*" one way and two another, you may take either the one or the other, at your option.

7. During the game, neither party can leave the room without mutual agreement; or the party so leaving forfeits the game. Such a rule, however, could only be carried out with certain limitations.

8. When, at the end of the game, a small degree of force

alone remains, the player appearing the stronger, may be required to win the game in a certain number of moves; and, if he cannot do this, the game must be abandoned as drawn. Suppose that three Black kings and two White kings were the only pieces remaining on the board; the White insists that his adversary shall win or relinquish the game as drawn, after forty* moves (at most) have been played by each player. The moves to be computed from that point at which notice was given. If two kings remain opposed to one king only, the moves must not exceed twenty on each side. The number of moves once claimed they are not to be exceeded even if one more would win the game. A move, it should be observed, is not complete until both sides have played; therefore, twenty moves, so called, consist of twenty on each side. In giving the odds of "the draw," the game must, however, be played to a more advanced state than is required in any other case. When in such a game the situations become so equal that no advantage can be taken, he who gives the draw shall not occasion any unnecessary delay by uselessly repeating the same manœuvres; but shall force his adversary out of his strong position, or, after at most 20 moves, lose the game through its being declared drawn.

9. By-standers are forbidden to make any remarks whatever, relative to the game, until that game shall be played out. Should the players be contending for a bet or stake, and the spectator say anything that can be construed into the slightest approach to warning or intimation, that spectator shall pay all bets pending on the losing side, should that side win which has received the intimation.

10. Should any dispute occur between the players, not satisfactorily determined by the printed rules, the question must be mutually referred to a third party, whose decision shall be considered final. Of course, should a player commit any breach of the laws, and refuse to submit to the penalty, his adversary is justified in claiming the game without playing it out.

11. Respecting a false move, such as giving a common man the move of a king, or any other impropriety of the same sort, the law varies in different countries as to the penalty to be exacted by the opposite party. We cannot but suppose that

* We think half the number would be better.

such mistakes are unintentional, and consider it sufficient penalty that in all such cases the piece touched must be moved to whichever square the adversary chooses; or, he has the option of allowing the false move to stand, if more to his advantage. Should the piece be unable to move at all, that part of the penalty cannot be inflicted.

12. The rule (almost universal with English Draughts) is to play on the white squares. The exception (limited we believe to Scotland) is to play on the *black*. When, therefore, players are pledged to a match without any previous agreement as to which squares are to be played on, white must be taken as the law. The colour of the squares, excepting so far as habit is concerned, makes no difference in their relative position on the board.

In all cases, a player refusing to take, to play, or to comply with any of the rules, loses the game. Hence the saying "Whoever leaves the game loses it."

EXAMPLES OF GAMES, FROM STURGES.

(*See Explanations at page* 410.)

GAME 1.	27. 23	27. 31	22. 13	6. 9	14. 18
	6. 10	*4. 8	15. 22	25. 21	**Drawn.**
11. 15	16. 12	31. 27	26. 17	9. 13	
22. 18	8. 11	24. 20	8. 12 A.	11. 7	**B.**
15. 22	28. 24	27. 23	27. 24	W. wins.	25. 21
25. 18	25. 29	8. 11	3. 7		10. 14
8. 11 var.	30. 25	23. 18	30. 25	**A.**	17. 10
29. 25	29. 22	11. 8	7. 10	9. 14	6. 15
4. 8	26. 17	18. 15	24. 19 B.	17. 10	13. 6
25. 22	11. 15	B. wins.	10. 14	6 15	2. 9
12. 16	20. 16		17. 10	27 24	24. 19
24. 20	15. 18	**Var.**	6. 24	8. 12	15. 24
10. 15	24. 20	12. 16	13. 6 D.	24. 19	28. 19
27. 24*	18. 27	29. 25	1. 10 E.	15. 24	9. 14
16. 19	31. 24	8. 11	28. 19	28. 19	19. 15
23. 16	14. 18	24. 20	2. 6	5. 9	11. 27
15. 19	16. 11	10. 15	31. 26 G.	13. 6	20. 11
24. 15	7. 16	25. 22	11. 15	1. 10	1. 6
9. 14	20. 11	4. 8	20. 11	32. 28	32. 23
18. 9	18. 23	21. 17	15. 24	3. 7	6. 9
11. 25	11. 8	7. 10	23. 19	28. 24	23. 19
32. 27	23. 27	17. 14	10. 14	10. 14	14. 17
5. 14	8. 4	10. 17	26. 22	31. 26	21. 14

* These asterisks, wherever they occur, denote the moves which cause the loss of the game.

9. 18
11. 7
18. 22
7. 3
5. 9
3. 7
9. 13
7. 10
22. 25 C.
10. 14
25. 29
31. 27
29. 25
Drawn.

C.
13. 17
10. 14
17. 21
14. 17
22. 25
17. 22
25. 29
22. 26
29. 25
31. 27
W. wins.

D.
28. 19
9. 14
25. 22
2. 6
22. 18
6. 10
18. 9
5. 14
13. 9
14. 17
9. 6
10. 14
6. 2
17. 22
19. 15
11. 27
20. 11
Drawn.

E.
2. 9
28. 19
9. 14
25. 22
1. 6
32. 28
6. 9 F.
31. 27
9. 13
27. 24
13. 17
22. 18
14. 17
23. 18
16. 23
24. 19
W. wins.

F.
6. 10
28. 24
5. 9
31. 27
9. 13
22. 18
13. 17
18. 9
17. 22
9. 6
22. 26
6. 2
26. 31
2. 7
10. 14
19. 15
11. 18
20. 11
31. 26
23. 19
26. 23
24. 20
23. 32
7. 10
32. 27
10. 17
27. 24
20. 16
24. 8
17. 14
12. 19
14. 16
8. 12
W. wins.

G.
25. 22
6. 9
32. 28
9. 13
28. 24
10. 14
31. 26
13. 17
22. 13
14. 17
19. 15
11. 27
B. wins.

GAME 2.
11. 15
24. 20
8. 11
22. 18
15. 22
25. 18
4. 8
29. 25
10. 15
25. 22
12. 16
21. 17
7. 10 var.
17. 13
8. 12
28. 24
9. 14
18. 9
5. 14
23. 19
16. 23
26. 19
3. 8
31. 26
15. 18
22. 15
11. 18
32. 28
2. 7
30. 25
7. 11
25. 21
18. 22
26. 17
11. 15
20. 16
15. 18
24. 20
18. 22
27. 24
22. 26
19. 15
12. 19
13. 9
6. 22
15. 6
1. 10
24. 6
Drawn.

Var.
9. 13
17. 14
16. 19
23. 16
8. 12
14. 10
7. 23 A.
16. 7
2. 11
26. 10
6. 15
28. 24
5. 9
27. 23
1 6
31. 26
6. 10
32. 28
3. 7
23. 19
W. wins.

A.
12. 19
27. 23
7. 14
23. 7
W. wins.

GAME 3.
11. 15
22. 18
15. 22
25. 18
8. 11
29. 25
4. 8
25. 22
12. 16
24. 19
16. 20
28. 24 var 1
8. 12
32. 28
10. 15
19. 10
7. 14
30. 25
11. 16
18. 15
3. 8
22. 17
14. 18
23. 14
9. 18
26. 23
6. 9
23. 14
9. 18
15. 10
8. 11
10. 7 var 2
11. 15
7. 3
2. 7
3. 19
16. 32
24. 19
32. 27
31. 24
20. 27
17. 14
27. 31
21. 17
31. 26
25. 21
26. 22
17. 13
22. 17
14. 10
17. 14
10. 7
18. 23
7. 3
23. 27
3. 7
14. 18
7. 11
27. 31
11. 16
31. 27
16. 20
18. 22
B. wins.

Var. 1
19. 15
10. 19
23. 16
9. 14
18. 9
5. 14
16. 12
11. 15
27. 23
6. 10
31. 27
8. 11
22. 17
15. 18
30. 25
2. 6 A.
23. 19 B.

11. 15
28. 24
6. 9
17. 13
1. 6
26. 22
7. 11
19. 16
3. 7
24. 19
15. 31
22. 8
W. wins.

A.

1. 6
17. 13
11. 15
28. 24
7. 11
23. 19
11. 16
26. 23
6. 9
13. 6
2 9
21. 17
Drawn.

B.

17. 13
11. 16
28. 24
1. 5
32. 28
7. 11
26. 22
11. 15
B. wins.

Var. 2.

17. 14
11. 15
21. 17
16. 19
31. 26
2. 6
17. 13
12. 16
25. 21
18. 23
Drawn.

GAME 4.

11. 15
22. 18
15. 22
25. 18
8. 11
29. 25
4. 8
25. 22
12. 16
24. 20
10. 14
27. 24
8. 12
24. 19
7. 10
32. 27
9. 13
18. 9
5. 14
22. 18
1. 5
18. 9
5. 14
19. 15 A.
11. 18
20. 11
18. 22
26. 17
13. 22
11. 8
22. 25
8. 4
25. 29
4. 8
2. 7
23. 19
29. 25
27. 24
14. 18
21. 17
25. 22
17. 13
18. 23
8. 4
10. 14
24. 20
22. 18
4. 8
18. 22
20. 16
22. 18
8. 11
7. 10
28. 24 B.
14. 17
24. 20
10. 14
11. 8
17. 22
8. 11
14. 17
11. 18
17. 21
B. wins.

A.

27. 24
3. 7
26. 22
14. 17
21. 14
10. 26
31. 22
7. 10
30. 25
10. 14
25. 21
13. 17
22. 13
6. 9
Drawn.

B.

11. 7
6. 9
13. 6
23. 27
31. 24
10. 15
19. 10
12. 19
24. 15
18. 9
28. 24
14. 18
24. 19 C.
18. 23
19. 16
9. 14
10. 6
23. 27
6. 1
14. 10
30. 25
27. 31
25. 21
31. 26
21. 17 D.
26. 23
17. 13
10. 14
1. 5
23. 19
16. 12
19. 15
5. 1
15. 10
1. 5
10. 6
B. wins

C.

30. 26
9. 14
10. 6
3. 8
24. 20
8. 11
6. 1
11. 15
1. 6
15. 19
20. 16
18. 23
26. 22
23. 26
16. 11
26. 30
11. 7
30. 26
B. wins.

D.

16. 12
10. 14
1. 5
26. 23
5. 1
23. 19
1. 6
19. 15
6. 2
15. 11
2. 6
3. 7
6. 10
14. 18
10. 3
18. 14
12. 8
B. wins.

GAME 5.

11. 15
22. 18
15. 22
25. 18
8. 11
29. 25
4. 8
25. 22
12. 16
24. 20
10. 15
21. 17
7. 10
27. 24
8. 12
17. 13
9 14
18. 9
5. 14 } var. 1, 2, & 3
24. 19
15. 24
28. 19
14. 47
32. 27
10. 14
27. 24 var 4
3. 7
30. 25 var 5
6. 9
13. 6
1. 10
22. 13
14. 18
23. 14
16. 30
25. 21
10. 17
21. 14
30. 25
14. 9
11. 15 var 6
9. 6
2. 9
13. 6
15. 18
6. 2
7. 10
2. 6
10. 14
6. 9
25. 21
31. 26
14. 17
Drawn.

Var. 1.

23. 19
16. 23
26. 19
3. 7
31. 27
14. 18
30. 25
11. 16
20. 11

7. 23
25. 21
18. 25
27. 11
25. 30
11. 8
30. 26
8. 3
26. 23
3. 8
23. 18
8. 11
10. 14
24. 19
18. 23
11. 16
14. 17
21. 14
6. 10
14. 7
2. 20
19. 15
1. 6
B. wins.

Var. 2.

30. 25
14. 17
25. 21
3. 7
21. 14
10. 17
24. 19
15. 24
28. 19
7. 10
32. 27
17. 21
22. 18
21. 25
18. 15
11. 18
20. 11
25. 30
23. 7
B. wins.

Var. 3.

31. 27
1. 5
23. 19 A
16. 23
27. 9
5. 14
24. 19
15. 24
28. 19
11. 15
32. 28
15. 24
28. 19
3. 8
26. 23
14. 17
22. 18
17. 22
B. wins.

A.

23. 18
14. 23
26. 19 B.
16. 23
27. 18
10. 14
18. 9
5. 14
30. 26
12. 16
26. 23
14. 17
24. 19
15. 24
28. 12
17. 26
23. 18
6. 10
B. wins.

B.

27. 18
16. 19
32. 27 C.
5. 9
20. 16
11. 20
18. 11
10. 15
22. 17
3. 7
11. 8
7. 10
8. 3
9. 14
3. 8
14. 21
8. 11
6. 9
B. wins.

C.

22. 17 D.
15. 31
24. 8
5. 9
30. 25
31. 26
B. wins.

D.

26. 23
19. 26
30. 23
10. 14
18. 9
5. 14
23. 19
6. 10
32. 27
B. wins.

Var. 4.

22. 18
1. 5
18. 9
5. 14
19. 15
11. 18
20. 11
12. 16
27. 24
18. 27
24. 20
27. 32
31. 27
32. 23
26. 12
17. 22
11. 8
14. 18
8. 4
18. 23
4. 8
22. 26
30. 25
26. 30
25. 22
30. 25
22. 17
25. 21
17. 14
21. 17
14. 9
17. 14
Drawn

Var. 5.

22. 18
1. 5
18. 9
5. 14
26. 22
17. 26
31. 22
14. 17
22. 18
17. 22
19. 15
16. 19
15. 8
19. 28
18. 14
28. 32
8. 3
7. 11
23. 19
32. 27
3. 8
2. 7
8. 15
7. 10
14. 7
6. 9
B. wins.

Var. 6.

25. 22†
9. 6 E.
2. 9
13. 6
22. 18
6. 2 F.
18. 23
2. 6
11. 15
6. 2
7. 11
2. 6
15. 18
6. 10
18. 22
10. 14
22. 25
14. 17
25. 29
17. 14
29. 25
14. 10
25. 22
10. 14
23. 27
14. 10
22. 17
31. 26
27. 32
26. 23
32. 28
23. 19
28. 32
B. wins.

E.

9. 5
22. 18
31. 26
11. 15
5. 1
7. 11
1. 5
12. 16
13. 9
16. 19
B. wins.

F.

31. 26
11. 15
6. 2
7. 11
2. 6
18. 14
26. 23
12. 16
B. wins.

GAME 6

11. 15
22. 18
15. 22
25. 18
8. 11
29. 25
4. 8
25. 22
12. 16
24. 20
10. 15
21. 17
7. 10
17. 13
8. 12
28. 24
10. 14 var
23. 19
16. 23
26. 10
14. 23
27. 18
6. 15
13. 6
1. 10
31. 26

5. 9
26. 23
9. 13
23. 19
13. 17
22. 13
15. 22
32. 28
10. 14
19. 16
12. 19
24. 8
3. 12
13. 9
14. 18
28. 24
18. 23
24. 19
23. 27
19. 15
27. 32
15. 11
32. 27
9. 5
27. 23
5. 1
22. 26
Drawn.

Var.
9. 14
18. 9
5. 14
23. 18 C.
14. 23
27. 18 A.
16. 19
32. 28
10. 14
18. 9
1. 5
26. 23
19. 26
30. 23
5. 14
24. 19
15. 24
28. 19
14. 17
22. 18
17. 22
18. 14
6. 10
14. 7
3. 10
23. 18
2. 6
B. wins.

A.
26. 19
16. 23
27. 18
12. 16
32. 28
16. 19
30. 26 B.
1. 5
31. 27
5. 9
20. 16
11. 20
18. 11
10. 15
22. 17
3. 7
11. 8
7. 10
B. wins.

B.
18. 14
10. 26
30. 7
B. wins.

C.
23. 19
16. 23
27. 9 F.
1. 5
26. 23 E.
5. 14
31. 27
3. 8
23. 18
14. 23
27. 18
12. 16
32. 27 D.
16. 19
18. 14
19. 28
14. 7
15. 18
22. 15
11. 18
7. 3
8. 12
27. 24
28. 32
24. 19
6. 10
3. 8
32. 28
8. 11
28. 24
11. 15 L.
18. 23
15. 6
2 9
13. 6
24. 15
30. 25
15. 10
6. 1
10. 14
1. 6
23. 26
25. 21
26. 30
6. 1
30. 26
1. 5
26. 22
5. 1
22. 17
1. 5
17. 13
5. 1
13. 9
1. 5
9. 6
5. 1
14. 10
1. 5
6. 1
5. 9
10. 15
9. 5
15. 18
21. 17
18. 22
17. 14
1. 6
5. 1
6. 2
14. 9
B. wins

D.
30. 26
16. 19
32. 28
8. 12
22. 17
15. 31
24. 8
31. 26
B. wins

E.
32. 28
5. 14
26. 23
3. 8
23. 19
15. 18
22. 15
11. 18
31. 26
18. 22
26. 17
14. 21
30. 26
21. 25
26. 23
25. 30
23. 18
30. 26
18. 15
26. 31
B. wins.

F.
26. 19
3. 8
31. 26 H.
15. 18
22. 15
11. 18
32. 28 I.
2. 7
30. 25
14. 17 G.
25. 21
18. 22
21. 14
10. 17
26. 23
17. 21
23. 18
22. 26
18. 14
1. 5
19. 15
26. 31
27. 23
7. 11
23. 19
11. 18
19. 15
18. 22
24. 19
31. 27
28. 24
Drawn.

G.
7. 11
25. 21
18. 22
26. 17
11. 15
20. 16
15. 18
24. 20
18. 22
27. 24
22. 26
19. 15
12. 19
13. 9
6. 22
15. 6
1. 10
24. 6
8. 12
Drawn.

H.
27.
15.
22. 15
11. 27
32. 23
8. 11
30. 26
14. 17
26. 22
17. 26
31. 22
10. 14
22. 18
1. 5
18. 9
5. 14
B. wins.

I.
26. 22
18. 25
30. 21
14. 18
32. 28 K.
10. 15
19. 10
6. 15
21. 17
8. 11
B. wins.

K.
21. 17
8. 11
27. 23
18. 27
32 23
11. 15
20. 16
15. 18
23. 7
2. 27
17. 14
27. 32
19. 15
32. 27
B. wins.

L.
19. 16
12. 19
11. 15
Drawn.

GAME 7.
22. 18
11. 15
18. 11
8. 15
21. 17
4. 8
23. 19
11 var 1
7. 13
9. 14
27. 23
5. 9
25. 22
14. 17
29. 25
17. 21
22. 17
11. 16
25. 22
16. 20
19. 16
20. 27
31. 24
12. 19
23. 16
10. 14
17. 10
7. 14
24. 19
15. 24
28. 19
1. 5
22. 17
14. 18
26. 23
18. 27
32. 23
6. 10
13. 6
2. 9
17. 13
9. 14
Drawn.

Var. 1.
15. 18
17. 13
9. 14
26. 23
14. 17
23. 14
17. 21
27. 23 var 2
10. 17
31. 26
5. 9
25. 22
9. 14
29. 25
8. 11
24. 20
11. 16
20. 11
7. 16
32. 27
3. 8
19. 15
16. 19
23. 16
12. 19
15. 10
6. 15
13. 9
15. 18
22. 15
14. 18
15. 10
8. 12
9. 5
2. 6
10. 7
6. 9
27. 24
9. 13
24. 15
17. 22
26. 17
13. 29
15. 10
29. 25
7. 2
25. 22
Drawn.

Var. 2.
31. 26
10. 17
25. 22
8. 11 D.
27. 23
7. 10
29. 25 A.
11. 15
32. 27
3. 7
19. 16
12. 19
23. 16
7. 11
16. 7
2. 11
27. 23
5. 9
24. 20
9. 14
28. 24
11. 16
20. 11
15. 18
22. 15
10. 28
11. 7
6. 10
7. 2
28. 32
2. 7
32. 27
23. 19
27. 31
25. 22
31. 27
7. 11
27. 24
19. 16
24. 27
16. 12
27. 31
12. 8
1. 6
8. 3
14. 18
22. 15
31. 22
11. 16
10. 19
16. 23
6. 10
3. 7
10. 14
7. 10
22. 26
23. 19
26. 22
10. 15
W. wins.

A.
24. 20
11. 15
19. 16
12. 19
23. 16
15. 19
32. 27
10. 14
16. 11 B. C.
19. 24
28. 19
21. 25
30. 21
14. 18
21. 14
18. 25
29. 22
6. 9
13. 6
2. 25
Drawn.

B.
27. 23
14. 18
23. 24
19. 23
26. 19
17. 26
30. 23
6. 9
13. 6
2. 27
B. wins.

C.
29. 25
3. 8
27. 23
8. 12
16. 11
5. 9
23. 16
12. 19
11. 8
19. 23
26. 19
17. 26
30. 23
21. 30
19. 16
30. 26
23. 19
Drawn.

D.
5. 9
22. 18
8. 11
26. 23
17. 22
18. 15
11. 18
23. 5
7. 11
24. 20
3 7
27. 23 E
6. 10
32. 27
11. 16
20. 11
7. 16
28. 24
22. 26
29. 25
26. 31
25. 22
2. 6
22. 18 F
16. 20
18. 14
10. 17
23. 18
17. 22
30. 26
22. 25
26. 22
25. 30
22. 17
30. 26
18. 14
26. 22
14. 9
6. 10
9. 6
22. 18
6. 2
31. 26
2. 7
10. 14
17. 10

26. 23
7. 2
23. 16
2. 6
21. 25
6. 9
18. 15
10. 7
B. wins.

E.

28. 24
6. 10
13. 9
10. 14
9. 6
1. 10
5. 1
14. 18
1. 5
11. 16
20. 11
7. 23
5. 9
21. 25
30. 21
22. 26
21. 17
26. 31
9. 13
10. 15
13. 9
15. 19
24. 15
31. 24
9. 14
12. 16
Drawn.

F.

22. 17
31. 26
23. 18
16. 32
30. 23
32. 27
24. 20
21. 25
23. 19
25. 30
18. 14
27. 24
10. 7
24. 15
7. 2
6. 10
2. 6
30. 25
6. 9
25. 21
9. 14
12. 16
14. 7
21. 14
20. 11
B. wins.

GAME 8.

22. 18
11. 15
18. 11
8. 15
21. 17
4. 8
23. 19
8. 11
17. 13
9. 14
27. 23
6. 9 var. 1
13. 6
2. 9
24. 20
15. 24
28. 19
14. 17
25. 22
9. 13
29. 25
5. 9
32. 28
9. 14
31. 27
1. 5
25. 21
11. 15
27. 24
7. 11
30. 25 A.
3. 7
19. 16
12. 19
23. 16
14. 18
21. 14
10. 17
24. 19
15. 24
22. 8
17. 21
28. 19
21. 30
16. 12
30. 16
20. 2
W. wins.

A.

19. 16
12. 19
23. 7
14. 18
21. 14
18. 25
30. 21
10. 17
21. 14
3. 17
24. 19
15. 24
28. 19
17. 21
Drawn.

Var. 1.

15. 18
19. 15 var 2
18. 27
15. 8
12. 16
32. 23
3. 12
24. 20
7. 11 C.
25. 22
14. 17
29. 25
10. 15
31. 27
2. 7
13. 9
6. 13 B.
25. 21
1. 6
21. 14
6. 9
23. 18
13. 17
22. 6
15. 30
27. 24
31. 27
6. 1
27 23
1. 6
23. 18
6. 10
W. wins.

B.

5. 14
22. 13
14. 17
13. 9
6. 13
25. 21
15. 18
23. 14
17. 22
26. 17
13. 22
28. 24
1. 6
27. 23
22. 25
21. 17
25. 29
24. 19
W. wins.

C.

10. 15
20. 11
7. 16
13. 9
6. 13
23. 18
15. 22
26. 10
16. 19
31. 27
5. 9
25. 22 D.
9. 14
29. 25
12. 16
25. 21
16. 20
27. 23
19. 26
30. 23
1. 5
22. 18
13. 17
18. 9
5. 14
Drawn.

D.

30. 26
13. 17
25. 21
19. 23
21. 5
23. 32
26. 22
32. 27
Drawn.

Var. 2.

32. 27
14. 17 G.
23. 14
17. 21
24. 20 H.
10. 17
27. 23
7. 10 E. F.
25. 22
11. 15
19. 16
12. 19
23. 16
10. 14
29. 25
15. 19
31. 27
3. 8
27. 23
8. 12
16. 11
5. 9
23. 16
12. 19
11. 8
19. 23
26. 19
17. 26
30. 23
21. 30
19. 16
Drawn

E.

5. 9
25. 22
11. 16
20. 11
7. 16
19. 15
9. 14
22. 18
1. 5
18. 9
5. 14
15. 11
16. 20
11. 8
2. 7
29. 25
7. 11

25. 22
6. 10
W. wins.

F.

11. 16
20. 11
7. 16
19. 15
3. 8
25. 22
2. 7
31. 27
5. 9
15. 10
7. 14
28. 24
8. 11
Drawn.

G.

11. 16
25. 22
18. 25
29. 22
14. 17
24. 20
10. 14
20. 11
7. 16
19. 15
3. 8
27. 24
16. 19
23. 16
12. 19
24. 20
14. 18
20. 16
18. 25
30. 14
6. 9
13. 6
2. 18
31. 27
8. 12
15. 10
5. 9
10. 7
9. 14
7. 2
14. 17
Drawn.

H.

25. 22
10. 17
29. 25
11. 16
27. 23
16. 20
31. 27
3. 8
23. 18
5. 9
19. 16
12. 19
24. 15
8. 12
27. 23
7. 10
15. 11
20. 24
28. 19
B. wins.

GAME 9.

22 18
11. 15
18. 11
8. 15
21. 17
4. 8
23. 19
8. 11
17. 13
9. 14
27. 23
5. 9
25. 22
14. 17
29. 25
11. 16
32. 27 var 1
16. 20
19. 16
12. 19
23. 16
17. 21
22. 17
15. 18
26. 23
18. 22
25. 18
10. 14
17. 10
6. 22
13. 6
1. 10
23. 18
22. 25
18. 15
10. 19
24. 15
7. 10
15. 6
2 9
27. 23
25. 29
23. 18
29. 25
31. 26
9. 13
18. 14
13. 17
14. 10
25. 22
26. 23
22. 26
23. 19
26. 23
10. 6
17. 22
6. 2
22. 26
16. 12
23. 16
30. 23
21. 25
2. 6
25. 30
6. 10
30. 26
23. 18
20. 24
B. wins.

Var. 1.

24. 20
15. 24
20. 11
7. 16
28. 19
17. 21
22. 18 var 2
2. 7
31. 27 B.C.
10. 14
18. 15
3. 8
26. 22
7. 11
22. 18
1. 5
25. 22
14. 17
30. 26
21. 25
27. 24
25. 30
15. 10
6. 15
13. 6
16. 20
19. 10
20. 27
22. 13
27. 31
26. 22
31. 26
22. 17
26. 19
Drawn.

Var. 2.

32. 28
2. 7
28. 24
7. 11
24. 20
11. 15 A.
20. 11
15. 24
23. 19
10. 14
11. 8
24. 28
8. 4
28. 32
4. 8
32. 28
8. 11
28. 24
19. 15
14. 18
22. 17
24. 19
17. 14
19. 17
26. 22
17. 26
31. 15
12. 16
11. 20
Drawn.

A.

3. 8
23. 18
16. 23
26. 19
10. 15
19. 10
6. 15
13. 6
1. 10
31. 26
Drawn.

B.

25. 22
7. 11
32. 28 D.
10. 14
28. 24
16. 20
19. 15
20. 27
31. 24
11. 16
15. 10
6. 15
13. 6
1. 10
18. 11
16. 20
Drawn.

D.

31. 27
3. 8 E.
19. 15
10. 19
22. 17
1. 5
17. 14
W. wins.

E.

10. 14
19. 15
3. 7
15. 8
21. 25
30. 21
16. 19
23. 16
14. 30
16. 11
Drawn.

C.

18. 15
3. 8 var 3
32. 27
16. 20
25. 22
7. 11
22. 18
10. 14
27. 24
Drawn.

Var. 3.
16. 20
25. 22 F.
20. 24
32. 28 G. H.
3. 8
23. 18
7. 11
26. 23
1. 5
22. 17
11. 16
31. 26
16. 20
19. 16
10. 19
18. 15
24. 27
23. 18
27. 31
26. 22
31. 26
30. 23
19. 26
16. 11
26. 30
11. 4
Drawn

F.
31. 27
9. 14
25. 22
21. 25
30. 21
14. 17
21. 14
10. 17
19. 16
12. 19
23. 16
7. 11
16. 7
3. 19
32. 28
17. 21
27. 23
Drawn.

G.
22. 18
3. 8
26. 22
7. 11
32. 28
11. 16
15. 11
8. 15
18. 11
24. 27
31. 24
16. 20
11. 7
Drawn.

H.
23. 18
3. 8
32. 28
7. 11
26. 23
1. 5
22. 17
11. 16
31. 26
16. 20
19. 16
12. 19
23. 16
10. 19
26. 23
19. 26
Drawn.

GAME 10.
22. 18
11. 15
18. 11
8. 15
21. 17
4. 8
23. 19
8. 11
17. 13
9. 14
27. 23
5. 9
25. 22
14. 17
29. 25
17. 21
22. 17 F.
11. 16 C.
25. 22
16. 20
19. 16
20. 27
31. 24
12. 19
23. 16
10. 14
9. 14 var 1
24. 19
15. 24
28. 19
10. 15
19. 10
6. 15
17. 10
7. 14
22. 17
2. 7
17. 10
7. 14
13. 9
14. 17 A.
16. 11
15. 18
26. 23
18. 27
Drawn.

A.
15. 19
16. 11
19. 24
26. 22
24. 28
9. 5
1. 6
5. 1
6. 9
1. 6
9. 13
W. wins.

Var. 1.
7. 11
16. 7
2. 11
26. 23
3. 8
23. 18
15. 19 B.
24. 15
10. 19
17. 14
1. 5
14. 10
6. 15
13. 6
19. 23
28. 24
5. 9
6. 2
15. 19
24. 15
9. 14
18. 9
11. 25
2. 7
25. 29
7. 10
29. 25
10. 15
25. 22
15. 19
W. wins.

B.
8. 12
24. 20
12. 16
28. 24
1. 5
32. 28
16. 19
17. 14
10. 26
30. 7
15. 22
7. 2
22. 26
24. 19
26. 31
19. 15
31. 26
2. 7
26. 23
W. wins.

C.
9. 14
25. 22
3. 8 D.
23. 18
14. 23
17. 14
10. 17
19. 3
11. 16
26. 19
17. 26
30. 23
16. 20
32. 27
21. 25
31. 26
25. 30
19. 15
30. 25 E.
23. 19
25. 30
26. 23
30. 25
15. 10
6. 15
19. 10
2. 7
10. 6
1. 10
23. 19
W. wins.

D.
14. 18
23. 14
1. 5
14. 9
5. 14
26. 23
W. wins

E.
1. 5
26. 22
30. 26
15. 11
8. 15
23. 19
26. 17
W. wins.

F.
24. 20
15. 24
28. 19
9. 14 K
22. 17
11. 15
25. 22
15. 24
22. 18
7. 11
18. 9
11. 15
9. 5
3. 7 G. H
20. 16
12. 19
23. 16
7. 11
16. 7
2. 11
26. 23
11. 16
31. 26
24. 27
26. 22
15. 19
23. 18

19. 23
18. 14
Drawn.

G.
2. 7
30. 25
W. wins.

H.
24. 28
31. 27
2. 7 I.
30. 25
21. 30
20. 16
W. wins.

I.
3. 7
30. 25
21. 30
20. 16
12. 19
23. 16
30. 23
27. 11
Drawn.

K.
11. 15
32. 28 L.
15. 24
28. 19
9. 14
22. 17 M.
10. 15
19. 10
6. 15
17. 10
7. 14
25. 22
Drawn.

L.
19. 16
12. 19
23. 16
7. 11
16. 7
2. 11
22. 17
15. 19
25. 22
10. 15
31. 27
19. 24
27. 23
24. 27
23. 18
27. 31
17. 14
15. 19
14. 5
3. 8
Drawn.

M.
22. 18
14. 17
19. 16
12. 19
23. 16
1. 5
25. 22
5. 9
26. 23
17. 26
31. 22
7. 11
16. 7
2. 11
21. 17
3. 8
23. 19
8. 12
17. 14
Drawn.

GAME 11.
22. 18
11. 15
18. 11
8. 15
21. 17
4. 8
23. 19
8. 11
17. 13
9. 14
27. 23
5. 9
25. 22
14. 17
29. 25
17. 21
22. 17
11. 16
25. 22
7. 11 } var. 1, 2, & 3.
24. 20
15. 24
28. 19
10. 14
17. 10
6. 24
13. 6
1. 10
22. 17 C.
24. 28
17. 13
3. 7
13. 9
16. 19
23. 16
12. 19
9. 5
19. 24
5. 1
11. 16
20. 11
7. 16
1. 5
16. 20
5. 9
24. 27
Drawn.

Var. 1.
23. 18
16 23
26. 19
11. 16
18. 11
16. 23
22. 18
10. 14
17. 10
6. 22
13. 6
1. 10
11. 8
23. 26
30. 23
21. 25
23. 19
10. 14
8. 4
25. 30
4. 8
30. 25
8. 11
22. 26
31. 22
25. 18
B. wins.

Var. 2.
31. 27
21. 25
30. 21
9. 14
B. wins.

Var. 3.
32. 27
3. 8
22. 18 B.
15. 22
19. 15 A.
11. 18
23. 5
22. 25
B. wins.

A.
24. 20
22. 25
27. 24
25. 29
19. 15
11. 27
20. 4
29. 25
B. wins.

B.
24. 20
15. 24
28. 19
10. 14
17. 10
6. 24
13. 6
1. 10
B. wins.

C.
23. 18
10. 15
18. 14
15. 19
32. 28
3. 7
22. 18
19. 23
28. 19
21. 25
30. 21
23. 30
19. 15
30. 25
15. 8
25. 22
20. 11
22. 15
8. 3
7. 16
3. 8
16. 19
14. 9
19. 24
21. 17
Drawn.

GAME 12.
22. 18
11. 15
18. 11
8. 15
25. 22
4. 8
29. 25
8. 11
23. 18
9. 13 var
18. 14
10. 17
21. 14
6. 10
25. 21
10. 17
21. 14
2. 6
24. 19
15. 24
28. 19
6. 10 A
22. 17
13. 22
26. 17
11. 15
32. 28
15. 24
28. 19
1. 6
30. 26
3. 8
26. 23
8. 11
23. 18
11. 16
27. 23
16. 20
31. 27
6. 9
18. 15
9. 18
23. 14
12. 16
19. 12
10. 19

12. 8
Drawn.

A.
11. 16
27. 23
6. 9
22. 18
1. 6
30. 25
6. 10
25. 21
10. 17
21. 14
7. 10
14. 7
3. 10
32. 28
10. 14
26. 22
14. 17
19. 15
Drawn.

Var.
12. 16
18. 14 C.
10. 17
22. 13
16. 20 B.
21. 17
7. 10
26. 23
9. 14
25. 21
15. 18
30. 25
10. 15
17. 10
18. 22
25. 18
15. 22
23. 19
6. 15
19. 10
22. 25
24. 19

2. 7
Drawn.

B.
9. 14
24. 20
6. 10
27. 24
16. 19
25. 22
14. 18
22. 17
1. 6
32. 27
19. 23
26. 19
18. 23
27. 18
15. 22
17. 14
10. 17
21. 14
6. 10
14. 9
5. 14
13. 9
14. 17
9. 5
17. 21
5. 1
22. 25
31. 26
Drawn.

C.
24. 20
16. 19
27. 23 D.
9. 13
B. wins.

D.
27. 24
10. 14
22. 16 E.
14. 23
31. 27

11. 20
27. 11
7. 16
24. 15
Drawn.

E.
22. 17
14. 23
25. 22
9. 13
17. 14
11. 16
20. 11
7. 16
14. 10 F.
16. 20
31. 27
15. 18
B. wins.

F.
14. 9
5. 14
22. 18
15. 22
24. 15
6. 10
15. 6
1. 10
26. 12
22. 25
28. 24
25. 29
24. 20
29. 25
31. 26
13. 17
26. 23
25. 22
20. 16
2. 7
B. wins.

GAME 13.
22. 18
11. 15

18. 11
8. 15
21. 17
4. 8
23. 19
8. 11
17. 13
9. 14
25. 21
14. 18
26. 23
18. 22
30. 26
15. 18
26. 17
18. 22
23. 18
11. 16
27. 23 A.
16. 20
32. 27
10. 14 var.
17. 10
7. 14
18. 9
5. 14
13. 9
6. 13
19. 15
1. 6
24. 19
3. 7
28. 24
22. 25
29. 22
14. 18
23. 14
6. 10
15. 6
2. 25
19. 15
25. 30
27. 23
20. 27
31. 24
30. 26
23. 18

26. 22
18. 14
12. 16
15. 11
Drawn.

A.
18. 14
16. 23
27. 18
10. 15
18. 11
7. 16
13. 9
6. 13
32. 27
Drawn.

Var.
3. 8†
18. 15 C.
7. 11
23. 18 D.
11. 16
27. 23
20. 27
31. 24
16. 20
15. 11
8. 15
18. 11
20. 27
23. 18
2. 7
11. 2
27. 31
2. 9
5. 23
17. 14 B.
10. 17
21. 14
31. 26
14. 10
22. 25
29. 22
26. 17
B. wins.

B.
13. 9
31. 27
17. 14
10. 17
21. 14
23. 26
19. 15
27. 23
15. 10
23. 18
10. 7
18. 15
B. wins.

C.
18. 14
8. 11
14. 9
5. 14
19. 15
11. 18
23. 19
22. 26
31. 15
14. 18
29. 25
18. 23
27. 18
20. 27
18. 14
27. 31
25. 22
31. 27
22. 18
27. 24
14. 9
24. 20
18. 14
20. 16
15. 11
16. 23
11. 8
23. 19
B. wins.

D.
31. 26
22. 31
29. 25
11. 18
23. 7
2. 11
17. 14
6. 9
13. 6
1. 17
21. 14
31. 26
14. 10
26. 30
25. 21
30. 25
10. 7
25. 22
7. 3
11. 16
19. 15
16. 19
3. 7
B. wins.

GAME 14.
22. 18
11. 15
18. 11
8. 15
21. 17
4. 8
23. 19
8. 11
17. 13
9. 14
25. 21
14. 18
26. 23
18. 22
23. 18 var.
11. 16
18. 11
16. 23
27. 18
7. 16
24. 20
16. 19
18. 15
19. 23
15. 11
10. 14
11. 8
22. 26
31. 22
14. 17
21. 14
6. 9
13. 6
1. 26
8. 4
Drawn.

Var.
21. 17
5. 9
23. 18
10. 14 A.
17. 10
7. 23
19. 10
6. 15
13. 6
2. 9
27. 18
1. 5 D.
24. 20
9. 14
18. 9
5. 14
32. 27
14. 18 B.
30. 25
12. 16 C.
31. 26
22. 31
25. 22
18. 25
29. 22
31. 24
28. 10
16. 19
22. 18
19. 23
10. 6
23. 26
6. 2
26. 31
2. 6
31. 27
6. 10
27. 23
18. 14
23. 19
14. 9
11. 15
20. 16
19. 12
10. 19
12. 8
9. 6
8. 11
6. 2
11. 8
19. 23
8. 11
23. 18
11. 16
Drawn.

A.
11. 16
18. 11
16. 23
27. 18
7. 16
18. 15
10. 19
24. 15
16. 19
30. 26
3. 7
32. 27
1. 5
27. 24
7. 10
15. 11
Drawn.

B.
14. 17
27. 23
12. 16
30. 26
W. wins.

C.
15. 19
27. 24
11. 15
20. 16
19. 23
16. 11
23. 26
24. 19
15. 24
28. 19
26. 30
25. 21
18. 23
11. 8
30. 25
8. 4
23. 26
4. 8
26. 30
8. 11
30. 26
19. 15
26. 23
15. 10
25. 30
10. 6
23. 18
6. 1
W. wins.

D.
12. 16
24. 20
1. 6
32. 27
6. 10
27. 23
10. 14
29. 25
22. 29
30. 26
15. 22
26. 10
29. 25
28. 24
3. 8
Drawn.

GAME 15.
22. 17
11. 15
25. 22
8. 11
29. 25
9. 13
17. 14
10. 17
21. 14
4. 8
24. 19
15. 24
28. 19
11. 16
22. 18
16. 20
26. 22
8. 11 var 1
30. 26
6. 9
19. 15
11. 16 var 2
25. 21
16. 19 var 3
23. 16
12. 19
32. 28
1. 6
15. 11
7. 16
14. 10
6. 15
18. 11
2. 6
22. 18
W. wins.

Var. 1
6. 9
25. 21
1. 6
30. 26
12. 16
19. 12
8. 11
22. 17
13. 22
26. 17
9. 13
23. 19
13. 22
19. 15
11. 16
15. 10
6. 15
18. 11
22. 25
11. 8
25. 29 A
8. 4
29. 25
4. 8
25. 22
8. 11
16. 19
11. 15
19. 23
27. 18
7. 10
15. 6
2. 9
Drawn

A.
16. 19
8. 4
25. 29
4. 8
29. 25
32. 28
25. 22
27. 24
20. 27
31. 15

22. 18
15. 10
18. 9
10. 6
9. 14
6. 1
14. 18
28. 24
Drawn.

Var. 2.
12. 16
15. 8
3. 12
18. 15
9 18
23. 14
1. 6
15. 11
6. 9
11. 8
9. 18
22. 15
7. 11
15. 10
11. 15
8. 4
5. 9
4. 8
9. 14
8. 11
14. 17
11. 18
17. 22
26. 17
13. 29
18. 22
16. 19
W. wins.

Var. 3.
7. 10
14. 7
3. 19
18. 15
1. 6
15. 11
6. 10
11. 8
10. 14
22. 17
13. 22
26. 10
19. 26
31. 22
16. 19
32. 28
9. 14
8. 4
5. 9
4. 8
19. 23
27. 18
14. 23
10. 7
2. 11
8. 15
23. 26
15. 18
26. 30
22. 17
9. 13
17. 14
W. wins.

GAME 16.
11. 15
22. 17
8. [illegible]
25. [illegible]
9. 13
23. 18
6. 9 A.
27. 23
9. 14 C.
18. 9
5. 14
30. 25
1. 6
24. 19
15. 24
28. 19
11. 15
32. 28
15. 24
28. 19
7. 11
22. 18
13. 22
18. 9
6. 13
25. 18
3. 8
18. 14
10. 17
21. 14
11. 16
14. 9
2. 7
9. 6
7. 10
Drawn.

A.
12. 16
17. 14
10. 17
21. 14
16. 19
24. 20
6. 10
29. 25
10. 17
25. 21
1. 6
21. 14
6. 10
30. 25 B.
10. 17
25. 21
19. 23
26. 10
17. 26
31. 22
7. 33
27. 18
3. 7
28. 24
7. 10
24. 19
4. 8
19. 16
10. 14
16. 7
2. 11
18. 9
5. 14
32. 27
8. 12
27. 23
11. 15
B. wins.

B.
27. 23
10. 17
23. 16
2. 6
32. 27
17. 21
27. 23
6. 9
28. 24
4. 8
16. 12
9. 14
18. 9
5. 14
W. wins.

C.
4. 8
23. 19
9. 14
18. 9
5. 14
26. 23
2. 6
22. 18
15. 22
31. 26
22. 31
30. 25
13. 22
25. 2
31. 27 D.
23. 18
27. 20
28. 24
20. 27
32. 23
1. 5
2. 6
11. 16
6. 15
5. 9
21. 17
9. 13
17. 14
7. 11
14. 10
13. 17
10. 7
3. 10
15. 6
17. 22
6. 10
22. 26
10. 14
26. 31
29. 25
31. 26
14. 17
26. 31
25. 21
31. 27
17. 14
27. 24
19. 15
24. 19
15. 10
19. 26
18. 15
11. 18
Drawn.

D.
10. 15
19. 10
7. 14
32. 27
31. 26
23. 19
11. 16
19. 15
16. 20
24. 19
14. 18
15. 10
26. 23
10. 7
23. 32
B. wins.

GAME 17
11. 15
22. 17
8. 11
25. 22
11. 16
23 18
3. 8 **var 1**
18. 11
8. 15
24. 19
15. 24
27. 11
7. 16
22. 18
9. 14
18. 9
5. 14
28. 24
4. 8
24. 19
16. 23
26. 19
8. 11
31. 26
2. 7 **var 2**
26. 23
11. 15
32. 28
15. 24
28. 19
7. 11
30. 26
11. 15
19. 16
12. 19
Drawn.

Var. 1.
7. 11
17. 14
10. 17
21. 14
16. 20
29. 25
9. 13
24. 19
15. 24
28. 19
3. 8
19. 15
6. 9
14. 10
12. 16
26. 23
20. 24
27. 20
9. 14
18. 9
11. 27
32. 23
5. 14
20. 11
8. 15
31. 26
4. 8
10. 7
2. 11
23. 18
14. 23
26. 10
Drawn.

Var. 2.
11. 15
32. 28
15. 24
28. 19
14. 18
17. 14
10. 17
21. 14
18. 23
19. 15
23. 27
15. 11
27. 32
11. 8
32. 27
8. 4
12. 16
4. 8
16. 20
8. 11
20. 24
14. 10
6. 15
11. 18
24. 28
26. 23
28. 32
29. 25
27. 31
18. 22
32. 27
23. 19
Drawn.

GAME 18.
11. 15
22. 17
8. 11
25. 22
11. 16
23. 18
15. 19
24. 15
10. 19
17. 13 var.
9. 14
18. 9
5. 14
22. 17
7. 10
27. 24
19. 23
26. 19
16. 23
31. 26
14. 18
26. 19
18. 22
17. 14
10. 17
21. 14
3. 7
14. 9
4. 8
9. 5
8. 11
32. 27
6. 10
27. 23
11. 15
13. 9
7. 11
24. 20
15. 24
28. 19
11. 15
30. 25
15. 24
25. 18
1. 6
5. 1
6. 13
Drawn.

Var.
18. 15
4. 8
27. 24
16. 20
32. 27
7. 10
17. 13
10. 14
22. 17
14. 18
17. 14 A.
18. 22
26. 17
9. 18
30. 26
18. 22
13. 9
6. 13
15. 10
12. 16
24. 15
2. 6
26. 23
8. 12
23. 18
16. 19
18. 14
6. 9
10. 7
9. 18
27. 24
20. 27
31. 24
3. 10
15. 6
1. 10
24. 6
18. 23
17. 14
Drawn.

A.
29. 25
12. 16
17. 14
8. 12
26. 23
19. 26
30. 26
16. 19
23. 16
12. 19
31. 26
18. 23
B. wins.

GAME 19.
22. 17
11. 15
25. 22
9. 13
23. 18 var 1
6. 9 var 2
18. 11
8. 15
27. 23
9. 14
30. 25
5. 9
24. 19
15. 24
28 19
7. 11
22. 18
13. 22
26. 17
3. 8
32. 28
11. 15
18. 11
8. 24
28. 19
4. 8
17. 13
2. 6
25. 22
8. 11
31. 26
11. 16
22. 17
14. 18
23. 7
Drawn.

Var. 1.
17. 14
10. 17
21. 14
6. 10
29. 25
10. 17
25. 21
1. 6
21. 14
6. 10
22. 17
13. 22
26. 17
15. 18
17. 13
10. 17
23. 14
17. 22
24. 19
8. 11
27. 24
2. 6
24. 20
6. 10
14. 9
5. 14
13. 19
14. 17
9. 6
17. 21
6. 1
22. 25
1. 5
25. 29
5. 9
29. 25
31. 26
11. 15
9. 6
15. 24
6. 15
3. 8
28. 19
7. 11
26. 22
25. 18
15. 22
11. 16
20. 11
8. 24
22. 26
12. 16
26. 31
16. 20
Drawn.

Var. 2
5. 9
15. 11
8. 15
27. 23
15. 19
24. 15
10. 19
23. 16
12. 19

29. 25
7. 10
17. 14
9. 18
22. 15
4. 8
Drawn.

GAME 20.

11. 15
22. 17
8. 11
17. 13
4. 8
23. 19
15. 18 var 1
24. 20
11. 15 var 2
28. 24
8. 11
26. 23
9. 14
31. 26
6. 9
13. 6
2. 9
26. 22
9. 13
32. 28*
1. 6
21. 17
14. 21
23. 14
10. 26
19. 1
13. 17
30. 23

* White ought to win thus—
20. 16
11. 20
22. 17
13. 22
21. 17
14. 21
23. 14
10. 17
25. 2
1. 6
2. 9
5. 14
19. 15
3. 8
24. 19

21. 30
1. 6
3. 8
6. 2
7. 10
23. 19
10. 14
Drawn.

Var. 1.

9. 14
27. 23
15. 18 B. C.
32. 27
11. 15
26. 22
7. 11
21. 17
14. 21
23. 7
3. 10
27. 23
5. 9
31. 26
9. 14
24. 20
15. 24
28. 19
11. 15
19. 16
12. 19
23. 16
8. 11
16. 7
2. 11
26. 23 A.
11. 16
20. 11
15. 18
22. 15
10. 26
30. 23
21. 30
Drawn.

A.

22. 17
15. 19
25. 22
1. 5
26. 23
19. 26
30. 23
11. 15
20. 16
21. 25
16. 11
14. 21
22. 17
25. 30
11. 7
30. 26
7. 3
26. 19
B. wins.

B.

5. 9
32. 27
1. 5
26. 22
14. 18
23. 14
9. 18
22. 17
11. 16
27. 23
18. 27
17. 14
16. 23
31. 26
10. 17
26. 1
17. 22
Drawn.

C.

6. 9
13. 6
2. 9
25. 22
14. 18 D.
23. 14
9. 25
29. 22
10. 14
19. 10
14. 18
22. 15
11. 18
24. 19
7. 14
19. 15
1. 6
28. 24
3. 7
24. 20
5. 9
31. 27
7. 10
21. 17
14. 21
26. 23
10. 26
30. 5
6. 9
5. 1
9. 13
1. 6
8. 11
6. 10
21. 25
27. 23
25. 30
23. 18
30. 25
18. 14
25. 22
14. 9
22. 17
10. 6
Drawn.

D.

9. 13
32. 27
1. 6
22. 17
13. 22
26. 17
14. 18
23. 14
6. 9
30. 26
9. 18
26. 22
18. 25
29. 22
5. 9
27. 23
9. 13
23. 18 E.
10. 14
18. 9
15. 18
22. 15
13. 22
Drawn.

E.

31. 26
15. 18
23. 14
11. 16
19. 15 F.
10. 19
24. 15
7. 11
Drawn.

F.

26. 23
16. 20
23. 18
20. 27
18. 15
27. 31
15. 6
Drawn.

Var. 2

10. 14
26. 23
6. 10 K.
13. 6
2. 9
31. 26 H.
11. 15 G.
28. 24
1. 6
26. 22
8. 11
32. 28
9. 13
20. 16
Drawn.

G.

9. 13
28. 24
1. 6
26. 22
5. 9
22. 15
11. 18
25. 22
18. 25
29. 22
8. 11
22. 18
13. 17
32. 28
17. 22
Drawn

H.

19. 16
12. 26
31. 6
1. 10
25. 22
10. 15 I
22. 17
15. 18
17. 10
7. 14
30. 26
8. 12
26. 22
18. 25
29. 22
9. 13
22. 18
14.
27. 10

3. 7
28. 24
7. 10
24. 19
10. 14
18. 9
5. 14
32. 27
13. 17
27. 23
17. 22
21. 17
14. 21
23. 18
11. 16
20. 11
22. 26
Drawn.

I.
9. 13
22. 18
14. 23
27. 18
5. 9
30. 26
10. 14
26. 23
7. 10
29. 25
10. 15
25. 22
Drawn.

K.
11. 15
19. 10
6. 15
13. 6
1. 10 L.
28. 24
8. 11
30. 26
2. 6
26 22
3. 8
22. 17

5. 9
24. 19
15. 24
25. 22
18. 25
29. 22
24. 28
22. 18
12. 16
W. wins.

L.
2. 9
28. 24
8. 11
30. 26
9. 13
26. 22
3. 8
23. 19
7. 10
27. 23
18. 27
32. 23
5. 9
31. 27
W. wins.

GAME 21.
11. 15
22. 17
8. 11
17. 13
4. 8
23. 19
15. 18
24. 20
11. 15
28. 24 var.
8. 11
26. 23
18. 22 B.
25. 18
15. 22
30. 26
11. 15
26. 17

15. 18
23. 14
9. 18
27. 23
18. 27
32. 23
7. 11 D.
29. 25
5. 9 A.
25. 22
11. 15
20. 16
9. 14
16. 11
12. 16
19. 12
15. 18
22. 15
10. 28
17. 10
6. 15
8. 11
28. 32
8. 4
32. 28
4. 8
2. 7
31. 26
28. 24
26. 22
24. 27
23. 18
15. 19
22. 17
27. 23
18. 14
23. 18
8. 4
18. 9
13. 6
1. 10
17. 13
7. 11
4. 8
10. 15
13. 9
19. 24

9. 6
24. 28
6. 2
28. 32
2. 6
32. 28
21. 17
28. 32
17. 14
32. 28
14. 10
28. 24
6. 2
Drawn.

A.
11. 15
17. 14
10. 17
19. 10
6. 15
21. 14
15. 18
31. 27
1. 6
24. 19
2. 7
25. 21
18. 22
23. 18
22. 26
27. 23
W. wins.

B.
3. 8
23. 14
9. 18
30. 26
6. 9 C.
13. 6
2. 9
26. 22
9. 14
27. 23
18. 27
32. 23

5. 9
31. 27
1. 5
22. 17
9. 13
25. 22
5. 9
29. 25
15. 18
22. 6
13. 29
6. 1
7. 10
1. 5
9. 13
5. 9
13. 17
9. 18
17. 22
18. 25
29. 22
23. 18
22. 15
27. 23
10. 14
19. 10
11. 15
10. 7
15. 18
21. 17
18. 27
17. 10
27. 32
24. 19
8. 11
10. 6
32. 28
7. 3
28. 24
3. 8
24. 15
W. wins.

C.
5. 9
26. 22
9. 14

22. 17
6. 9
13. 6
2. 9
17. 13
1. 6
27. 23
18. 27
32. 23
15. 18
31. 27
11. 15
25. 22
18. 25
29. 22
7. 11
22. 17
Drawn

D.
10. 14
17. 10
7. 14
13. 9
6. 13
19. 15
1. 6
23. 19
6. 9
15. 10
14. 17
21. 14
9. 18
19. 15
18. 22
15. 11
13. 17
11. 8
17. 21
8. 4
21. 25
4. 8
25. 30
8. 11
30. 26
29. 25
22. 29

31. 22
29. 25
22. 17
25. 22
17. 13
22. 18
10. 6
2. 9
13. 6
Drawn

Var.
27. 24 F
8. 11
25. 22 E
18. 25
29. 22
9. 14
22. 17
11. 16
20. 11
7. 23
26. 19
2. 7
31. 26
7. 11
26. 23
15. 18
24. 20
18. 27
32. 23
11. 15
30. 26
15. 24
28. 19
3. 8
20. 16
5. 9
26. 22
10. 15
17. 10
15. 24
23. 19
6. 15
19. 10
Drawn.

F.
26. 22
15. 24
28. 19
9. 14
22. 15
7. 11
30. 26
11. 18
26. 22
2. 7
22. 15
7. 11
31. 26
11. 18
26. 22
3. 7
22. 15
7. 11
25. 22
11. 25
29. 22
8. 11
27. 23
11. 15
32. 28
15. 24
28. 19
10. 15
19. 10
6. 15
Drawn.

E.
26. 22
9. 14
31. 27
6. 9
13. 6
2. 9
27. 23
18. 27
32. 23
14. 18
23. 14
10. 26
30. 23
7. 10
23. 18
15. 22
25. 18
3. 8
B. wins.

GAME 22.
11. 15
22. 17
8. 11
17. 13
4. 8
23. 19
15. 18
24. 20
11. 15
28. 24
8. 11
26. 23
9. 14 B.
31. 26 {var 1
14. 17 {var 2
21. 14
10. 17
23. 14
6. 10
25. 22
17. 21
22. 17
15. 18
26. 22
18. 25
29. 22
11. 15
13. 9
7. 11
14. 7
3. 10
9. 6
2. 9
17. 13
9. 14
22. 17
1. 6
32. 28
5. 9
27. 23
15. 18
19. 15
18. 27
15. 8
14. 18
8. 3
W. wins.

Var. 1.
5. 9
21. 17
14. 21
23. 5
15. 18
26. 23
18. 22
25. 18
10. 15
19. 10
6. 22
23. 18
7. 10
32. 28
10. 15
27. 23
22. 26
18. 14
15. 18
23. 19
26. 31
14. 9
W. wins.

Var. 2.
11. 16
20. 11
7. 16
21. 17
14. 21
23. 7
2. 11
19. 10
6. 15
25. 22 A.
16. 19
32. 28
5. 9
13. 6
1. 10
29. 25
10. 14
24. 20
Drawn.

A.
24. 20
16. 19
27. 23
3. 7
23. 16
12. 19
25. 22
7. 10
22. 17
19. 24
29. 25
1. 6
25. 22
5. 9
26. 23
24. 27
20. 16
11. 20
23. 18
27. 31
18. 11
9. 14
11. 7
14. 18
22. 15
10. 19
7. 2
6. 10
2. 7
10. 15
7. 11
15. 18
11. 15
18. 23
15. 24
20. 27
17. 14
31. 26
14. 9
26. 22
9. 6
27. 31
6. 2
22. 18
2. 6
18. 15
13. 9
23. 26
30. 23
31. 26
Drawn.

B.
18. 22
25. 18
15. 22
30. 26
11. 15
26. 17
15. 18
23. 14
9. 18
29. 25
7. 11 B
17. 14
10. 17
21. 14
6. 9
13. 6
1. 17
25. 21
17. 22
19. 15
3. 8
15. 10
11. 15
21. 17
22. 26
31. 22
18. 25
17. 13
25. 30
10. 6
2. 9
13. 6

30. 25 C.
27. 23
25. 22
23. 18
8. 11
24. 19
15. 24
32. 28
22. 15
28. 10
5. 9
6. 2
9. 13
10. 7
11. 15
2. 6
15. 18
6. 10
18. 22
10. 14
22. 25
7. 2
25. 29
2. 7
29. 25
7. 10
25. 21
10. 15
13. 17
15. 19
17. 22
19. 23
W. wins.

C.

30. 26
6. 2
5. 9
2. 6
9. 13
6. 10
15. 18
10. 14
18. 22
32. 28
Drawn.

D.

18. 23
27. 18
10. 15
18. 11
7. 23
24 19
6. 10
25. 22 E.
23. 26
22. 18
26. 30
18. 15
30. 25
15. 6
1. 10
32. 27
25. 22
27. 23
2. 7
31. 27
7. 11
27. 24
22. 26
23. 18
26. 22
18. 14
3. 7
19. 15
Drawn.

E.

20. 16
3. 8
17. 14
10. 17
21. 14
2. 6
31. 27
23. 26
25. 21
26. 31
27. 23
31. 27
23. 18
27. 23
14. 9
23. 14
9. 2
14. 10
13. 9
5. 14
2. 6
10. 7
6. 10
8. 11
10. 3
11. 20
3. 7
14. 18
Drawn.

GAME 23.

11. 15
22. 17
8. 11
17. 13
4. 8
23. 19
15. 18
24. 20
11. 15
28. 24
8. 11
26. 23
9. 14
31. 26
6. 9
13. 6
2. 9
26. 22
9. 13 B.
20. 16†
11. 20
22. 17
13. 22
21. 17
14. 21
23. 14
10. 17
25. 2
1. 6 A.
2. 9
5 14
19. 15
3. 8
24. 19
W. wins.

A.

17. 22
19. 15
21. 25
30. 21
22. 26
15. 10
26. 31
29. 25
12. 16
25. 22
16. 19
24. 15
31. 24
15. 11
24. 19
11. 7
19. 15
2. 6
15. 11
7. 2
20. 24
22. 18
11. 16
21. 17
W. wins.

B.

1. 6
30. 26 C.D.
9. 13
32. 28
6. 9
B. wins.

C.

32. 28
9. 13 E.
20. 16
11. 20
Drawn.

E.

3. 8
30. 26
9. 13
19. 16
12. 19
23. 16
8. 12 F.
24. 19
15. 31
22. 8
12. 16
8. 3
W. wins.

F.

13. 17
22. 13
8. 12
25. 22
12. 19
22. 17
5. 9
26. 22
18. 25
29. 22
14. 18
27. 23
19. 26
17. 14
18. 25
14. 5
15. 18
21. 17
11. 15
5. 1
Drawn.

D.

22. 17
18. 22 G.
25. 18
15. 22
23. 18
14. 23
27. 18
9. 13
17. 14
10. 17
21. 14
6. 10
30. 25
10. 17
25. 21
22. 26
21. 14
26. 30
19. 15
30. 26
15. 8
26. 22
32. 28
22. 15
24. 19
15. 24
28. 19
13. 17 H
8. 4
17. 22
4. 8
22. 26
19. 15
26. 30
15. 10
Drawn.

G.

9. 13
25. 22
18. 25
29. 22
14. 18
23. 14
6. 9
22. 18
15. 22
32. 28
9. 18
17. 14
10. 17
21. 14
13. 17
19. 15
17. 21

15. 8
22. 25
24. 19
25. 29
19. 15
29. 25
15. 10
25. 22
10. 6
22. 17
6. 2
17. 10
2. 11
Drawn.

H.
7. 10
14. 7
3. 10
8. 3
10. 14
3. 7
14. 17
7. 10
17. 21
10. 14
13. 17
19. 15
17. 22
14. 17
22. 26
15. 10
Drawn.

GAME 24.
11. 15
22. 17
15. 18
23. 14
9. 18
17. 14 var.
10. 17
21. 14
8. 11
24. 20
6. 9
26. 23
3. 8
23. 19
18. 22
25. 18
11. 16
20. 11
8. 22
30. 25
9. 18
27. 23
18. 27
25. 18
5. 9
32. 23
4. 8
29. 25
12. 16
19. 3
2. 6
3. 10
6. 29
Drawn.

Var.
17. 13
8. 11
26. 23
10. 14
24. 20
11. 15
28. 24
4. 8
30. 26
8. 11
26. 22
3. 8
32. 28
7. 10
24. 19
15. 24
28. 19
11. 15 A.
27. 24
18. 27
13. 9
6. 13
22. 17
13. 22
25. 4
27. 32
4. 8
32. 27
29. 25
5. 9
25. 22
9. 13
8. 11
1. 5
11. 8
2. 7
8. 3
7. 11
3. 7
27. 23
Drawn.

A.
2. 7
22. 15
11. 18
31. 26
8. 11
19. 16
12. 19
23. 16
14. 17 B.
21. 14
10. 17
16. 12
11. 15
12. 8
17. 21
25. 22
18. 25
Drawn.

B.
10. 15
27. 24
6. 10
16. 12
14. 17
21. 14
10. 17
25. 21
18. 22
21. 14
22. 31
W. wins.

GAME 25.
22. 18
11. 16
25. 22
10. 14
29. 25
16. 20
24. 19
8. 11
19. 15
4. 8
22. 17 A.
*7. 10 var.
25. 22
10. 19
17. 10
6. 15
23. 7
2. 11
21. 17
1. 6
17. 13
3. 7
28. 24
12. 16
26. 23
8. 12
53. 19
16. 23
31. 26
7. 10
26. 19
11. 16
18. 11
16. 23
27. 18
W. wins.

A.
28. 24
7. 10
24. 19
3. 7
19. 16
10. 19
32. 28
7. 10
16. 7
2. 11
23. 7
14. 32
7. 3
32. 27
31. 24
20. 27
22. 18
27. 31
26. 22
10. 14
18. 15
14. 18
B. wins.

Var.
9. 13
17. 10
7. 14
18. 9
5. 14
26. 22
11. 18
22. 15
2. 7
30. 26
7. 10
23. 19
3. 7 B.
19. 16
12. 19
28. 24
19. 28
25. 22
10. 19
22. 17
13. 22
26. 3
8. 12
27. 24
20. 27
31. 15
6. 10
15. 6
1. 10
W. wins.

B.
1. 5
19. 16
12. 19
28. 24
19. 28
25. 22
10. 19
22. 17
13. 22
26. 1
19. 24
1. 6
8. 11
21. 17
11. 15
Drawn.

GAME 26
22. 18
11. 16
25. 22
10. 14
29. 25
16. 20
24. 19
8. 11
19. 15
4. 8
22. 17
12. 16
17. 10
7. 14
26. 22
2. 7
28. 24
16. 19
23. 16
14. 23
27. 18

20. 27
31. 24
11. 27
32. 23
7. 10 var.
15. 11 C.
8. 15
18. 11
10. 15
21. 17 D. E.
3. 7
11. 2
9. 13
2. 9
5. 21
23. 18
15. 19
18. 14
19. 23
22. 18
13. 17 A.
18. 15
23. 26
30. 23
21. 30
14. 10
30. 26
23. 19
26. 23
19. 16
23. 18
16. 11
Drawn.

A.

23. 26†
30. 23
21. 30
18. 15
30. 26
23. 18
26. 22
14. 10
13. 17
10. 7
17. 21
7. 2
21. 25
2. 7
25. 30
7. 11
30. 26
18. 14
26. 23
14. 10
22. 18
B. wins.

Var.

8. 12
23. 19
7. 10
21. 17
9. 13 B.
25. 21
3. 7
30. 26
12. 16
19. 12
10. 19
12. 8
7. 11
8. 3
11. 16
3. 7
16. 20
7. 11
19. 24
11. 16
24. 27
17. 14
6. 9
14. 10
27. 31
10. 7
20. 24
7. 3
24. 28
3. 7
28. 32
7. 10
32. 27
18. 15
27. 24
15. 11
31. 27
10. 15
9. 14
15. 10
5. 9
10. 17
27. 23
26. 19
24. 8
16. 19
8. 11
19. 23
11. 16
23. 27
16. 19
27. 32
19. 23
32. 28
Drawn.

B.

12. 16
19. 12
10. 19
17. 14
19. 23
14. 10
6. 15
18. 11
23. 27
11. 8
27. 31
8. 4
31. 27
4. 8
27. 23
8. 11
9. 13
11. 16
5. 9
16. 20
9. 14
22. 18
14. 17
18. 14
17. 21
25. 22
23. 19
14. 9
19. 15
Drawn.

C.

30. 26
10. 19
23. 16
8. 12
B. wins.

D.

23. 18
15. 19
22. 17
3. 7
11. 2
9. 13
2. 9
5. 23
17. 14
23. 27
14. 10
27. 31
10. 7
31. 27
25. 22
27. 23
21. 17
19. 24
17. 14
24. 27
14. 10
27. 31
Drawn.

E.

30. 26
3. 7
11. 2
9. 13
2. 9
5. 14
23. 19
15. 24
26. 23
24. 27
22. 18
1. 5
18. 9
5. 14
B. wins.

F.

23. 19
27. 31
19. 15
31. 26
B. wins.

GAME 27.

11. 15
22. 17
9. 13
17. 14
10. 17
21. 14
8. 11
24. 19
15. 24
28. 19
11. 16
25. 21
6. 9
29. 25
9. 18
23. 14
16. 23
26. 19
4. 8
25. 22
8. 11
22. 18
11. 16
27. 23
16. 20
31. 27
13. 17
30. 26
1. 6
19. 16
12. 19
23. 16
6. 9
18. 15
9. 18
21. 14
7. 11
15. 8
3. 19
27. 23
18. 27
32. 16
20. 24
14. 10
24. 27
23. 19
27. 31
19. 15
31. 27
15. 11
27. 24
16. 12
24. 19
Drawn.

GAME 28

11. 15
22. 17
9. 13
17. 14
10. 17
21. 14
8. 11
24. 19
15. 24
28. 19
11. 16
25. 21
6. 9 var.
29. 25
9. 18
23. 14
16. 23
26. 19
4. 8
25. 22
8. 11
22. 18

1. 16
27. 23
16. 20
31. 27
13. 17
30. 26
1. 6
18. 15*A.
20. 24
27. 20
7. 10
14. 7
2. 27
21. 14
6. 9
32. 23
B. wins.

A.

14. 9
6. 13
21. 14
13. 17
14. 9
5. 14
18. 9
17. 21
26. 22
21. 25
22. 17
25. 30
17. 13
30. 26
9. 6
2 9
13. 6
7. 11
6. 2
11. 16
2. 6
26. 31
B. wins

Var.

4. 8
26. 22
8. 11 B.

22. 18
16. 20
30. 26
6. 9
29. 25
1. 6
19. 15
11. 16
25. 22
7. 10 E.
14. 7
3. 19
18. 15
2. 7
15. 11
7. 10
11. 7
9. 14
7. 3
6. 9
3. 8
10. 15
22. 18
15. 22
26. 10
19. 26
31. 22
16. 19
32. 28
9. 14
10. 6
5. 9
6. 1
19. 23
27. 18
14. 23
1. 5
9. 14
5. 9
W. wins.

B.

6. 9
29. 25 C.
9. 18
22. 15
7. 11

31. 26
11. 18
23. 14
16. 23
26. 19
1. 6
25. 22
8. 11
22. 18
6. 9
19. 15
12. 16
15. 8
3. 12
30. 26
2. 7
27. 24
16. 20
32. 27
7. 11
14. 10
9. 14
18. 9
5. 14
26. 23
14. 18
23. 14
11. 15
Drawn.

C.

22. 18
13. 17
18. 15
9. 18
21. 14
7. 11
29. 25 D.
1. 6
25. 22
18. 25
30. 21
11. 15
14. 10
6. 24
27. 4
18. 27

31. 24
12. 16
21. 17
5. 9
Drawn.

D.

14. 10
18. 22
30. 25
11. 18
23. 14
16. 23
27. 18
8. 11
32. 27
2. 6
18. 15
11. 18
27. 23
6. 15
B. wins.

E.

16. 19
23. 16
12. 19
15. 11 var 2
7. 16
14. 10
6. 15
18. 11
2. 6
22. 18 F.
19. 24
Drawn.

F.

32. 28
20. 24
27. 20
6. 10
11. 8 G.
3. 12
20. 11
19. 23
26. 19

10. 14
Drawn.

G.

11. 7
10. 15
20. 11
3. 10
31. 27 H.
10. 15
B. wins.

H.

11. 7
19. 23
26. 19
15. 24
28. 19
10. 14
Drawn.

Var. 2

27. 23
7. 10
23. 16 I.
10. 19
14. 10
6. 15
18. 11
2. 6
32. 28 K.
6. 10
7. 11
10. 14
16. 11
3. 10
11. 8
19. 23
26. 19
10. 15
Drawn.

I.

14. 7
3. 10
23. 16
10. 19

18. 15
2. 7
15. 11
7. 10
11. 7
19. 23
26. 19
10. 14
19. 15
14. 17
Drawn.

K.

16. 12
6. 10
11. 8
19. 23
26. 19
10. 14
22. 18
14. 23
Drawn

GAME 29

11. 16
22. 18
16. 19
23. 16
12. 19
24. 15
10. 19
25. 22
9. 14
18. 9
5. 14
22. 17
7. 10
27. 24
2. 7
24. 15
10. 19
17. 10
7. 14
32. 27
3. 7
27. 24
7. 10 var

24. 15
10. 19
31. 27
8. 11
29. 25
6. 10
27. 23
11. 16
25. 22
10. 15
22. 17 A.
15. 18
Drawn.

A.

21. 17†
14. 21
23. 18
16. 20
18. 11
20. 24
11. 7
24. 27
7. 3
27. 31
3. 7
31. 27
7. 11
1. 5
11. 16
27. 23
28. 24
19. 28
26. 19
28. 32
19. 15
32. 27
16. 19
5. 9
15. 11
9. 13
11. 7
4. 8
7. 3
8. 12
3. 7
27. 32
7. 10
23. 27
10. 14
27. 32
14. 18
32. 27
22. 17
13. 22
18. 25
27. 31
25. 22
31. 27
30. 26
27. 23
19. 15
23. 30
15. 19
W. wins.

Var.

7. 11
24. 15
11. 18
28. 24
8. 11
29. 25
4. 8
24. 19
6. 9
26. 22
1. 5 B.
22. 15
11. 18
19. 16
18. 22
25. 18
14. 23
21. 17
8. 12
16. 11
9. 13
17. 14
12. 16
11. 7
16. 20
7. 2
23. 27
31. 24
20. 27
2. 6
27. 31
6. 10
31. 27
10. 15
27. 23
30. 25
23. 26
25. 21
26. 22
21. 17
22. 26
15. 18
13. 22
18. 25
Drawn.

B.

18. 23
22. 17
14. 18
17. 14
1. 5
19. 15
9. 13
14. 10
23. 27 C.
31. 24
18. 23
10. 7
15. 18
7. 3
8. 12
3. 8
23. 27
8. 11
27. 32
24. 20
18. 23
11. 15
32. 28
25. 22
Drawn.

C.

11. 16
10. 7
8. 12
7. 3
5. 9
3. 8
9. 14
8. 11
16. 20
31. 26
W. wins.

GAME 30.

11. 16
22. 18
8. 11
25. 22
4. 8
29. 25
10. 14
24. 19
7. 10
27. 24
16. 20
19. 16
20. 27
16. 7
2. 11
31. 24
12. 16
24. 19
8. 12
32. 27
16. 20
21. 17
14. 21
19. 16
12. 19
23. 7
10. 14
26. 23
3. 10
28. 24
10. 15
18. 11
9. 13
22. 18
6. 9
11. 7
13. 17
18. 15
14. 18
23. 14
9. 18
24. 19
17. 22
Drawn.

GAME 31.

11. 16
22. 18
10. 14
25. 22
16. 20
29. 25
12. 16
18. 15
8. 12
15. 11
7. 10
22. 18
10. 15
25. 22
6. 10 A.
24. 19
15. 24
28. 19
9. 13 B.
18. 9
5. 14
19. 15
10. 19
22. 17
13. 22
26. 10
19. 26
30. 23
3. 8 C.
11. 7
2. 11
10. 7
11. 15
7. 3
15. 19
23. 18
19. 23
18. 15
23. 26
31. 22
16. 19
15. 10
19. 24
27. 23
24. 27
23. 18
27. 31
18. 14
8. 11
10. 7
Drawn.

A.

3. 8
11. 7
2. 11
24. 19
15. 24
28. 19
6. 10
19. 15
10. 19
22. 17
19. 24
17. 10
24. 28
10. 7
11. 15
18. 11
8. 15
7. 3
15. 18
23. 14
9. 18
3. 7
W. wins.

B.

3. 8
11. 7
2. 11

19. 15
10. 19
22. 17
19. 24
17. 10
24. 28
10. 7
11. 15
18. 11
8. 15
7. 3
15. 18
23. 14
9. 18
3. 7
W. wins.

C.
16. 19
23. 16
12. 19
32. 28
2. 6
10. 7
3. 10
11. 8
4. 11
27. 24
20. 27
31. 8
Drawn.

GAME 32.
22. 18
10. 15
25. 22
6. 10
29. 25 var 1
10. 14
24. 19 var 2
15. 24
28. 19
11. 16
18. 15
7. 11
22. 18
16. 20
26. 22
11. 16
15. 10
9. 13
18. 9
5. 14
19. 15
16. 19
23. 16
12. 19
22. 18
14. 23
27. 18
2. 6
25. 22
19. 24
18. 14
24. 27
32. 23
8. 11
15. 8
4. 11
23. 18
6. 15
14. 10
20. 24
18. 14
11. 16
30. 26
16. 20
22. 17
13. 32
26. 17
Drawn.

Var. 1.
22. 17
15. 22
17. 13
9. 14
26. 17
11. 15
29. 25
8. 11
25. 22
4. 8
23. 19
14. 18
30. 25
11. 16 A.
13. 9
16. 23
17. 13
W. wins.

A.
2. 6
31. 26
11. 16
26. 23
16. 20
23. 14
7. 11
14. 7
3. 10
27. 23
20. 27
28. 24
27. 31
23. 18
5. 9
32. 27
31. 26
17. 14
26. 17
14. 7
15. 29
21. 5
11. 16
27. 23
16. 20
7. 2
20. 27
2. 9
29. 25
19. 15
25. 22
9. 14
12. 16
15. 10
B. wins.

Var. 2
23. 19
14. 23
19. 10
7. 14
26. 19
14. 18 E.F.
22. 15
11. 18
21. 17
8. 11 B.
24. 20 C.
9. 13
17. 14
2. 7
28. 24
4. 8
19. 15
7. 10
15. 6
1. 17
25. 22
17. 26
30. 14
3. 7
24. 19
13. 17
19. 16
12. 19
27. 23
19. 26
31. 13
8. 12
13. 9
7. 10
14. 7
5. 14
7. 2
Drawn.

B.
9. 13
17. 14
13. 17
31. 26
8. 11
24. 20
3. 7
27. 23
18. 27
32. 23
1. 6
23. 18
17. 22
26. 17
11. 16
20. 11
7. 23
25. 22
2. 7
17. 13
23. 27
18. 15
Drawn.

C.
17. 14
2. 7
19. 15
4. 8
24. 19 D.
9. 13
31. 26
11. 16
Drawn.

D.
24. 20
1. 6
30. 26
9. 13
26. 22
Drawn.

E.
9. 13
19. 15
11. 18
22. 15
12. 16
15. 10
14. 18
31. 26
2. 6
26. 23
6. 15
23. 14
16. 20
25. 22
8. 11
27. 23
20. 27
23. 18
13. 17
22. 13
15. 22
32. 23
22. 26
23. 18
26. 31
14. 10
31. 27
30. 26
Drawn.

F.
11. 16
19. 15
16. 19
15. 10 H
19. 23
27. 18
14. 23
22. 18
8. 11
25. 22
4. 8
22. 17 G.
9. 13
17. 14
2. 6
10. 7
3. 17
21. 14
13. 17
24. 20
17. 22
28. 24
23. 26
30. 23
22. 25
24. 19
25. 30

31. 26
6. 9
14. 10
9. 14
Drawn.

G.
24. 19
11. 16
19. 15
2. 6
31. 27
9. 13
15. 11
8. 15
18. 11
6. 15
27. 18
15. 19
18. 14
19. 23
21. 17
16. 19
11. 7
3. 10
14. 7
Drawn.

H.
22. 18
14. 23
27. 18
1. 6
21. 17 I.
3. 7
17. 14
9. 13
24. 20
13. 17
31. 26
17. 21
32. 27
6. 9
27. 24
7. 11
25. 22
9. 13

15. 10
11. 15
18. 11
8. 15
20. 16
4. 8
Drawn.

I.
25. 22
9. 14
18. 9
5. 14
22. 17
14. 18
17. 14
3. 7
21. 17
18. 22
17. 13
7. 10
14. 7
2. 18
24. 15
8. 11
15. 8
4. 11
28. 24
11. 15
31. 27
6. 10
13. 9
10. 14
9. 6
12. 16
Drawn.

GAME 33.
22. 18
10. 15
25. 22
6. 10
29. 25
10. 14
24. 19
15. 24

28. 19
11. 16
18. 15 var 1
7. 11
22. 18
16. 20
26. 22
11. 16 var 2
31. 26
2. 6
32. 28
3. 7
28. 24 var 3
7. 10 var 4
15. 11
8. 15
18. 11
10. 15
19. 10
6. 15
22. 17
14. 18 A.
23. 14
9. 18
26. 23
16. 19
23. 14
19. 28
25. 22
28. 32
27. 23
32. 27
23. 18
27. 24
11. 7
Drawn.

A.
16. 19
23. 16
12. 28
17. 10
15. 19
27. 23
19. 24
Drawn.

Var. 1.
27. 24
16. 20
31. 27
8. 11 B.
19. 15 C.
4. 8
2. 17
7. 10
15. 6
1. 10
23. 19
14. 23
27. 18
20. 27
32. 23
11. 16
17. 13
2. 6
21. 17
16. 20
25. 21
20. 24
17. 14
10. 17
21. 14
24. 27
19. 15
27. 31
26. 22
3. 7
14. 10
7. 14
15. 10
6. 15
18. 4
14. 18
13. 6
18. 27
Drawn.

B.
7. 10
32. 28
1. 6
19. 15
10. 19

24. 15
12. 16
22. 17
6. 10
15. 6
16. 19
17. 10
2. 7
23. 16
7. 32
6. 1
32. 27
25. 22
Drawn.

C.
18. 15
11. 18
22. 15
4. 8
26. 22
14. 18
23. 14
9. 18
21. 17
1. 6 D.
30. 26
7. 10
17. 14
10. 17
22. 13
3. 7
26. 22
7. 10
22. 17
2. 7
25. 21
18. 22
17. 14
10. 17
21. 14
7. 11
15. 10
6. 15
19. 10
12. 16
10. 7

8. 12
7. 3
Drawn

D.
2. 6
30. 26
7. 10
17. 14
10. 17
22. 13
12. 16
19. 12
6. 9
13. 6
1. 22
26. 21
20. 24
Drawn.

Var. 2.
2. 6 E.
27. 24
20. 27
31. 24
6. 10
15. 6
1. 10
32. 28
9. 13
18. 9
5. 14
30. 26
11. 15
19. 16
12. 19
23. 16
8. 12
16. 11
12. 16
17. 14
24. 20
16. 19
11. 7
19. 23
Drawn.

E.
2. 7
15. 10
W. wins.

Var. 3.
22. 17
6. 10
15. 6
1. 10
19. 15
10. 19
17. 3
20. 24
27. 11
8. 31
23. 16
Drawn.

Var. 4
8. 11 H.I.
15. 8
4. 11
22. 17
7. 10 F.
26. 22
9. 13
18. 2
1. 6
2. 9
5. 14
19. 15
11. 18
22. 6
13. 29
6. 2
29. 22
2. 6
25. 22
30. 25
22. 29
6. 10
14. 17
21. 14
29. 25
10. 7
25. 22
7. 10
Drawn.

F.
6. 10
17. 13
1. 6
18. 15
11. 18
26. 22
14. 17
22. 15
9. 14
15. 11 G.
14. 18
11. 2
17. 22
23. 7
22. 29
Drawn.

G.
13. 9
6. 13
15. 6
14. 18
21. 14
5. 9
14. 5
7. 11
Drawn.

H.
6. 10
15. 6
1. 10
21. 17
14. 21
18. 15
W. wins.

I.
7. 11
22. 17
6. 10
15. 6
1. 10
18. 15
11. 18
17. 13
8. 11
13. 6
Drawn.

GAME 34.
22. 18
10. 15
25. 22
6. 10
29. 25
10. 14
24. 19
15. 24
28. 19
11. 16
18. 15
7. 11
22. 18
16. 20
26. 22
11. 16
15. 10 var.
20. 24
27. 11
8. 24
18. 15
4. 8
32. 28
2. 6
28. 19
8. 11
15. 8
6. 24
23. 19
24. 28
8. 4
28. 32
4. 8
32. 28
8. 11
28. 24
19. 15
14. 17
22. 6
1. 19
21. 17
19. 23
17. 14
23. 27
25. 21
Drawn.

Var.
31. 26
1. 6
22. 17 A.
6. 10
15. 6
20. 24
17. 10
24. 31
26. 22
9. 13
6. 1
2. 6
32. 28
6. 24
28. 19
31. 27
19. 15
8. 15
15. 8
4. 11
1. 6
3. 8
6. 10
16. 20
30. 26
20. 24
21. 17
24. 28
25. 21
28. 32
17. 14
27. 31
21. 17
32. 27
10. 15
27. 24
14. 10
24. 27
10. 7
Drawn.

A.
32. 28
9. 13 B.
18. 9
5. 14
22. 18
6. 9
26. 22
2. 6
28. 24
8. 11
15. 8
4. 11
18. 15
11. 18
22. 15
Drawn.

B.
3. 7
22. 17 C.
6. 10
15. 6
7. 11
17. 10
11. 15
18. 11
8. 31
26. 22
9. 13
6. 1
31. 27
23. 18
27. 23
18. 15
4. 8
B. wins.

C.
28. 24
7. 10 D.
15. 11
8. 15
18. 11
14. 18
22. 15
9. 14
21. 17
14. 21
25. 22
5. 9
22. 18
9. 14
18. 9
6. 13
15. 6
2. 9
W. wins

D.
7. 11
22. 17 F.
6. 10
15. 6
11. 15 E.
18. 11
8. 15
19. 10
9. 13
25. 22
2. 9
10. 7
14. 18
23. 14
9. 25
Drawn.

E.
9. 13
17. 14
2. 9
25. 22
11. 15
18. 11
8. 15
10. 7
15. 18
22. 15
13. 17
21. 14
9. 18

23. 14
16. 32
24. 19
W. wins.

F.
21. 17
14. 21
22. 17
9. 13 H.
26. 22
6. 9 K.
17. 14
13. 17 G.
22. 6
2. 9
25. 22
9. 13
15. 10
11. 15
18. 11
8. 15
10. 7
5. 9
14. 5
13. 17
19. 10
17. 26
23. 18
26. 31
7. 3
16. 19
24. 15
W. wins.

G.
2. 6
14. 10
9. 14
18. 2
11. 18
22. 15
5. 9
10. 6
9. 14
15. 11
8. 15
19. 10
4. 8
2. 7
8. 11
6. 1
14. 17
10. 6
11. 15
7. 10
16. 19
23. 16
12. 28
10. 19
W. wins.

H.
6. 10
15. 6
9. 14 I.
18. 9
5. 14
17. 10
2. 9
19. 15
11. 18
23. 5
8. 11
Drawn.

I.
9. 13
26. 22
2. 9
17. 14
11. 15
19. 10
8. 11
10. 7
11. 15
18. 11
9. 18
23. 14
W. wins.

K.
2. 7
15. 10
6. 15
19. 3
11. 15
18. 11
8. 15
3. 8
4. 11
17. 14
13. 17
22. 13
15. 18
14. 10
11. 15
23. 14
16. 19
25. 22
19. 24
27. 23
28. 32
23. 18
15. 19
22. 17
19. 23
Drawn.

GAME 35.
22. 18
11. 16
25. 22
8. 11
29. 25
4. 8
18. 14
10. 17
21. 14
9. 18
23. 14
6. 10
22. 18
10. 17
25. 21
1. 6
21. 14
6. 10
24. 20
10. 17
18. 15
11. 18
20. 4
17. 21
4. 8
5. 9
28. 24
9. 13
27. 23
18. 27
32. 23
12. 16
8. 12
16. 20
26. 22
20. 27
31. 24
7. 11
23. 18
3. 7
18. 14
11. 15
14. 9
7. 10
12. 8
10. 14
8. 11
14. 18
24. 20
18. 25
11. 18
25. 29
9. 5
W. wins.

GAME 36.
11. 16
22. 18
8. 11
25. 22
4. 8
29. 25
16. 19
24. 15
10. 19
23. 16
12. 19
27. 24 A.
9. 14
18. 9
5. 14
24. 15
11. 18
22. 15
7. 10
32. 27
10. 19
27. 23
8. 12
23. 16
12. 19
31. 27
3. 8
27. 24
2. 7
Drawn.

A.
21. 17
9. 14
17. 10
7. 23
27. 18
11. 16
18. 15
6. 9
22. 17
1. 6
26. 22
3. 7
22. 18
7. 10
17. 13
16. 20
25. 22
9. 14
18. 9
5. 14
22. 18
14. 23
31. 27
8. 12
Drawn.

GAME 37
11. 15
22. 17
15. 19
24. 15
10. 19
23. 16
12. 19
25. 22
7. 10
27. 24
10. 15
22. 18
15. 22
24. 15
*3. 7 A.
30. 25
9. 13
25. 18
13. 22
26. 17
7. 10
31. 26
10. 19
32. 27
2. 7
17. 14
7. 11
27. 24
11. 15
18. 11
8. 15
14. 10
6. 9
10. 7
9. 14
W. wins.

A.
9. 13
26. 23
8. 11
15. 8
4. 11
28. 24
3. 7
24. 19

6. 10
17. 14
10. 17
21. 14
1. 6
30. 25
6. 10
25. 18
10. 17
19. 15
11. 16
15. 11
7. 10
Drawn.

GAME 38.
22. 18
11. 16
18. 14
10. 17
21. 14
9. 18
23. 14
8. 11
25. 22
6 10 var 1
29. 25 var 2
10. 17
22. 13
4. 8
26. 23
2. 6
23. 18
16. 20
24. 19
11. 16
27. 23
8. 11
31. 27
7. 10
18. 15
11. 18
23. 7
3. 10
25. 22 A.
16. 23
27. 18
5. 9
32. 27
12. 16
27. 23
10. 14
18. 15
14. 17
23. 18
17. 26
30. 23
1. 5
15. 11
6. 10
13. 6
10. 15
Drawn.

A.
25. 21
16. 23
27. 18
12. 16
30. 26
16. 19
32. 27
5. 9
18. 15
9. 14
15. 11
14. 18
11. 7
Drawn.

Var. 1.
11. 15
24. 19
15. 24
27. 11
7. 16
22. 18
4. 8 B.
29. 25
8. 11
28. 24
16. 20
31. 27
11. 16
26. 23
2. 7
25. 21
6. 9
24 19
1. 6
21. 17
9. 13
19. 15
13. 22
14. 10
7. 14
18. 2
22. 26
23. 19
16. 23
27. 18
26. 31
2. 6
12. 16
15. 11
16. 19
18. 14
19. 23
6. 10
31. 26
11. 7
20. 24
7. 2
24. 27
2. 7
27. 31
7. 11
31. 27
11. 15
3. 8
15. 18
8. 12
10. 6
12. 16
14. 10
W. wins.

B.
16. 20
26. 23
12. 16
32. 27
4. 8
28. 24
8. 12
29. 25
2. 7
25. 21 C.
16. 19
24. 15
7. 10
14. 7
3. 26
30. 23
6. 10
21. 17
12. 16
31. 26
1. 6
26. 22
5. 9
17. 13
10. 14
18. 15
14. 17
22. 18
17. 22
18. 14
9. 18
23. 14
16. 19
Drawn.

C.
25. 19
6. 10
25. 21
10. 17
21. 14
7. 10
14. 7
3. 10
31. 26
10. 14
18. 9
5. 14
26. 22
1. 5
30. 25
5. 9
25. 21
9. 13
Drawn.

Var. 2.
22. 17
4 8
29. 25
2. 6 D.
24. 20
16. 19
27. 24
11. 15
25. 22
6. 9
22. 18
15. 22
24. 6
1. 10
17. 13
9. 18
26. 17
18. 22
32. 27
8. 11
27. 24
11. 15
31. 27
7. 11
27. 23
22. 26
23. 18
15. 22
30. 23
22. 26
23. 19
11. 15
17. 14
10. 17
19. 10
26. 31
10. 7
Drawn.

D.
16. 20
24. 19
11. 15 F
28. 24
8. 11
25. 22
11. 16
26. 23
7. 11
14. 7
3. 10
23. 18
16. 23
18. 14
2. 7
27. 18
20. 27
31. 24
12. 16 E
24. 20
1. 6
30. 25
6. 9
25. 21
16. 19
32. 27
19. 23
27. 24
23. 27
20. 16
11. 20
18. 2
9. 25
24. 19
Drawn.

E.
1. 6
30. 25
6. 9
25. 21
12. 16
32. 28
16. 20
24. 19
15. 24

28. 19
20. 24
19. 15
10. 19
17. 13
11. 16
13. 5
Drawn.

F.
11. 16
25. 22
16. 23
26. 19
8. 11 G.
19. 16
12. 19
27. 24
20. 27
31. 8
3. 12
28. 24
10. 15
32. 28
12. 16
24. 20
16. 19
30. 25
1. 6
25. 21
6. 10
20. 16
19. 23
16. 12
23. 27
12. 8
27. 31
8. 3
30. 26
28. 24
26. 23
24. 20
23. 18
Drawn.

G.
10. 15

19. 10
2. 6
17. 13
6. 15
13. 9
8. 11
30. 26
11. 16
27. 23
16. 19
23. 16
12. 19
32. 27
7. 10
14. 7
3. 10
Drawn.

GAME 39.
22. 18
10. 14
24. 19
11. 16 var 1
27. 24
8. 11 var 2
25. 22
16. 20
31. 27
11. 16
19. 15 A.
16. 19
23. 16
12. 19
15. 11
14. 23
24. 15
7. 16
26. 12
4. 8
28. 24
9. 14
24. 19
2. 7
30. 26
14. 18
26. 23
18. 25

29. 22
7. 10
23. 18
5. 9
27. 24
20. 27
32. 23
W. wins.

A.
29. 25
7. 10
19. 15
10. 19
24. 15
16. 19
23. 16
12. 19
27. 23
19. 24
24. 19
20. 24
15. 10
6. 15
18. 11
24. 27
19. 15
27. 31
23. 18
14. 23
26. 19
9. 14 B.
22. 17
14. 18
15. 10
18. 23
17. 13
23. 26
30. 23
31. 27
21. 17
27. 18
17. 14
18. 9
13. 6
2. 9
11. 7

9. 14
25. 22
5. 9
7. 2
9. 13
2. 6
14. 17
22. 18
17. 22
6. 9
22. 26
9. 14
26. 31
18. 15
31. 26
Drawn.

B.
1. 6
19. 16
3. 7
21. 17
7. 10
16. 12
10. 19
11. 8
4. 11
17. 14
9. 18
22. 8
19. 23
8. 3
6. 10
3. 8
10. 14
8. 11
14. 17
25. 21
17. 22
21. 17
31. 27
11. 15
22. 26
15. 18
W. wins.

Var. 1.
6. 10
25. 22
11. 15
18. 11
8. 24
28. 19
4. 8
27. 24
8. 11
24. 20
11. 15
19. 16
12. 19
23. 16
14. 18
29. 25
1. 6
16. 11
7. 16
20. 11
18. 23
26. 19
15. 24
22. 17
10. 15
25. 22
24. 28
30. 26
15. 19
17. 13 C.
9. 14
22. 17
6. 10
13. 9
10. 15
17. 10
5. 14
26. 22
14. 18
22. 17
19. 23
17. 13
23. 26
31. 22
18. 25
10. 6

2. 9
3. 6
25. 30
6. 1
30. 26
1. 6
26. 23
21. 17
Drawn.

C.
31. 27
6. 10
27. 23
19. 24
Drawn.

Var. 2
16. 20
31. 27
8. 11
19. 16
12. 19
24. 8
4. 11
28. 24
6. 10
24. 19
9. 13
18. 9
5. 14
25. 22
11. 16
19. 16
15. 19
32. 28
2. 6
22. 18 D. E.
14. 17
21. 14
10. 17
18. 15 G.
17. 22
26. 17
19. 26
30. 23
13. 22

15. 11
7. 10
11. 7
10. 14
7 2
6 9
16. 11
1. 6
23. 19
22. 26
11. 7
3. 10
2. 7
9. 13
27. 23
14. 18
7. 14
18. 27
19. 15
26. 30
14. 9
27. 31
9. 2
13. 17
Drawn.

D.
16. 12
19. 24
28. 19
3. 8
12. 3
14. 17
21. 14
10. 17
3. 10
6. 31
23. 19
17. 21
19. 15
20. 24
B. wins.

E.
29. 25
19. 24
28. 19
10. 15
19. 10
6. 15
27. 24 F.
20. 27
16. 11
7. 16
23. 18
14. 23
26. 10
27. 31
22. 18
31. 27
18. 15
27. 23
15. 11
23. 18
11. 7
16. 19
7. 2
19. 23
2. 7
1. 6
B. wins.

F.
16. 12
7. 10
21. 17
14. 21
23. 18
15. 19
27. 23
19. 24
18. 15
10. 19
23. 16
24. 27
26. 23
27. 31
23. 19
31. 26
30. 23
B. wins.

G.
16. 12
19. 24
28. 19
3. 8
12. 3
17. 21
B. wins.

GAME 40.
22. 18
10. 14
24. 19
11. 16
27. 24
16. 20
31. 27
8. 11
25. 22
4. 8
29. 25
11. 16
19. 15
7. 11 var.
24. 19 A.
9. 13
18. 9
5. 14
22. 18*
1. 5
18. 9
5. 14
26. 22
11. 18
22. 15
3. 7
28. 24
7. 10
30 26
14 17
21. 7
2. 18
23. 14
16. 30
14. 9
B. wins.

A.
22. 17†
16. 19
17. 10
2. 6
23. 16
12. 19
21. 17
7. 21
27. 23
20. 27
23. 7
3. 19
32. 16
6. 10
16. 12
W. wins.

Var.
16. 19
23. 16
14. 23
26. 19
7. 11 D. E. F.
16. 7
3. 10 C.
22. 17
9. 13 B.
17. 14
10. 17
21. 14
6. 9
19. 16
12. 19
15. 10
9. 18
24. 15
2. 6
10. 7
W. wins.

B.
2. 7
17. 13
7. 11
21. 17
11. 18
19. 15
10. 19
24. 15
9. 14
17. 10
18. 23
27. 18
8. 11
15. 8
6. 29
8. 3
W. wins.

C.
2. 18
22. 15
3. 7
25. 22
9. 13
30. 26
5. 9
26. 23
7. 10
15. 11
8. 15
23. 18
W. wins.

D.
9. 13
22. 18
6. 9
25. 22
9. 14
18. 9
5. 14
15. 11
8. 15
19. 10
12. 19
24. 15
14. 18
30. 25
7. 14
15. 11
3. 7
22. 15
7. 16
15. 11
W. wins.

E.
6. 10
15. 6
1. 10
22. 18
10. 14
18. 15
7. 11
16. 7
2. 18
19. 16
12. 19
24. 15
18. 23 G.
27. 18
14. 23
15. 10
8. 11
10. 6
11. 15
6. 2
9. 13
2. 6
3. 7
W. wins.

G.
8. 11
15. 8
3. 12
30. 26
12. 16
28. 24
9. 13
26. 22
5. 9
22. 15
16. 19
25. 22
19. 28
15. 10
W. wins.

F.
9. 14

15. 10
6. 15
19. 10
12. 19
24. 15
14. 18 H.
22. 17
7. 14
17. 10
2. 7
20. 26
7. 14
26. 22
3. 7
15. 10
7. 11
22. 15
11. 18
10. 7
5. 9
7. 3
8. 12
27. 23
18. 27
32. 23
1. 5
25. 22
W. wins.

H.

7. 11
30. 26
11. 18
22. 15
5. 9
26. 23
2. 6
28. 24
9. 13
25. 22
8. 12
22. 18
6. 9
23. 19
W. wins.

GAME 41.

22. 18
10. 14
24. 19
11. 16
27. 24
16. 20
31. 27
8. 11
25. 22
4. 8
29. 25
11. 16
19. 15
7. 11
24. 19 A.
9. 13
18. 9
5. 14
28. 24
11. 18
22. 15
6. 10
15. 6
1. 10
26. 22
3. 7
22. 18
14. 17
21. 14
10. 17
18. 14
8. 11
14. 9
7. 14
9. 5
10. 14
25. 21
17. 22
5. 1
22. 25
1. 5
25. 29
5. 9
13. 17
9. 18
17. 22
18. 25
29. 22
19. 15
11. 18
23. 14
2. 7
21. 17
Drawn.

A.

22. 17†
16. 19
17. 10
12. 16
10. 7
3. 10
18. 14
9. 18 B.
23. 7
11. 18
24. 15
2. 11
21. 17
6. 9
17. 14
9. 13
14. 10
13. 17
10. 7
1. 6
7. 3
8. 12
15. 8
W. wins.

B.

10. 17
21. 14
9. 18 C.
23. 14
11. 18
24. 15
2. 7
26. 23
6. 10
15. 6
1. 17
23. 14
8. 11
28. 24
W. wins.

C.

11. 18
24. 15
9. 13
28. 24
8. 12
15. 11
6. 9
14. 10
9. 14
10. 7
13. 17
W. wins.

GAME 42.

22. 18
10. 14
24. 19
11. 16
27. 24
8. 11
31. 27
16. 20
25. 22
4. 8
29. 25
11. 16 var
19. 15
7. 11
22. 17
16. 19
17. 10
2. 7
23. 16
12. 19
25. 22
7. 23
27. 18
20. 27
32. 7
3. 19
21. 17
6. 10
17. 14
10. 17
22. 6
1. 10
18. 15
10. 14
15. 10
Drawn.

Var.

9. 13
18. 9
5. 14
22. 18 var 2
6. 9 R
26. 22 U
11. 16 Q.
18. 15 N.
7. 10
15. 6
1. 10
30. 26
3. 7
19. 15 A.
10. 19
24. 15
2. 6
28. 24
Drawn.

A.

22. 18
7. 11
19. 15 C.D.
10. 19
24. 15
16. 19
23. 7
14. 30
7. 3
9. 14
25. 22 B.
30. 26
22. 18
14. 23
27. 18
26. 23
15. 10
23. 7
3. 10
12. 16
B. wins.

B.

27. 23
30. 26
23. 19
2. 7
3. 17
13. 29
15. 10
26. 23
19. 15
23. 19
B. wins

C.

25. 22
2. 7
19. 15
10. 19
24. 15
16. 19
B. wins.

D.

26. 22
2. 6
18. 15
11. 18
22. 15
13. 17
B. wins.

Var. 2.

19. 15
11. 18
22. 15
7. 10
25. 22 E.
10. 19
23. 16
12. 19
24. 15

14. 18
30. 25
2. 7
15. 10 F.I.
7. 14
22. 15
3. 7
28. 24
14. 17
21. 14
6. 10
15. 6
1. 17
25. 21
17. 22
26. 17
13. 22
24. 19
22. 26
19. 15
Drawn.

E.

23. 18
14. 23
26. 19
2. 7
25. 22
1. 6
22. 18
7. 11
30. 26
11. 16
26. 23
5. 9
B. wins.

F.

27. 24
20. 27
32. 14
7. 10
14. 7
3. 19
22. 18
8. 11
18. 14 G.
1. 5
25. 22 H.
11. 15
14. 10
6 9
10. 7
9. 14
7. 3
14. 18
3. 7
18. 25
26. 22
19. 23
Drawn.

G.

26. 22
6. 10
21. 17
B. wins.

H.

26. 22
19. 23
28. 24
23. 26
24. 19
26. 30
19. 15
11. 18
22. 15
6. 9
B. wins.

I.

28. 24
7. 11
24. 19 K.
20. 24
27. 20
18. 23
B. wins.

K.

26. 23
11. 16
23. 14
6. 10
B. wins.

L.

27. 23
18. 27
32. 23
7. 10
22. 18 M.
10. 19
23. 16
8. 12
B. wins.

M.

23. 19
1. 5
22. 18
5. 9
25. 22
3. 7
B. wins.

N.

19. 15
16. 19
23. 16
14. 23
27. 18
12. 19
21. 17 O.P.
20. 27
32. 16
8. 11
15. 8
3. 19
B. wins.

O.

30. 26
20. 27
32. 16
8. 11
B. wins.

P.

15. 11
8. 15
18. 11
B. wins.

Q.

1. 5
19. 15
2. 6
24. 19
7. 10
28. 24
12. 16
19. 12
10. 28
18. 15
11. 18
22. 15
Drawn.

R.

1. 5
18. 9
5. 14
25. 22
6. 9 S.T.
22. 18
W. wins.

S.

11. 16
22. 18
6. 9
18. 15
W. wins.

T.

6. 10
19. 16
12. 19
24. 6
W. wins.

U.

25. 22
1. 6
19. 15 V.Y.
7. 10
24. 19
2. 7
19. 16
12. 19
23. 16
B. wins.

V.

19. 16
12. 19
24. 15
7. 10
23. 19
14. 23
27. 18
9. 14
B. wins.

Y.

30. 25
11. 16
18. 15
7. 10
22. 18
3. 7
B. wins.

GAME 43.

22. 18
10. 14
24. 19
11. 16
27. 24
8. 11
25. 22
16. 20
31. 27
4. 8
29. 25
9. 13
18. 9
5. 14
22. 18
6. 9
19. 16
12. 19
24. 15
7. 10 va.
15. 6
1. 10
23. 19 E.
14. 23
27. 18
20. 24
18. 14 A.
9. 18
19. 15
10. 19
26. 23
18. 27
32. 7
3. 10
28. 19
8. 11
25. 22 B.
11. 15
19. 16
10. 14
16. 11
14. 18
30. 25
18. 23
11 8
23 26
8 3
26 30
3. 8
2. 7
8. 3
7. 10
3. 8
10. 14
8. 11
15. 19
11. 15
19. 24
15. 19
24. 27
19. 23
27. 31
22. 18
31. 26
18. 9
26. 19

9. 5
19. 15
5. 1
15. 18
1 5
18. 14
5. 1
30. 26
1. 6
26. 23
6. 1
23. 18
1. 5
13. 17
5. 1
B. wins.

B.
30. 26
11. 15
19. 16
15. 18
16. 11
10. 15
11. 8
15. 19
26. 22
18. 23
22. 18
23. 26
18. 15
26. 30
15. 10
19. 24
8. 4
24. 27
4. 8
27. 31
Drawn.

A.
19. 16
11. 20
28. 19
20. 24 O
18. 15
2. 6
25. 22
3. 7
22. 18
7. 11 D.
26. 22
10. 14
19. 16
11. 20
15. 10
14. 23
10. 1
24. 27
1. 5
27. 31
5. 14
23. 27
32. 23
31. 26
14. 18
26. 19
21. 17
20. 24
17. 14
Drawn.

C.
8. 11
32. 27
10. 14
26. 23
3. 8
30. 26
8. 12
26. 22
11. 16
18. 15
14. 18
23. 5
16. 32
5. 1
32. 27
Drawn.

D.
24. 28
26. 23
10. 14
30. 26
13. 17
19. 16
8. 12
15. 11
12. 19
23. 16
14. 30
21. 5
7. 10
5. 1
30. 26
11. 7
26. 23
W. wins.

E.
28. 24
10. 15
25. 22
2. 7 F.
23. 19
14. 23
19. 10
7. 14
26. 19
14. 18
22. 15
11. 18
19. 15
8. 11
15. 8
Drawn.

F.
13. 17
22. 6
15. 31
6. 1
31. 26
23. 19
26. 22
1. 5
14. 18
19. 15
18. 23 G.
27. 18
20. 27
32. 23
22. 26
15. 10
W. wins.

G.
11. 16
5. 9
18. 23
27. 18
20. 27
32. 23
22. 26
Drawn.

Var.
2. 6 H.
28. 24
7. 10
24. 19
1. 5
25. 22
3. 7
30. 25
14. 17
21. 14
10. 17
25. 21
W. wins.

H.
11. 16
28. 24
7. 10 L.
15. 6
1. 10
24. 19
8. 11
19. 12
10. 15
26. 22
2. 6 I.
30. 26
W. wins.

I.
2. 7
30. 26
15. 19 K.
23. 16
14. 30
22. 18
W. wins.

K.
13. 17
22. 6
18. 31
32. 28
W. wins.

L.
16. 19
23. 16
14. 23
26. 19
7. 11 M.N.
16. 7
2. 18
30. 26
8. 11
19. 15
11. 16
15. 10
W. wins.

M.
9. 14
16. 11
7. 23
27. 9
20. 27
32. 23
1. 5
25. 22
W. wins.

N.
8. 12
15. 11
9. 14
25. 22
1 6
22. 18
14. 23
27. 18
20. 27
32. 23
W. wins.

GAME 44.
22. 18
10. 14
24. 19
11. 16
27. 24
8. 11
25. 22
16. 20
31. 27
4. 8
29. 25
11. 16
19. 15
7. 11
22. 17
16. 19
23. 7var
14. 23
26. 19
2. 18
17. 14
9. 13
14. 10
6. 15
19. 10
12. 16
30. 26
8. 11
26. 23
11. 15
23. 14
15. 18
10. 7
3. 17
21. 14
Drawn.

Var.
17. 10†
2. 7
23. 16
12. 19
21. 17
7. 21
27. 23
20. 27
23. 7
3. 19
32. 16
6. 10
25. 22
9. 14
18. 9
W. wins.

GAME 45.
22. 18
10. 14
24. 19
11. 16
27. 24
8. 11
25. 22
16. 20
31. 27
4. 8
29. 25
11. 16 var
19. 15
7. 11
22. 17
16. 19
17. 10
2. 7
23. 16
12. 19
21. 17†
7. 23
27. 18
20. 27
32. 7
3. 19
17. 13
8. 11
25. 22
11. 16
22. 17
16. 20
26. 23
19. 26
W. wins.

Var.
9. 13
18. 9
5. 14
22. 18
6. 9
19. 16
12. 19
24. 15
7. 10
15. 6
1. 10
23. 19
14. 23
27. 18
20. 24
26. 22
10. 15 A.
19. 10
2. 7
28. 19
7. 23
19. 15
11. 18
22. 15
8. 11
15. 8
3. 12
25. 22
12. 16
22. 18
Drawn.

A.
10. 14
18. 15
11. 18
22. 15
14. 18 F.G.H.
15. 11 B.
8. 15
19. 10
2. 7
28. 19
7. 14
19. 15
18. 22 D.E.
25. 18
14. 23
15. 10
9. 14
10. 6
14. 18
6. 2
18. 22
21. 17
22. 25
Drawn.

B.
19. 16
8. 11
28. 19
11. 20
32. 27
9. 14
30. 26
13. 17
19. 16 C.
2. 6
16. 12
6. 9
15. 11
9. 13
11. 8
3. 7
8. 3
7. 11
3. 7
11. 16
7. 11
16. 19
11. 15
19. 24
15. 22
24. 31
12. 8
20. 24
Drawn.

C.
15. 11
18. 22
25. 9
3. 7
21. 14
7. 30
14. 10
30. 25
10. 6
25. 22
6. 1
22. 17
27. 23
17. 14
1. 5
20. 24
23. 19
24. 27
19. 16
27. 31
16. 11
B. wins.

D.
13. 17
30. 26
3. 8
26. 23
18. 27
32. 23
W. wins.

E.
18. 23
15. 10
14. 18
10. 6
9. 14
6. 2
23. 27
32. 23
18. 27
25. 22
27. 31
2. 6
W. wins.

F.
3. 7
15. 10
7. 11
10. 7
8. 12
7. 3
11. 16
3. 8
W. wins.

G.
2. 7
15. 10
7. 11
25. 22
8. 12
W. wins.

H.
8. 12
15. 10
14. 18
19. 15
2. 7
28. 19
7. 14
15. 11 I.
18. 22
25. 18
14. 23
19. 15
9. 14
15. 10
14. 18
10. 6
18. 22
6. 1
22. 26
1. 6
26. 31
11. 7
3. 10
6. 15
12. 16
15. 11
16. 20
11. 15
20. 24
15. 10
Drawn.

I.
15. 10
13. 17
30. 26
17. 22
26. 17
9. 13
10. 6
13. 29
6. 1
29. 25
1. 6
18. 22
6. 9
25. 29
9. 35
29. 22
32. 27
3. 7
27. 24
7. 11
B. wins

K.
10. 6
17. 22
6. 1
22. 29
1. 6
9. 13
6. 9
18. 22
9. 25
29. 22
19. 15
3. 7
B. wins

GAME 46.
22. 18
11. 16
25. 22
10. 14
24. 19
16. 20
22. 17
9. 13
17. 10
6. 22
26. 17
13. 22
30. 26
2. 6
26. 17
7. 10
17. 14
10. 17
21. 14
3. 7
29. 25
6. 10
25. 21
10. 17
21. 14
1. 6
19. 15
8. 11
15. 8
4. 11
23. 19
6. 9
14. 10
7. 14
19. 16
Drawn.

GAME 47.
22. 17
11. 15
23. 19
8. 11
25. 22
11. 16
24. 20
16. 23
27. 11
7. 16
20. 11
3. 8
26. 23
8. 15
23. 18
15. 19
30. 26
9. 14
18. 9
5. 14
32. 27
4. 8
27. 24
12. 16
24. 15
10. 19
17. 10
6. 15
21. 17
8. 12
31. 27
1. 6
17. 14
16. 20
27. 23
15. 18
22. 15
6. 10
23. 16
12. 19
14. 7
2. 18
Drawn.

GAME 48.
11. 15
23. 19
9. 13
26. 23 A.
8. 11 var
23. 18
4. 8
27. 23
6. 9
30. 26
9. 14
18. 9
5. 14
32. 27
1. 5
19. 16
12. 19
23. 16
11. 20
22. 17
13. 22
25. 4
5. 9
29. 25
9. 13
25. 22
14. 17
21. 14
10. 17
26. 23
17. 26
31. 22
7. 11
24. 19
2. 7
W. wins.

A.
21. 17
5. 9
25. 21
9. 14
27. 23
8. 11
24. 20
15. 24
28. 19
4. 8
30. 25
11. 15
32. 28
15. 24
28. 19
8. 11
22. 18
13. 22
26. 17
1. 5
18. 9
5. 14
B. wins.

Var.
5. 9
22. 18
15. 22
25. 18
10. 14 B.
29. 25
8. 11
25. 22
7. 10 E.
30. 26
3. 8 C.D.
24. 20
11. 15
18. 11
8. 24
28. 19
4. 8
32. 28
8. 11
19. 16
12. 19
23. 7
2. 11
27. 23
W. wins.

B.
1. 5
29. 25
13. 17
21. 14
10. 17
31. 26
9. 13
25. 22
8. 11
24. 20
4. 8
27. 24
6. 9
32. 27
17. 21
19. 16
12. 19
23. 16
2. 6
16. 12
6. 10
27. 23
9. 14
18. 9
5. 14
22. 18
14. 17
18. 14
17. 22
26. 17
13. 22
14. 9
22. 26
9. 6
26. 31
6. 2
31. 26
23. 19
27. 23
3. 6
W. wins.

C.
4. 8
24. 20
10. 15
19. 10
6. 15
27. 24
2. 7
24. 19
15. 24
28. 19
7. 10
22. 17
13. 22
26. 17
9. 13
18. 9
13. 22
21. 17
11. 15
32. 28
15. 24
28. 19
8. 11
23. 18
22. 25
9. 6
25. 29
6. 2
29. 25
Drawn.

D
10. 15
19. 10
6. 15
24. 19
15. 24
28. 19
2. 6
27. 24
11. 16
32. 27
Drawn.

E.
6. 10
24. 20 F.
2. 6
30. 26
10. 15 G.
19. 10
6. 15
21. 17
14. 21
20. 16
12. 19
23. 16
11. 20
18. 2
21. 25
22. 18
Drawn

F.
31. 26

4. 8
19. 15
10. 19
24. 15
12. 16
28. 24
16. 20
24. 19
2. 6
19. 16
8. 12
15. 8
12. 19
23. 16
B. wins.

G.

4. 8
27. 24
10. 15
19. 10
6. 15
21. 17
14. 21
Drawn.

GAME 49.

11. 15
23. 19
9. 13
26. 23
8. 11
23. 18
4. 8 C.D.
27. 23
6. 9
30. 26
9. 14
18. 9
5. 14
32. 27
14. 17
21. 14
10. 17
19. 10
7. 14
25. 21
11. 15
24. 19
15. 24
28. 19
8. 11
22. 18
1. 5
18. 9
5. 14
29. 25
11. 16
19. 15 B.
2. 6
15. 11
16. 19
23. 16
12. 19
27. 23
19. 24
25. 22
24. 28
22. 18
6. 9
18. 15
28. 32
23. 19
32. 28
11. 7
3. 10
15. 6
28. 24
19. 16
24. 19 A.
6. 2
19. 12
2. 7
12. 16
31. 27
W. wins.

A.

24. 20
16. 11
20. 24
6. 2
24. 19
2. 7
W. wins.

B.

25. 22
14. 18
22. 15
3. 7
21. 14
7. 10
15. 6
2. 18
23. 14
16. 30
14. 10
30. 25
10. 6
25. 22
6. 2
Drawn.

C.

5. 9
27. 23
10. 14
19. 10
6. 15
30. 26
7. 10
32. 27
1. 5
24. 19
15. 24
28. 19
11. 16
22. 17
13. 22
26. 17
4. 8
17. 13
3. 7
13. 6
2. 9
25. 22
8. 11
29. 25
9. 13
18. 9
5. 14
22. 18
14. 17
21. 14
10. 17
19. 15
16. 19
23. 16
11. 20
25. 22
17. 26
31. 22
12. 16
27. 23
20. 24
18. 14
24. 27
Drawn.

D.

11. 16
18. 11
16. 23
27. 18
7. 16
24. 20 E.
16. 19
30. 26
12. 16
20. 11
2. 7
11. 2
4. 8
2. 9
5. 30
22. 17 H.
13. 22
25. 18
8. 11
18. 14
10. 17
21. 14
1. 6
32. 27
6. 10
14. 7
3. 10
27. 24
10. 15
24. 20
19. 23
31. 26
23. 27
26. 23
27. 32
23. 19
15. 24
28. 19
32. 27
19. 16
11. 15
16. 12
27. 24
12. 8
24. 19
8. 4
15. 18
4. 8
18. 22
8. 12
30. 26
20. 16
19. 15
12. 8
Drawn.

E.

18. 15
10. 19
24. 15
16. 19
30. 26
12. 16
32. 27
3. 7
15. 11
7. 10 F.
11. 8
4. 11
27. 24
11. 15
22. 17
13. 22
25. 11
10. 15
24. 20
W. wins

F.

6. 10
11. 8 G.
4. 11
27. 24
11. 15
22. 17
13. 22
25. 11
16. 20
24. 6
7. 16
29. 25
1. 10
21. 17
5. 9
17. 13
2. 6
25. 22
9. 14
26. 23
10. 15
31. 26
15. 19
22. 18
14. 17
18. 14
20. 24
23. 18
24. 27
18. 15
27. 31
Drawn.

G.

27. 23
10. 15
23. 18
1. 6
21. 17
4. 8
11. 4

6. 10
Drawn.

H.
32. 27
8. 11
27. 24
19. 23
24. 19
3. 8
28. 24
23. 27
24. 20
1. 5
31. 24
8. 12
22. 18
10. 14
18. 9
5. 14
19. 15
11. 18
24. 19
30. 26
19. 15
18. 23
15. 10
23. 27
10. 6
27. 31
6. 1
31. 27
1. 6
26. 23
25. 22
23. 19
6. 10
27. 23
10. 17
23. 26
22. 18
13. 22
21. 17
26. 23
18. 14
19. 15
14. 9
23. 19
9. 5
15. 10
5. 1
19. 15
17. 13
15. 11
1. 5
11. 7
B. wins.

GAME 50.
11. 15
23. 19
9. 13
26. 23
6. 9
22. 18
15. 22
25. 18
8. 11
29. 25
9. 14
18. 9
5. 14
23. 18
14. 23
27. 18
10. 15 E.
19. 10
7. 23
31. 27
12. 16 G.
27. 18
4. 8
24. 20
16. 19
30. 26
3. 7
32. 27
8. 12
27. 24 A.
19. 23
26. 19
11. 16
20. 11
7. 23
Drawn.

A.
27. 23
2. 6
23. 16
12. 19
26. 22
7. 10 B.
18. 15
11. 18
22. 15
6. 9
15. 6
1. 10
20. 16
9. 14
16. 11
Drawn.

B.
19. 23
18. 15 C.
11. 18
22. 15
6. 10
15. 16
1. 10
20. 16
23. 26
16. 12
26. 31
12. 8
31. 27
8. 3
Drawn.

C.
28. 24
6. 10
24. 19
23. 27
19. 16
27. 31
16. 12
31. 26 D.
12. 8
26. 17
21. 14
10. 17
25. 21
17. 22
8. 3
7. 10
3. 7
10. 14
Drawn.

D.
31. 27
21. 17
27. 23
18. 14
23. 26
12. 8
26. 30
25. 21
30. 25
22. 18
13. 22
8. 3
10. 17
21. 14
Drawn.

E.
11. 16
18. 15
16. 23
15. 6
1. 10
31. 26
10. 14
26. 19
14. 18
32. 27
7. 11
19. 15
11. 16
15. 10 F.
4. 8
30. 26
18. 23
27 18
16. 20
24. 19
20. 24
26. 22
24. 27
28. 24
27. 31
24. 20
31. 27
18. 15
27. 24
20. 16
24. 27
16. 11
27. 23
8. 4
23. 16
4. 8
16. 11
8. 4
Drawn.

F.
30. 26
16. 19
15. 11
19. 23
26. 19
3. 7
19. 15
7. 11
15. 11
2. 6
11. 7
6. 10
7. 2
Drawn.

G.
23. 26
30. 28
12. 16
24. 20 H.
4. 8
28. 24
8. 12
24. 19
3. 7
25. 22
7. 10
27. 24
1. 5
32. 28
10. 14
22. 18
13. 17
18. 9
5. 14
23. 18
16. 23
18. 9
17. 22
21. 17
23. 26
17. 14
26. 31
14. 10
31. 27
10. 7
27. 23
7. 3
23. 18
9. 5
11. 15
24. 19
15. 24
28. 19
22. 26
3. 8
26. 31
8. 11
31. 27
19. 15
27. 23
15. 10
23. 19
1. 5
19. 24
10. 7
18. 23
7. 3
12. 16
Drawn.

H.
23. 18
4. 8
27. 23
16. 20
31. 27
8. 12
24. 19
11. 16
25. 22
2. 7
28. 24 M.
7. 11
18. 14
3. 7
14. 9 N.
7. 10
21. 17 I.K.L.
1. 5
9. 6
5. 9
6. 2
11. 15
2. 7
9. 14
7. 11
14. 21
11. 18
21. 25
18. 15
10. 14
22. 18
14. 17
18. 14
25. 30
14. 10
30. 26
10. 7
17. 22
7. 2
13. 17
B. wins.

I.
9. 6
10. 14
6. 2
13. 17
22. 13
14. 18
23. 14
16. 32
24. 19
32. 27
B. wins.

K.
9. 5
11. 15
21. 17
1. 6
17. 14
10. 26
19. 1
26. 31
21. 18
31. 26
B. wins.

L.
22. 18
1. 5
18. 14
10. 17
21. 14
13. 17
9. 6
17. 22
6. 2
22. 26
B. wins.

M.
21. 17
1. 6
B. wins.

N.
22. 18
13. 17
14. 10
7. 14
18. 9
17. 22
19. 15
11. 18
23. 14
22. 25
14. 10
1. 5
9. 6
5. 9
6. 2
9. 14
2. 6
14. 18
6. 9
18. 22
9. 14
25. 30
Drawn.

GAME 51.
11. 15
22. 17
8. 11
25. 22
9. 13
29. 25 var
15. 18
23. 14
11. 15
24. 19
15. 24
28. 19
4. 8
26. 23
8. 11
23. 18
6. 9
27. 24
1. 6
32. 28
11. 15
18. 11
9. 18
22. 15
13. 29
11. 8
29. 25
31. 26
5. 9
B. wins.

Var.
23. 19
4. 8
27. 23
6. 9
23. 18
9. 14
18. 9
5. 14
26. 23
2. 6
24. 20
15. 24
28. 19
10. 15
19. 10
6. 15
17. 10
7. 14
31. 27
3. 7
23. 18
Drawn.

GAME 52.
11. 15
23. 19
8. 11
22. 15
9. 14 var
25. 22
11. 16 C.
24. 20
16. 23
27. 11
7. 16
20. 11
3. 7
28. 24
7. 16
24. 19
16. 23
26. 19
4. 8
30. 26
8. 11
26. 23
11. 15 B.
32. 28
15. 24
28. 19
5. 9
29. 25
9. 13
31. 27
1. 5 A.
27. 24
6. 9
24. 20
2. 7
20. 16
14. 18
23. 14
9. 18
22. 6
13. 29
6. 2
7. 10
16. 11
10. 14
2. 6
29. 25
Drawn.

A.
6. 9
27. 24
2. 7
19. 15
10. 26
17. 3
9. 14
3. 7
26. 31
24. 19
31. 27
7. 10
27. 24
10. 17
24. 15
17. 14
1. 5
21. 17
Drawn.

B.
6. 9
17. 13
1. 6
22. 18
2. 7
29. 25
11. 16
32. 27
14. 17
21. 14
10. 17
25. 22
17. 26
31. 22
16. 20
22. 17
W. wins

C.
3. 8
26. 23
5. 9
17. 13
11. 16
24. 20
15. 24
28. 19
1. 5
20. 11
8. 24
27. 20
14. 17
Drawn.

Var.
11. 16
24. 20
16. 23
27. 11
7. 16
20. 11
3. 7

28. 24
7. 16
25. 22
16. 20 C. D.
29. 25
20. 27
31. 24
9. 14 F.
26 23
4 8
24. 19
8. 11
30. 26
11. 16
17. 13
2. 7
22. 18
14. 17
21. 14
10. 17
25. 21
6. 10
21. 14
10. 17
18. 14
17. 21
19. 15
Drawn.

C.
4. 8
26. 23
9. 14
24. 19
8. 11
30. 26
16. 20
17. 13
20. 24
22. 17
11. 16
26. 22
16. 20
31. 27
24. 28
29. 25
20. 24
W wins.

D.
10. 15
24. 20
16. 19
17. 13
4. 8
31. 27 E.
8. 11
32. 28
9. 14
29. 25
6. 10
27. 24
5. 9
13. 6
2. 9
22. 17
9. 13
25. 22
1. 5
26. 23
19. 26
30. 23
5. 9
24. 19
15. 24
28. 19
11. 15
20. 16
15. 24
16. 11
24. 27
11. 7
27. 31
7. 3
31. 27
23. 19
27. 23
19. 15
10. 19
17. 10
19. 24
10. 6
B wins.

E.
30. 25
2. 7
22. 18
15. 22
25. 18
7. 10
29. 25
10. 14
18. 15
14. 17
21. 14
9. 18
20. 16
18. 23
26. 22
19. 24
16. 11
12. 16
11. 4
23. 27
Drawn.

F.
12. 16
24. 20
16. 19
17. 14
9. 18
22. 15
6. 9
15. 6
1. 10
20. 16
2. 7
32. 27
9. 14
8. 12
5. 9
25. 22
9 13
27. 23
19. 24
22. 18
14. 17
21. 14
10. 17
18. 15
24. 27
23. 18
27. 31
26. 23
31. 26
23. 19
26. 23
18. 14
23. 16
15. 11
17. 22
11. 2
13. 17
14. 10
16. 19
2. 7
19. 23
7. 3
Drawn.

GAME 53.
11. 15
22. 17
8. 11
23. 19
4. 8
25. 22
15. 18
22. 15
11. 18
17. 13
9. 14
29. 25
14. 17 var
21. 14
10. 17
26. 22 A.
17. 26
31. 15
7. 11
30. 26
11. 18
26. 22
5. 9
22. 15
9. 14
24. 20
14. 17
27. 24
2. 7
25. 21
17. 22
20. 16
22. 26
32. 27
26. 31
15. 10
7. 14
16. 11
8. 15
19. 10
6. 15
24. 20
31. 24
28. 10
14. 18
13. 9
18. 23
Drawn.

A.
24. 20
17. 21
26. 23
6. 10
23. 14
10. 17
27. 23
8. 11
31. 26 E.
1. 6
28. 24
7. 10 C
32. 28
11. 15
25. 22
3. 7
20. 16
7. 11
16. 7
2. 11
23. 18 B.
6. 9
13. 6
5. 9
22. 13
15. 31
24. 20
31. 27
6. 2
27. 24
13. 6
24. 15
6. 1
10. 14
1. 6
14. 18
Drawn.

B.
24. 20
15. 24
28. 19
11. 15
23. 18
15. 24
18. 14
10. 15
14. 10
24. 27
10. 1
27. 31
1. 6
15. 18
Drawn

C.
6. 10
25. 22
11. 15 D
32. 27
7. 11
23. 18
5. 9
13. 6
2. 9
22. 6
15. 31
6. 1
10. 14

14. 17
6. 10
17. 22
10. 14
22. 25
14. 18
25. 29
19. 15
3. 8
15. 10
W. wins.

D.
2. 6
22. 18
5. 9
32. 27
10. 14
19. 15
3. 8
24. 19
7. 10
27. 24
12. 16
19. 3
10. 28
3. 7
28. 32
7. 16
32. 28
W. wins.

E.
28. 24
7. 10
31. 26
3. 7 F.
25. 22
1. 5
22. 18
10. 14
18. 9
5. 14
32. 28
14. 18
Drawn.

F.
11. 15
25. 22
1. 6 G.
20. 16
3. 7
22. 18
W. wins.

G.
3. 7
20. 16
7. 11
16. 7
2. 11
32. 28
1. 6
24. 20
15. 24
28. 19
11. 15
19. 16
12. 19
23. 16
Drawn.

Var.
5. 9 M.
26. 23
1. 5
30. 26
14. 17 L.
21. 14
10. 17
23. 14
9. 18
26. 22
17. 26
31. 15
7. 10 K.
24. 20
2. 7 H.
27. 23
10. 14
28. 24
14. 17
15. 11
W. wins.

L.
7. 11
19. 15
10. 19
24. 15
3. 7
26. 22
W. wins.

H.
3. 7
27. 23
5. 9
25. 21 I.
9. 14
13. 9
6. 13
15. 6
2. 9
19. 15
7. 11
15. 10
11. 15
28. 24
13. 17
10. 6
9. 13
6. 2
17. 22
2. 6
22. 26
W. wins.

I.
23. 18
7. 11
32. 27
10. 14
27. 23
14. 17
25. 21
9. 14
18. 9
11. 27
21. 14
8. 11
9. 5
6. 9
13. 6
W. wins.

K.
5. 9
27. 23
7. 10
24. 20
9. 14
25. 21
3. 7
13. 9
6. 13
15. 6
2. 9
19. 15
7. 11
15. 10
11. 15
28. 24
8. 11
10. 6
11. 15
24. 19
W. wins.

M.
7. 11
24. 20
11. 15
26. 22
15. 24
28. 19
10. 15
19. 10
6. 15
30. 26
8. 11
26. 23
12. 16
22. 17
2. 6 N.
17. 10
18. 22
25. 18
15. 22
10. 7
3. 10
27. 24
W. wins.

N.
2. 7
17. 10
7. 14
31. 26
1. 6
32. 28
5. 9
26. 22
3. 7
28. 24
7. 10
W. wins.

GAME 54.

11. 15
22. 17
8. 11
23. 19
4. 8
25. 22
9. 13
17. 14
10. 17
19. 10
6. 15
21. 14
15. 19
24. 15
11. 25
30. 21
8. 11
29. 25
11. 15
25. 22
12. 16
27. 23
2. 6
32. 27
16. 20
23. 19
15. 24
28. 19
6. 10
22. 17
13. 22
26. 17
1. 6
31. 26
20. 24
Drawn.

GAME 55.

11. 15
22. 17
8. 11
23. 19
4. 8 var.
25. 22
9. 13
27. 23
6. 9
23. 18
9. 14
18. 9
5. 14
26. 23
2. 6
30. 25
6. 9
31. 27
1. 5
23. 18
14. 23
27. 18
9. 14
18. 9
5. 14
24. 20
15. 24
28. 19
11. 15
22. 18
14. 23
19. 16
12. 19

32. 28
13. 22
Drawn.

Var.
9. 13
17. 14
10. 17
21. 14
15. 18
19. 15
4. 8
24. 19
6. 9F.G.
28. 24
13. 17 E.
24. 20
9. 13
32. 28
2. 6 D.
28. 24
17. 21
26. 23
18. 22A.B.
25. 18
6. 10
15. 6
1. 17
18. 15
11. 18
23. 14
8. 11
29. 25
11. 15
19. 10
17. 22
25. 18
5. 9
14. 5
7. 32
24. 19
13. 17
Drawn.

A.
6. 10
15. 6
1. 17
28. 14
11. 15
19. 10
17. 22
25. 18
5. 9
14. 5
7. 32
31. 27
32. 23
24. 19
Drawn.

B.
13. 17
31. 26
6. 9
14. 10
7. 14
25. 22
18. 25
29. 6
11. 18
6. 2
5. 9
19. 15
9. 13
23. 19
13. 17
26. 23
18. 22 C.
20. 16
22. 26
16. 11
26. 31
11. 4
31. 26
W. wins.

C.
17. 22
15. 10
22. 26
19. 15
W. wins.

D.
1. 6
28. 24
17. 21
26. 23
13. 17
31. 26
6. 9
20. 16
11. 20
25. 22
18. 25
29. 6
2. 18
23. 14
7. 11
15. 10
11. 16
26. 23
8. 11
10. 6
W. wins.

E.
11. 16
15. 11
8. 15
19. 10
16. 20
24. 19
13. 17
25. 22
18. 25
19. 6
2. 18
20. 6
1. 10
19. 16
12. 19
W. wins.

F.
13. 17
28. 24
11. 16
26. 23
16. 20
31. 26
17. 21
15. 10
6. 15
19. 10
8. 11
25. 22
18. 25
29. 22
11. 15
23. 19
2. 6
26. 23
6. 9
22. 17
Drawn.

G.
6. 10
15. 6
1. 17
25. 22
18. 25
30. 14
13. 17 I.
27. 23
2. 6 H.
23. 18
17. 21
26. 23
11. 16
28. 24
6. 9
32. 27
Drawn.

H.
11. 16
26. 22
17. 26
31. 22
16. 20
32. 27
8. 11
22. 18
7. 10
14. 7
3. 10
18. 15
11. 18
23 7
2. 11
Drawn.

I.
2. 6
29. 25
13. 17
25. 21
11. 16 K.
14. 10
16. 30
21. 14
6. 15
31. 26
30. 23
27. 2
8. 11
2. 6
11. 15
6. 10
15. 18
W. wins.

L.
6. 10
27. 23 M.
11. 16
28. 24
16. 20
32. 28
20. 27
31. 24
8. 11
24. 20
W. wins.

M.
27. 24
11. 15
24. 20
15. 24
28. 19
8. 11
32. 27
3. 8 N.
27. 23
17. 22
Drawn.

N.
11. 15
19. 16
12. 19
20. 16
3. 8
W. wins.

GAME 56.
11. 15
22. 17
8. 11
23. 19
4. 8var.
25. 22
9. 13
27. 23
6. 9
23. 18
9. 14
18. 9
5. 14
26. 23
2. 6
24. 20
15. 24
28. 19
10. 15 C.
19. 10
6. 15
17. 10
7. 14
31. 28
3. 7A.B
23. 18
14. 23
27. 18
15. 19
30. 26
19. 24
29. 25

1. 6
21. 17
7. 10
17. 14
10. 17
25. 21
12. 16
21. 14
8. 12
14. 9
6. 10
9. 6
10. 15
18. 14
15. 19
6. 2
19. 23
26. 19
16. 23
22. 18
24. 27
14. 10
27. 31
10. 7
31. 26
7. 3
26. 22
18. 14
11. 15
3. 7
Drawn.

A.
1. 6
22. 17
18. 22
30. 26
22. 31
32. 28
31. 24
28. 1
11. 15
1. 6
8. 11
29. 25
12. 16
6. 10
15. 18
W. wins.

B.
15. 18
22. 15
11. 18
29. 25
1. 6
30. 26
3. 7
23. 19
13. 17
27. 23
W. wins.

C.
6. 9
30. 26
11. 15 E.
23. 28
15. 24
28. 19
8. 11
19. 16
12. 19
23. 16
1. 6 D.
26. 23
11. 15
22. 18
15. 22
16. 11
7. 16
20. 11
W. wins.

D.
11. 15
16. 11
7. 16
20. 11
15. 19
11. 7
19. 24
7. 2
W. wins.

E.
1. 5
32. 27
11. 15
20. 16
15. 24
27. 20
12. 19
23. 16
8. 12 F.
16. 11
7. 16
20. 11
W. wins.

F.
8. 11
26. 23
11. 15
16. 11
7. 16
20. 11
W. wins.

Var.
9. 13
25. 22
6. 9
27. 23
9. 14
24. 20
15. 24
28. 19
11. 15
32. 28
15. 24
28. 19
7. 11 I.
19. 16
12. 19
23. 7
2. 11
26. 23
11. 15 G.H.
20. 16
3. 7
22. 18
15. 22
23. 19
14. 18
17. 14
10. 17
21. 14
1. 6
19. 15
18. 23
30. 25
23. 26
25. 18
26. 30
Drawn.

G.
5. 9
23. 19
11. 15
19. 16
15. 19
16. 11
3. 8
11. 7
8. 11
7. 2
1. 6
22. 18
13. 22
2. 7
14. 23
7. 5
W. wins.

H.
4. 8
22. 18
13. 22
18. 9
5. 14
30. 25
22. 26
31. 22
3. 7
22. 18
14. 17
21. 14
10. 17
25. 21
17. 22
23. 19
22. 26
21. 17
1. 6
18. 14
6. 10
14. 9
8. 12
9. 6
Drawn.

I.
4. 8
30. 25
8. 11 K.
22. 18
13. 22
18. 9
5. 14
29. 5
1. 5 L.
26. 22
5. 14
22. 18
14. 17
21. 14
10. 17
19. 15
Drawn.

K.
7. 11
22. 18
13. 22
18. 9
5. 14
25. 9
11. 15
19. 16
12. 19
23. 16
8. 12
16. 11
1. 5
9. 6
2. 9
11. 7
10. 14
7. 2
3. 7
2. 18
14. 30
21. 17
9. 13
10. 14
13. 17
14. 10
17. 22
Drawn.

L.
11. 15
19. 16
12. 19
23. 16
1. 5
16. 11
7. 16
20. 11
5. 14
26. 23
15. 18
29. 25
18. 27
31. 24
14. 18
21. 17
18. 23
24. 19
23. 26
25. 21
26. 31
17. 14
10. 17
21. 14
Drawn

GAME 57
22. 17
11. 15
23. 19

8. 11
25. 22
4. 8
29. 25
9. 13
17. 14
10. 17
19. 10
7. 14
22. 18
14. 23
21. 14
11. 16
27. 18
3. 7
24. 20
16. 19
32. 27
6. 10
25. 21
10. 17
21. 14
1. 6
27. 24
19. 23
26. 19
6. 10
30. 26
10. 17
26. 22
17. 26
31. 22
2. 6
18. 15
7. 10
20. 16
10. 14
15. 11
8. 15
19. 1
12. 19
24. 15
14. 18
1. 6
Drawn.

GAME 58.

11. 16
22. 18
10. 14
25. 22
8. 11
29. 25
4. 8
24. 20
16. 19
23. 16
14. 23
27. 18
12. 19
32. 27
9. 14
18. 9
5. 14
22. 17 A.
19. 23
26. 19
8. 12
17. 10
6. 24
28. 19
11. 16
20. 11
7. 32
B. wins.

A.

27. 23
8. 12
23. 16
12. 19
31. 27
6. 10
27. 23
3. 8
23. 17
8. 12
26. 23
12. 36
30 23
10. 15
22. 17
7. 10
25. 22
3. 7
28. 24
1. 5
23. 19
14. 18
Drawn.

GAME 59.

11. 16
22. 18
10. 14
25. 22
8. 11
29. 25
4. 8
18. 15
11. 18
22. 15
16. 20
26. 22 A.
14. 18
23. 14
9. 18
24. 19
7. 11
27. 24
20. 27
32. 14
11. 18
22. 15
6. 10
14. 7
2. 18
28. 24
3. 7
21. 17
7. 10
17. 14
10. 17
25. 22
18. 25
30. 14
8. 11
Drawn.

A.

24. 19
7. 10
19. 16
10. 19
25. 22
2. 7
22. 18
7. 10
18. 15
3. 7
27. 24
20. 27
31. 24
14. 17
Drawn.

GAME 60.

11. 15
22. 17
8. 11
23. 19
4. 8
25. 22
9. 13
27. 23
6. 9
23. 18
9. 14
18. 9
5. 14
26. 23
2. 6 B.
30. 25
6. 9
31. 27
1. 5
23. 18
14. 23
27. 18
12. 16†
19. 12
10. 14
17. 10
7. 23
24. 19
15. 24
28. 19
23. 26
19. 15 A.
11. 18
22. 15
26. 30
32. 28
13. 17
21. 14
9. 18
25. 21
30. 26
28. 24 D.
26. 23
15. 10
8. 11
10. 6
18. 22
21. 17 E.
23. 18
6. 1
11. 16
24. 20
16. 19
1. 6
18. 15
17. 14
19. 23
6. 1
15. 11
1. 6
23. 26
6. 1
26. 30
1. 6
30. 26
B. wins.

A.

32. 28
26. 31
28. 24
31. 27
24. 20
3. 7
12. 3
27. 24
3. 10
24. 6
21. 17
6. 10
25. 21
10. 6
29. 25
B. wins.

B.

1. 5
30. 25
5. 9
32. 27
2. 6
22. 18
15. 22 C.
25. 18
13. 22
24. 20
12. 16
19. 12
W. wins.

C.

13. 22
24. 20
15. 24
28. 19
12. 16
19. 12
W. wins.

D.

21. 17
26. 23
15. 10
8. 11
10. 6
18. 22
6. 1
23. 18
1. 6
18. 15
17. 14
11. 16
6. 9

16. 19
9. 13
19. 23
13. 9
23. 26
9. 6
26. 30
14. 10
5. 9
B. wins.

E.
24. 20
23. 18
6. 1
5. 9
1. 5
18. 14
21. 17
14. 21
5. 14
22. 26
14. 18
26. 31
18. 23
11. 15
B. wins.

GAME 61.
22. 17
11. 15
23. 19
8. 11
25. 22
9. 13
17. 14
10. 17
19. 10
7. 14
29. 25
2. 7
27. 23
6. 10 A.
31. 27
4. 8
24. 20
12. 16 D.
27. 24
8. 12
24. 19
5. 9 B.
19. 15
10. 19
23. 18
14. 23
21. 5
7. 10
25. 21
10. 15
28. 24
19. 28
26. 10
16. 19
21. 17
Drawn.

A.
11. 16
31. 27
16. 20
23. 18
14. 23
21. 14
6. 9
27. 18
20. 27
32. 23
4. 8
23. 19
8. 11
28. 24
11. 16
24. 20
16. 23
26. 19
1. 6
25. 21
6. 10
21. 17
7. 11
14. 7
3. 10
19. 16
12. 19
17. 14
10. 26
Drawn.

B.
3. 8
32. 27
5. 9 C.
22. 18
17. 22
26. 17
13. 29
18. 15
11. 18
20. 2
8. 11
21. 17
14. 21
23. 7
11. 16
Drawn.

C.
11. 15
20. 4
15. 31
4. 8
1. 6
8. 3
Drawn.

D.
10. 15
23. 18
14. 23
21. 14
7. 10 F.
27. 18
10. 17
32. 27
12. 16 G. H.
27. 23
8. 12 E.
28. 24
5. 9
23. 19
16. 23
26. 10
17. 26
30. 23
13. 17
23. 19
17. 22
25. 21
22. 26
21. 17
9. 13
17. 14
26. 30
19. 15
30. 26
15. 8
26. 22
14. 9
22. 6
9. 2
Drawn

E.
15. 19
25. 21
1. 6
21. 14
6. 10
14. 7
3. 10
30. 25
Drawn.

F.
15. 18
26. 19
1. 6
22. 15
11. 18
27. 24
13. 17
32. 27
17. 21
19. 15
6. 9
15. 10
9. 13
10. 6
13. 17
6. 2
8. 11
2. 6
11. 15
6. 10
15. 19
Drawn.

G.
3. 7
25. 21
1. 6
21. 14
13. 17
22. 13
15. 31
30. 25
31. 24
28. 19
5. 9
Drawn.

H.
17. 21
20. 16
12. 19
27. 23
19. 24
28. 10
11. 16
23. 19
16. 23
26. 19
8. 12
18. 14
3. 8
10. 7
8. 11
19. 15
W. wins.

GAME 62.
11. 15
22. 17
8. 11
23. 19
4. 8
25. 22
9. 13
17. 14
10. 17
19. 10
7. 14
29. 25
2. 7
27. 23
11. 16 B.
22. 18
6. 10
18. 9
5. 14
24. 20
16. 19 C.
23. 16
12. 19
32. 27
1. 6
27. 23
8. 12
23. 16
12. 19
31. 27
14. 18
21. 14 A.
10. 17
25. 22
18. 25
Drawn.

A.
10. 15
25. 22
6. 10
27. 23
19. 24
28. 19
15. 24
20. 16
10. 15
16. 12
7. 10
23. 18
14. 23

21. 7
3. 10
26. 19
24. 27
12. 8
15. 24
22. 18
27. 31
8. 3
31. 27
3. 7
27. 23
7. 14
13. 17
14. 21
23. 14
Drawn.

B.

11. 15
31. 27
8. 11
24. 20
15. 19
23. 16
12. 19
27. 23
3. 8
23. 16
8. 12
32. 27
12. 19
27. 23
11. 15
23. 16
15. 19
16. 11
7. 16
Drawn.

C.

8. 11
28. 24
10. 15
23. 19
16. 23
26. 10
11. 15
30. 26
7. 11
26. 23
15. 18
31. 26
18. 27
32. 23
11. 15
25. 22
W. wins.

GAME 63.

11. 15
22. 17
8. 11
23. 19
4. 8
25. 22
9. 13
17. 14
10. 17
19. 10
7. 14
29. 25
3. 7
27. 23
11. 16 B.
31. 27
8. 11 A.
22. 18
16. 20
18. 9
5. 14
23. 19
11. 16
19. 15
7. 10
25. 22
10. 19
24. 15
14. 18
21. 14
Drawn.

A.

6. 10
22. 18
8. 11
18. 9
5. 14
24. 20
11. 15
20. 11
7. 16
25. 22
16. 19
23. 16
12. 19
27. 23
1. 6
23. 16
14. 18
21. 7
18. 25
30. 21
2. 20
Drawn.

B.

6. 10
24. 20
1. 6
28. 24
6. 9
24. 19
2. 6
32. 28
14. 18
22. 15
11. 27
31. 24
10. 14
25. 22
7. 11
30. 25
14. 18
22. 15
11. 18
Drawn.

GAME 64.

11. 15
22. 17
8. 11
23. 19
4. 8
25. 22
9. 13
17. 14
10. 17
19. 10
7. 14
29. 25
2. 7
27. 23
6. 10
24. 20
11. 15 B.
28. 24
8. 11
31. 27 E.
12. 16
23. 18
14. 23
26. 12
17. 26
30. 23
5. 9 A.
25. 22
1. 5
21. 17
9. 14
20. 16
14. 21
23. 18
11. 20
Drawn.

A.

13. 17
21. 14
10. 17
32. 28
17. 22
25. 18
15. 22
12. 8
3. 12
23. 19
7. 10
19. 16
12. 19
24. 8
10. 14
Drawn.

B.

12. 16
28. 24
10. 15 C.
23. 18
14. 23
26. 12
17. 26
30. 23
5. 9
32. 28
1. 5
24. 19
15. 24
28. 19
13. 17
21. 14
9. 27
31. 24
Drawn.

C.

8. 12
24. 19
10. 15
19. 10
16. 19
23. 16
12. 19
22. 18
15. 23
21. 14
13. 17 D.
25. 21
11. 15
20. 16
5. 9
14. 5
7. 14
16. 11
15. 18
31. 27
W. wins.

D.

5. 9
14. 5
7. 14
25. 22
3. 7
31. 27
14. 17
27. 18
19. 24
18. 14
W. wins.

E.

32. 28
5. 9 E.
24. 19
15. 24
28. 19
1. 5 G
19. 16
12. 19
23. 16
10. 15
31. 27
15. 18
22. 8
3. 19
26. 22
13. 26
30. 16
7. 10
16. 11
10. 15
27. 24
15. 18
11. 7
13. 17
7. 2
9. 13
2. 6
17. 22
6. 9
22. 29

24 19
29 25
19. 15
25. 22
15. 10
22. 26
20. 16
26. 23
16. 12
23. 19
10. 7
19. 15
7. 2
15. 10
12. 8
13. 17
8. 3
17. 22
2. 7
25. 22
9. 13
18. 23
13. 9
Drawn.

F.

14. 18
23. 14
1. 6
24. 19
15. 24
28. 19
11. 15
20. 16
15. 24
16. 11
Drawn.

G.

3. 8
23. 18
14. 23
21. 5
11. 15
25. 21
15. 24
26. 19
8. 11
22. 18
24. 28
30. 26
28. 32
21. 17
13. 22
26. 17
32. 28
17. 14
10. 17
19. 15
28. 24
15. 8
24. 19
18. 14
19. 15
8. 3
7. 11
3. 8
17. 22
14. 10
15. 6
8. 15
22. 25
31. 27
25. 30
27. 24
30. 26
24. 19
26. 30
19. 16
Drawn.

GAME 65.

9. 14
22. 18
5. 9
25. 22
11. 16
29. 25
16. 20
24. 19
8. 11 A.
21. 17
14. 21
18. 15
11. 18
23. 5
4. 8
22. 18
7. 11
5. 22
1. 16
18. 15
16. 23
26. 19
3. 7
22. 17
7. 11
31. 26
11. 18
27. 24
20. 27
32. 7
2. 11
17. 14
11. 16
28. 24
16. 23
26. 19
Drawn.

A.

1. 5
18. 15
8. 11
15. 8
4. 11
22. 18
9. 13
18. 9
5. 14
25. 22
11. 15
22. 17
15. 24
28. 19
Drawn.

GAME 66.

9. 14
22. 18
11. 15
18. 9
5. 14
23. 19
6. 9 C.
25. 22
9. 13
22. 17
13. 22
26. 17
8. 11
29. 25
14. 18
27. 23
18. 27
32. 23
11. 16 A.
24. 20
15. 24
20. 11
7. 16
28. 19
10. 15
19. 10
2. 6
Drawn.

A.

2. 6
30. 26
6. 9 B.
26. 22
9. 14
31. 26
4. 8
17. 13
1. 6
24. 20
15. 24
28. 19
Drawn.

B.

4. 8
25. 22
6. 9
17. 13
1. 6
22. 17
9. 14
24. 20
15. 24
28. 19
11. 15
W. wins.

C.

8. 11
25. 22
3. 8
22. 17
11. 16
26. 22
16. 23
27. 9
6. 13
30. 26
12. 16 D.
32. 27
16. 20
24. 19
15. 24
28. 19
8. 11
17. 14
10. 17
21. 14
4. 8
29. 25
8. 12
26. 23
1. 6
14. 9
6. 10
22. 18
11. 15
18. 11
7. 16
25. 22
10. 14
19. 15
16. 19
23. 16
12. 19
Drawn.

D.

8. 11
17. 14
10. 17
21. 14
4. 8
24. 19
15. 24
28. 19
11. 16
26. 23
16. 20
32. 27
8. 11
29. 25
Drawn.

GAME 67

22. 18
9. 13
25. 22
5. 9 A.
29. 25
10. 15
21. 17
7. 10
25. 21
1. 5
23. 19
9. 14
18. 9
5. 14
26. 23
6. 9 B.
30. 26
11. 16 C. D.
24. 20
15. 24
28. 19
3. 7 E.
20. 11
8. 24
27. 20
12. 16 F.
20. 11
7. 16
32. 28

4. 8
28. 24
16. 20
24. 19
8. 11
19. 16
20. 24
16. 7
2. 11
22. 18
13. 22
26. 17
10. 15
Drawn.

B.
15. 18
22. 15
13. 22
30. 26
11. 18
Drawn.

A.
11. 16
29. 25
16. 19
23. 16
12. 19
24. 15
10. 19
27. 24
7. 10
24. 15
10. 19
31. 27
2. 7
27. 24
7. 10
24. 15
10. 19
32. 27
3. 7
18. 14
7. 11
27. 24
6. 9

24. 15
11. 18
22. 15
9. 18
15. 10
5. 9
10. 7
8. 12
7. 3
4. 8
26. 22
18. 23
21. 17
23. 27
17. 14
9. 18
22. 15
27. 31
3. 7
1. 6
7. 2
6. 9
2. 7
13. 17
7. 11
9. 14
11. 4
17. 21
25. 22
14. 18
22. 17
W. wins.

C.
2. 6
24. 19
15. 24
28. 19
Drawn.

D.
3. 7
24. 20
15. 24
28. 19
11. 15
20. 16

15. 24
27. 20
12. 19
23. 16
Drawn.

E.
8. 11
27. 24
3. 7
32. 28
4. 8
22. 18
13. 22
26. 17
9. 13
18. 9
13. 22
21. 17
22. 25
17. 13
10. 14
9. 6
W. wins.

F.
7. 11
23. 19
4. 8 G.
32. 28
11. 15
28. 24
14. 18
Drawn.

G.
11. 15
32. 28
15. 24
28. 19
4. 8
19. 15
Drawn.

GAME 68.
22. 18
9. 14

18. 9
5. 14 B.
25. 22
11. 15
23. 19
8. 11
22. 17
3. 8 D.
29. 25
11. 16
17. 13
16. 23
27. 9
1. 5
25. 22
5. 14
22. 17
12. 16 E.
26. 23
16. 20
24. 19 F.
15. 24
28. 19
7. 11
30. 25 G.
20. 24
25. 22
11. 15
19. 16
8. 12
16. 11
12. 16
11. 7 A.
2. 11
32. 28
24. 27
31. 24
16. 20
24. 19
15. 24
28. 19
11. 15
19. 16
4. 8
16. 11
15. 19
23. 16

8. 15
16. 11
14. 18
Drawn.

A.
32. 28
16. 19
23. 16
14. 18
28. 19
18. 25
17. 14
15. 24
14. 7
24. 27
31. 24
4. 8
Drawn.

B.
6. 13
25. 22
11. 15
23. 18
5. 9
18. 11
8. 15
26. 23
4. 8
23. 18
8. 11
27. 23
10. 14
24. 19
15. 24
28. 19
7. 10
32. 27
3. 7
29. 25
11. 16
18. 15 C.
1. 5
15. 6
13. 17
22. 13

14. 18
23. 14
16. 32
14. 10
7. 14
6. 1
14. 17
13. 6
2. 9
21. 14
9. 18
Drawn.

C.
30. 26
16. 20
18. 15
2. 6
15. 11
7. 16
22. 18
10. 15
18. 11
14. 18
23. 5
16. 30
11. 7
Drawn

D.
6. 9
17. 13
1. 5
13. 6
2. 9
29. 25
4. 8
27. 23
14. 17
21. 14
9. 27
32. 23
5. 9
25. 22
9. 14
30. 25
14. 18

23. 14
10. 17
22. 13
W. wins.

E.

7. 11
26. 23
15. 18
23. 19
18. 22
19. 15
11. 18
24. 19
6. 9
W. wins.

F.

32. 27
8. 11
24. 19
15. 24
28. 19
11. 15
19. 16
7. 11
16. 7
2. 11
30. 26
4. 8
26. 22
8. 12
27. 24
Drawn.

G.

19. 16
8. 12
16. 7
2. 11
31. 26 H.
11. 15
32. 28
15. 18
23. 19
18. 22
26. 23
4. 8
19. 15
Drawn.

H.

23. 19
4. 8
30. 25
20. 24
32. 28
11. 25
25. 22
8. 11
22. 18
15. 22
19. 15
Drawn.

GAME 69.

9. 13
22. 18
10. 15
25. 22
6. 10
18. 14
10. 17
21. 14
15. 19 A.
24. 15
11. 25
30. 21
8. 11
29. 25
11. 15
25. 22
4. 8
23. 18
8. 11
28. 24
12. 16
24. 20
16. 19
27. 23
19. 24
14. 9
5. 14
18. 9
24. 28
9. 5
7. 10
23. 18
15. 19
18. 14
10. 17
21. 14
2. 7
22. 18
7. 10
14. 7
3. 10
18. 15
11. 18
26. 23
18. 27
31. 6
Drawn.

A.

15. 18
22. 15
11. 18
29. 25
8. 11
24. 19
4. 8
28. 24
1. 6
24. 20
6. 10
32. 28
10. 17
23. 14
2. 6 B.
27. 24
17. 21
25. 22
6. 9 C.
22. 18
13. 17
26. 22
17. 26
31. 22
9. 13
19. 15
W. wins.

B.

11. 16
20. 4
3. 8
4. 11
7. 32
14. 10
17. 21
25. 22
5. 9
10. 6
9. 14
6. 1
W. wins

C.

6. 10
22. 17
13. 22
26. 17
11. 15
31. 26
8. 11
26. 22
3. 8
19. 16
12. 19
22. 18
15. 22
24. 6
W. wins

STURGES' CELEBRATED COLLECTION OF 150 CRITICAL POSITIONS, TO BE WON OR DRAWN BY SCIENTIFIC PLAY.

*** Throughout these Critical Situations the White are supposed to have occupied the lower half of the board: their men are, consequently, moving upwards.

No. 1. *White to move and win* *

No. 2. *White to move and win.*

No. 3. *White to move and draw.*†

No. 4. *Either to move, W. win.*

* This situation occurs in a great number of games, and ought to be well understood.

† This situation often occurs when each player has equal men on different parts of the board; Black, however, not being able to extricate those men, it becomes a draw.

No. 5. *White to move and win.*

No. 6. *White to move and draw.**

No. 7. *Either to move, B. win.*†

No. 8. *White to move and win.*

No. 9. *White to move and win.*

No. 10. *Black to move and win.*

* This situation, though apparently simple, should be noted.

† White loses through being unable to keep command of square 20.

No. 11. *White to move and win.*

No. 12. *White to move and draw.*

No. 13. *White to move and win.*†

No. 14. *White to move and win.*

No. 15. *B. to move, W. to win.**

No. 16. *White to move and win.*

* Similar endings often occur.

No. 17. *B. to move, W. to draw.**

No. 18. *White to move and win.*†

No. 19. *B. to move W. to win.*‡

No. 20. *White to move and win.*

No. 21. *White to move and win.*

No. 22. *White to move and win.*

* An instructive position. ‡ A very neat piece of play.

† White can force the game in a few moves. Three kings win against two, whenever the Black are in the double corners, as above.

No. 23. *White to move and draw.*

No. 24. *White to move and win.*

No. 25. *White to move and win.*

No. 26. *Black to move and draw.*

No. 27. *White to move and win.*

No. 28. *White to move and win.*

DRAUGHTS.

No. 29. *White to move and win.*

No. 30. *White to move and win.*

No. 31. *White to move and win.*

No. 32. *White to move and win.*

No. 33. *Black to move and win.*

No. 34. *White to move and win.*

No. 35. *White to move and win.*

No. 36. *B. to move, W. to draw.*

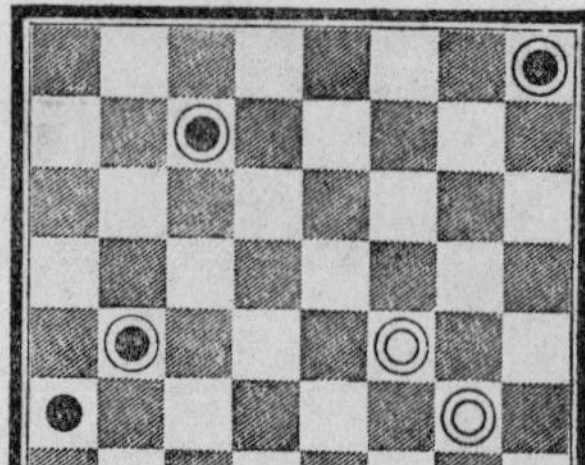
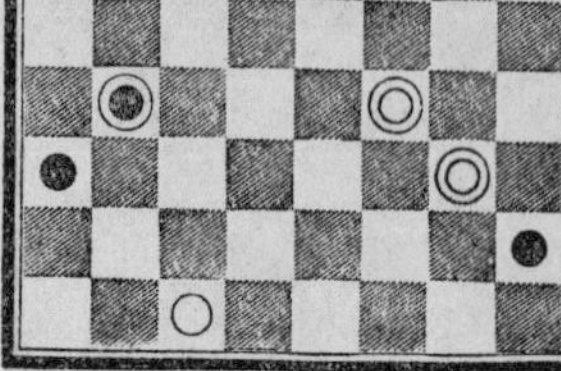

No. 37. *White to move and win.*

No. 38. *White to move and win.*

No. 39. *White to move and win* *

No. 40. *B. to move, W. to win.*

* This position, though it could never occur in play, is not the less curious.

No. 41. *B. to move, W. to draw.*

No. 42. *White to move, B. wins.**

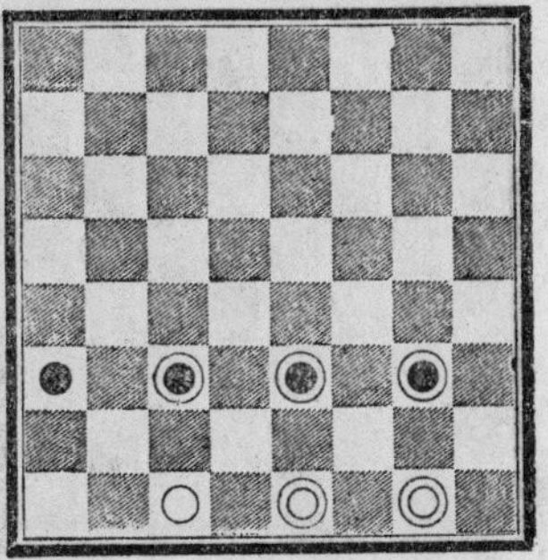

No. 43. *White to move and win.*

No. 44. *Black to move and win.*

No. 45. *White to move and win.*

No. 46. *White to move and win.*

* The same as No. 41, with the difference of the move.

No. 47. *White to move and win.*

No. 48. *White to move and win.*

No. 49. *White to move and win.*

No. 50. *Black to move and win.*

No. 51. *White to move and win.*

No. 52. *White to move and win.*

No. 53. *White to move and win.*

No. 54. *White to move and win.*

No. 55. *White to move and win.*

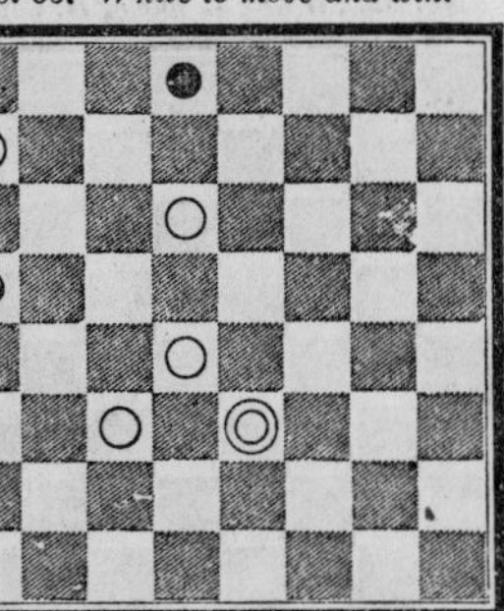

No. 56. *White to move and win.*

No. 57. *B. to move, W. to win.*

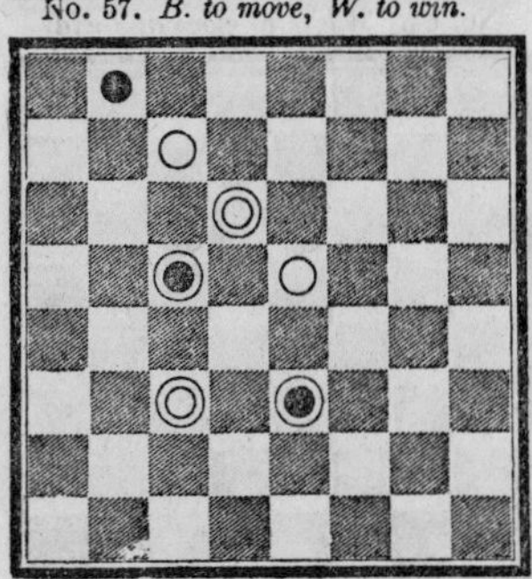

No. 58. *White to move and win.*

No. 59. *White to move and win*

No. 60. *White to move and win.*

No. 61. *White to move and win.*

No. 62. *White to move, B. wins.*

No. 63. *White to move and win.*

No. 64. *White to move and win.*

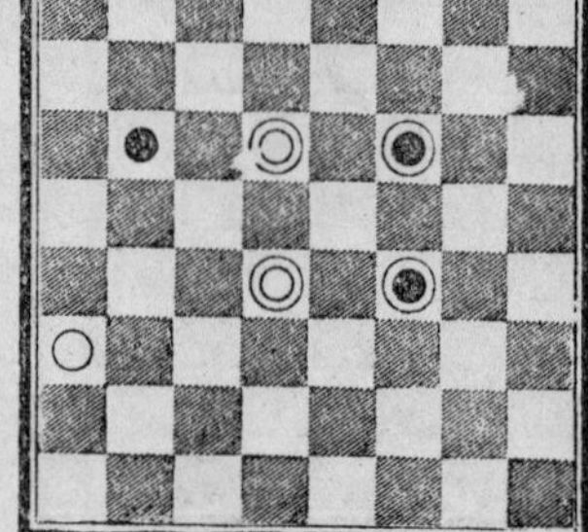

No. 65. *White to move and win.*

No. 66. *White to move and win.*

No. 67. *White to move and win.*

No. 68. *Black to move and win.*

No. 69. *White to move and win.*

No. 70 *White to move and win.*

No. 71. *White to move and win.*

No. 72. *White to move and win.*

No. 73. *White to move and win.*

No. 74. *White to move and win.*

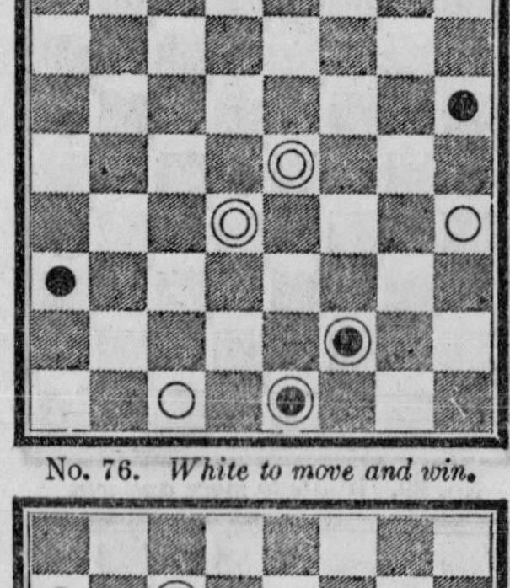

No. 75. *White to move and win.*

No. 76. *White to move and win.*

No. 77. *White to move and win.*

No. 78. *Black to move and win.*

No. 79. *Black to move and draw.*

No. 80. *White to move and win.*

No. 81. *White to move and win.*

No. 82. *White to move and win.*

No. 83. *White to move and win*

No. 84. *White to move and win.*

No. 85. *White to move and win.*

No. 86. *White to move and win.*

No. 87. *White to move and win.*

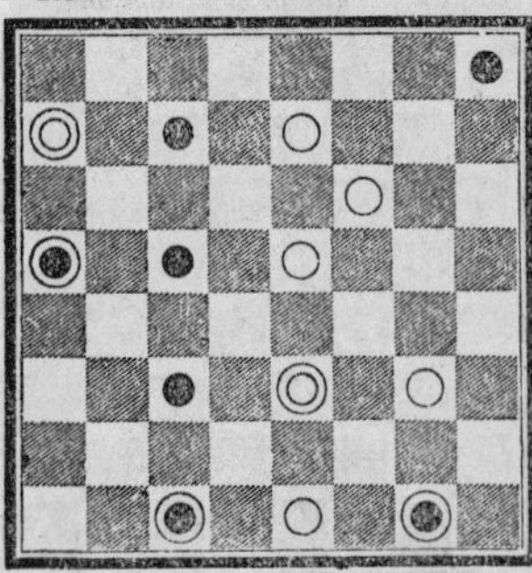

No. 88. *White to move and win.*

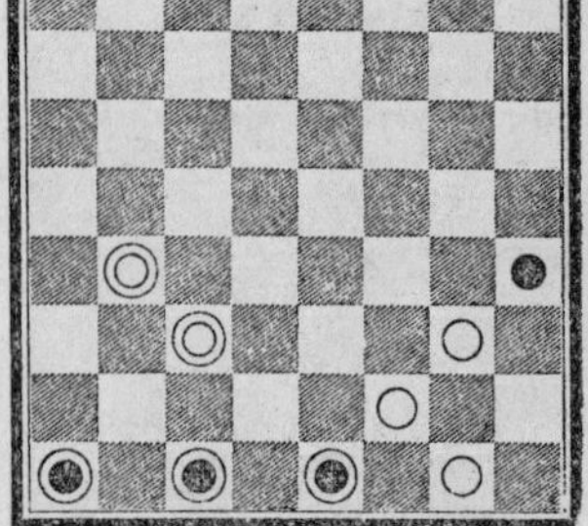

No. 89. *Black to move and win.*

No. 90. *White to move and win.*

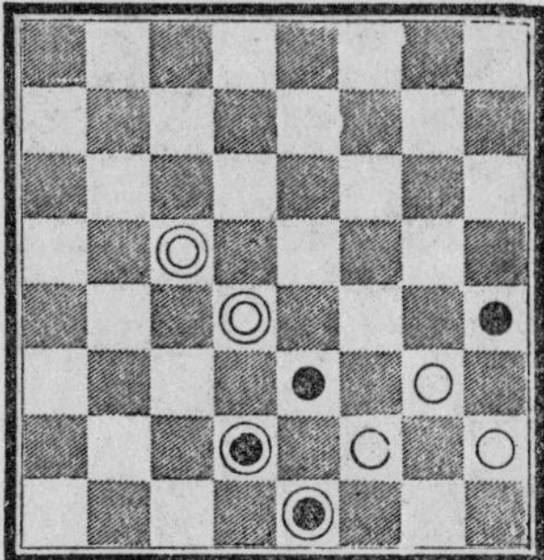

No. 91. *Black to move and draw.*

No. 92. *White to move and win.*

No. 93. *White to move and win.*

No. 94. *White to move and win.*

No. 95. *Black to move and win.*

No. 96. *Black to move and win.*

No. 97. *White to move and win.*

No. 98. *Black to move, W. to win.*

No. 99. *White to move and win.*

No. 100. *Black to move and win.*

No. 101. *Black to move and win.*

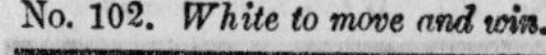

No. 102. *White to move and win.*

No. 103. *White to move and win.*

No. 104. *White to move and win.*

No. 105. *White to move and win.*

No. 106. *Black to move and win.*

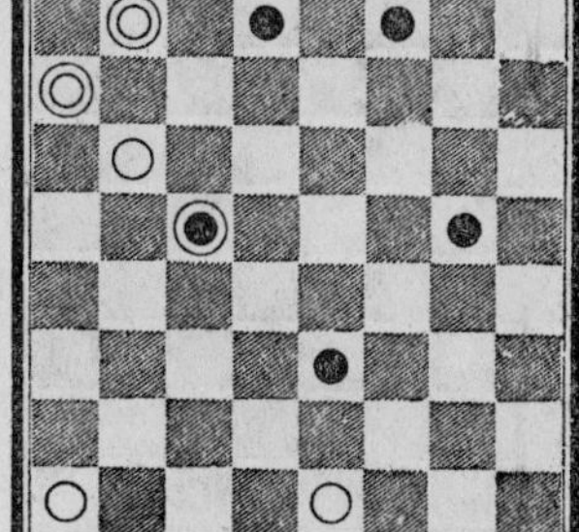

No. 107. *White to move and win.*

No. 108. *White to move and win.*

No. 109. *White to move and win.*

No. 110. *White to move and win.*

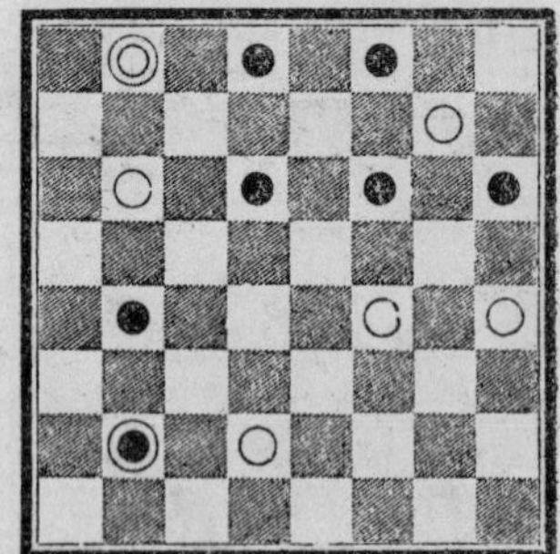

No. 111. *White to move and win.*

No. 112. *White to move and win.*

No. 113. *White to move and win.*

No. 114. *White to move and win.*

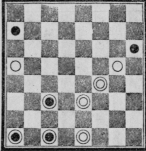

No. 115. *White to move and win.*

No. 116. *White to move and win.*

No. 117. *White to move and win*

No. 118. *White to move and win.*

No. 119. *White to move and win.*

No. 120. *Black to move and win.*

No. 121. *White to move and win.*

No. 122. *White to move and win.*

No. 123. *Black to move and win.*

No. 124. *White to move and win.*

No. 125. *White to move and win.*

No. 126. *White to move and win.*

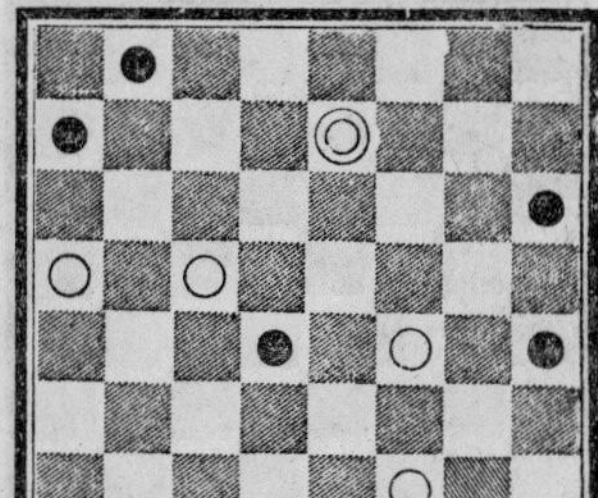

No. 127. *White to move and win.*

No. 128. *White to move and win.*

No. 129. *White to move and win.*

No. 130. *White to move and win.*

No. 131. *White to move and win.*

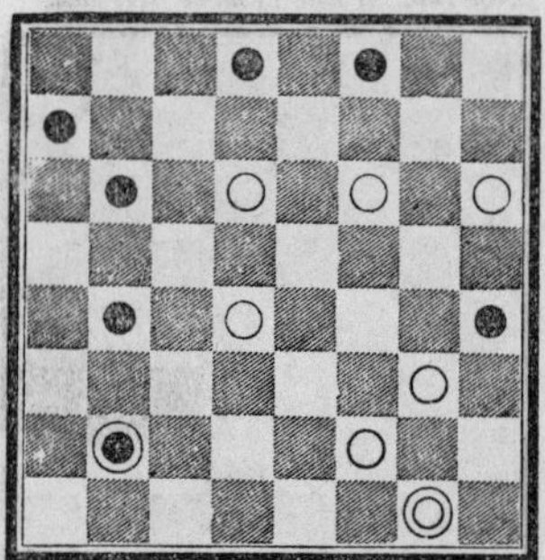

No. 132. *White to move and win.*

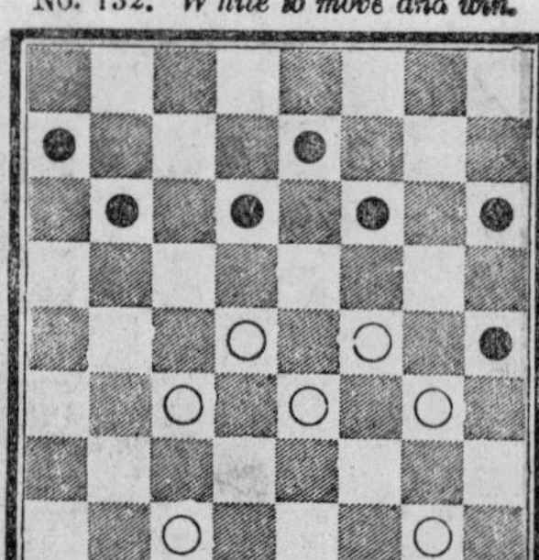

No. 133. *White to move and win.*

No. 134. *Black to move and win.*

No. 135. *White to move and win.*

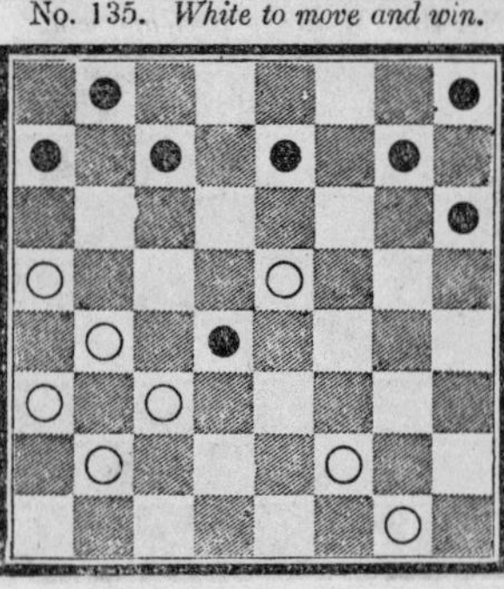

No. 136. *White to move and win.*

No. 137. *White to move and win.*

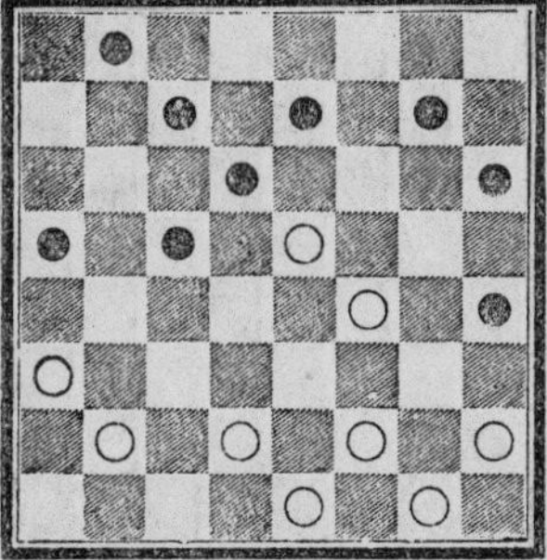

No. 138. *White to move and win.*

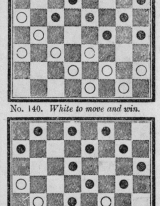

No. 139. *Black to move and win.*

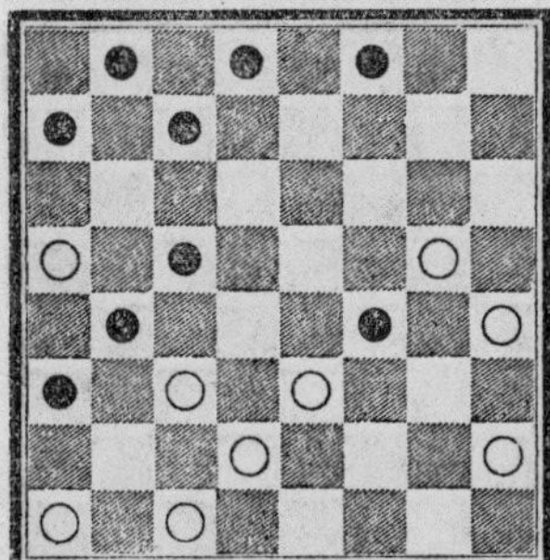

No. 140. *White to move and win.*

No. 141. *White to move and win.*

No. 142. *White to move and win.*

No. 143. *White to move and win.*

No. 144. *White to move and win.*

No. 145. *White to move and win.*

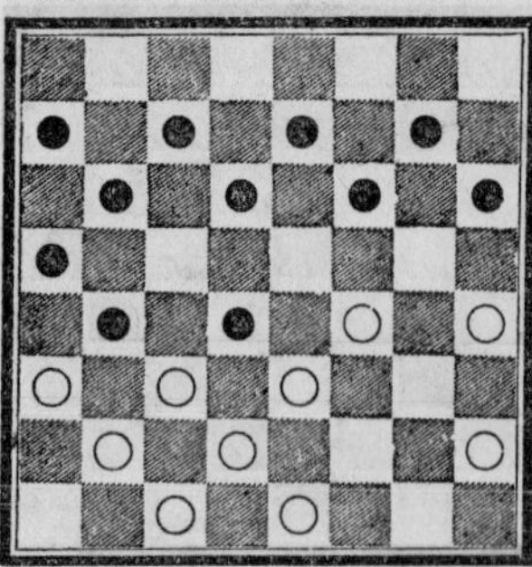

No. 146. *White to move and draw.*

No. 147. *White to move and win.*

No. 148. *White to move and win.*

No. 149. *White to move and win.*

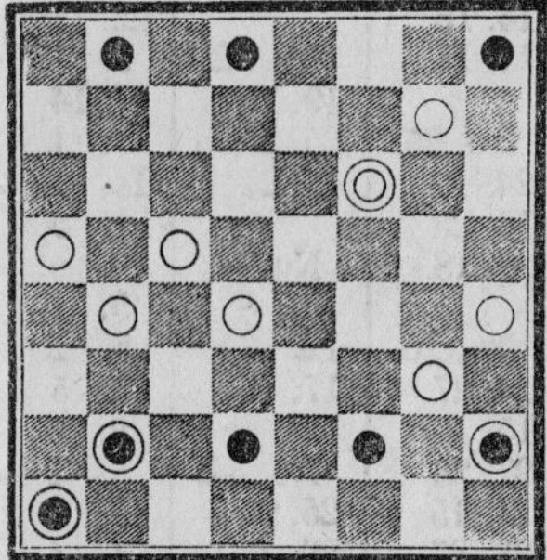

No. 150. *White to move and win.*

SOLUTIONS OF THE FOREGOING HUNDRED AND FIFTY POSITIONS.

No. 1.
27. 32
28. 24
23. 18
24. 28 A.
18. 15
28. 24
32. 28
24. 27
15. 18
12. 16
28. 32
27. 24
18. 15
24. 28
15. 11
16. 19
32. 27
28. 32
27. 31
19. 23
11. 15
32. 28
15. 19

A.
12. 16
18. 15
16. 20
15. 18
24. 19
32. 28
19. 16
18. 23
16. 11
23. 19
11. 8
28. 32
8. 11
32. 27
11. 8
27. 23
8. 3
23. 18
3. 8
18. 15

No. 2.
30. 26
27. 23
19. 15
23. 30
15. 19
21. 25
22. 29
30. 26
29. 25
26. 31
25. 22
31. 27
22. 18
27. 32
18. 23
32. 28
23. 27
28. 32
19. 23
32. 28
See No. 1.

No. 3.
7. 10
9. 13
10. 14
13. 9
14. 10

No. 4.
27. 23
25. 29
23. 18
29. 25
26. 30

No. 5.
24. 19
15. 24
30. 26
21. 30
6. 9

No. 6.
27. 24
18. 15
24. 20
15. 11
20. 24
19. 23
24. 20

No. 7.
31. 27
22. 18
27. 24
18. 15
24. 27
23. 19
27. 24
19. 16
24. 20
15. 11
20. 24
16. 20
24. 27
11. 15
27. 31
20. 24
32. 27
15. 19
27. 20
28. 32

No. 8.
32. 27
28. 32
27. 24
19. 28
26. 23

No. 9.
13. 9
6. 13
15. 6
2. 9
19. 15
7. 11
15. 10
11. 15
28. 24
8. 11
10. 6
15. 18
24. 19

No. 10.
12. 16
24. 20
15. 10
20. 11
10. 1
11. 7

No. 11.
26. 23
32. 28
27. 32
28. 24
32. 28
24. 20
23 19
20. 24
19. 15
24. 27
15. 18
3. 8
18. 15
8. 12
28. 32
27. 24
15. 11
24. 28
32. 27
28. 32

27. 24
32. 28
24. 19
28. 32
11. 15
32. 28
15. 18
28. 32
18. 23
32. 28
23. 27
28. 32
19. 23
32. 28
See No. 1.

No. 12.
15. 11
3. 8
10. 15
8. 3
15. 19
12. 8

No. 13.
18. 22
17. 26
27. 31

No. 14.
26. 22
12. 19
22. 15
19. 23
20. 16
23. 27
25. 21
17. 22
21. 17
27. 32
17. 14
32. 27
15. 11

No. 15.
13. 17
30. 26
5. 9
12. 8
9. 13
26. 30
17. 22
8. 4
13. 17
4. 8
17. 21
8. 11
22. 25
11. 15
25. 29
15. 18
29. 25
30. 26

No. 16.
17. 22
18. 25
27. 23

No. 17.
14. 17
23. 26
15. 10
22. 25
17. 21
25. 22
10. 14
26. 30
14. 17
22. 18

No. 18.
18. 15
6. 1
14. 9
24. 28
23. 19
1. 5
9. 6
28. 32
19. 24
5. 1
24. 19

No. 19.
6. 10
19. 23

No. 20.
7. 10
15. 19
21. 17
9. 14
10. 15

No. 21.
27. 23
32. 27
23. 18
27. 23
18. 15
23. 19
15. 10
19. 12
10. 6
12. 16

No. 22.
26. 23
18. 22
23. 18
16. 19
18. 15
22. 26
30. 16
12. 19
13. 9
6. 13
15. 11
13. 17

No. 23.
15. 19
8. 11
19. 23
11. 15
23. 27

No. 24.
18. 15
9. 14
26. 22
14. 18
15. 11

No. 25.
24. 19
16. 23
22. 18

No. 26.
24. 27
15. 11
27. 23
11. 15
23. 27
15. 19
27. 32

No. 27.
22. 18
15. 22
17. 26
28. 32
27. 24
19. 28
26. 23

No. 28.
11. 7
3. 10
2. 7

No. 29.
30. 25
21. 30
8. 11

No. 30.
32. 27
28. 32
7. 10
32. 23
10. 14

No. 31.
12. 8
11. 4
6. 2

No. 32.
19. 23
25. 29
17. 21

No. 33.
3. 8
12. 3
17. 13

No. 34.
25. 21
26. 17
29. 25

No. 35.
10. 7
15. 8
2. 6

No. 36.
4. 8
19. 23
8. 11
24. 28
11. 16
23. 27
6. 10
28. 32
16. 20
32. 28

No. 37.
10. 6
1. 10
23. 19
8. 11
31. 27
5. 9
27. 23

No. 38.
29. 25
1. 6
25. 22
6. 9
22. 17
9. 6
17. 14
6. 1
14. 9
1. 5
9. 6
5. 1
6. 2
1. 5
2. 6
5. 1
6. 9
1. 5
9. 14
5. 1
14. 18
1. 5
18. 22
5. 9
30. 26
9. 14
26. 23
11. 9
23. 18
9. 5
18. 14
5. 1
14. 9
1. 5
22. 17
5. 14
27. 10

No. 39.
18. 22
17. 26
19. 24
20. 27

No. 40.
28. 24
20. 16
24. 8
17. 14

No. 41.
24. 28
31. 27
23. 19
27. 31
19. 24
32. 27
24. 20
27. 32
22. 18
31. 27
3. 8
24. 20
8. 11
6. 1
11. 15
1. 6
15. 19
20. 16
18. 23
26. 22
23. 26
16. 11
26. 30
11. 7
30. 26

A.
24. 19
18. 23
19. 16
9. 14
10. 6
23. 27
6. 1
14. 10
30. 25
27. 31
25. 21
31. 26
16. 12 B.
10. 14
1. 5
26. 23
5. 1
23. 19
1. 6
19. 15
6. 2
15. 11
2. 6
3. 7
6. 10
14. 18
10. 3
18. 14

B.
21. 17
26. 23
17. 13
10. 14
1. 5
23. 19
16. 12
19. 15
5. 1
15. 10
1. 5
10. 6
2. 6

No. 42.
32. 28
24. 20
28. 32
22. 18
31. 27
23. 19
27. 31
19. 24
32. 27
24. 28
27. 32
18. 22
31. 27
22. 26
30. 23
28. 24

No. 43.
22. 17
21. 25
17. 13
25. 30
14. 9
6. 10
3. 7
11. 2
9. 6

No. 44.
14. 18
30. 26 A.
9. 14
10. 6

No. 45.
7. 10
14. 7
6. 2

No. 46.
15. 10

No. 47.
11. 7

No. 48.
11. 8

No. 49.
10. 7
2. 11
19. 15

No. 50.
21. 25
2. 7
25. 30
7. 11
30. 26
18. 14
26. 23
14. 10
22. 18

No. 51.
9. 6
1. 10

No. 52.
17. 14
10. 17
9. 13

No. 53.
30. 26
22. 31
7. 11

No. 54.
28. 24
20. 27
25. 22

No. 55.
10. 6
23. 14
5. 1
2. 9
1. 5

No. 56.
13. 9
5. 14
6. 10

No. 57.
22. 18
14. 17
18. 11
10. 14

No. 58.
10. 15
17. 21
19. 16
12. 19
15. 24
22. 25
24. 19

No. 59.
30. 26
22. 18
19. 24
28. 19
26. 23

No. 60.
32. 27
23. 32
26. 23

No. 61.
11. 15
23. 30
32. 27

No. 62.
6. 10
27. 32
10. 19
32. 28

No. 63.
19. 24
20. 27
18. 22

No. 64.
21. 17
9. 13
10. 15
19. 10
18. 14
13. 22
14. 16

No. 65.
22. 25
21. 30
6. 2

No. 66.
22. 18
13. 17
10. 6
2. 9
18. 14

No. 67
2. 6
15. 18
6. 10
18. 22
10. 14
22. 25
7. 2
25. 29
2. 7
29. 25
7. 10
25. 21
10. 15
13. 17
15. 19
17. 22
19. 23

No. 68
13. 9
11. 20
9. 2
20. 24
12. 16
24. 28
16. 19
28. 32
19. 24

No. 69
18. 14
9. 18
26. 22
18. 25
24. 19

No. 70
20. 16
19. 10
11. 7

No. 71
21. 17
14. 21
15. 18

No. 72.
24. 20
19. 10
20. 11
10. 7
29. 25
7. 16
31. 26
17. 21
4. 8

No. 73.
15. 11
8. 15
30. 26
22. 31
32. 28

No. 74.
30. 26
31. 22
18. 25
21. 30
20 16

No. 75.
29. 25
21. 30
31. 26
30. 23
22. 18
23. 14
15. 10

No. 76.
28. 24
19. 28
10 19
20. 24
19. 15

No. 77.
27. 24
16. 20
23. 18

No. 78.
5. 9
13. 6
1. 10
7. 14
22. 26

No. 79.
23. 18
11. 7
18. 9
7. 2

No. 80.
22. 18
13. 22

No. 81.
10. 6
1. 10
14. 7
3. 10
17. 14

No. 82.
26. 23
17. 26
19. 16

No. 83.
22. 18
13. 22
8. 3

No. 84.
6. 9
13. 6
2. 9
14. 17
9. 13
17. 22
13. 17
22. 25
17. 22

No. 85.
16. 19
22. 26
11. 16
20. 11
32. 27

No. 86.
12. 8
26. 19
14. 10
4. 11
18. 14

No. 87.
23. 26
30. 23
24. 19
23. 16
31. 27
32. 23
15. 10
6. 15
5. 9
13. 6
7. 3

No. 88.
27. 23
20. 27
17. 21
30. 26
21. 17

No. 89.
6. 9
13. 6
15. 18

No. 90.
14. 9
23. 32
9. 13
20. 27
18. 22

No. 91.
3. 8
12. 3
15. 18

No. 92.
20. 16
12. 19
14. 18

No. 93.
30. 26
18. 9
26. 19
11. 15
10. 6

No. 94.
19. 16
12. 19
21. 17
22. 13
27. 23

No. 95.
11. 15
19. 16
10. 14
16. 11
14. 18
30. 25
18. 23

No. 96.
11. 15
13. 6
15. 19
6. 15
24. 20

No. 97.
3. 7
11. 16
13. 9
6. 13
4. 8

No. 98.
8. 11 B.
14. 9
6. 10
9. 6
10. 14
6. 2
14. 17
2. 7
11. 16
7. 10
17. 22
13. 9
22. 26
9. 6
26. 30 A.
6. 2
30. 26
2. 7
26. 22
10. 15
1. 6
7. 11

A.
1. 5
10. 14
26. 30
6. 2
30. 26
2. 6
26. 22
6. 10
22. 26
10. 15
26. 22
14. 10
5. 9
10. 7
9. 14
7. 11
14. 17
11. 8

B.
8. 12
14. 9
6. 10
9. 6
10. 14
6. 2
14. 18
2. 7
18. 22
13. 9
22. 26
7. 10
1. 5
10. 14
26. 30
9. 6
30. 26
6. 2
26. 31
2. 7
31. 24
28. 19
20. 24
7. 11
24. 28
11. 16
28. 32
16. 20
32. 27
19. 15
27. 23
15. 10
23. 19
10. 6
19. 15
6. 2
15. 11
2. 6
12. 16 C.
14. 18
16. 19
6. 10
5. 9
10. 6
9. 13
6. 10
11. 8
10. 15

C.
11. 15
14. 10

15. 11
6. 9
5. 14
10. 17
12. 16
17. 22
16. 19
22. 18
11. 7
18. 15
19. 23

No. 99.
26. 22
18. 25
19. 16
12. 19

No. 100.
31. 26
25. 22
26. 23
22. 13
12. 16

No. 101.
14. 18
5. 14
23. 19

No. 102.
28. 24
20. 27
26. 23
27. 18
9. 5

No. 103.
23. 19
24. 15
14. 17

No. 104.
30. 25
29. 22
14. 10
5. 14
6. 1

No. 105.
17. 22
25. 18
28. 24
20. 27
2. 6
1. 10
3. 7
11. 2
9. 6

No. 106.
23. 27
31. 24
16. 19
23. 15
14. 10

No. 107.
24. 19
15. 24
30. 25
21. 30
32. 28

No. 108.
23. 19
16. 23
22. 18
13. 22
14. 9

No. 109.
24. 19
15. 24
32. 28
22. 15
28. 10
5. 9
6. 2
9. 13
10. 7
11. 15
2. 6
15. 18
6. 10
18. 22
10. 14
22. 25
7. 2
25. 29
2. 7
29. 25
7. 10
25. 21
10. 15
13. 17
15. 19
17. 22
19. 23

No. 110.
26. 22
25. 18
9. 6
2. 9
19. 16
12. 19
1. 5

No. 111.
30. 25
29. 22
31. 27
32. 23
15. 10
14. 7
8. 3

No. 112.
13. 9
23. 32
30. 25
29. 22
8. 3

No. 113.
30. 25
21. 30
23. 26
30. 23
22. 17
13. 22
6. 9

No. 114.
13. 9
5. 14
23. 26
30. 23
19. 10
12. 19
31. 27

No. 115.
30. 25
29. 22
14. 9
5. 14
10. 19
3. 10
19. 23
10. 14
4. 8
14. 17
8. 11
17. 21
11. 15
21. 25
15. 18

No. 116.
17. 14
18. 9
15. 10
6. 15
13. 6
2. 9
11. 25
9. 13
25. 22
5. 9
3. 7
9. 14
7. 10
14. 17
22. 25

No. 117.
28. 24
12. 16
24. 19
16. 23
20. 25
29. 22
13. 9

No. 118.
30. 25
29. 22
23. 18
22. 15
6. 1

No. 119.
22. 18
15. 22
31. 26
22. 31
30. 26
31. 22
21. 17
22. 13
6. 1

No. 120.
20. 16
11. 20
19. 24
28. 19
18. 14
17. 10
27. 24

No. 121
27. 23
18. 27
31. 24
20. 27
30. 26
22. 31

No. 122.
32. 27
31. 24
15. 11
7. 16
30. 26
21. 30
8. 11

No. 123.
19. 23
26. 19
17. 26
30. 23
14. 18

No. 124.
6. 10
14. 17
10. 15
17. 26
27. 24
20. 27
19. 16

No. 125.
17. 14
10. 17
22. 18
15. 22
31. 27
22. 31
5. 1

No. 126.
19. 16
12. 19
14. 10
31. 24
10. 6

No. 127.
21. 17
14. 21
28. 24

No. 128
10. 7
3. 10
23. 18

14. 23
24. 19
23. 16
9. 6

No. 129.
32. 27
31. 24
13. 9
5. 14
21. 17
14. 21
22. 25
21. 30
6. 2

No. 130.
14. 10
7. 14
20. 16
12. 19
27. 23

No. 131.
11. 7
3. 11
27. 23
20. 27
18. 15

No. 132.
22. 17
20. 27
18. 15

No. 133.
12. 8
3. 12
6. 2
23. 16
10. 6
1. 10
7. 14
16. 7
2. 11
5. 9
14. 5
13. 17
5. 9
17. 22
9. 14
22. 26
14. 18
26. 31
18. 22
4. 8
11. 4
12. 16
4. 8
16. 19
8. 11
19. 23
22. 25
31. 26
25. 30

No. 134.
6. 9
13. 6
23. 27
31. 24
10. 15

No. 135.
13. 9
6. 13
15. 10
7. 14
17. 10

No. 136.
26. 22
17. 26
32. 28
10. 17
28. 32
1. 10
27. 24
20. 27
16. 11
7. 16
12. 8
4. 11
19. 12
26. 19
32. 30

No. 137.
19. 16
12. 19
28. 24
19. 28
25. 22
10. 19
22. 17

No. 138.
22. 18
15. 22
13. 9
6. 13
27. 24

No. 139.
14. 18
22. 15
17. 22
26. 17
19. 26
30. 23
6. 9

No. 140.
13. 9
16. 23
17. 13
5. 14
24. 19
15. 24
22. 6
2. 9
13. 6
1. 10
27. 9

No. 141.
28. 24
7. 11
24. 19
4. 8
6. 2
8. 12
2. 7
11. 16
7. 10
16. 23
30. 25
29. 22
14. 9

No. 142.
12. 8
3. 12
19. 16
12. 19
28. 24
19. 28
26. 23
17. 26
20. 24

No. 143.
29. 25
32. 23
2. 7
30. 21
22. 17
13. 22
14. 17

No. 144.
25. 22
23. 16
15. 11
6. 15
13. 6
1. 10
28. 24

No. 145.
22. 15
11. 27
31. 24
10. 14
25. 22
7. 11
30. 25
14. 18
22. 15
11. 18
21. 14
13. 17
14. 10
6. 15
19. 10
9. 18
25. 21
18. 22
21. 14
22. 31
10. 6
13. 17
6. 2
31. 27
2. 6
8. 11
6. 10
11. 16

No. 146.
24. 19
15. 24
28. 19
1. 6
30. 26
6. 10
26. 23
3. 8
19. 16
8. 15
16. 11
2. 6
22. 17
6. 9
17. 13
15. 18
13. 6
18. 27
6. 2
10. 15
2. 6
15. 19
6. 10

No. 147.
23. 18
14. 23
3. 7
5. 14
15. 19
24. 6
7. 10
6. 15
8. 3
15. 8
3. 10
4. 8
10. 15
13. 17
21. 14
29. 25
14. 18

No. 148.
15. 10
19. 12
3. 7
2. 11
32. 27
12. 3
27. 24

No. 149.
14. 9
28. 19
18. 15
19. 10
17. 14
10. 17
9. 6
1. 10
11. 16

No. 150.
18. 15
11. 18
24. 19
2. 11
20. 16
11. 20
29. 25
22. 29
17. 22
18. 25
19. 24
20. 27
14. 10

A SERIES OF ORIGINAL GAMES, BY MR. R. MARTIN.

GAME 1.
11. 15
22. 18
15. 22
25. 18
8. 11
29. 25
4. 8
24. 20
10. 15
25. 22
12. 16
21. 17
8. 12
17. 13
7. 10
27. 24
9. 14
18. 9
5. 14
32. 27
*14. 17 C.
23. 18
17. 21 A.
27. 23
6. 9 B.
13. 6
2. 9
24. 19
15. 24
28. 19
1. 5
22. 17
9. 13
18. 14
13. 22
26. 17
11. 15
14. 7
15. 24
20. 11
3. 10
11. 7
10. 15
7. 2
15. 19
23. 16
12. 19
2. 7
19. 23
7. 11
23. 27
11. 15
27. 32
17. 13
W. wins.

A.
32. 28
18. 14
3. 7
13. 9
6. 13
27. 23
17. 21
23. 19
16. 23
26. 19
10. 26
19. 3
11. 15
31. 22
5. 9
3. 8
9. 14
24. 19
15. 24
28. 19
14. 17
22. 18
17. 22
18. 14
22. 25
8. 11
25. 29
11. 15
29. 25
15. 18
W. wins.

B.
2. 7
23. 19
16. 23
26. 19
W. wins.

C.
2. 7
24. 19
15. 24
28. 19
10. 15 E.
19. 10
6. 15
22. 18
15. 22
26. 10
7. 14
13. 9
14. 17 D.
23. 18
16. 19
9. 6
1. 10
18. 15
11. 18
27. 23
19. 26
31. 6
3. 8
6. 2
8. 11
2. 6
11. 15
6. 10
15. 19
10. 14
17. 21
14. 18
W. wins.†

D.
3. 7
27. 24
14. 17
31. 26
17. 21
26. 22
7. 10
9. 6
10. 15
6. 2
W. wins.

E.
14. 17
13. 9
6. 13
22. 18
10. 14 G.
18. 9
7. 10
27. 24
10. 14 I.
9. 5
17. 21 F.
26. 22
14. 17
31. 26
3. 7
22. 18
17. 22
26. 17
13. 22
19. 15
16. 19
15. 8
19. 28
8. 3
7. 10
3. 7
W. wins.

F.
3. 7
26. 22
17. 26
31. 22
14. 17
22. 18
17. 22
19. 15
W. wins.

G.
10. 15
19. 10
7. 14
18. 9
17. 22 H.
26. 17
13. 22
27. 24
3. 7
24. 19
7. 10
9. 6
11. 15
20. 11
15. 24
6. 2
10. 14
2. 7
14. 17
7. 10
17. 21
10. 14
21. 25
14. 18
25. 29
18. 22
12. 16
11. 7
16. 20
7. 2
24. 27
31. 24
20. 27
23. 18
W. wins

H.
3. 7
27. 24
17. 21
26. 22
W. wins.

I.
17. 22
26. 17
13. 22
9. 6
10. 14
6. 2
14. 18 K.
23. 14
16. 23
24. 19
3. 7
19. 15
11. 18
2. 11
W. wins

K.
14. 17 L.
31. 27
17. 26
19. 15
11. 18
23. 14
16. 19
24. 15
26. 31
27. 24

* This move loses the game.

† See Sturges' 38th critical situation.

31. 27
15. 11
17. 22
14. 10
27. 23
11. 8
23. 27
8. 4
12. 16
20. 11
27. 20
2. 7
20. 16
11. 8
3. 12
10. 6
1. 10
7. 14
W. wins.

L.
3. 7
23. 18
16. 23 N.
18. 9
23. 27 M.
24. 19
27. 32
19. 15
11. 18
2. 11
32. 28
11. 7
18. 23
9. 6
1. 10
W. wins.

M.
7. 10
24. 19
11. 15
2. 6
15. 24
6. 15
W. wins.

N.
14. 23
19. 15
11. 18
2. 11
23. 27
11. 7
27. 32
20. 11
32. 28
24. 20 O.
18. 23
7. 10
23. 27
31. 24
28. 19
10. 14
19. 23
Draw.

O.
24. 19
28. 24
19. 15
24. 19
15. 10
19. 15
10. 6
15. 8
30. 26
1. 10
7. 23
Draw.

GAME 2.
11. 15
22. 18
15. 22
25. 18
8. 11
29. 25
4. 8
24. 20
10. 15
25. 22
12. 16
21. 17
8. 12
17. 13
7. 10
27. 24
9. 14
18. 9
5. 14
32. 27
2. 7 I.
24. 19
15. 24
28. 19
14. 17
19. 15 D.
10. 19
22. 18
17. 22
26. 17
19. 26
30. 23 A.
16. 19
23. 16
12. 19
17. 14
6. 10
14. 9
19. 23
27. 24
10. 15
18. 14
23. 27
31. 26
27. 32
26. 23
15. 18
23. 19
32. 28
B. wins.

A.
31. 22
16. 19
18. 14 B.
6. 10
13. 9
10. 15
30. 25
19. 24
27. 23
24. 27
25. 21
27. 31
23. 18
31. 26
9. 5
B. wins.

B.
27. 23 C.
19. 26
30. 23
6. 10
13. 9
10. 15
B. wins.

C.
30. 25
11. 16
20. 2
1. 5
2. 9
5. 30
22. 17
30. 26
27. 23
19. 24
B. wins.

D.
27. 24
10. 15
19. 10
6. 15
22. 18 G.
15. 22
13. 9
3. 8
24. 19 E.
7. 10
9. 6
10. 14
6. 2
22. 25
30. 21
14. 18
23. 14
16. 30
B. wins.

E.
23. 18
7. 10
18. 14
10. 15
26. 23
17. 21
9. 5 T.
22. 25
14. 9
25. 29
31. 26
21. 25
30. 21
29. 25
9. 6
1. 10
5. 1
10. 14
1. 6
25. 30
6. 10 F.
15. 18
10. 17
18. 27
26. 23
27. 32
B. wins.

F.
23. 19
30. 23
19. 10
23. 18
6. 2
16. 19
24. 15
14. 17
21. 14
18. 9
B. wins.

G.
23. 19
16. 23
26. 10
7. 14
24. 19
17. 26
30. 23
14. 17
23. 18
1. 6 H.
19. 15
3. 8
31. 26
17. 21
26. 22
21. 25
18. 14
W. wins

H.
17. 22
19. 15
3. 8
15. 10
22. 25
10. 7
25. 30
7. 3
30. 25
18. 14
25. 22
14. 10
22. 18
10. 7
11. 15
20. 16
12. 19
3. 12
19. 24
13. 9
1. 5
12. 16
Draw.

I.
1. 5

24. 19
15. 24
28. 19
3. 7
22. 18
14. 17
26. 22 S.
17. 26
31. 22
10. 14 R.
18. 9
5. 14
22. 18 K.
6. 10
18. 9
11. 15
20. 11
15. 31
11. 8
31. 27
8. 3
27. 18
9. 6
2. 9
13. 6
7. 11
B. wins.

K.

27. 24
7. 10 Q.
22. 18
6. 9
13. 6
2. 9
30. 25
14. 17
25. 21
17. 22
21. 17
9. 13
17. 14
10. 17
19. 15
22. 26
15. 8
26. 31
20. 11
31. 26 P.
24. 19
17. 21
18. 14
21. 25
14. 9
25. 30
9. 6
30. 25
6. 1
25. 22
8. 3
13. 17
1. 6
17. 21
6. 10
21. 25
11. 7
25. 30
7. 2
30. 25
2. 7
25. 21
7. 11
21. 25
11. 15
25. 21
3. 8
21. 17
8. 11
17. 21 M.
11. 16
21. 17
16. 20
17. 21
15. 11
21. 17
20. 24
17. 21 L.
24. 28
21. 17
11. 15
17. 21
19. 16
W. wins.

L.

17. 14
10. 17
22. 13
24. 20
13. 9
11. 15
9. 14
15. 18
14. 10
19. 15
W. wins.

M.

17. 14
10. 17
22. 13
15. 18
13. 9
11. 16
9. 13 N.
18. 14
26. 22
14. 17
22. 26
17. 21
26. 22
16. 20
13. 9
19. 15
9. 14
15. 11
14. 10
11. 8
W. wins.

N.

26. 31
18. 22
31. 27 O.
22. 17
27. 18
17. 14
18. 15
14. 9
15. 24
16. 20
24. 28
5. 9
W. wins.

O.

9. 14
23. 18
14. 23
16. 20
W. wins.

P.

31. 27
24. 20
17. 22
7. 11
22. 25
23. 19
W. wins.

Q.

14. 17
22. 18
17. 22
19. 15
16. 19
15. 11
19. 28
18. 14
28. 32
8. 3
6. 10
23. 18
10. 17
3. 10
32. 27
13. 9
27. 23
18. 15
23. 18
10. 14
18. 11
14. 21
22. 25
21. 17
25. 29
9. 5
12. 16
Draw.

R.

5. 9
22. 17
9. 14
18. 9
11. 15
20. 11
15. 31
23. 18
7. 16
Draw.

S.

27. 24
5. 9
26. 22
17. 26
31. 22
10. 14
19. 15
16. 19
15. 8
19. 28
8. 3
7. 10
3. 8
28. 32
8. 11
32. 27
11. 8
14. 17
8. 11
17. 26
18. 15
10. 19
23. 16
12. 19
30. 16
Draw.

T.

14. 10
22. 25 U.
9. 6
25. 29
6. 2
29. 25
2. 6
25. 22
6. 9
22. 17
9. 13
17. 22
Draw.

U.

1. 5
9. 6
5. 9
6. 2
9. 14
2. 6
22. 25
6. 9
14. 18
23. 14
16. 10
10. 7
19. 28
7. 3
28 32
14. 10
15. 19
9. 14
32. 28
10. 6
19. 23
6. 2
11. 15
20. 16
12. 19
3. 12
19. 24
14. 10
15. 18
10. 15
18. 22
15. 19
Draw.

GAME 3.
11. 15
23. 19
9. 14
22. 17
6. 9
17. 13
2. 6
25. 22
8. 11
22. 17
14. 18
26. 23
4. 8
23. 14
9. 18
27. 23
18. 27
32. 23
10. 14 E.
17. 10
7. 14
19. 10
6. 15
24. 19
15. 24
28. 19
11. 16
31. 26 D.
16. 20
26. 22
20. 24
22. 17
24. 27
17. 10
27. 31
30. 25
8. 11
23. 18
31. 27
10. 7 B.
3. 10
21. 17
27. 24
18. 14
24. 15
14. 7
11. 16
25. 21
16. 19
7. 2
1. 6
2. 9
5. 14
17. 10
15. 6
29. 25
19. 23
25. 22
23. 26
22. 18
27. 30
18. 15
30. 26
15. 11 A.
26. 22
11. 7
6. 10
7. 2
10. 14
B. wins.

A.
21. 17
26. 23
17. 14
6. 1
13. 9
23. 18
15. 11
18. 15
11. 8
15. 11
8. 4
11. 7
4. 8
7. 2
8. 11
1. 5
11. 15
12. 16
B. wins.

B.
21. 17
27. 23
18. 14
23. 16
10. 7
3. 10
14. 7
16. 19 C.
25. 21
19. 15
7. 2
1. 6
2. 9
5. 14
17. 10
15. 6
21. 17
11. 15
17. 14
15. 18
14. 9
6. 1
29. 25
Draw.

C.
11. 15
25. 21
16. 11
7. 2
15. 18
13. 9
5. 14
17. 10
18. 22
10. 7
Draw.

D.
29. 25
14. 18
23. 14
16. 23
14. 10
12. 16
21. 17
16. 20
17. 14
23. 27
31. 24
20. 27
25. 21
8. 12
21. 17
27. 31
10. 7
3. 10
14. 7
5. 9
Draw.

E.
5. 9
29. 25
9. 14 I.
24. 20
15. 24
28. 19
11. 15 F.
25. 22
15. 24
22. 18
6. 9
13. 6
1. 5
18. 9
5. 14
6. 1
25. 22
1. 6
22. 18
17. 13
7. 11
13. 9
12. 16
9. 5
24. 28
5. 1
28. 32
1. 5
32. 28
5. 9
W. wins.

F.
14. 18
23. 14
1. 5
31. 27
11. 15
27. 24
15. 18
30. 26
8. 11 H.
26. 22
18. 23 G.
14. 9
5. 14
22. 18
W. wins.

G.
11. 15
20. 16
18. 23
16. 11
7. 16
14. 7
3. 10
24. 20
15. 24
20. 11
W. wins.

H.
18. 23
26. 22
23. 26
14. 9
5. 14
19. 15
10. 28
17. 1
8. 11
1. 6
11. 15
13. 9
15. 19
9. 5
19. 24
5. 1
24. 27
6. 2
7. 11
1. 6
Draw.

I.
1. 5
31. 26 K
12. 16
19. 12
15. 19
24. 15
11. 27
B. wins.

K.
30. 26
15. 18
23. 14
9. 18
31. 27
6. 9 L
13. 6
18. 22
25. 18
10. 15
19. 10
7. 30
6. 2
12. 16
24. 20
16. 19
17. 14
30. 25
14. 10
25. 22
2. 7
19. 23
7. 16
23. 32
16. 19
Draw.

L.
11. 16
19. 15

10. 19
24. 15
16. 19
17. 14
7. 10
14. 7
3. 10
21. 17
5. 9
27. 24
9. 14 M.
25. 21
18. 23
26. 22
23. 26
22. 18
14. 23
17. 14
10. 17
21. 14
26. 30
24. 20
30. 26
14. 9
6. 10
15. 6
Draw.

M.

18. 23
26. 22
23. 26
22. 18 N.
8. 11
15. 8
26. 30
24. 15
30. 23
15. 11
9. 14
11. 7
10. 15
7. 2
6. 10
2. 6
14. 17
8. 3
10. 14
3. 7
15. 19
B. wins.

N.

25. 21
9. 14
22. 18
14. 23
17. 14
Draw.

GAME 4.

11. 15
23. 19
9. 14
22. 17
6. 9
17. 13
2. 6
25. 22
8. 11
29. 25
4. 8
24. 20
15. 24
28. 19
11. 15
27. 24
14. 17
21. 14
9. 18
26. 23
18. 27
32. 23
10. 14
19. 10
6. 15
13. 9
7. 11
23. 19 G.
15. 18
22. 15
11. 18
31. 26 B.
18. 23
19. 15
23. 27
24. 19
27. 31
26. 22
14. 17
22. 13
5. 14
20. 16
31. 27
16. 11
27. 23
11. 4
23. 16
13. 9
14. 18
30. 26 A.
18. 23
26. 19
16. 23
15. 10
23. 18
10. 6
12. 16
6. 2
16. 19
2. 7
19. 23
25. 21
18. 22
7. 11
23. 26
11. 16
22. 18
16. 11
18. 14
11. 7
14. 9
7. 2
26. 30
21. 17
9. 13
17. 14
30. 26
B. wins.

A.

25. 21
18. 22
21. 17
16. 19
15. 10
19. 15
17. 13
15. 6
9. 2
12. 16
2. 7
3. 10
4. 8
16. 19
8. 11
19. 23
11. 7
10. 14
7. 10
14. 18
10. 14
22. 26
14. 10
26. 31
10. 15
18. 22
15. 18
22. 25
30. 21
1. 5
18. 27
31. 24
B. wins.

B.

19. 15
18. 22
25. 18
14. 23
31. 26
5. 14
26. 19
14. 18
15. 10 F.
18. 23
30. 25 E.
23. 26
25. 22
26. 31
22. 18
31. 26
18. 15
26. 22
20. 16 D.
22. 18
24. 20 C.
18. 11
16. 7
8. 11
B. wins.

C.

16. 11
1. 5
11. 4
18. 11
B. wins.

D.

10. 6
1. 10
15. 6
8. 11
6. 1
22. 17
1. 6
17. 14
6. 1
14. 9
1. 5
9. 6
5. 1
6. 2
1. 5
3. 7
B. wins.

E.

19. 15
23. 27
24. 19
27. 31
20. 16
31. 27
10. 6
3. 10
15. 6
27. 24
16. 11
24. 15
11. 4
12. 16
6. 2
15. 18
2. 6
18. 14
B. wins.

F.

20. 16
3. 7
30. 25
7. 10
15. 6
1. 10
24. 20
10. 14
B. wins.

G.

31. 27 H.
12. 16
25. 21
14. 18
23. 14
16. 19
27. 23
19. 28
B. wins.

H.

23. 18
14. 23
31. 26
5. 14
26. 10
11. 15 N.
30. 26
8. 11 O.
26. 23

12. 16
25. 21
14. 18 I.
23. 14
16. 19
21. 17
19. 28
10. 7
3. 10
14. 7
15. 19
22. 18
28. 32
7. 3
32. 27
17. 14
W. wins.

I.
3. 8
10. 7 K.
16. 19
23. 16
8. 12
24. 19
15. 24
22. 17
12. 19
17. 10
11. 15
Draw.

K.
22. 17 M.
8. 12
10. 7
1. 5 L.
17. 10
16. 19
23. 16
12. 28
7. 3
15. 19
3. 8
W. wins.

L.
15. 18
17. 10
18. 27
7. 3
27. 32
10. 7
32. 27
7. 2
11. 15
16. 11
27. 20
Draw.

M.
24. 19
15. 24
10. 7
24. 27
7. 3
8. 12
22. 17
11. 15
17. 10
27. 31
20. 11
31. 26
Draw.

N.
14. 18
22. 15
11. 18
25. 22
18. 25
30. 21
8. 11
21. 17
11. 15
17. 14
15. 18
14. 9
18. 23
9. 6
23. 27
6. 2
27. 32
24. 19
32. 27
19. 15
27. 23
15. 11
23. 19
11. 8
12. 16
Draw.

O.
14. 18
10. 6
1. 10
24. 19
Draw.

GAME 5.
11. 15
23. 19
9. 14
22. 17
6. 9
17. 13
2. 6
25. 22
8. 11
29. 25
4. 8
24. 20
15. 24
28. 19
11. 15
27. 24
14. 17
21. 14
9. 18
26. 23
18. 27
32. 23
10. 14
19. 10
6. 15
13. 9
14. 18 D.
23. 14
7. 11 H.
31. 26 B.
12. 16 A.
24. 19
15. 24
14. 10
5. 14
10. 7
3. 10
22. 18
14. 23
26. 3
W. wins.

A.
3. 7
22. 17
12. 16
24. 19
15. 24
14. 10
7. 21
25. 22
5. 14
22. 18
14. 23
26. 3
11. 15
3. 7
24. 28
B. wins.

B.
30. 26
3. 7
31. 27
12. 16
26. 23 C.
8. 12
14. 10
7. 14
25. 21
14. 18
23. 14
16. 19
21. 17
19. 28
9. 6
1. 10
14. 7
28. 32
B. wins.

C.
27. 23
8. 12
14. 10
7. 14
25. 21
14. 18
23. 14
16. 19
22. 17
19. 28
26. 22
28. 32
9. 6
1. 10
14. 7
32. 27
10. 3
27. 23
17. 13
15. 19
3. 8
11. 15
8. 11
23. 18
22. 17
19. 24
17. 14
18. 9
13. 6
15. 18
11. 15
18. 22
15. 18
22. 26
21. 17
26. 31
6. 2
31. 27
2. 6
24. 28
6. 10
28. 32
10. 15
27. 24
17. 13
32. 27
18. 14
27. 23
13. 9
23. 19
15. 10
19. 23
9. 6
23. 19
6. 2
19. 23
2. 7
23. 19
7. 11
19. 23
11. 15
23. 19
14. 17
5. 9
15. 11
9. 13
17. 22
19. 23
10. 14
23. 19
22. 26
19. 16
11. 15
16. 19
15. 10
24. 27
14. 18
27. 31
26. 30
31. 27
Draw.

D.
14. 17
22. 13
5. 14
25. 22
1. 6

23. 19 E.
7. 10
30. 25
14. 17
25. 21
17. 26
31. 22
8. 11
22. 17
15. 18
17. 14
10. 17
21. 14
6. 10
14. 6
3. 10
13. 9
18. 23
9. 6
23. 27
6. 2
27. 32
2. 7
10. 15
Draw.

E.
31. 26
7. 10 F.
23. 18
14. 23
26. 19
3. 7
30. 26
15. 18
22. 15
7. 11
13. 9
B. wins.

F.
14. 17
30. 25
17. 21 G.
23 19
21 30
19 1

30. 23
24. 19
W. wins.

G.
7. 11
25. 21
3. 7
21. 14
15. 18
22. 15
11. 27
14. 9
6. 10
9. 6
27. 32
6. 2
8. 11
26. 23
32. 28
23. 19
11. 16
20. 11
7. 23
2. 6
28. 19
6. 24
Draw.

H.
7. 10
14. 7
3. 10
30. 26
5. 14
26. 23
1. 6
23. 19
8. 11
25. 21
6. 9
31. 27
14. 18
22. 17
18. 22
17. 13
9. 14

13. 9
22. 26
9. 6
26. 31
6. 2
31. 26
27. 23*
26. 22
2. 7
11. 16 I.
20. 11
22. 18
24. 20
18. 27
7. 2
15. 24
2. 6
Draw.

I.
15. 18
7. 16
18. 27
19. 11
22. 18
11. 7
18. 15
21. 17
14. 21
7. 14
15. 11
14. 18
27. 32
19. 15
11. 8
15. 10
Draw.

GAME 6.
11. 15
23. 19
9. 14
22. 17
5. 9
26. 23
9. 13
30. 26

13. 22
25. 9
6. 13
29. 25
8. 11
25. 22
4. 8
22. 17
13. 22
26. 17
1. 5
17. 13 M.
2. 6
21. 17 E.
12. 16
19. 12
5. 9
23. 19 A.
9. 14
27. 23
14. 21
2. 7
21. 25
7. 11
15. 18
22. 15
11. 27
32. 23
25. 30
23. 18
30. 26
24. 20
8. 11
B. wins.

A.
31. 26 B.
9. 14
26. 22
14. 21
23. 18
21. 25
27. 23
15. 19
23. 16
11. 27
32. 23

25. 30
22. 17
30. 25
28. 24
8. 11
18. 14
25. 21
B. wins.

B.
17. 14 D.
9. 18
23. 14
10. 17
24. 19 C.
15. 24
28. 19
11. 16
27. 23
17. 22
31. 27
7. 10
27. 24
8. 11
31. 27
22. 26
B. wins.

C.
27. 23
15. 19
24. 15
11. 27
32. 23
17. 22
23. 18
7. 10
28. 24
8. 11
24. 20
22. 25
31. 26
25. 30
26. 23
30. 26
23. 19
26. 23

19. 16
23. 14
16. 7
10. 15
7. 2
15. 18
2. 9
14. 5
B. wins.

D.
24. 19 Y.
15. 24
28. 19
9. 14
23. 18
14. 21
27. 23
21. 25
31. 26
25. 29
26. 22
29. 25
22. 17
11. 16
32. 27
16. 20
18. 14
25. 21
19. 16
8. 11
23. 18
10. 15
B. wins.

E.
24. 20 L.
15. 24
28. 19
11. 15
27. 24 G.
8. 11 F.
31. 26
5. 9
26. 22
9. 14
21. 17

* If White plays 2. 7., Black should win in two moves.

14. 21
22. 17
12. 16
19. 12
21. 25
23. 19
15. 18
20. 16
11. 27
32. 14
7. 11
14. 7
3. 10
Draw.

F.

5. 9
31. 26
9. 14
26. 22
7. 11
21. 17 G.
14. 21
22. 17
15. 18
23. 7
3. 10
32. 27
21. 25
27. 23
25. 30
23. 18
30. 25
18. 14
25. 21
14. 7
21. 14
7. 2
14. 9
2. 7
9. 14
7. 16
14. 10
16. 11
8. 15
20. 16

6. 9
B. wins.

G.

23. 18
14. 23
22. 17
15. 18
32. 28
3. 7
17. 14
10. 17
21. 14
6. 10
14. 9
10. 14
9. 6
18. 22
6. 2
14. 18
19. 16
12. 19
24. 15
Draw.

H.

32. 28
15. 24
28. 19
8. 11
31. 26
10. 14
19. 16 I.
12. 19
23. 16
14. 18
27. 24
6. 10
B. wins.

I.

26. 22 K.
3. 8
22. 18
6. 10
18. 9
5. 14

13. 9
11. 15
27. 24
15. 18
9. 6
18. 27
6. 1
8. 11
1. 6
11. 15
6. 2
7. 11
B. wins.

K.

27. 24
3. 8
26. 22
7. 10
22. 18
5. 9
B. wins.

L.

31. 26
11. 16
26. 22
8. 11
22. 17
5. 9
17. 14
9. 18
23. 14
16. 23
27. 18
10. 17
21. 14
15. 22
B. wins.

M.

17. 14 U.
10. 17
21. 14
15. 18
31. 26
2. 6

19. 15 O.
18. 22
26. 17
11. 18
23. 19 N.
18. 22
27. 23
22. 26
23. 18
26. 31
32. 27
31. 26
27. 23
26. 31
17. 13
6. 10
14. 9
5. 14
18. 9
31. 27
9. 6
27. 20
B. wins.

N.

24. 20
18. 22
23. 18
22. 26
27. 23
26. 30
32. 27
30. 26
23. 19
26. 30
27. 23
30. 26
17. 13
7. 10
14. 7
3. 10
20. 16
26. 31
28. 24
31. 27
24. 20
27. 24

18. 15
24. 27
B. wins.

O.

24. 20
6. 10
28. 24
10. 17
23. 14
17. 21
26. 22
21. 25
22. 17 R.
25. 30
17. 13
30. 26
13. 9
26. 22
9. 6
22. 17
6. 2
17. 10
20. 16
11. 20
2. 4
5. 9
32. 28 Q.
10. 7
4. 8 P.
9. 14
8. 4
14. 18
4. 8
18. 22
8. 4
22. 26
4. 8
26. 31
8. 4
31. 26
4. 8
26 22
8. 4
22. 18
4. 8
7. 2

8. 11
2. 6
11. 8
6. 9
8. 11
9. 14
11. 8
14. 17
8. 11
17. 22
19. 16
12. 19
24. 15
22. 26
B. wins

P.

19. 16
12. 19
24. 15
9. 13
27. 23
13. 17
23. 18
17. 22
18. 14
22. 26
15. 10
7. 2
14. 9
26. 31
10. 6
31. 26
6. 1
26. 23
1. 5
23. 19
5. 1
20. 24
1. 5
24. 27
5. 1
27. 31
1. 5
31. 27
5. 1
27. 24

1. 6
3. 8
4. 11
19. 23
28. 19
23. 7
B. wins.

Q.

4. 8
10. 7
8. 4
9. 14
32. 28
14. 18
19. 15
7. 11
15. 8
12. 16
B. wins.

R.

19. 15 T.
11. 18
22. 15
25. 30
15. 10
30. 26
10. 6
26. 22
6. 2
8. 11
2. 6
22. 18
6. 9
7. 10
14. 7
5. 14
7. 2
18. 22
24. 19
14. 17
32. 28
17. 21
27. 24
3. 8
2. 7 S.
22. 26
7. 16
26. 23
19. 15
12. 19
15. 10
23. 18
24. 15
18. 11
B. wins.

S.

2. 6
21. 25
6. 9
25. 30
9. 14
22. 26
14. 10
26. 31
10. 14
30. 25
19. 15
11. 18
14. 23
25. 30
24. 19
31. 26
20. 16
26. 22
28. 24
22. 26
23. 27
Draw.

T.

22. 18
25. 30
27. 23
30. 26
32. 28
26. 22
19. 15
22. 26
23. 19
26. 22
B. wins.

U.

3. 7
11. 16
17. 14
10. 17
21. 14
15. 18 X.
24. 20
7. 11
19. 15
2. 7 W.
15. 10
18. 22 V.
26. 17
5. 9
14. 5
7. 21
27. 24
3. 7
23. 18
W. wins.

V.

16. 19
23. 16
12. 19
27. 23
18. 27
32. 16
8. 12
10. 6
12. 19
6. 2
W. wins.

W.

16. 19
23. 7
3. 17
26. 23
18. 22
23. 19
22. 26
28. 24
26. 31
20. 16
2. 7
32. 28
W. wins.

X.

7. 10
14. 7
3. 10
26. 22
8. 11
22. 17
16. 20
23. 18
15. 22
19. 16
12. 19
24. 8
22. 26
27. 24
20. 27
32. 23
Draw.

Y.

24. 20
9. 14
13. 9
6. 22
20. 16
11. 20
23. 18
14. 23
27. 2
10. 14
2. 6
14. 17
6. 10
17. 21
10. 15
21. 25
31. 27
25. 30
27. 23
30. 26
Draw

TWELVE ORIGINAL CRITICAL POSITIONS, BY. R MARTIN.

No. 1. *White to move and win.*

No. 2. *White to move and win.*

No. 3. *White to move and win.*

No. 4. *White to move and win.*

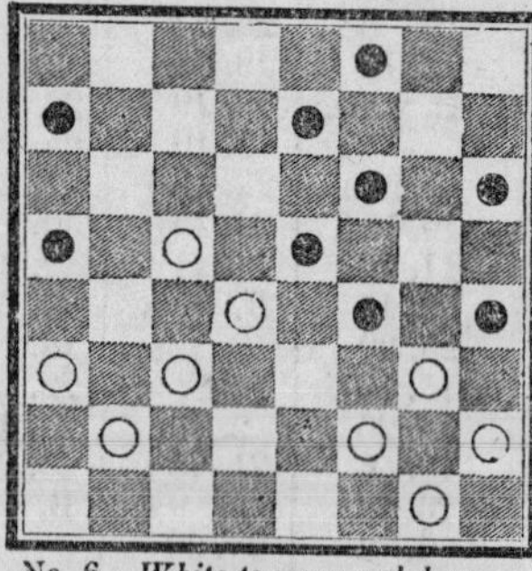

No. 5. *White to move and win.*

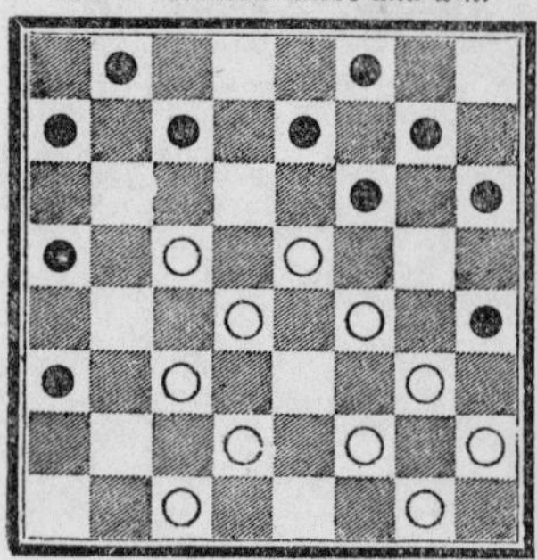

No. 6. *White to move and draw.*

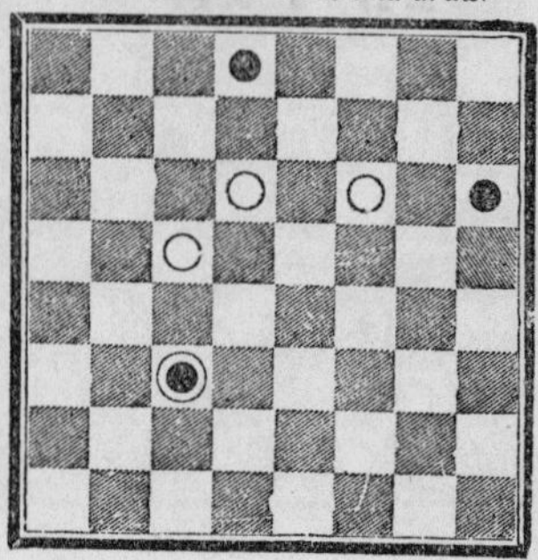

No. 7. *White to move and win.*

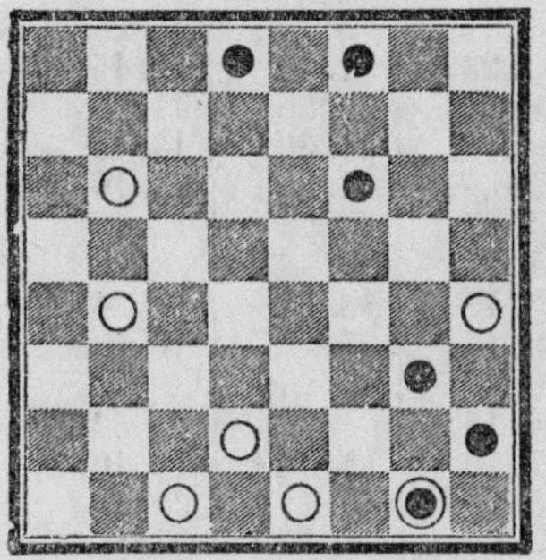

No. 8. *White to move and win.*

No. 9. *White to move and win.*

No. 10. *White to move and win.*

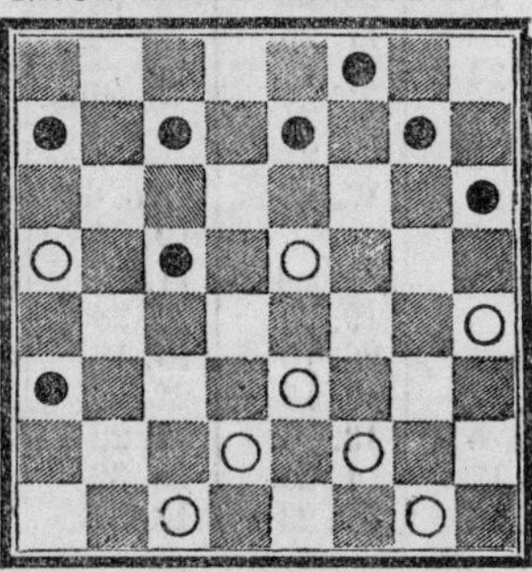

No. 11. *White to move and win.*

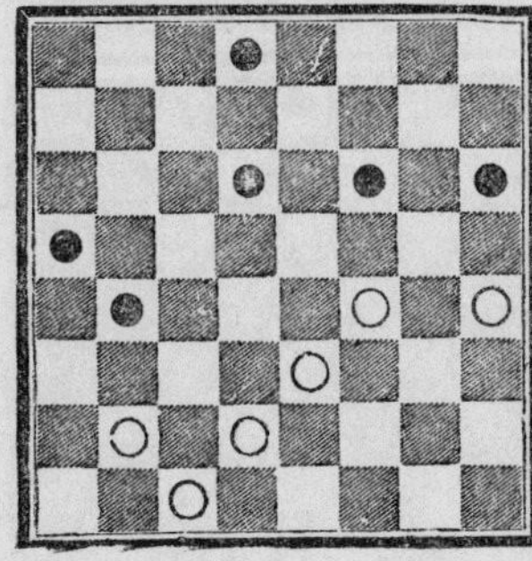

No. 12. *White to move and win.*

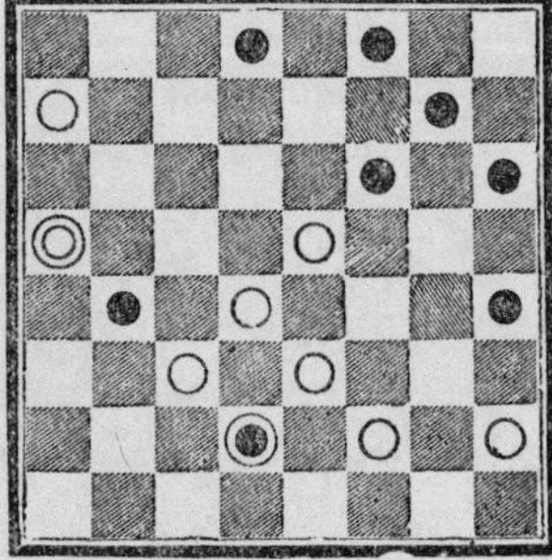

SOLUTIONS OF MR. MARTIN'S 12 CRITICAL POSITIONS.

No. 1.
10. 6
1. 10
32. 27
23. 32
30. 16
12. 19
2. 6
W. wins.

No. 2.
15. 11
8. 15
24. 20
15. 24
20. 18
17. 21
18. 22
1. 5
10. 6
5. 9
6. 1
9. 13
1. 6
21. 17
22. 18
17. 21
6. 10
13. 17
18. 23
17. 22
10. 14
22. 25
23. 26
25. 29
26. 30
W. wins.

No. 3.
26. 22
17. 26
19. 15
11. 27
24. 22
W. wins.

No. 4.
19. 23
26. 10
6. 15
13. 6
1. 26
30. 23
15. 22
W. wins.

No. 5.
19. 16
12. 19
15. 10
6. 15
14. 10
7. 23
27. 18
20. 27
32. 7
3. 10
18. 4
W. wins.

No. 6.
19. 24
11. 15
24. 28
15. 18
22. 26
31. 22
28. 32
18. 27
32. 23
Draw.

No. 7.
24. 27
31. 24
13. 17
22. 13
16. 19
24. 15
7. 10
15. 6
W. wins.

No. 8.
2. 7
3. 10
19. 24
20. 27
11. 16
12. 19
17. 13
10. 17
13. 15
W. wins.

No. 9.
9. 6
1. 10
30. 26
21. 30
24. 20
30. 23
20. 4
18. 25
27. 2
W. wins.

No. 10.
15. 11
8. 15
30. 25
21. 30
20. 16
12. 19
23. 16
30. 23
27. 2
W. wins.

No. 11.
8. 12
16. 11
7. 16
20. 11
10. 15
11. 8
15. 19
23. 16
12. 19
8. 4
19. 24
W. wins.

No. 12.
15. 10
26. 19
5. 1
17. 26
27. 24
20. 27
10. 7
3. 10
18. 15
11. 18
1. 6
2. 9
13. 15
W. wins

POLISH DRAUGHTS.

	1		2		3		4		5
6		7		8		9		10	
	11		12		13		14		15
16		17		18		19		20	
	21		22		23		24		25
26		27		28		29		30	
	31		32		33		34		35
36		37		38		39		40	
	41		42		43		44		45
46		47		48		49		50	

THIS variety is played with a table divided into one hundred squares, fifty of each colour, and with forty counters, (called indifferently either pieces, pawns, or men,) one-half black and the other white, each player having twenty of one colour. (In Germany, however, Polish Draughts is now frequently played on the ordinary board, with the usual complement of twenty-four pieces.) The counters are moved forward, as in the English game, and upon the same system, namely, obliquely, from square to square; but in taking, they move in the Polish game either backwards or forwards. The King,* too have the privilege of passing over several squares, and even the whole length of the diagonal, when the passage is free, at one move, which vastly adds to the amount of combinations.

It is usual both in France and England to arrange the counters on the white squares; but they may by consent

* In the Polish game, almost the only one played on the Continent, the crowned piece is called a Queen, instead of King. Indeed, the common name for Draughts is Damen (women,) it follows therefore naturally that the principal piece should be a queen.

be placed on the black. The colour adopted a matter of indifference, excepting that the black pieces are not seen quite so well on their own colour as the white on theirs.

The table is so placed, that each of the players has a double corner of the colour played on, to his right, viz. the squares numbered 45 and 50. The board, in first placing the pieces, is divided into two portions: that occupied by the black counters, comprising the twenty squares, from 1 to 20, and that occupied by the white, comprising those numbered from 31 to 50, leaving between them two rows of squares unoccupied, upon which the first moves take place.

The laws which regulate the English game are with a few additions equally applicable to the Polish. We have therefore merely to give the directions for playing, and the two or three additional rules which belong peculiarly to this variety.

The march of the Pawn, as already observed, is the same as in the English game, with this addition, that when there are pieces *en prise* (but not else) the taking Pawn may move backwards. Thus, White having a pawn at 25, and Black unsupported Pawns at 20, 9, 8, 17, 27, 38 and 39, White having the move would take them all, and finish at square 34. It will be observed that in this *coup* White passes a crowning square at 3, but he does not therefore become entitled to be made a King, nor has he the option of stopping *en route*, but must go on to the termination of his move at 34 or be huffed.

The piece which captures, whether Pawn or King, cannot in the course of one *coup* repass any covered square which it has leaped over, but must halt behind that piece which, but for this restriction, would be *en prise*. For example, suppose *White* to have a Pawn upon 22, 32, 33, and 37, with a King at 43, and *Black* a Pawn at 3, 4, 9, and 19, with Kings at 10 and 13. The black Queen at 13 takes the four Pawns, 22, 33, 43 and 73, and must stop at 28, which he would have to touch in preparing to take 32, but is prohibited from going to square 37 in consequence of having passed over it before. A square which is vacant may be passed or repassed several times in the course of one *coup*, provided no piece is passed over a second time. It is the intricacy of such moves which renders the rule imperative that the pieces taken be not removed till the capturing Pawn is at its destination or "en repos." The White Pawn at 32, then takes the Black Pawn jeopardized at 28, as well as the pieces at 19 and 10, making a King.

As regards huffing at this game the player is bound to take the greatest number of pieces where he has the choice, notwithstanding the smaller number may be most to his advantage, and failing to do so he may be huffed or compelled to take at the option of his adversary. Thus if on the one hand there are three Pawns *en prise*, and on the other two Kings, you are compelled to take the Pawns, but were there only two Pawns instead of three, you must take the Kings, as being of greatest value. When pieces, at the option of taking, are numerically and intrinsically the same, you may take which you please. The rule resolves itself into this, that you are controlled by numerical value, excepting when the numbers are equal, and then by the actual value of the pieces.

Kings are made in the same manner as in the English game. It has already been said that you cannot claim to have your Pawn crowned if it touches a King's square merely in its passage over it *en coup*. Good players, when they cannot prevent the adversary from reaching a King's square, commonly endeavour to lead him out again by placing a man or two in take, so as to disentitle him from being crowned. Indeed, it is sometimes good play to sacrifice three men, either for the object of gaining or capturing a King, especially towards the end of the game, when he is of the greatest importance, much greater in proportion than at the English game.

The movement of the King is the great feature in this game, and in *coup* he may accomplish more angles on the draught-board than a billiard-ball can be made to perform, even in the hands of a Kentfield. He has the privilege of traversing the board from one extremity to the other (if the line be unoccupied) or of halting on any of the intermediate squares, like the Bishop at chess. Thus, if he stand at 28, he may move anywhere on the line between 5 and 46, or between 6 and 50, but he can only move on one line at a time, unless there are pieces *en prise*, and then he may move diagonally all over the board, in which respect he has an advantage over the Bishop at chess. For example, place isolated black Pawns or Kings at 37, 17, 20, 30, 40, and a white King at 48. He will take all the pieces, by touching at the following squares, viz., 26, 3, 25, 34, and 45, where he rests, which squares, it will be perceived, though not close to the pieces, are within the angles. Indeed, it is possible so to place the pieces that a single King might capture a dozen in rotation. The following example is a case in which 19 may be taken at one *coup*. Pace a white King at 45, and he may take all the intervening pieces, by touching at the following squares, viz., 29, 18, 4, 15, 29, 38, 27, 18, 7, 16, 27, 36, 47, 28, 49, 35, 24, 13, and 2 where he rests. The player who may wish to try this experiment, will have to place the pieces on squares 8, 9, 10, 11, 12, 19, 20, 21, 22, 23, 30, 31, 32, 33, 34, 41, 42, 43, 44.

Between equal and skilful players the game would of necessity be "drawn" in many positions, when the uninitiated would lose; it is difficult therefore to define what are drawn games, but one or two of the simplest may be instanced. Suppose that at the end of the game one party, say White, has a King on the great central line, between Nos. 5 and 46, and Black has two or even three Kings, the game is drawn, as White cannot be driven from his hold, or captured, if he play correctly, and takes care to keep on the other side of a trap; thus, if he finds White preparing to get his pieces at 37, 38, and 49, he must be between 5 and 28, and *vice versâ*, that is, always on the adversary's unfortified or weak side But when the single King does not occupy the central line, there are many ways of winning, especially against an inferior player, but as these cannot be forced, the game must be considered drawn after 15 moves, and this rule holds good although the stronger party may have given odds. Should the odds, however, consist in ceding the draw as a game won, then twenty moves may be claimed by the party giving such odds.

When at the conclusion of a game, a player, who has only one King, offers to his adversary, who has a King and two men, or two Kings and a man, to crown his two men, or the man, for the purpose of counting the limited moves, the latter is obliged to accept the offer, otherwise the former can leave the game as a draw.

When one party at the end of a game has a King and a man against three Kings, the best way is to sacrifice the man as soon as possible, because the game is more easily defended with the King alone.

In Polish Draughts especially it is by exchanges that good players parry strokes and prepare them; if the game is embarrassed, they open it by giving man for man, or two for two. If a dangerous stroke is in preparation, they avoid it by exchanging man for man. If it is requisite to strengthen the weak side of your game, it may be managed by exchanging. If you wish to acquire the move, or an advantageous position, a well managed exchange will produce it. Finally, it is by exchanges that one man frequently keeps many confined, and that the game is eventually won.

When two men of one colour are so placed that there is an empty square behind each and a vacant square between them, where his adversary can place himself, it is called a *lunette*, and this is much more likely to occur in the Polish than the English game. In this position one of the men must necessarily be taken, because they cannot both be played, nor escape at the same time. The lunette frequently offers several men to be taken on both sides. As it is most frequently a snare laid by a skilful player, it must be regarded with suspicion; for it is not to be supposed that the adversary, if he be a practised player, would expose himself to lose one or more men for nothing. Therefore, before entering the lunette look at your adversary's position, and then calculate what you yourself would do in a similar game.

Towards the end of a game when there are but few Pawns left on the board, concentrate them as soon as possible. At that period of the game the slightest error is fatal.

The King is so powerful a piece, that one, two, or three Pawns may be advantageously sacrificed to obtain him. But in doing so it is necessary to note the future prospects of his reign. Be certain that he will be in safety, and occupy a position that may enable him to retake an equivalent for the Pawns sacrificed, without danger to himself. An expert player will endeavour to snare the King as soon as he is made, by placing a Pawn in his way, so as to cause his being retaken.

GAME I.

WHITE.	BLACK.
32 to 28	20 to 25
37 to 32	14 to 20
41 to 37	10 to 14
31 to 27	17 to 21
37 to 31	21 to 26
42 to 37	4 to 10
47 to 42	20 to 24
28 to 22	14 to 20
33 to 28	10 to 14
34 to 30	25 to 34
	(taking 30)
39 to 30	20 to 25
(taking 34)	
44 to 39	25 to 34
	(taking 30)
40 to 20	14 to 25
(tak. 34 & 24)	(taking 20)
35 to 30	25 to 34
	(taking 30)
39 to 30	18 to 23
(taking 34)	
45 to 40	15 to 20
40 to 35	12 to 18
43 to 39	7 to 12
39 to 33	20 to 24
49 to 43	5 to 10
50 to 45	10 to 15
45 to 40	15 to 20
30 to 25	2 to 7
25 to 14	9 to 20
(taking 20)	(taking 14)
40 to 34	20 to 25
33 to 29	24 to 33
	(taking 29)
28 to 39	12 to 17
(taking 33)	

WHITE.	BLACK.
46 to 41	17 to 28
	(taking 22)
34 to 29	23 to 34
	(taking 29)
32 to 14	8 to 12
(tak. 28 & 19)	
39 to 30	25 to 34
(taking 34)	(taking 30)
27 to 22	18 to 27
	(taking 22)
31 to 22	3 to 9
(taking 27)	
14 to 3	12 to 17
(crn'd, tak. 9)	
3 to 21	26 to 28
(taking 17)	(tak. 21 & 22)
36 to 31	7 to 12
31 to 27	12 to 18
41 to 36	11 to 17
27 to 22	18 to 27
	(taking 22)
37 to 32	28 to 37
	(taking 32)
42 to 11	6 to 17
(tak. 37, 27,	(taking 11)
& 17)	
38 to 33	17 to 22
43 to 39	34 to 43
	(taking 39)
48 to 39	16 to 21
(taking 43)	
39 to 34	21 to 27
34 to 29	13 to 18
29 to 24	27 to 31
36 to 27	22 to 31
(taking 31)	(taking 27,

WHITE.	BLACK.	WHITE.	BLACK.
24 to 20	31 to 37	9 to 4	47 to 14
20 to 14	37 to 41	(a King)	(taking 33)
14 to 9	41 to 47	4 to 36	
	(a King)	(taking 18)	

Drawn, each player remaining with a King and Pawn.

GAME II.

*** *The variations are given as notes at the foot of the page.*

WHITE.	BLACK.	WHITE.	BLACK.
34 to 30	20 to 25	31 to 26	24 to 29(*a*)
40 to 34	14 to 20	33 to 24	20 to 29
45 to 40	10 to 14	(taking 29)	(taking 24)
50 to 45	5 to 10	39 to 33	17 to 22(*b*)
33 to 28	20 to 24	33 to 24	22 to 33
39 to 33	15 to 20	(taking 29)	(taking 28)
44 to 39	18 to 23	38 to 29	11 to 17
49 to 44	12 to 18	(taking 33)	
31 to 27	7 to 12	37 to 31	7 to 11
37 to 31	2 to 7	42 to 37	17 to 21
41 to 37	10 to 15	26 to 17	11 to 22
47 to 41	4 to 10	(taking 21)	(taking 17)

(*a*) Here Black in playing from 24 to 29 commits a false move, which causes the loss of a pawn. It might have been avoided by playing

	17 to 21	36 to 27
26 to 17	11 to 31	(taking 31)
(taking 21)	(taking 17 & 27)	

This would have caused a mutual exchange of two pieces.

(*b*) The pawn at 29 is necessarily lost, as the sequel of the game will show, and if to save it Black had played 14 to 20, he would have lost a *coup*, thus:

	14 to 20	31 to 22	17 to 28
33 to 24	20 to 29	(taking 27)	(taking 22)
(taking 29)	(taking 24)	38 to 27	
27 to 22	18 to 27	(taking 32)	
	(taking 22)	5 to 32	It is immaterial how these moves are played.
32 to 21	16 to 27	(taking 28)	
(taking 27)	(taking 21)	40 to 29	
37 to 31	23 to 32	(taking 34)	
	(taking 28)	White having	
34 to 5	25 to 34	gained a King	
tak. 29, 19 & 10,	(taking 30)	and three	
and crowned)		pawns.	

WHITE.	BLACK.
43 to 38	14 to 20 (*c*)

(*c*) Black, in playing 14 to 20, makes a false move, which causes him to lose the game, through a skilful *coup*, and he would not the less have lost, if White, in lieu of making the *coup*, had played as follows :

48 to 42	10 to 14
31 to 26	22 to 31 (taking 27)
36 to 27 (taking 31)	12 to 17
44 to 39	6 to 11
39 to 33	1 to 6
26 to 21	17 to 26 (taking 21)
27 to 22	18 to 27 (taking 22)
29 to 18 (taking 23)	20 to 29 (taking 24)
33 to 24 (taking 29)	13 to 22 (taking 18)
24 to 4 (taking 19 & 9 & crowned)	8 to 13
4 to 18 (taking 13)	22 to 13 (taking the King)
32 to 21 (taking 27)	26 to 17 (taking 21)
30 to 24	14 to 20
37 to 32	20 to 29 (taking 24)
34 to 23 (taking 29)	3 to 9
35 to 30	25 to 34 (taking 30)
40 to 29 (taking 34)	9 to 14
29 to 24	16 to 21
38 to 33	17 to 22
42 to 38	22 to 27
33 to 28	21 to 26
32 to 21 (taking 27)	26 to 17 (taking 21)
38 to 32	17 to 22
28 to 17 (taking 22)	11 to 22 (taking 17)

23 to 18 (in the lunette)	22 to 17
18 to 20 (taking 13 & 14)	27 to 38 (taking 32)
20 to 14	38 to 43
4 to 9	43 to 49 (a King)
9 to 3 (a King)	49 to 27
45 to 40	6 to 11
40 to 35	11 to 16
41 to 36	27 to 43
24 to 19	43 to 27
35 to 30	27 to 49
Or	
19 to 13	15 to 20
3 to 15 (taking 20	49 to 35
Immaterial where	35 takes 2 Drawn.
Or 30 to 24	49 to 44
19 to 13	44 to 22
13 to 9	22 to 4 (taking 9)
36 to 31	4 to 36 (taking 31)
46 to 41	36 to 20 (taking 41 & 24)
3 to 25 (taking the King)	16 to 21 (*d*)
25 to 43	21 to 26
43 to 48	15 to 20
48 to 42	20 to 25
42 to 48	25 to 30
48 to 25 (taking 30)	26 to 31
25 to 14	31 to 36
14 to 46	36 to 41
46 to 37 (taking 41)	Lost.

(*d*) Here commence a series of moves necessary, in order with a single King, to arrest the two pawns which are advancing from the right and left of the board to the crowning line.

WHITE.	BLACK.	WHITE.	BLACK.
31 to 26	22 to 33 (tak. 27, 37, & 38)	34 to 5 (a King, taking 29, 19, & 10)	25 to 34 (taking 30)
29 to 38 taking 33)	20 to 29 (taking 24)	48 to 30 (tak. 43 & 34)	Lost.
32 to 28	23 to 43 (tak. 28 & 38)		

We nevertheless continue the game to its conclusion, that nothing may be omitted which the learner could desire.

WHITE.	BLACK.
	12 to 17
5 to 37	9 to 14
37 to 5 (taking 14)	18 to 23
5 to 11 (tak. 23 & 17)	6 to 17 (tak. the King)
30 to 24	16 to 21
35 to 30	3 to 9
40 to 35	1 to 7
44 to 39	7 to 12
39 to 33	12 to 18
41 to 37	21 to 27
36 to 31	27 to 36 (taking 31)
46 to 41	36 to 47 (crn'd, tak. 41)
30 to 25	47 to 20 (tak. 33 & 24)

WHITE.	BLACK.
25 to 23 (taking 20, 9, 8, & 18)	17 to 22
26 to 21	15 to 20
35 to 30	13 to 18
23 to 12 (taking 18)	22 to 28
45 to 40	28 to 33
40 to 34	33 to 38
37 to 28	38 to 16 (tak. 32 & 21)
12 to 8	16 to 21
8 to 3	21 to 27
3 to 25 (taking 20)	27 to 32
25 to 20	32 to 37
20 to 47	Lost.

LOSING GAME.

THIS game, which is lively and amusing, may for variety's sake be occasionally played. Although not ranked as scientific, it has its niceties, and requires considerable attention and management.

The player who first gets rid of all his men wins the game. Your constant object, therefore, is to force your adversary to take as many pieces as possible, and to compel him to make Kings, which is accomplished by opening your game freely, especially the back squares. Huffing, and the other rules, apply equally to this game.

THE GAME OF CHESS.

THIS Game is played on a board the same as that used draughts or chequers, containing sixty-four squares. The board must be so placed that each player will have a white square at his right hand. The squares are named from the pieces, viz. that on which the king is placed is called the king's square, and that on which the king's pawn is placed, the king's second square, that before the pawn the king's third square, and the next the king's fourth, and so of all the pieces of each side. Each player has eight pieces and eight pawns, which are thus placed; the white king on the fourth square from the right hand, which is black, and the queen on the fifth, which is white, the black king on the fifth square from the right hand on the other side the board, directly opposite the white king, and the queen on the fourth, opposite the white queen; each queen being on a square of her own colour. The bishops, one on the third and one on the sixth square of each side; the knights on the second and seventh, and the rooks on the first and eighth, or corner squares; the pawns on the lines of squares immediately in front of the pieces of each side. The pieces and pawns before the king, and on his side the board, are called the king's pawn, king's bishop, king's bishop's pawn, &c.; those before the queen, and on her side, are called the queen's pawn, queen's bishop, queen's bishop's pawn, &c.

The white queen being on the *left* of her king, and the black queen on the *right* of hers, players should accustom themselves to play with either colour.

The pawns move *forward* only; they may move one or two squares the first move, but afterward only one; the pawns can only take by moving *angularly* forward.

The knights move obliquely three squares at a time, vaulting over any piece which may be in their way, from black to white, and from white to black; a move which may be better learnt from the games hereafter stated, than from description.

The bishops move angularly, forward or backward, on the colour on which they are originally placed.

The rooks move in straight lines, forward, backward, or sidewise.

The queen has the moves of the bishop and of the rook.

The king moves in every direction, but one square only at a time, *except in castleing.* He may castle once in the game, which is done by placing the rook with which he castles, on the square next to the king, and then placing the king on the square next to the other side of the rook.

The queen, rooks, and bishops, move the whole extent of the board, unless impeded by some other piece of pawn.

The player is not compelled, as at draughts, to take any piece offered him, but may refuse if he thinks proper. When any piece is captured, it is removed from the board, and the capturing piece placed in the same square.

When the king is exposed to the attack of any of the adversary's pieces or pawns, he is said to be in *check*, and if he is unable to avoid the attack, by taking the attacking piece, interposing one of his own, or retiring out of check, he is *check-mated*, and his adversary wins the game.

When the pieces and pawns on each side are so much reduced, or so situated, that neither party can check-mate the other's king, the game is *drawn.*

When a player has no piece or pawn which he can move, except his king, and his king not being in check, is yet so situated that he cannot move without going into check, he is *stale-mated.* Phillimore, Hoyle, and many others, say that he who is stale-mate *wins the game;* but Sarrat, in his work, published in London, 1808, states, that "in Italy, France, Germany, &c., and by all Italian players of eminence, stale-mate is considered a *drawn game;*" and gives this as an established law.

LAWS OF THE GAME.

1. If the board, or pieces, be improperly placed, the mistake cannot be rectified after four moves on each side are played

2. When a player has touched a piece, he must move it, unless it is only to replace it; when he must say, "*J'adoube*," or *I replace*.

3. When a player has quitted a piece, he cannct recall the move.

4. If a player touch one of his adversary's pieces, without saying *J'adoube*, he may be compelled to take it, or if it cannot be taken to move his king.

5. When a pawn is moved two steps, it may be taken by any adversary's pawn which it passes, and the capturing pawn must be placed in that square over which the other leaps.

6. The king cannot castle if he has before moved, if he is in check, if in castling he passes a check, or if the rook has moved.

7. Whenever a player checks his adversary's king, he must say *Check*, otherwise the adversary need not notice the check. If the player should, on the next move, attack the queen or any other piece, and then say *check*, his adversary may replace his last move, and defend his king.

8. When a pawn reaches the first row of the adversary's side, it may be made a queen, or any other piece the player chooses.

9. If a false move is made, and is not discovered until the next move is completed, it cannot be recalled.

10. The king cannot be moved into check, nor within one square of the adverse king, nor can any player move a piece or pawn that leaves his king in check.

MR. HOYLE'S GENERAL RULES FOR THE GAME OF CHESS

1. Before you stir your pieces, you ought to move your pawns, and afterward bring out your pieces to support them. Therefore, in order to open your game well, the king's, the queen's, and the bishop's pawns should be first played.

2. You are not, therefore, to play out any of your pieces in the early part of your game, because you thereby lose moves, in case your adversary should have it in his power by playing a pawn upon them, to make them retire, which also

opens his game at the same time; more particularly avoid playing your queen out, until your game is tolerably well opened.

3. Never give check unless some advantage is thereby gained, because you lose the move if he is able either to take or drive your piece away.

4. Do not crowd your game by having too many pieces together, choking up your passage, so as to impede your advancing or retreating your men as occasion may render necessary.

5. If your game is crowded, endeavour to free it by making exchanges of pieces or pawns, and castle your king as soon as possible.

6. Endeavour, on the other hand, to crowd your adversary's game, thus: when he plays out his pieces before he does his pawns, attack them as soon as you can with your pawns, by which you may make him lose moves, and thus crowd him.

7. If the adversary attacks your king, and it should not be in your power to attack his, offer exchanges with him: and if he retires when you present a piece to exchange, he may lose a move, and thus you gain an advantage.

8. Play your men in so good guard of one another, that if any man you advance be taken, the adverse piece may be taken also by that which protected yours, and witn this view, be sure to have as many guards to your piece as you perceive your adversary advances pieces upon it; and if you can, let them be of less consideration than those he attacks with. If you find that you cannot well support your piece, see if by assailing one of his that is better, or as good, you cannot thereby save yours.

9. Avoid making an attack unless well prepared for it, for you open thereby your adversary's game, and make him ready prepared to pour in a strong attack upon you when your weak one is over.

10. Never play any man till you have examined whether you are free from danger by your enemy's last move: nor offer to commence an attack till you have considered what injury he would be able to do you by his next move, in consequence of yours, that you may frustrate his designs, if hurtful, before it is too late.

11. When your attack is prosperous, never be diverted

from following up your scheme (if possible) on to giving him mate, by taking any piece, or other advantage, your adversary may purposely throw in your way, with this intention, that by your taking that bait he might gain a move that would make your design prove abortive.

12. When you are pursuing a well-conceived attack, but judge it necessary to force your way through your adversary's defence with the loss of a few pieces; if, upon reckoning as many moves forward as you can, you see a prospect of success, rush on boldly, and sacrifice a piece or two to achieve your object: these bold attempts make the finest games.

13. Never let your queen so stand before your king, as that your adversary by bringing a rook or a bishop, might check your king, if she was not there, for you hardly have a chance to save her.

14. Let not your adversary's knight (particularly if duly guarded) come to check your king and queen, or your king and rook, or your queen and rook, or your two rooks at the same time: for in the first two cases, the king being compelled to go out of check, the queen or the rook must be lost: and in the last two cases, a rook must be lost, at best, for a worse piece.

15. Be careful that no guarded pawn of your adversary's fork two of your pieces.

16. When the kings have castled on different sides of the board, the enemy must advance upon the other king the pawns he has on that side of the board, taking care to bring up his pieces, especially his queen and rooks, to support them: and the king that has castled is not to stir his three pawns till compelled to it.

17. Endeavour to have a move as it were in ambuscade, in playing the game: that is, place the queen, bishop, or rook, behind a pawn, or a piece, in such a way, as that upon playing that pawn, or piece, you discover a check upon your adversary's king, and thus get a piece, or some other advantage by it.

18. Never protect an inferior piece with a better, if you can do it with a pawn, because that better piece may in such a case be, as it were, out of play; on the same account, you ought not to guard a pawn with a piece, if you have it in your power to guard it with a pawn.

19. A pawn passed, and well supported, frequently costs the adversary a piece. And if you play to win the game only, whenever you have gained a pawn, or any other advantage, and are not in danger of losing the move thereby, make as frequent exchanges of pieces as possible.

20. If you have three pawns each upon the board, and no piece, and you have one of your pawns on one side of the board, and the other two on the opposite, and your adversary's three pawns also are opposite to your two, march with your king as soon as possible, to take his pawns: and if he tries with his king to protect them, go on to the queen with your single pawn, and if he goes to prevent it, take his pawns, and push the others to the queen.

21. Toward the end of a game, each party having only three or four pawns on opposite sides of the board, the kings should endeavour to gain the move, in order to win the game. For instance, if you bring your king opposed to your adversary's king, with only one square between you, you will have gained the move.

22. When your adversary has his king and one pawn on the board, and you have your king only, you cannot lose that game, if you can bring your king to be opposite to your adversary's when he is directly either before or on one side of his pawn, and there is only one square between the kings.

23. When your adversary has a bishop and one pawn on the rook's line, and bishop is not of the colour that commands the square his pawn is going to, and you have only king, if you can get into that corner, that game cannot be lost, but may be won by a stale.

24. When the game is to your disadvantage, having only your queen left in play, and your king is in the position of stale-mate, keep giving check to your adversary's king taking especial care not to check him where he can interpose any of his pieces that make the stale; you will at last force him, by so doing, to take your queen, and then you conquer by being in a stale-mate. (See p. 520.)

25. Never cover a check with a piece that a pawn pushed upon it may take, for fear of only getting that pawn for it.

26. Always be careful that your adversary's king has a move: therefore do not crowd him up with your pieces, for fear you inadvertantly give stale-mate.

EXPLANATORY OBSERVATIONS ON SOME OF THE PRECEDING RULES.

1. Whether it is the open or the close game you play, be sure bring out all your pieces into play before you commence the assault; for if you do not, and your adversary does, you will attack or be attacked always disadvantageously; this is so decided, that you had better forego a benefit than deviate from it, and no one will ever play well at this game, who does not put this rule strictly in practice. It must not be concluded that these preparatory moves are useless, because you receive not an immediate success from them; they are equally important as it is at Whist to deal thirteen cards round before play. With a view of bringing out your pieces properly, push on your pawns first, and support them with your pieces, and you will receive this advantage from it, that your game will not be choked. By this I mean, that all your pieces will be at liberty to play and assist each other, and thus co-operate towards completing your purpose; and this may be farther observed, that, either in your attack or defence, you bring them out so as not to be driven back again.

2. When you have brought out your pieces, which you will have done very well, if you have your choice on which side to castle, (which I would always recommend to do) you should then stop and consider thoroughly your own and your adversary's game, and from his situation, and noticing where he is weakest, you should not only make your decision where to castle, but also where to begin your attack; and it is certainly clear you cannot do it in a better place than where you are strongest, and your adversary weakest. By this mode, it is very probable that you will be able to break through your adversary's game, in which contest some pieces must of course be exchanged. But now rest awhile, and survey both games attentively, and do not let your impetuosity hurry you away with this first success; and my advice to you in this critical juncture (especially if you still find your enemy pretty strong) is to rally your men again, and put them in good order for a second or third attack, if requisite, still keeping your men close and well connected together, so as to be of use to each other: for want of this method, and a little coolness, I have

often known an almost sure victory snatched out of a player's hands, and a total overthrow the consequence. But if, after all, you cannot penetrate so far as to win the game, nevertheless, by observing these rules, you may still be sure of having a well-disposed game.

3. And now that I am arrived at the last period of the game, which abounds also with difficulties and niceties, it must be remarked, where your pawns are strongest, most united together, and nearest to queen, you must likewise bear in mind how your adversary's pawns are disposed, and their degree of preferment, and compare these things together; and if you find you can get to queen before him, you must proceed without hesitation; if not, you must hasten on with your king to prevent him. I speak now, as supposing the noblemen to be gone: if not, they are to attend your pawns and likewise to hinder your adversary from going to queen.

SOME OTHER GENERAL RULES.

1. Do not be over cautious about losing a rook for an inferior piece: although a rook is better than any other, except the queen, yet it does not often come into play, so as to operate, until the end of the game; and therefore it often turns out that it is better to have a less good piece in play than a better out.

2. When you have moved a piece, so that your adversary drives you away with a pawn, you may be sure (generally speaking) that it is a bad move, your enemy gaining that double advantage over you of advancing himself, and making you retire; I think this merits attention; for although between equal and good players the first move may not be much, yet the loss of one or two more, after the first, makes the game almost irretrievable. Also, if you defend and can recover the move, or the attack, (for they both go together,) you are in a fair way of winning.

3. If you make such a move as that, having liberty to play again, you can make nothing of it, take it for granted, it is an exceeding bad one; for in this nice game every move is important.

4. If your game is such, that you have scarcely any thing to play, it is your own fault, either for having brought out

your pieces wrong, or, which is worse, not at all; for had they been brought out right, you must have sufficient variety to play.

5. Do not be too cautious of doubling a pawn; three pawns together are strong, but four, that make a square, with the help of other pieces, well managed, create an invincible strength, and in time of need may probably produce you a queen: on the other hand, two pawns, with an interval between, are no better than one; and if, carelessly, you should have three over each other in a line, your game cannot be in a worse plight; examine this on the table, and the truth will be self-evident. You are therefore to keep your pawns closely cemented and well connected together; and it must be great strength on your adversary's side that can overpower them.

6. When a piece is so attacked as that you cannot save it, give it up, and bestow your thoughts how to annoy your enemy elsewhere, while he is taking it; for it frequently occurs, that while your adversary is running madly after a piece, you either get a pawn or two, or such a situation as ends in his discomfiture.

7. Supposing your queen and another piece are attacked at the same time, and by removing your queen you must lose your piece; in this situation, if you can get two pieces in exchange for your queen, you should rather do it than retire; for it is the difference of three pieces, which is more than the value of a queen; besides that, you keep your game entire, and preserve your situation, which very often is better than a piece; nay, rather than retire, I would give my queen for a piece, and a pawn or two, nay, almost for what I can get; for observe this one thing, among good players, (to convince you this advice is not bad,) that when the attack and defence is well formed, and every thing prepared for the storm, if he that plays first is obliged by the act of the person that defends to retire, it generally ends in the loss of the game of the attacked side.

8. Do not aim at changing without sufficient reason; it is so far from being right, that a good player will take this advantage of it, that he will spoil your situation, and of course mend his own; but it is quite right in these following cases; when you are strongest especially by a piece, then every time you change your advantage is increasing; this is

so plain, it requires no argument. Again, when you have played a piece, and your adversary opposes one to you, change directly, for it is clear he wants to remove you; prevent him, therefore, and do not lose the move.

9. Cast up your game every now and then, make a balance, and then take your measures accordingly.

10. At the conclusion of the game especially, remember your king is a capital piece, and do not let him be idle; it is by his means, generally, you get the move and the victory.

11. Notice this also, that as the queen, rook, and bishop, operate at a distance, it may not always be necessary in your attack to have them near your adversary's king: they do better at a distance, cannot be driven away, and prevent a stalemate.

12. When a piece presents that you can take, and that cannot escape you, avoid being in too great a hurry; see that there is not a better move elsewhere, and take it at your leisure.

13. To take your adversary's pawn with your king is not always right, for it very often turns out to be a safeguard and protection to your king.

14. If you can take a man with different pieces, do it not hastily with the first that occurs, but consider thoroughly with which you had best take it.

SELECT GAMES AT CHESS.

THE FIRST GAME;

Beginning with white. Illustrated by observations on the most material moves; and two back games; one commencing at the 12th, and the second at the 37th move.

1. White. The king's pawn two steps.
   Black. The same.
2. W. The king's bishop at his queen's bishop's 4th square.
   B. The same.
3. W. The queen's bishop's pawn one move.
   B. The king's knight at his bishop's 3d square.

4. W. The queen's pawn two moves.(*a*)
   B. The pawn takes it.
5. W The pawn retakes the pawn.(*b*)
   B. The king's bishop at his queen's knight's 3d square.(*c*)
6. W. The queen's knight at his bishop's 3d square.
   B. The king castles.
7. W. The king's knight at his king's 2d square.(*d*)
   B. The queen's bishop's pawn one move.
8. W The king's bishop at his queen's 3d square.(*e*)
   B The queen's pawn two moves.
9. W. The king's pawn one move.
   B. The king's knight at his king's square.
10. W. The queen's bishop at his king's 3d square.
    B. The king's bishop's pawn one move.(*f*)
11. W. The queen at her 2d square.(*g*)

(*a*) This pawn is played two moves for important reasons : 1st, to hinder the adversary's king's bishop from playing upon your king's bishop's pawn; 2d, to place the strength of your pawns in the middle of the board; of great consequence to achieve the making of your queen.

(*b*) When the game is in this situation, viz. one of your pawns at your king's, and another at your queen's 4th square, do not push either of them before your adversary proposes to change one for the other; in such case advance the attacked pawn. Pawns, when sustained in a front line, obstruct very much the adversary's pieces from entering in our game, or taking a desirable post.

(*c*) If he gives check with his bishop instead of withdrawing it, you are to cover the check with your bishop in order to retake his bishop with your knight; in case he takes yours, your knight will then defend your king's pawn, otherwise defenceless. But perhaps he may not choose to take your bishop, because a good player endeavours to retain his king's bishop as long as possible.

(*d*) You should not play your knights at your bishop's 3d square before the bishop's pawn has moved two steps, because the motion of the pawn is hindered by the knight.

(*e*) Your bishop retires to avoid being attacked by the black queen's pawn, which would force you to take that pawn with yours; and thus decrease the strength of your game, spoiling entirely the project already mentioned, in the first and 2d observations.

(*f*) He plays this to give an opening to his king's rook, which cannot be avoided, whether you take his pawn or not.

(*g*) If you should take the pawn, in lieu of playing your queen, you would commit a great error, for your royal pawn would then lose its line; whereas if your king's pawn is taken by the adversary, that of your queen supplies the place, and you may sustain it with that of your king's bishop; these two pawns will evidently win the game, because they can now no more be parted without the loss of the piece, or one of them will make a queen, as will be seen in the end. Besides, it is of no little consequence to play your queen in that place, and for two reasons: 1st, to support and

B. The king's bishop's pawn takes the pawn.(*h*)
12. W. The queen's pawn retakes it.
B. The queen's bishop at his king's 3d square.(*i*)
13. W. The king's knight at his king's bishop's 4th square.(*k*)
B. The queen at her king's 2d square.
14. W. The queen's bishop takes the black bishop.(*l*)
B. The pawn takes the white queen's bishop.
15. W. The king castles with his rook.(*m*)
B. The queen's knight at his queen's 2d square.
16. W. The knight takes the black bishop.
B. The queen takes the knight.
17. W. The king's bishop's pawn two steps.
B. The king's knight at his queen's bishop's 2d square.
8. W. The queen's rook at its king's place.
B. The king's knight's pawn one move.(*n*)
19. W. The king's rook's pawn one move.(*o*)

defend your king's bishop's pawn; and 2d, to sustain your queen's bishop, which, being taken, would oblige you to retake his bishop with the above mentioned last pawn; and thus your best pawns would have been totally divided, and the game lost.

(*h*) He takes the pawn in order to give an opening to his king's rook.

(*i*) He plays this bishop to protect his queen's pawn, with a view afterward to push that of his queen's bishop.

N. B. He might have taken your bishop, but he rather chooses to let you take his, to clear a way for his queen's rook, though his knight's pawn is doubled by it; you are again to take notice, that a double pawn is no way disadvantageous when surrounded by three or four others. However, this is the subject of a back game beginning from this 12th move; the black bishop there taking your bishop, shows, that playing well on both sides it makes no alteration in the case. The king's pawn, together with the queen's, or the king's pawn, well played, and well supported, must certainly win the game.

(*k*) Your king's pawn not being in danger, your knight attacks his bishop, in order to take or have it removed.

(*l*) It is always unsafe to let the adversary's king's bishop batter the line of your king's bishop's pawn; and as it is likewise the most dangerous piece to form an attack, it is not only necessary to attack him at times by your queen's bishop, but you must get rid of that piece as soon as a convenient opportunity presents.

(*m*) Castle on the king's side, with a view to strengthen and protect your king's bishop's pawn, which advance two steps as soon as your king's pawn is attacked.

(*n*) He is forced to play this pawn, to deter you from pushing your king's bishop's pawn upon his queen.

(*o*) This move is made to concentrate all your pawns together, and push them afterward with vigour.

B. The queen's pawn one move.
20. W. The knight at his king's 4th square.
B. The king's rook's pawn one move.(*p*)
21. W. The queen's knight's pawn one move.
B. The queen's rook's pawn one move.
22. W. The king's knight's pawn two steps.
B. The king's knight at his queen's 4th square.
23. W. The knight at his king's knight's 3d square.(*q*)
B. The king's knight at the white king's 3d square.(*r*)
24. W. The queen's rook takes the knight.
B. The pawn takes the rook.
25. W. The queen takes the pawn.
B. The queen's rook takes the pawn of the opposite rook.
26. W. The rook at his king's place.(*s*)
B. The queen takes the white queen's knight's pawn.
27. W. The queen at her king's 4th square.
B. The queen at her king's 3d square.(*t*)
28. W. The king's bishop's pawn one move.
B. The pawn takes it.
29. W. The pawn takes again.(*u*)
B. The queen at her 4th square.(*x*)
30. W. The queen takes the queen.
B. The pawn takes the queen.
31. W. The bishop takes the pawn in his way.
B. The knight at his 3d square.
32. W. The king's bishop's pawn one move.(*y*)

(*p*) He plays this pawn to hinder your knight from entering in his game, and forcing his queen to remove; else your pawns would have an open way.

(*q*) You should play this knight in order to push your king's bishop's pawn next; it will be then strengthened by three pieces, the bishop, the rook, and the knight.

(*r*) He plays this knight to subvert your scheme by breaking the strength of your pawns, by pushing his king's knight's pawn; but baulk his design by changing your rook for his knight.

(*s*) Play your rook to protect your king's pawn, which else would remain in the lurch when you push your king's bishop's pawn.

(*t*) The queen returns to prevent the check-mate.

(*u*) You would run the risk of losing the game, were you not to take with your pawn.

(*x*) He offers to change queens in order to frustrate your plan of giving him check-mate with your queen and bishop.

(*y*) When your bishop runs upon white, put your pawn always upon black, because then your bishop serves to drive away your adversary's king or rook when between your pawns; and *vice versa*, wher your bishop runs black, then you have your pawns upon white.

B. The queen's rook at the white queen's knight's 2d square.

33. W. The bishop at his queen's 3d square.
B. The king at his bishop's 2d square.

34. W. The bishop at the black king's bishop's 4th square.
B. The knight at the white queen's bishop's 4th square.

35. W. The knight at the black king's rook's 4th square.
B. The king's rook gives check.

36 W. The bishop covers the check.
B. The knight at the white queen's 2d square.

37. W. The king's pawn gives check.
B. The king at his knight's 3d square.(z)

38. W. The king's bishop's pawn one move.
B. The rook at its king's bishop's square.

39. W. The knight gives check at the 4th square of his king's bishop.
B. The king at his knight's 2d square.

40. W. The bishop at the black king's rook's 4th square.
B. Plays any where, the white pushes to queen.

FIRST BACK GAME;

From the twelfth move.

12. W. The queen's pawn retakes it.
B. The king's bishop takes the white queen's bishop.

13. W. The queen takes the bishop.
B. The queen's bishop at his king's 3d square.

14. W. The king's knight at his king's bishop's 4th square
B. The queen at her king's 2d square.

15. W. The knight takes the bishop.
B. The queen takes the knight.

16. W. The king castles with his rook.
B. The queen's knight at his queen's 2d square.

17 W. The king's bishop's pawn two moves.
B. The king's knight's pawn one move.

(z) As his king may retire to his bishop's square, the second back game will inform you how to act in this case.

18. W. The king's rook's pawn one move.
B. The king's knight at his 2d square.
19. W. The king's knight's pawn two steps.
B. The queen's bishop's pawn one move.
20. W. The knight at his king's 2d square.
B. The queen's pawn one move.
21. W. The queen at her 2d square.
B. The queen's knight at his 3d square.
22. W. The knight at his king's knight's 3d square.
B. The queen's knight at his queen's 4th square.
23. W The queen's rook at its king's square.
B. The queen's knight at the white king's 3d square.
24. W The rook takes the knight.
B. The pawn takes the rook.
25. W The queen takes the pawn.
B. The queen takes the white queen's rook's pawn.
26. W. The king's bishop's pawn one move.
B. The queen takes the pawn.
27. W. The king's bishop's pawn one move.
B. The knight at his king's square.
28. W. The king's knight's pawn one move.
B. The queen at the white queen's 4th square.
29 W. The queen takes the queen.
B. The pawn takes the queen.
30. W. The king's pawn one move.
B. The knight at his queen's 3d square.
31. W. The knight at his king's 4th square.
B. The knight at his king's bishop's 4th square.
32. W. The rook takes the knight
B. The pawn takes the rook.
33. W. The knight at the black queen's 3d square
B. The king's bishops pawn one move anywhere, the game being lost.
34. W. The king's pawn one move.
B. The king's rook at its queen's knight's square.
35. W. The bishop gives check.
B. The king retires, having but one place.
36. W. The knight gives check.
B. The king removes.
37. W. The knight at the black queen's square discovering check.

B. The king moves where he can.
38. W. The king's pawn making a queen, gives checkmate at the same time.

SECOND BACK GAME;

Commencing from the thirty-seventh move.

37. W. The king's pawn gives check.
    B. The king at his bishop's square.
38. W. The rook at its queen's rook's square.
    B. The rook gives check at the white queen's knight's square.
39. W. The rook takes the rook.
    B. The knight retakes the rook.
40. W. The king at his rook's 2d square.
    B. The knight at the white queen's bishop's third square.
41. W. The knight at the king's bishop's fourth square.
    B. The knight at the white king's 4th square.
42. W. The knight takes the pawn.
    B. The rook at its king's knight's 4th square.
43. W. The king's pawn one move, and gives check.
    B. The king at his bishop's 2d square.
44. W. The bishop gives check at the black king's third square.
    B. The king takes the bishop.
45. W. The king's pawn makes a queen, and wins the game.

GAME THE SECOND;

Commencing with the black; wherein is seen that playing the king's knight the second move, is wrong play, because it gives the advantage of the attack to the adversary. The learner will see by these three different back games, that a good attack keeps the adversary always embarrassed.

1. B. The king's pawn two steps.
   W. The same.
2. B. The king's knight at his bishop's 3d square.

W. The queen's pawn one move.

3. B. The king's bishop at the queen's bishop's fourth square.

W. The king's bishop's pawn two moves.(*a*)

4 B. The queen's pawn one move.

W. The queen's bishop's pawn one move.

5. B. The king's pawn takes the pawn.(*b*)

W. The queen's bishop retakes the pawn.

6. B. The queen's bishop at the white king's knight's 4th square.

W. The king's knight at his bishop's 3d square.(*c*)

7. B. The queen's knight at his queen's 2d square.

W. The queen's pawn one move.

8. B. The bishop retires.

W. The king's bishop at his queen's 3d square.(*d*)

9. B. The queen at her king's 2d square.

W. The same.

10. B. The king castles with his rook.(*e*)

(*a*) Had your adversary played anything else, this was still your best move, it being highly advantageous to change your king's bishop's pawn for his royal pawn, because your king and queen's pawns place themselves in the middle of the chess board, and are thus enabled to stop all the progress of your adversary's pieces; besides this, you gain the attack by his having played his king's knight at the second move. You have also another advantage by losing your king's bishop's pawn for his king's pawn: viz. when you do castle with your king's rook the same rock finds itself instantly free and fit for action. This will be made clear by the first back game, the third move.

(*b*) Observe, if he refuses taking your pawn, leave it exposed in the same situation and place; unless he should choose to castle with his king's rook, in such case you must undoubtedly push that pawn forwards, in order to attack his king with all the pawns of your right wing. The effect will be best understood by a second back game, beginning from this fifth move. Take notice again, as a general rule, not easily to push on the pawns either of your right or left wings before your adversary's king has castled, otherwise he will retire where your pawns are less strong or less advanced.

(*c*) If he takes your knight, you must take his with your pawn, which being joined to his, increases their strength.

(*d*) This is the best square your king's bishop can choose, except the fourth of his queen's bishop, particularly when you have the attack, and it is not in your adversary's power to hinder that bishop from playing on his king's bishop's pawn.

(*e*) Had he castled on his queen's side, then it would have been your game to castle on your king's side, that you might attack him more conveniently with your pawns on the left. Be cautious in pushing your pawns forward till they are well sustained both by one another, and also by your pieces. The form of this attack at your left will be best understood by a third back game, commencing from this tenth move.

W. The queen's knight at his queen's 2d square.
11 B. The king's knight at his rook's 4th square.(*f*)
W. The queen at her king's 3d square.
12. B. The king's knight takes the bishop.(*g*)
W. The queen retakes the knight.
13. B. The queen's bishop takes the knight.(*h*)
W. The pawn retakes the bishop.
14. B. The king's bishop's pawn two moves.
W The queen at her king's knight's 3d square.
15. B. The pawn takes the pawn.
W. The bishop's pawn retakes it.
16. B. The king's rook at its king's bishop's 3d square.(*i*)
W. The king's rook's pawn two steps.(*k*)
17. B. The queen's rook at its king's bishop's square.
W. The king castles with his queen's rook.
18. B. The queen's bishop's pawn two steps.
W. The king's pawn one step.(*l*)

(*f*) He plays this knight to make room for his king's bishop's pawn, in order to advance it two steps, and thus to break the chain of your pawns.

(*g*) Had he pushed his king's bishop's pawn instead of taking your bishop, in that case you must have attacked his queen with your queen's bishop, and pushed your king's rook's pawn the next move upon his bishop, to force him to take your knight: in which case your best game is to retake his bishop with your pawn, in order to support your royal pawn, and replace it in case it be taken.

(*h*) If he did not take your knight, his bishop would remain imprisoned by your pawns, or he would lose at least three moves to set him at liberty.

(*i*) He plays this rook either with an intention to double it, or remove your queen.

(*k*) You push this pawn two steps to give your queen more room, who, being attacked, can retire behind this pawn, and then remain, menacing her adversary's king's rook's pawn. Your pawn advancing afterward will become dangerous to your adversary's king.

(*l*) This move is most difficult to comprehend as well as to explain. You are to observe, when you find yourself with a chain of pawns succeeding one another upon one and the same coloured squares, the pawn who has the van must not be abandoned, but should strive to keep his post. Here again observe, that your king's pawn being not in the line of his comrades, your adversary has pushed his queen's bishop's pawn two steps, for two reasons. The first, to engage you to push that of your queen forwards, which in this case would be always stopped by that of his queen, and thus leaving behind that of your king, would render it totally useless. The second is to hinder your king's bishop from battering his king's rook's pawn: it is best, therefore, to push your king's pawn upon his rook and lose it; because then your adversary, by taking it, opens a free passage to your queen's pawn, which you are to advance immediately, and support, in case of need, with your other pawns, with a view to make a queen with it, or draw some other valuable advantage to win the game. His queen's pawn (now become his king's apparently has the same advantage of having

19. B. The queen's pawn takes the pawn.
W. The queen's pawn one move.
20. B. The bishop at his queen's bishop's 2d square.
W. The knight at his king's 4th square.(*m*)
21. B. The king's rook at the white king's bishop's third square.
W. The queen at her king's knight's 2d square.
22. B. The queen at her king's bishop's 2d square.(*n*)
W. The knight at the black king's knight's 4th square.
23. B. The queen gives check.
W. The king at his queen's knight's square.
24. B. The rook takes the bishop.(*o*)
W. The rook retakes the rook.
25. B. The queen at her king's bishop's 4th square.
W. The queen at her king's 4th square.(*p*)
26. B. The queen takes the queen.
W. The knight takes the queen.
27. B. The rook at the white king's bishop's fourth square
W. The knight at the black king's knight's fourth square.
28. B. The queen's bishop's pawn one move.
W. The queen's rook at her king's knight's 3d square.
29. B. The knight at his queen's bishop's 4th square.
W. The knight at the black king's 3d square.
30. B. The knight takes the knight.

no opposition from your pawn's to make a queen: the difference, however, is great, because his pawn being entirely parted from his comrades, will always be in danger in his road, by a multitude of your pieces all waging war against it.

(*m*) In order to stop his king's pawn, it became necessary to play that knight: the more, because this very pawn, in its present situation, blocks up the passage of his own bishop, and even of his knight.

(*n*) He plays his queen to give check next: but if he had played his king's rook's pawn to frustrate the attack of your knight, you must then have attacked his bishop and his queen with your queen's pawn; hence he would have been forced to take your pawn, and you should have retaken his bishop with your knight, which he could not have taken with his queen, because she would have been lost by a discovered check with your bishop.

(*o*) He takes your king's bishop: in the first place, to save his king's rook's pawn, and because your bishop proves more inconvenient to him than any other of your pieces: and secondly, to put his queen upon the rook that covers your king.

(*p*) Having the advantage of a rook against a bishop at the end of a game, it is your interest to change queens; because his queen being at present troublesome in the post where he just played it, you compel him to change, which he cannot avoid, if he will save his being check-mate.

W. The pawn retakes the knight.

31 B. The rook at its king's bishop's 3d square.

W. The king's rook at its queen's square.

32. B. The rook takes the pawn.

W. The king's rook at the black queen's 2d square, and must win the game.(q.)

FIRST BACK GAME;

From the third move.

3. B. The queen's pawn two steps.

W. The king's bishop's pawn two steps.

4. B. The queen's pawn takes the pawn.(a)

W. The king's bishop's pawn takes the pawn.

5. B. The king's knight at the white king's knight's 4th square.

W. The queen's pawn one step.

6. B. The king's bishop's pawn two steps.

W. The king's bishop at his queen's bishop's fourth square.

7. B. The queen's bishop's pawn two steps.

W. The queen's bishop's pawn one step.

8. B. The queen's knight at his bishop's 2d square.

W. The king's knight at his king's 2d square.

9. B. The king's rook's pawn two steps.(b)

W. The king's rook's pawn one move.

10. B. The king's knight at his rook's 3d square.

W. The king castles.

11. B. The king's knight at his rook's 4th square.

W. The bishop gives check.

12. B. The bishop covers the check.

W. The bishop takes the black bishop.

13. B. The queen takes the bishop.

(q) Anything he could have played could not hinder you from doubling your rooks, unless he had sacrificed his bishop, or let you make a queen with your pawn; thus he loses the game all ways.

(a) If he had taken your king's bishop's pawn in lieu of this, you must have pushed your king's pawn upon his knight, and his pawn you must afterward have retaken with your queen's bishop.

(b) He pushes this pawn two steps, avoiding having a double pawn upon his king's rook's line, which by pushing your king's rook's pawn upon his knight, he had no chance of escape, and you taking it afterward with your queen's bishop, would have given him a bad game

W. The queen's pawn one move.
14. B. The queen's bishop's pawn one move.(*c*)
W. The queen's knight's pawn two moves.
15. B. The queen's bishop's pawn takes it by passing by
W. The rook's pawn retakes the pawn.
16. B. The queen's knight's pawn one move.
W. The queen's bishop at his king's 3d square.
17. B. The bishop at his king's 2d square.
W. The king's knight at his king's bishop's 4th square.(*d*)
18. B. The king's knight at his own square.
W. The king's knight at the black king's knight's 3d square.
19. B. The king's rook at his 2d square.
W. The king's pawn one move.
20. B. The queen at her knight's 2d square.
W. The queen's pawn one move.
21. B. The king's bishop at his 3d square.
W. The king's rook takes the pawn.
22. B. The king castles.
W. The king's rook takes the black queen's knight.
23. B. The queen's pawn takes the rook.
W. The queen's rook takes the pawn.
24. B. The queen's rook's pawn one move.
W. The rook gives check.
25. B. The king retires.
W. The rook at the black queen's bishop's 2d square
26. B. The queen at her knight's 4th square.
W. The queen's knight at his rook's 4th square
27. B. The queen at her king's bishop's 4th square
W. The queen's knight at her bishop's 4th square.
28. B. The queen takes the knight.
W. The bishop gives check.
29. B. The king retires where he can.
W. The knight gives check-mate.

(*c*) He plays in this manner to cut the communication of your pawns; but you escape it by pushing immediately your queen's knight's pawn upon his knight, which retreat forces your adversary to take the pawn by the way. This joins your pawns again, and makes them invincible.

(*d*) This knight gives the mortal blow to this game, because he has at present all your adversary's pieces in some measure locked up, till you can re the check-mate

SECOND BACK GAME;

From the fifth move.

5. B. The king castles.
   W. The king's bishop's pawn one move.
6. B. The queen's pawn one move.
   W. The queen at her king's bishop's 3d square.
7. B. The queen's pawn takes the pawn.
   W. The queen's pawn retakes the pawn.
8. B. The queen's rook's pawn two moves.
   W. The king's knight's pawn two moves.
9. B. The queen at her 3d square.
   W. The king's knight's pawn one move.
10. B. The king's knight at his king's square.
    W. The king's bishop at his queen's bishop's 4th square.
11. B. The queen's bishop's pawn one move.
    W. The queen at the black king's rook's 4th square.
12. B. The queen's knight's pawn two steps.
    W. The king's knight's pawn one move.
13. B. The king's rook's pawn one move.
    W. The bishop takes the king's bishop's pawn, and gives check.
14. B. The king at the rook's square.
    W. The queen's bishop takes the black king's rook's pawn.
15. B. The king's knight at his bishop's 3d square.
    W. The queen being at her king's rook's 5th square, wins the game on removing the bishop.

THIRD BACK GAME,

From the tenth move.

10. B. The bishop castles on his queen's side.
    W. The king castles on his own side.
11. B. The king's rooks pawn one move.
    W. The queen's knight at his queen's 2d square
12. B. The king's knight's pawn two steps.
    W. The queen's bishop at his king's 3d square.
13. B. The queen's rook at his king's knight's square
    W. The queen's knight's pawn two steps.
14. B. The king's rook's pawn one move.
    W. The queen's rooks pawn two moves.(a)
15. B. The bishop takes the knight.
    W. The queen takes the bishop.
16. B. The king's knight's pawn one move.
    W. The queen at her king's 2d square.
17. B. The queen's bishop's pawn one step.
    W. The queen's rooks pawn one step.
18. B. The bishop at his queen's bishop's 2d square
    W. The queen's bishop's pawn one move.
19. B. The king's rook's pawn one move.
    W. The king's rook at its queen's knight's square.
20. B. The king's rook at its 4th square.
    W. The queen's bishop's pawn one move.
21. B. The queen's pawn one move.
    W. The king's pawn one move.
22. B. The king's knight at his king's square.
    W. The queen's knight's pawn one move.
23. B. The pawn takes the pawn.
    W. The king's rook retakes the pawn.
24. B. The queen's rook's pawn one move.
    W. The king's rook at its queen's knight's 4th square.

(a) When the king is behind two or three pawns, and the adversary falls upon them in order to attack your king, you must avoid pushing any of those pawns till forced; as it would have been very indifferent policy to have pushed your king's rook's pawn upon his bishop, because he would then have got the attack by taking your knight with his bishop, and would have got an opening upon your king by pushing his king's knight's pawn which would have lost you the game.

25. B. The king's bishop's pawn one move.
    W. The king's bishop takes the queen's rook's pawn.
26. B. The pawn takes the bishop.
    W. The queen takes the pawn and gives check.
27. B. The king retires.
    W. The queen gives check.
28 B. The knight covers the check.
    W. The queen's rook's pawn one move.
29 B. The king at his queen's 2d square.
    W. The queen takes the queen's pawn and gives check.
30. B. The king retires.
    W. The queen's rook's pawn one move, and by different ways wins the game.

ECARTÉ.

The following treatise, for which we are indebted to the kindness of the Author, was written ten years ago; in the first instance merely for the use of a circle of friends among whom he was at the time residing, and by whom the game was frequently played. A long residence on the Continent, where it was in very general esteem, and a personal aptitude for games of calculation, peculiarly fitted him for the self-imposed task. The spirit and style of his essay are evidences that it is the production of one on the best of terms with his subject, and by no means without confidence in himself. "For convenience of reference," as he tells us, "it is divided into parts. The first Part lays down clear and concise Rules for the Game, as played and acknowledged by the 'Académie de Paris.'

"The Second Part relates to the probabilities of chances, with tables for calculating the relative value of any card. The reader by studying these tables, which are extremely simple, may acquire, in a short period, a scientific method of play.

"The Third Part gives some examples of difficult games, and the method of playing them: by an attention to which the reader may get an insight into the niceties of Ecarté. There are a few passages marked, which refer to rules necessary to be observed when playing with Foreigners; but which scarcely apply to the game as played in our clubs and drawing-rooms. Further notice will be taken of this peculiarity.

"The Author confidently offers this little treatise to the public as a *safe guide*—long experience of the game having made him acquainted with all its mysteries. Said a worldly Parisian to his son, whom he discovered lamenting over an empty purse, 'My son, until you have four eyes in your head, risk not your gold at Ecarté.'—The Author has but one better counsel to offer—

'PLAY NOT AT ALL!'"

PART I.—ON THE RULES.

Of all Games of Commerce, the most fashionable at this moment is Ecarté; yet, strange to say, we have never yet been furnished with a complete Treatise on its Rules—still less has any writer indicated the method of playing, or explained its niceties and different combinations.* Hence was the atuhor determined to compile a Treatise, in which should be layed down, not only the rules recognized and adopted by the clubs, but also be pointed out, how to detect and punish the different errors which might be committed in the course of the rubber.

It became necessary to give an example of the ordinary games, and the manner of playing them; hence he has added to this Treatise directions how the cards ought to be played in different games, whether with a view to win points, or to avoid losing them,—taking for his basis, every probable combination which the doctrine of chances presents in a game composed of thirty-two cards.

ON THE GAME OF ECARTE.

1. Ecarté is played by two persons, with a pack or game of thirty-two cards,—the deuce, three, four, five, and six of each suit being discarded.

2. Five points scored are game,—unless there be any mutual agreement to the contrary.

3. The score is always marked on the side of the stakes.

4. The money, whether stakes or bets is always put on the table.

5. Whoever wins three tricks, scores *one* point: whoever wins *all* the tricks, scores *two*. This is called in French, making the "*vole.*"

6. Only two points can be scored in a single deal, unless one of the parties hold or turn up the king.

7. It may be either played in games or rubbers. A rubber consists in winning two games out of three.

* No person really understanding cards will aver that there is "no play in Ecarté." This is a silly sophistry, arising from the false data that it is easier to manage five cards than thirteen; and a person acting on this principle will soon find his mistake to his cost.

8. The winner cannot refuse giving "a revenge;" the loser is not obliged to accept it.

9. It is usual to have two packs of cards, used alternatively: to prevent mixing them, the backs of one are generally dotted or coloured: the latter method is preferable.

10. The king is the highest card: the ace ranks next after the knave.

ON CUTTING, AND CUTTING FOR DEAL.

1. First see who is eldest hand: at this game the eldest hand deals: there is a slight advantage in dealing, because the king turned up, scores a point, as we shall see presently.

2. Many players imagine it is as advantageous to be younger, as elder hand; in other words, as advantageous to play first, as to be played up to;* they are in error,—for it is only 7 to 1 against the king being turned up and it is more than 7 to 1 against the first player making the point, from the sole reason that he is first player, *i. e.*, with cards which win because he is first, and which would lose were he last.

3. Another advantage in dealing is, that if the first to play (younger hand) proposes, the dealer presumes that his adversary has a weak hand, and can profit by this knowledge by refusing to give cards, whilst the younger hand, playing without throwing out, (écarté, signifies "thrown out,") can have no clue to the strength of the dealer's cards.

4. The eldest hand has choice of cards: this choice once made must last throughout the game, unless fresh cards be called for, which is allowable.

5. The deal is decided by cutting into the pack and showing the last card of the cut; highest deals.

6. If in cutting for deal, several cards are shown, the lowest of those turned up is accounted the cut.

7. Whoever neglects to show his cut, is supposed to have the cut lowest of all.

8. The cut holds good, even if the pack be incomplete.

* As in Ecarté the eldest deals, and consequently plays last, (contrary to the usual mode,) to avoid the confusion which the terms "elder hand" and "younger hand" would make, the two players are throughout this work called the one "dealer," the other "player,"—the latter designating him who leads the first card.

9. When a pack of cards is discovered to be incorrect, all preceding deals—even that in which the discovery is made, provided the deal be already played out—hold good.

10. A cut must consist of more than one card.

ON DEALING.

1. The cards are dealt by two and three, or by three and two. Five are given to each player, and the eleventh is turned up.

2. The turned up card indicates the suit of the trumps.

3. A trump is superior to every other card of a different suit.

4. When once the cards are dealt by two and three, or by three and two, this order cannot be changed during the game, unless by giving notice to the adversary previously to his cutting.

5. If this order of dealing should be changed, the adversary a right to call a fresh deal, provided he has not seen his hand. Once, however, the hand seen, the deal holds good.

6. The residue of the pack (Fr. *talon*) is placed on the right of the dealer, and the écart (or cards rejected) on the left, both to avoid confusion, and to show, if forgotten, which party was dealer.

7. The dealer ought always to shuffle the cards, and the adversary always cut; but the latter is entitled to shuffle also before cutting, and the dealer to re-shuffle afresh, or to present the pack for the cut without re-shuffle, or to call for fresh cards.

8. It is allowable to shuffle the cards each time they are presented for cutting, but not to do so twice following in the same deal.

9. The party receiving cards plays first.

10. The king counts as one point in favor of the person either turning it up or holding it.

[Note. The following rule is important, and ought to be read with attention, as an ignorance of it gives rise to frequent discussions.]

14. It is not sufficient that the holder of the king mark it; he ought to distinctly announce "that he has the king." If the holder is also "the player," he ought to make this announcement before he leads his first card, except when he plays king first, and in that case it is allowable to announce it *after* it is on the table, but *before* it is covered by the ad-

versary's card. This rule is only applicable to the younger hand (or first to play,) the second to play (or eldest hand) should invariably announce the king just before covering his adversary's first card, otherwise he cannot score it; for his own interest he ought not to announce it until just after the opponent's first card is played.

12. When a player deals out of his turn, and the error is perceived before the trump is turned up, there is a fresh deal by the proper dealer; if the trump is turned up, the deal is put aside, and is a good deal for the next time; if the error is only perceived after the hand is played, the deal holds good, since the fault lies between the two players, the one in having dealt, the other in having allowed the deal.

13. A player who plays before his turn is only obliged to take back his card; if however it is covered, the *coup* (or trick) is good, this fault also being committed through the negligence of both players.

14. When the player is not satisfied with his hand, he proposes to take other cards, saying "I throw out," or "I propose" (usually however the French terms are adopted in this game, "*J'écarte*" or "*Je propose*;") the dealer accepts or refuses, according to whether satisfied or not with what he holds; if he accept, he gives as many cards as his adversary requires, and then serves himself with as many as he may want.

15. Whoever plays without changing cards, or whoever refuses to change cards, looses two points if he make not three tricks; and making them, scores but one.

16. When a proposition is once made or refused, there can be no retracting; also, when once a certain number of cards are asked for, that number can neither be diminished nor increased.

17. If after the second time of giving cards, the player still wishes to propose, he has the power of so doing; likewise after the third, and so on until the pack is exhausted; but the dealer in refusing, no longer loses two points if he does not make three tricks.

18. When after having changed (or écarté'd) several times, the player proposes again, without paying attention as to whether sufficient cards remain or not, and that the dealer inconsiderately accepts, the former takes as many cards as he needs; so much the worse for the latter if there remain not

sufficient for him, or even none at all—as he dealt, it was his duty to pay proper attention; in this case he keeps his own hand and if he has already écarté'd, takes at hazard, from the cards thrown out, the necessary number to complete his hand.

OF FAULTS IN GENERAL.

1. Each player previously to receiving fresh cards, puts his écart (or those he rejects) on one side, and once this écart made can no longer touch it. Should either happen to look at the rejected cards, even his own, not only is it forbidden to retake them, were they even trumps, but he is obliged to play with his cards on the table, being supposed to have cognizance of his adversary's écart

[Note. The following rules (2 and 3) apply to Foreigners, who are often vociferous in their play, calling out the suit of the card before they throw it on the table. To our quiet and gentlemanly English habits, this rule can never be but a dead letter. But as many who read this little treatise may perhaps either play with Foreigners abroad or at home, I insert the rule, in order that they may not fall into the very commonly laid trap of a false card being called.]

2. It is obligatory to play the colour announced: thus any one calling "club," and playing spade or any other suit, is obliged, if the adversary desire, to retake his card and to play the suit announced; if he has none the adversary can call a suit.

3. If, however, the adversary deem the card played more favorable to him than the suit announced, he has the right to hinder its being taken back.

4. Whichever from mistake, or otherwise, announces "the king," and has it not, loses one point independently of the result of that *coup* or deal: that is to say, instead of marking the king thus falsely announced, the adversary marks it unless the mistake is declared previously to a card being played. It easy to see the necessity of this forfeit, since a *ruse* of this nature might cause the other party to lose the point or miss the *vole*, from not daring to lead trumps, thinking the king to be in his adversary's hand.

[Note. Although the following is the rule, it is seldom attended to, as players generally omit to take up their tricks.]

5. It is not allowable to look at the adversary's tricks, under pain of playing with cards on table.

6. Whichever through error, or purposely, throws his cards on the table, loses one point, if he have already made a trick, and two points if he has not.

7. The cards are considered as thrown on the table, if being embarrassed to keep a suit, a player lowers them so as to show them to his adversary; since it is possible by this movement, to make him believe that the *coup* is abandoned, and induce him to show *his* cards also.

8. A player who quits the game, loses it.

9. If a faced card is found in the pack, and it is perceived in dealing, the deal is null, except when the faced card happens to be the eleventh, because in that case there is no interference with its destiny, which was "to have been turned up."

10. If it be only detected after the écart, and the faced card falls to the party receiving cards, he may either keep it, or begin the deal afresh, *and take the deal*, the fault lying with the dealer, it being possible to have been committed purposely, with a fraudulent intention, by an unscrupulous player.

11. If the faced card fall (after the écart) to the dealer, the deal holds good; equally good is it should the faced card remain unperceived till both players have finished taking in cards.

ON REVOKING OR UNDER-FORCING.

1. It is forbidden to either revoke or under-force (*sous-forcer*). This term means the answering a card with one of the same suit, but inferior value to those remaining in hand; for instance—putting the nine of clubs on the ten, having the ace in hand.

2. When a player revokes or underforces, he is obliged to retake his card, and the hand is played over again; but a player committing this fault does not score if he make the point, and only scores one if he make the *vole*.

[*Note.* Some persons imagine that there is nothing gained by sub-forcing, and that they are only obliged to withdraw their card, and take with a stronger, without punishment; they are wrong,—for there are games which are lost because of this necessity of taking, and games which might be won if this practice were allowed.]

ON BETS.

1. It is allowed to bet on either player, and the betters have the right of advising; but their advice, and what they say, is counted for nothing by the adversary, so long as the player has not spoken:—thus, if a better calls "the king," and the player has not announced it before playing his card, he no longer has the right to score it, save in the case already cited in the chapter on "Dealing."

2. The players have the privilege of taking all bets on the opposite side, in preference to the *gallery*, which can only take the amount of what the player has declined to cover.

[*Note.* The gallery is a technical term, used for all except the two players.]

3. It is forbidden to look over the hand of the party betted against.

4. The betters have no right to speak about the hand of their "partners" (or player whom they back), and when they advise, they ought to *point* at the card to be played or kept, but they ought neither to *name* the card nor its suit.

5. Bets can be made on the rubber, the game, and the point; also when either or both players are at the two, three, or four first points; on the king and the queen of trumps; or on the suit of the trump.

6. The gallery has a right to give notice of all errors which would be frauds, could it be supposed they were done intentionally:—for example, if a player scored a point too many, or took tricks not belonging to him

7. We have said further back, that a player who quits the game loses it; but in this case, one of the betters is obliged by his own interest, and that of the others, to take the vacant seat and finish the game.

8. At the end of each game the winning player first takes whatever is due to him, and then divides the remainder amongst the betters, giving to each his due, without however being responsible for errors which may result from the inexactitude of the accounts; the deficit (if any) must be borne by the betters amongst them.

ON MIS-DEALING.

1. When the dealer turns up two or more cards instead of one, the player has the right to pick out that which ought to be the trump; or to put aside the cards thus exposed and take the next remaining on the pack for trump; or to recommence the hand, taking the deal; but he has only this last choice provided he has not seen his hand.

2. When the dealer shows or turns up one or more cards of his adversary's hand, he must finish dealing, and the adversary has then the choice of recommencing the hand, taking the deal, or counting the deal good.

3. If the cards exposed belong to the dealer, neither party has the choice of recommencing the deal, the fault being prejudicial to the dealer who has chosen his cards, and advantageous to the player who has seen them.

4. If, however, this happen after the écart (or change,) the party who has exposed the cards can only require another or others, but cannot recommence the deal.

5. If the dealer after changing, turn up a card as if he were turning up the trump at the beginning of the hand, he can neither refuse a fresh change to his adversary, nor to give him the card thus turned up.

ON MIS-DEALING THE ENTIRE HAND.

[*Note.* The entire hand (called in French *D'Emblée*), is the *first hand* dealt by each dealer; when five cards are given to each party and one turned up, making the full number of eleven.]

1. If the dealer gives one or more cards too many, the player has the right either to look at his hand and throw out the supernumerary cards, first showing them to the dealer, or to recommence the hand, taking to himself the deal.

2. If he has given too few, the player has the right to take the number wanting from the *talon* or residue of the pack, without however changing the trump; or to recommence, taking the deal.

3. If, on the contrary, the dealer has dealt himself too many cards, the adversary has a right either to pick out at hazard the supernumerary cards, or to recommence the hand, taking the deal.

4. If the dealer deals himself too few cards, the adversary has a right either to make him take the number wanting from the *talon;* or recommence the hand, taking the deal.

5. If one of the two players, having too many, or too few, cards, should écart without giving notice to his adversary, and if the latter should perceive it, either from counting the cards thrown out, or in any other way, the player who thus makes a false écarte, loses two points, *and the right of marking the king, even if he had turned it up.*

ON MIS-DEALING AFTER CHANGING CARDS.

1. If the dealer gives more or less cards than asked for, he loses the point and the right of marking the king if he has it in his hand, but not if he has turned it up, the turn up being anterior to the mis-deal.

2. If the dealer deals himself more cards than he has thrown out, he loses the point and the right of marking the king if he has it in his hand.

3. If he deals himself fewer, he completes his hand from the first cards of the *talon*, since they are his by right.

4. If he only perceives it when he has played, the player counts as tricks those cards which cannot be covered.

5. If, however, the fault is not the dealer's, as in the case where the player has asked for more or less cards than he has thrown out, then the player loses one point and the right of marking the king. But if he has too few cards he may mark it, for the simple reason, that holding the king with too few cards, he would of course have equally held it, if he had asked fer his proper number.

6. Whichever (after having changed cards) holds more than five, loses a point, and the right to score the king.

7. Any case not mentioned in this treatise, ought always to be decided against the player who commits the fault.

There only now remains to treat of the principles of the game, the manner of playing it, its niceties or *finesses*, its combinations, and the advantages to be derived from a knowledge of these points.

PART II.—ON THE PRINCIPLES.

All Games of Hazard are subject to an analysis founded on mathematical principles.

Many calculators have exercised their talents in analyzing different games, but not one has entered into any details on the game of Ecarté, either because it is but lately in fashion, or because it has not attracted their attention.

The following are the fundamental principles of this game:—

1. As five cards are dealt to each, and one turned up, it is evident that a player after having looked at his hand, has a knowledge of six cards, and that there remain twenty-six unknown to him, viz.,—twenty-one in the *talon*, and five in his adversary's hand, making altogether thirty-two, of which number the pack is composed.

2. It is then on the six known, and the twenty-six unknown cards, that he must reason, and base his calculations.

For example:—if in the six known cards there are two of the same colour turned up, (or trumps,) there remain six trumps in the twenty-six unknown.

Hence—if in the twenty-six unknown, there are six trumps, or rather less than a quarter, it is probable that in the adversary's five cards there is, at most, but one trump, since one is also a trifle less than the quarter of five.

This principle is the basis of all; from it arise all others; and in order to place it in a more obvious light, and more copious in consequences, we have given in the following table, the number of the principal combinations of twenty-six cards, calculated mathematically.

Twenty-six cards can form 65,780 combinations of five cards,—or in other words, 65,780 different hands of five cards each.

	IF IN THE SIX KNOWN CARDS						
	there is not one club.	there is one club.	there are two clubs.	there are three clubs.	there are four clubs.	there are five clubs.	there are six clubs.
The science of combinations teaches that the number of hands of five cards, which will be without a club, in the twenty-six unknown cards, is...	8568	11628	15504	20349	26334	33649	42504
With one club......	24480	27132	29070	29925	29260	26565	21252
With two clubs......	22848	20349	17100	13300	9240	5313	2024
With three clubs....	8568	5985	3800	2100	924	253	....
With four clubs.....	1260	665	300	105	22	....	....
With five clubs......	56	21	6	1	....	....	....
Total.........	65780	65780	65780	65780	65780	65780	65780

To point out the method of using this table,—suppose the player has but one club in the hand first dealt him, and that the trump card is also a club, making *two known* clubs, and that it is desired to ascertain what are the chances of probability which can also give two or more to the adversary.

It will be seen in the third column, that of the 65,780 hands which the twenty-six unknown cards can form, there are—

Without one club	15,504	
With one club	29,070	
Total of hands which have not two clubs		**44,574**
Hands with two clubs	17,100	
" three clubs	3,800	
" four clubs	300	
" five clubs	6	
Total of hands which have two or more clubs		**21,206**
Total of hands which twenty-six cards can form		65,780

From these combinations we may draw the conclusion that a player can risk with probability of success, a first hand, (called in French "*un jeu d'emblée*," being the first five cards

dealt previously to changing, and which, for brevity's sake, we shall denominate a first hand,) which ought to win the point if it does not encounter two trumps in that of his adversary, (such as will be seen in the paragraph which treats of the "*Jeux de Regles*," see p. 247) since the odds are 44,574 against 21,206, or reduced to simple terms, a little more than 2 to 1 that two clubs will not be found in the adversary's first hand.

The kings being superior cards, and that turned up of double importance, (as the king gives one point, moreover as a trump taking all other trumps,) it is an interesting enquiry, how many, according to the doctrine of chances, there are likely to be in the adversary's hand after the cards have been distributed to each of the players, and the trump ascertained.

To resolve this question we have compiled the following table.

	IF IN THE SIX KNOWN CARDS				
	there is not one king.	there is one king.	there are two kings.	there are three kings.	there are four kings.
The number of hands without a king in the 26 unknown cards is..	26334	33649	42504	53130	65780
With one king...........	29260	26565	21252	12650	....
With two kings........	9240	5313	2024	...	....
With three kings........	924	253	....	....	....
With four kings..........	22	....	....	....	....
Total.........	65780	65780	65780	76780	65780

Hence—if there were one king in the six known caıds, it would be seen in the second column that in 65,780 different hands which the adversary can have, there will be 33,649, that is to say, more than half, which are without kings, and consequently, it is probably that he has no king in his hand

This rule about kings, applies also to queens, knaves, &c.

This same table serves to ascertain the probability of finding the king of trumps in the adversary's hand; it is sufficient to glance down the fourth column where it is seen that when one king only fixes the attention, there are 12,650 games that contain it, and that there are 53,130 which do not.

Consequently the odds are 53,130 against 12,650, or in simple terms, 21 against 5, that the adversary has not the king of trumps, first hand.

It will perhaps be noticed that the three first columns of the last table, are the same as the three last of the preceding table; this arises from the circumstance that when there are four, five, or six clubs known, and that there consequently remain four, three, or two, in the twenty-six unknown cards, the case as to the probability of finding four clubs is exactly similar to that of finding four kings.

We will not swell this little work with more tables. Volumes might be written, and it would be easy to lose oneself in endless calculations; we must leave to players the task of appreciating those principles *by practice*, without a further demand on their memory and attention.

PART III.—ON THE METHOD OF PLAYING.

GENERAL RULES.

When a player holds (comprising the king of trumps) three cards which ensure the point, *he ought always to propose*, if the two remaining cards are not sufficiently strong to give reasonable expectation of the *vole*. It is even good play to propose, were it only for *one card*, in order to hazard receiving a refusal, or to make the *vole* if the proposal is accepted, and there should be five cards in the *rentrée* (or take in).

When a player has hopes of making the *vole*, and the adversary cannot answer a lead of trumps, it is better to play a king if single, than to continue trump; because the system of the game being to play double cards (*i. e.* two or more of a suit,) if the adversary is dubious which to retain, he will by preference keep the suit in which he was attacked. If the player is engaged with an adversary who is acquainted with this *ruse*, it may be still advantageous to act in a similar manner, but in an inverse sense; that is to say, equally play the king, although guarded, before continuing trump, because imagining that it is done to induce him to keep the suit of the king already played, he will part with it more readily than any other suit.

When a player expects to make the *vole*, and has not trumps sufficiently strong to begin by playing them, he must be careful to keep changing his suit in order not to be roughed, and to be able to make a trump, whatever it may be, at the fourth card after having secured the point.

When a player has made two tricks, and remains with the queen of trumps and two small ones, knowing the king to be in the adversary's hand, he ought to lead with one of the small trumps, and wait with the queen guarded. Nothing could prevent his making the odd trick even against king third.

When there is a fear lest the adversary should make the *vole*, and the player has but one trump and four weak cards, without any hope of making the point, he must play his strongest single card, in order to get a chance of employing his trump in case the suit of his single card should be lead up to him.

When the game is three against four, and the player who is at four makes his adversary play, or plays himself without changing, the one who is at three, if he have the king, would do well *not to announce it*, in order to draw his antagonist into the error of leading trump to *pass* his good cards, and be taken by the king which he did not expect, thus losing the point which he would perhaps have won, had he known that the king was in the adversary's hand: in this case it is the less consequence for the player who is at three to announce his king and mark it, inasmuch as he gains two points, that is,—the game, if he make three tricks; his adversary having played, or forced him to play, without changing.

[*Note.* To *pass* a card, means to lead it and make a trick with it, without its being taken by a higher of the same suit or roughed. By some writers this latter word is spelt "ruffed,"—but we think erroneously.]

HANDS TO BE PLAYED WITHOUT CHANGING; AND METHOD OF PLAYING THEM.

These are termed "*Jeux de Regles.*" No hand ought to be played without changing, excepting when the odds are 2 to 1 that the player make three tricks, for the risk is 2 to 1 against him if he do not make them, excepting the cases where the adversary is at four, because as he then wants but one point to win, the risk is no longer 2 to 1, and by playing without a change the chance of giving him the king is avoided.

On this principle all "*Jeux de Regles*" are played without changing (although there be a few which can scarcely reckon in their favor 2 to 1.)

The following are "*Jeux de Regles:*"—all those hands which

cannot fail making three tricks, except from finding two trumps (first hand) in the adversary's hand.

Example 1st.—A has one trump, no matter how small; a tierce major, and a small card of either remaining suit; the odds are more than 2 to 1 that he wins the point;—the probability is demonstrated in the first table.

Method of playing.—Begin with the king of the tierce, and continue the suit, if not roughed, until you are roughed; if it happens at the second card, your trump will bring you back to your suit, and enable you to make the third trick

Example 2nd.—Two trumps,—a queen second, and a small card. This hand ought always to be risked by the player, although the odds are scarcely 2 to 1.

Method of playing.—If the trumps are small, begin by playing the single card, being certain if it is taken, the adversary will not return the suit, and that he will prefer playing a king if he has one; should it be of that suit of which you hold queen second, you make her, later, with the two trumps, supposing he has not superior ones.

But if one of the two trumps is strong, for instance, the queen or the knave, you must then begin with the queen guarded; because you hope if she is roughed, to regain the lead with one of your trumps, and then make a trick with your knave or queen of trumps, in order to pass the second card of the queen which has been roughed.

Example 3rd.—Two trumps; a knave and ace of another suit; and another knave.

Method of playing.—Begin with the knave guarded; if it passes, and the trumps are sequences, and pretty high, risk one; if that makes, play the other, and then your ace, &c.

[*Note.* Generally speaking, a player ought to commence with a card which is guarded, except when he fears the *vole*, or when he can only hope for the point *by being played up to.*]

Example 4th.—Two kings, and queen second.

Method of playing.—As necessarily one king is guarded, begin with this; if it makes a trick, continue the suit; should it be roughed, the chance remains of regaining the lead through the other king, or through the queen, and returning afterwards to the suit of the king first played.

Example 5th.—One trump; a king single; and a queen third.

[*Note.* This is a weak hand if the player has not the lead.]

Method of playing.—If you have the lead, commence with the queen; if she passes, continue the colour; if she is roughed, immediately you regain the lead, again play the suit of the queen that has been roughed.

Example 6th.—One trump, and king fourth.

Method of playing.—If your trump happen to be the queen, play her; for the odds are 21 to 5, that is, rather more than 4 to 1, that the king is not in the adversary's hand; more than 2 to 1, that he has not two trumps; and 55,594 to 10,186, or more than 5 to 1, that he has not two cards of the suit of which you hold king fourth; but it is especially necessary when you are at three, and your adversary four, that you should not hesitate playing the hand in this manner. For be it observed, that in every other position, probabilities which would appear only to offer favorable chances isolatedly, present also the contrary when united: for, firstly, you may encounter the king of trumps; and then probably lose two points: you would likewise lose if you encountered two cards of the suit of which you hold the king; and if the adversary is enabled to take, you might equally lose against an adversary who has no trump; whilst by beginning with the king fourth, you can win against an adversary who has two trumps, if after having roughed, he should lead trump in order to pass a king.

Example 7th.—Two trumps, and three cards of a suit.

[*Note.* This is a very strong hand, and ought *always* to be risked by the player.]

Method of playing.—Having the lead, you commence with the highest card of your suit; if it is roughed, your adversary must have three trumps in order to get the point.

Example 8th.—Four court cards; provided they be not the four knaves, nor the card second, the knave of trumps.

Method of playing.—Very often the way to play this is, to begin with trump, even if it is single; the order in which hands like this ought to be played, can scarcely be pointed out; it depends on the nature of the court cards, more particularly of that which is guarded.

Example 9th.—All hands which require only two cards to be thrown out.

In this class are found those "*Jeux de Regles*" of which we have spoken, where the odds are not 2 to 1 that they will win the point; and yet they are played, because in two cards a player has much less chance of taking in advantageously, than has his adversary in the five which he perhaps requires, and amongst which he may find the king; hence there are very few hands and very few cases wherein a player ought to change for two cards only.

If you play with two trumps and a king unguarded, begin with a low card and *never with a king,* in order to avoid getting it roughed; but on the contrary to be enabled to regain the lead with one trump, play the other to protect the king, and then pass it.

Holding three trumps, especially when sequences, it is almost always the game to lead trump, no matter how inferior they may be.

There are so very few hands which can be reckoned more advantageous to be led up to, than to lead, that we will not mention them; with such sort of hands, never refuse to change *once* and never accede to it a *second time.*

ON HANDS WHICH WIN OR LOSE THE POINT, ACCORDING TO THE MANNER IN WHICH PLAYED.

Example.—Suppose a club the trump. The dealer has ace of trumps, king and nine of diamonds; knave and nine of spades.

The player has queen of trumps, queen of spades, ace of hearts, eight and seven of diamonds.

The right game of the player is, to lead his eight of diamonds, as it is guarded by the seven; if the dealer take with the nine, he ought to lose the point, and if he take with the king, he ought to win it; because taking with the king, he intimates that he has no other diamond, and as he is certain that the adversary led the strongest of his suit he runs no risk in employing this *ruse;* then he plays his knave of spades which is also his guarded card; the player takes with the queen, and then leads queen of trumps, in order to pass his seven of diamonds, which he imagines to be a sure card, the eight having brought out the king, and he loses the point; whereas if the dealer, who took with the king, had taken with nine, the player, after having played the queen of trumps, would have preferred endeavouring to pass his ace of hearts, which had but three cards superior to it, rather than his seven of diamonds, which had five, and he would thus have gained the point.

As it is necessary to make three tricks in order to win the point, it often happens that after having trumped once, it is advisable to *lead trumps,* in order to pass a king, or some high card;—again, there are cases where this would be bad play, as is demonstrated by the following example:—

Suppose a spade the trump card:—the player has the knave and ten of trumps; the king of clubs; and the king and ten of diamonds. The dealer has queen and nine of trumps; knave and ten of hearts; and seven of diamonds.

Should the player not find the king of trumps in his adversary's hand, he has a game which warrants his hoping to make the *vole:* he ought then to commence by playing his king single, in preference to his king second; having more chance of escaping the rough with it, than with that which is guarded; and of being able afterwards to win a trick with a lead from the knave of trumps, having only to fear the queen, (if the dealer has not announced the king,) and endeavour to get the *vole;* the right play therefore is, to commence with the king of clubs; if the dealer trump it, adieu to all hopes of the *vole:*—there only remains to secure the point; the adversary then leads the knave of hearts, which the player takes with his ten of trumps: and *now* comes the nicety; he loses the point if he lead knave of trumps in order to pass his king of diamonds,—whereas he gains it, if he plays his king first. For if he lead his knave of trumps, the dealer takes it with the queen, and makes his second heart, whereas had he played his king of diamonds, it would have been answered with the seven:—he plays diamonds again—the ten,—the adversary is obliged to trump with queen, and then play his ten of hearts, which the player takes by roughing it with the knave of trumps, thus making the third trick.

We have given one reason why it was preferable to play the king of clubs, rather than that which was guarded; we may add add another which confirms the rule, that king single ought to be played first; which is, that if the adversary with two diamonds to the queen, and two clubs to the queen in hand, has any hesitation which suit to keep, he will prefer keeping the queen of clubs, which is his suit first attacked, to keeping the queen of diamonds second

Final Example.—Be particular in holding your cards well up, so that none can see them but yourself, for fear of any indiscreet exclamations on the part of the betters,—as the following *coup* is not so easy that it can be learnt by every player.

The object is to win the point with a hand which would infallibly lose if it were played naturally, that is to say, without *finesse.*

Suppose a heart the trump. The player has the king, ace, and ten of trumps: the king of diamonds; and the king of spades. The dealer has the queen, knave, and seven of trumps; the eight and seven of clubs.

The player would feel almost sure of making the *vole*, if to his king of trumps, with which he ought to open the game, he sees fall the queen; and yet this would cause him to lose the point, if the dealer is sufficiently adroit to throw her away, instead of the seven, on the king; because the player would then continue leading trumps, by playing his ace, and the dealer take it whith his knave, and then play his eight of clubs, which the player would rough with his ten of trumps, and play one of his kings,—the dealer would rough this with his seven of trumps, and then pass his second club; the player having no more trumps to rough with, loses the point; whereas had the dealer thrown the seven, instead of the queen of trumps on the king, the player, fearful of meeting the queen and knave of trumps accompanied by clubs, would not have continued leading trumps, but played one of his kings, and would necessarily have won the point.

CONCLUSION.

It would exceed the limits of this little work to give more examples of hands which are susceptible of *finesse;* it being essential only to cite a few of the most remarkable, in order to lay down the principles; to establish fixed and complete rules; to indicate the method of playing the cards to advantage; and to give the power, by means of a recognized code, of avoiding, smoothing down, or settling all the discussions which continually arise in society, where this game is undoubtedly very fashionable; disputes having hitherto been generally decided according to the usages of localities; which a traveller would find to vary very much.

This is the object we have aimed at; whether successfully, the Reader must decide.

RULES FOR CALCULATING BETS ON ANY EVENT.

Add together the odds for and against; divide the given sum: or, (as a general example,) say—£1 into as many parts as there are odds, and give to each party as many shares as he has chances.

Example.—Odds 5 to 1 against A.—7 to 3 against B.—11 to 4 against C.

What are the odds between the field and the favourites?—$5+1=6$. Divide £1 by 6; then A's value will be one-sixth, or 3*s.* 4*d.*—B's value three-tenths, or 6*s.*—and C's value four-fifteenths, or 5*s.* 4*d.*,—being altogether, 14*s.* 8*d.* for the favourites, leaving 5*s.* 4*d.* for the field; or, reduced to fractions, 11 to 4 against the field.

The odds, A against B, will be 3*s.* 4*d.* to 6*s.* = 18 to 10, or 9 to 3 against A. The same rule can be applied in comparing the value of any of the other odds. The odds may be readily computed by the following rule:—reduce the odds, in each case, to a vulgar fraction; then multiply all the denominators for a common denominator, and each numerator by all the denominators, except its own, for a new numerator.

In the last case, A's value = one-sixth, B's = three-tenths, and C's = four-fifteenths, giving a new denominator of 900: and A's numerator = 150, B's = 279, and C's = 250; leaving the remainder, or 230, for the field; or, reduced to 30ths, A = 5, B = 9, C = 8, and field = 8.—Total 30.

The value which ought to be paid to cancel a bet, where either party has betted too high, is found as follows:—deduct the value which ought to be staked, from the amount actually staked; then divide the surplus stakes by the total odds between the parties, and the party in whose favour the bet stands, will be entitled to receive such a proportion of the surplus as is equal to his odds on the event.

Example.—I bet 9 to 6 against C, the odds being as above. In this case my opponent ought to stake four-fifteenths, or 5*s.* 4*d.*, instead of six-fifteenths, or 8*s.*, and, consequently, he stakes 2*s.* 8*d.* beyond the correct amount; and the odds in my favour being eleven-fifteenths, I am entitled to that proportion of the 2*s.* 8*d.*, or surplus amount staked, to cancel the bet.

VOCABULARY OF THE PRINCIPAL TERMS USED IN PLAYING ECARTE.

[*Note.* Those marked with an * are words which are commonly used even amongst English at this game; the rest are useful to be acquainted with when playing with foreigners.]

Abattre—To lower the cards and show them.
**Atout*—Trump.
Avoir la main—The action of dealing.
Battre—To shuffle the cards before dealing.
Carte doublée }
Carte Gardée } Two cards of the same suit.
**Couper*—To cut.
Défausser—To refuse a suit.
**Donner*—To deal.
**Ecart*—The cards which are thrown aside.
Etre à la devine—To be embarrassed which suit to keep.
Faire—The same as "*donner*" to deal.
Faire un main—To make a trick.
**Forcer*—To play a superior card on an inferior.
La Belle—The highest card of any suit.
**La Vole*—To make all the tricks.
**Le Point*—One score of the five which compose the game.
Levee—One trick made whilst playing.
**Proposer*—The asking fresh hands, or part of fresh hands
Refaire—To recommence distributing the cards.
**Renouncer*—Not to answer the suit led.
**Retourner*—When the cards are dealt to turn up the first of the *Talon*.
Sous-forcer—To play a card inferior to what remains of some suit in hand.
Talon—What remains of the pack after there has been distributed to each player what he requires

LOTO.

F... this game, which may be played by an unlimited number of persons, boxes containing 100 counters; 14 fishes, every one reckoned as ten counters; 12 contracts, valued at ten fish a-piece; a pack of 24 very large cards, with fifteen different numbers marked on each, and in a bag 90 knobs or balls, numbered from 1 to 90; besides a board with ten cavities cut therein, for the purpose of placing the knobs as drawn; are sold at the Tunbridge-ware or turners' shops. Fresh covers for the cards may be purchased, ready printed, and any bookbinder can easily make a new or repair the old pack.

RULES.

1. Every player should draw two cards, and deposit a stake previously agreed upon; and if the party is not too numerous, then any may take four or six cards, laying down a double or treble stake accordingly; and when the players are more than twelve, then some are only to have one card, paying half a stake, and likewise should the players not take all the cards among them, the remainder of the pack is to be laid aside until some other persons join the set. From the cards not taken, players may exchange one or more of those drawn, or they may change with one another; similar exchanges, if the company consent, may also be made previous to each drawing, and likewise prior to replenishing the pool. Cards may be thrown up, or additional ones drawn from those put by; stakes being paid proportionably.

2. The stakes are to be put together in a pool, placed on the middle of the table, and also on the table a quantity of counters sufficient for the number of cards taken; upon the counters a value is to be fixed adequate to the stakes first deposited, from the whole of which a sum must be reserved, enough to pay, at the conclusion of the game, all the counters laid upon the table.

3. Then after counting the 90 knobs so as to be certain they are right, the eldest hand shall first shake them well together in the bag, and afterwards draw out ten successively,

not only declaring the number of each as drawn, but also placing the same conspicuously on the board.

4. As soon as the number is declared, each player having the same on one or more cards, is to take up counters sufficient to lay one upon that number every time it occurs, and so on until the ten knobs are drawn.

5. When only part of the pack is taken, and a number drawn happens not to be upon any player's card, then the players may put away that knob till some person takes the card on which it is printed.

6. When ten knobs are drawn out, every player examining the cards separately, and having only one counter upon any horizontal line, wins for that no more than the said counter, which is styled gaining by *abstract;* where two counters are on the same horizontal line of a separate card, the player gains an *ambo*, and becomes entitled to five counters, besides the two; when three are upon the same line, the player obtains a *terne*, and is to receive 25 additional counters; if four are on the same line, that is called a *quaterne*, winning 100 counters additional; when five occur on the same line, that makes a *quinterne*, gaining 250 additional counters, and the player is entitled to payment out of the pool for all the abovementioned acquisitions previous to another drawing. Instead of giving counters, payment for the same may at once be made from the stock in the pool.

7. The knobs are then to be returned, and the bag given to the next player in rotation, who is to shake the same, and draw, &c., as before stated.

8. Whenever the pool is exhausted, the players must contribute again, according to the number of cards taken; and when it is resolved to finish the game, they agree among themselves to have only a fixed number of drawings more.

9. At the last drawing each player proceeds as heretofore directed, but the drawing concludes when no more counters are left on the table. The players then beginning with the eldest-hand, are to be paid out of the pool, as far as the money will go; and when that is expended, the others remain unpaid, which is styled a Bankruptcy; next the players are to re-unite the counters with those that were on their cards, and receive payment for them out of the fund reserved at the commencement of the game.

10. There are also cards of a new combination, which may be played by 6 = 12 = 18 = or 24, observing that when six cards only are taken, but one counter is given; if 12, two; if 18, three; and when 24, four counters; and also when but six cards are taken, they must be either from 1 to 6—7 to 12—13 to 18—or 19 to 24; if 12 cards, from 1 to 12—or 13 to 24—for 18 cards, from 1 to 18; and when 24, the whole number.

11. The counters may refer for the payment to the amount of the stakes deposited in the stock.

For 24 cards	. . . .	144 times	10
" 18 "	. . . .	108 "	10
" 12 "	. . . .	72 "	10
" 6 "	. . . .	36 "	10

There are other methods of playing at Loto, but the before-mentioned is the most approved.

POPE, OR POPE JOAN.

POPE, a game somewhat similar to that of Matrimony, is played by a number of people, who generally use a board painted for this purpose, which may be purchased at most turners' or toy shops.

The eight of diamonds must first be taken from the pack, and after settling the deal, shuffling, &c., the dealer dresses the board by putting fish, counters, or other stakes, one each to ace, king, queen, knave, and game; two to matrimony, two to intrigue, and six to the nine of diamonds, styled Pope. This dressing is in some companies at the individual expense of the dealer, though in others the players contribute two stakes apiece towards the same.

The cards are next to be dealt round equally to every player, one turned up for trump, and about six or eight left in the stock to form stops; as for example, if the ten of spades is turned up, the nine consequently becomes a stop; the four kings and the seven of diamonds are always fixed stops, and the dealer is the only person permitted in the course of the game to refer occasionally to the stock for information what other cards are stops in that respective deal.

If either ace, king, queen, or knave, happens to be the turned-up trump, the dealer takes whatever is deposited on that head; but when Pope is turned up, the dealer is entitled both to that and the game, besides a stake for every card dealt to each player. Unless the game is determined by Pope being turned up, the eldest hand begins by playing out as many cards as possible; first the stops, then Pope if he has it, and afterwards the lowest card of his longest suit, particularly an ace, for that never can be led through; the other players are to follow when they can, in sequence of the same suit, till a stop occurs, and the party having the said stop, thereby becomes eldest-hand, and is to lead accordingly, and so on, until some person parts with all his cards, by which he wins the pool (game,) and becomes entitled besides to a stake for every card not played by the others, except from any one holding Pope, which excuses him from paying; but if Pope has been played, then the party having held it is not excused, having already received the stakes for that card.

King and queen form what is denominated matrimony, queen and knave make intrigue, when in the same hand; but neither they, nor ace, king, queen, knave, or pope, entitle the holder to the stakes deposited thereon, unless played out, and no claim can be allowed after the board is dressed for the succeeding deal; but in all such cases the stakes are to remain for future determination.

This game only requires a little attention to recollect what stops have been made in the course of the same; as for instance, if a player begins by laying down the eight of clubs, then the seven in another hand forms a stop, whenever that suit is led from any lower card, or the holder when eldest may safely lay it down in order to clear his hand.

VINGT-UN.

VINGT-UN, or twenty-one, is very similar to Quinze, and may be played by two or more people. It is essentially a family game, and when played as such, the stakes are usually represented by counters, which may be of any value; say, sixpence the dozen, or more. It is common to limit the stakes to be laid to a dozen of counters, or the amount in money which they represent. As the deal is advantageous, and often continues long with the same person, it is usual to determine it at the commencement by the first ace turned up, or any other mode that may be agreed upon.

The deal is retained by the person who commences, until a natural vingt-un occurs, when it passes to the next in rotation.* (The old mode of play, however, is, that in the case of a natural vingt-un the deal passes to the holder, and many still adhere to this custom. This item of the game must, therefore, be regulated by the custom of the table, or be previously agreed.) The pony or youngest hand should collect the cards that have been played, and shuffle them together ready for the dealer against the period when he shall have distributed the whole pack.

The dealer begins by giving two cards, one at a time, face downwards, to each player, including himself. After the first card has been dealt round, each places his stake upon it (which may, if he chooses, be as low as a single counter,) and then receives the second card; but the dealer, upon the stakes being all laid, and before proceeding with the deal, looks at his own card, and if he thinks proper (having perhaps an ace, ten, or court card,) he may double the stakes, which he announces by crying 'double.' He then distributes a second card to each, and lastly to himself. Should he chance to have a natural vingt-un, he declares it at once, before any more cards are dealt, and collects the stakes (which, by a vingt-un, are doubled,) but should he have drawn less than 21, the game proceeds thus:—The dealer enquires of each player in rotation, beginning with the eldest hand on the left, whether he stands, or wishes for another card, which, if required, must be given from off the top (face upwards) of the pack, and afterwards another, or more, if requested, till the points of the additional card or cards, added to those dealt, exceed or make 21 exactly, or such a number less than 21, as the player may choose to stand upon; but when the points exceed 21, the player is technically said to have overdrawn, and his cards are to be thrown up forthwith, and the stake laid on them paid to the dealer. When the dealer has gone the

* Should a natural vingt-un occur in the first round it does not put o t, the dealer being allowed a *misericorde*.

round of the table in this manner, he turns up his own cards to the view of the company, and should he have any number of points, between, say from 17 to 20, he usually "stands," that is, pits his cards against the other players. Those under his number, as well as ties,* pay; those above it receive. If the dealer should have only 14 or 15 points in his first hand, the chances would be against him, were he to stand on so small a number. He would therefore draw another card, and should this be a very low one (an ace or a deuce,) and he have reason to suppose, by the extra cards dealt round, that he had to contest high numbers, he would draw again, and if he obtained 19 or 20 points would then probably win on more than he loses; the average of chances being in his favor; if by drawing he should happen to make up 21, he would receive double from all, excepting from the ties and those who had already thrown up; if more than 21, he would have to pay all who stand, paying the vingt-uns double.

Should either the dealer or a player happen to turn up two cards of the same denomination, for instance, two aces, deuces, or any other number, or two kings, two queens, &c., he would have the choice of going on both, and should the next card he draws be a triplicate, he may go on all three. If the cards happen to be aces, which count either as 1 or 11, at the option of the player, and if by great luck he should successively draw three tens, or Court cards, thus making three natural vingt-uns, he would obtain double stakes upon each, therefore six times as much as the stakes placed on the various hands, and should he, on laying his first card, have cried "double," the stakes payable, would, in such case, be twice doubled, therefore upon the three cards twelve-fold. This is an extreme case, cited merely to show the nature of the game. It commonly happens, however, that when either dealer or player "goes" on several cards, he loses on one or more, and thus neutralizes his gains. Players, as already intimated, have the same right of "going" on several cards. as the dealer.

When any player has a vingt-un, and the dealer not, then the player wins double stakes from him; in other cases, except a natural vingt-un happens, the dealer pays single stakes

* Ties are the principal advantage of the dealer.

to all whose numbers under 21 are higher than his own, and receives from those who have lower numbers; players who have similar numbers to the dealer pay; and when the dealer draws more than 21, he overdraws, and has to pay to all who have not thrown up, as already stated.

Twenty-one, whensoever dealt in the first two cards, is styled a Natural Vingt-un, and should be declared immediately. Hoyle says that this entitles the possessor to the deal, besides double stakes from all the players, unless there shall be more than one natural vingt-un, in which case the younger hand or hands so having the same, are exempted from paying to the eldest. But this rule, like that mentioned at page 318, is nearly obsolete. It is not now customary to allow any except the dealer to take double stakes from the company, in respect to his natural vingt-un.

One of the first thoughts of the dealer, after the cards have been cut, should be to look for BRULET, which is a natural vingt-un formed by the bottom and top card, when they happen to be an ace and tenth card. The card or cards looked at must be thrown out, and mixed with those collected by the pony. Brulet either clears the board of the stakes laid, (usually one or two counters levied on each player, at the commencement of every game, and collected into a tray,) or takes the amount of the limit (perhaps 6*d.*) from each, as may be agreed.

The deal, it should be observed, may be sold to the best bidder, and, as it is undoubtedly of some advantage, a buyer will generally be found. But should a timid player object to the deal, and no buyer be found, he may decline it, and so let it pass to the next.

N. B. An ace, as already intimated, may be reckoned either as 11 or 1: every court-card is counted as 10, and the rest of the pack according to their points.

The odds of this game merely depend upon the average quantity of cards likely to come under or exceed 21; for example, if those in hand make 14 exactly, it is 7 to 6 that the one next drawn does not make the number of points above 21, but if the points be 15, it is 7 to 6 against that hand; yet it would not therefore always be prudent to stand at 15, for as the ace may be calculated both ways, it is rather above an even bet that the adversary's two first cards amount to more than 14. A natural vingt-un may be expected once in 7 coups when two, and twice in 7, when four people play, and so on according to the number of players.

LANSQUENET.

THIS game may be played by almost any number of people, although only one pack of cards is used at a time, during each deal.* The dealer, who has rather an advantage, begins by shuffling the cards, and having them cut by any other person of the party; after which he deals out two cards on his left-hand, turning them up; then one for himself, and a fourth, which he places in the middle of the table for the company, called the *rejouissance* card. Upon this card any, or all of the company, except the dealer, may put their money, either a limited or unlimited sum, as may be agreed on, which the dealer is obliged to answer, by staking a sum equal to the whole that is put upon it by different persons. He continues dealing, and turning the cards upwards, one by one, till two of a sort appear; for instance, two aces, two deuces, &c. which in order to separate, and that no person may mistake for single cards, he places on each side of his own card; and as often as two, three, or the fourth card of a sort comes up, he always places them, as before said, on each side of his own. Any single card the company has a right to take and put their money upon, unless the dealer's own card happens to be double, which often occurs by this card being the same as one of the two cards which he first of all dealt out on his left-hand. Thus he continues dealing till he brings either their cards, or his own. As long as his own card remains undrawn he wins; and whichever card comes up first, loses. If he draws or deals out the two cards on his left, which are called the hand-cards, before his own, he is entitled to deal again; the advantage of which is no other, than being exempted from losing when he draws a similar card to his own, immediately after he has turned up one for himself.

* As the game is now played in France, four, and even more, packs of cards are mixed together.

This game is often played more simply without the *rejouissance* card, giving every person round the table a card to put their money upon. Sometimes it is played by dealing only two cards, one for the dealer, and another for the company.

PUT.

WE will borrow the opinions and views of this little contrivance against time—as broached by Mr. Seymour in his volume written for the especial behoof of the young princesses—and append to them Mr. Hoyle's observations on it.

"Put is the ordinary rooking-game of every place; and seems, by the few cards that are dealt, to have no difficulty in the play; but there is great craft and cunning in it.

"If you play at either Two or Three-handed Put, the best put-card deals. Having shuffled the cards, the adversary cuts them; then the dealer deals one to his antagonist, and another to himself, till they have three a-piece: five up, or a Put is commonly the game. The eldest, if he hath a good game and thinks it better than his adversary's, puts to him; if the other will not, or dare not see him, he then wins one; but if he will see him, they play it out, and he who wins two tricks, or all three, wins the whole set; but if each wins a trick, and third tied, neither win, because it is trick and tye.

"Sometimes they play without putting; and then the winner is he that wins most tricks. In playing keep up your cards very close; for the least discovery of any one of them, is a great advantage to him who sees it.

"This game consists very much in daring; for a mettled gamester will put boldly upon very bad cards sometimes, as upon a five, seven and a nine; the other thinking there are good cards in his adversary's hand, having very indifferent ones in his own, dares not see him; and so by going to stock, loseth one. He who once hath the confidence to put on bad cards, cannot recal his putting, by which means he frequently pays for his bravado.

"The best Put-cards are, first, the tray, next, the deuce, then the ace; the rest follow in pre-eminence, as king, queen, knave ten, and so onwards, to the four, which is the meanest card at Put.

"Put, played with a complete pack, generally by two people, sometimes by three, and often by four, is a game at which the cards rank differently from all others, tray being the best, next the deuce, then ace, king, and so on in the usual order. After cutting for deal, &c., at which the highest Put-card wins, three cards, by one at a time, are given to each player, then the game is played in the following way. If the non-dealer throws up his cards, he loses a point; if he plays, and the dealer does not lay down another to it, he gains a point; but, should the dealer either win the same, pass it, or lay down one of equal value, forming what is termed a tie, the non-dealer is still at liberty to put, that is play, or not, and his opponent then only gains a point; then if both parties agree to go on, whoever gains all the tricks or two out of three, wins five points, which are the game; if each player obtains one trick, and the third is a tie, then neither party scores.

"Four-handed Put differs only in that any two of the players give each their best card to his partner, who then lays out one of his, and the game is afterwards played as in two-handed Put.

"If the dealer turns up any of his adversary's cards, another deal may be demanded; but when he shows his own, he is to abide by them: and should a faced card occur, the pack must be shuffled and dealt again: when more cards than necessary are given to the non-dealer, he may either claim a fresh deal, or have the extra cards drawn out; but should the dealer give himself too many, then his opponent is entitled to a point, and may either have another deal, or draw the supernumerary cards. Bye-standers ought never to interfere, under penalty of paying the stakes. Either party saying 'I put,' must abide the event of the game, or pay the stakes."

LOTTERY.

Of the minor games of cards, Lottery is without doubt one of the most amusing. A great excellence of the game is, that it is most agreeable when there is a great number of players; for it may be played by ten, twelve, or more; but not well with less than four or five players. Two entire packs of cards are employed, one of which serves for the tricks, and the other for the lots or prizes. Each player should take a certain number of counters, more or less, that and their value depending on the will of the players. These points being settled, every one gives the counters he has, for his stake, and these being collected into a box or purse, on the middle of the table, compose the fund of the Lottery.

The players being all ranged round the table, two of them take the two packs of cards, and as it is of no importance who deals, as there is no advantage in being eldest or youngest, the cards are commonly presented in compliment to some two of the players. The dealers, after well shuffling the cards, have them cut by their left-hand neighbours, and one of them deals a card to each player; all these cards are to remain turned, and are called the *lots;* each player then places on his lot what number of counters he thinks proper; they should observe, however, to make them one higher than the other, that there may be as few as possible of the same value. The lots being thus prized, he who has the other pack deals likewise to each player one card, which are called the *tickets;* each player having received his card, the lots are then turned, and each examines whether his ticket answers to any of the lots; for example, if any of the lots are, the knave of clubs, the queen of hearts, the ace of spades, the eight of clubs, the six of diamonds, the four of hearts, the three of spades, and the two of diamonds; he or they, whose cards correspond to any of those, take up the lot or prize that is marked on that card.

The two dealers then collect those cards that belong to their respective packs, and after having shuffled them, deal again in the same manner as before, the lots being laid down and drawn by the tickets, in the manner we have just mentioned; and such lots as remain undrawn, are to be added to the fund of the lottery. This continues till the fund is all drawn out, after which each player examines what he has won, and the stakes are paid in money by him who drew the lottery; whose business it is to collect and divide it.

If the party should last too long, instead of giving only one card to each for his ticket, you may give two, three, or even four, one after the other, according as you would have the party continue; the increasing the value of the lots likewise, helps greatly to shorten the party.

Another method is, to take at random three cards out of one of the packs, and place them, face downward, on a board or in a bowl on the table for the prizes, then every player purchases from the other pack any number of cards for tickets as may be most agreeable, paying a fixed sum or certain quantity of counters for each, which sums or counters are put in different proportions on the three prizes to be gained by those who happen to have purchased corresponding cards, and such that happen not to be drawn are continued till the next deal.

This game may be played with a single pack, by separating the same into two divisions, each containing a red and black suit.

COMMERCE.

Of this there are two distinct methods of playing, the new and the old mode. The new way is played by any number of persons, from three to twelve, with a complete pack of 52 cards, bearing the same import as at Whist, only the ace is reckoned as eleven. Every player has a certain quantity of counters on which a fixed value is put, and each, at every fresh deal, lays down one for the stake. Sometimes the game is continued until, or finished when, one of the players has lost all the counters given at the commencement; but in order to prevent it from being spun out to an unpleasant length, or concluded too soon, it is often customary to fix the duration to a determinate number of tours or times, that the whole party shall deal once each completely round.

After determining the deal, the dealer, styled also the banker shuffles the pack, which is to be cut by the left hand player; then three cards, either altogether or one by one, at the dealer's pleasure, are given to each person, beginning on the right hand, but none are to be turned up. If the pack proves false, or the deal wrong, or should there be a faced card, then there must be a fresh deal.

At this game are three parts: 1st, That which takes place of all others, called the tricon, or three cards of the same denomination, similar to pair-royal at Cribbage: 2dly, the next in rank is the sequence, or three following cards of the same suit, like tierce at Piquet: and lastly, the point, being the greatest number of pips on two or three cards of a suit in any one hand; of all which parts the highest disannuls the lower.

After the cards have been dealt round, the banker enquires, "Who will trade?" which the players beginning with the eldest hand, usually and separately answer by saying, "For ready money," or "I barter." Trading for money is giving a card and a counter to the banker, who places the card under the stock or remainder of the pack styled the bank, and returns in lieu thereof another card from the top. The counter is profit to the banker, who consequently trades with the stock free from expense. Barter is exchanging a card without pay with the next right hand player, which must not be refused, and so on, the players trade alternately, till one of them obtains the object aimed at, and thereby stops the Commerce; then all show their hands, and the highest tricon, sequence, or point wins the pool. The player who first gains the wished for tricon, &c., should show the same immediately, without waiting till the others begin a fresh round, and if any one chooses to stand on the hand dealt, and show it without trading, none of the junior players can trade that deal, and if the eldest hand stands, then of course no person can trade.

The banker always ranks as eldest hand, in case of neither tricon or sequence, when the game is decided by the point. Whenever the banker does not gain the pool, then he is to pay a counter to that player who obtains the same, and if the banker possesses tricon, sequence, or point and does not win the pool, because another player has a better hand, then he is to give a counter to every player.

Commerce the old way is played by several persons together, every one depositing a certain sum in the pool, and receiving three fish or counters a-piece, on which a value is fixed; as suppose sixpences are pooled, the counters then may be rated at 1*d*. or 1½*d*. each, so as to leave a sum for that player who gains the final sweep. After determining the deal, three cards, beginning on the left hand, are given to every player and as many turned up on the board by one at a time.

This game is gained, as at the other, by pairs, sequences, or flushes, and should the three cards turned up be such as the dealer approves of, he may, previous to looking at the hand dealt to himself, take them so turned up in lieu of his own, but then must abide by the same, and cannot afterwards exchange any during that deal. All the players, beginning with the eldest hand, may in rotation change any card or cards in their possession for such as lie turned up on the table, striving thereby to make pairs-royal, sequences, or flushes, and so on round again and again, till all have refused to change, or are satisfied, but every person once standing cannot change again that deal. Finally the hands are all shown, and the possessor of the highest pair-royal, &c., or the eldest hand if there are more than one of the same value, takes the sum agreed upon out of the pool, and the person having the worst hand, puts one fish or counter therein, called "Going up." The player, whose three are first gone off, has the liberty of purchasing one more, called, "Buying a Horse," for a sum as agreed, usually one-third of the original stake, to be put into the pool. After that, every player, whose fish are all gone, sits by till the game is concluded, which finishes by the person who continues the longest on the board, thereby gaining the pool or final sweep.

BLIND HOOKEY.

THIS is purely a game of chance, without any limit as to the number of players, but is best suited to a party of four, six, or ten. Each player cuts for the deal, which is decided in the same manner as at Whist. The pack being then shuffled by the player on the dealer's right hand, may be again shuffled by the dealer himself, and being cut by the right hand player, is placed by the dealer before the player on his left hand. He cuts a parcel for himself, consisting of not less than four cards, nor of more than shall allow an equal number at least to all the players, and lays them before him with the faces downwards. All the players having done the same, and a small parcel being left for the dealer, he also lays it before him, face downwards. Each player then places upon the parcel of cards before him, the stake which he is inclined to go for, and all the party having followed his example, the dealer forthwith turns up his parcel, for he is obliged to set the players in the amount they decide to venture. The dealer having turned up his parcel, the left-hand player does the same, and whoever turns up the highest card wins the stake, but should the cards "tie," that is, be of equal value, the dealer wins. This is a considerable advantage, and consequently the deal is many points in the favor of the holder. It may be sold, and the buyer being out, which results from his turn-up card being lower than any that is turned up by any of the players, it returns to the player on the left-hand of the dealer who sold it. This is the principle upon which Blind Hookey is commonly played.

MATRIMONY.

MATRIMONY may be played by any number of persons from 5 to 14. This game is composed of 5 chances, usually marked on a board or sheet of paper, as follows:

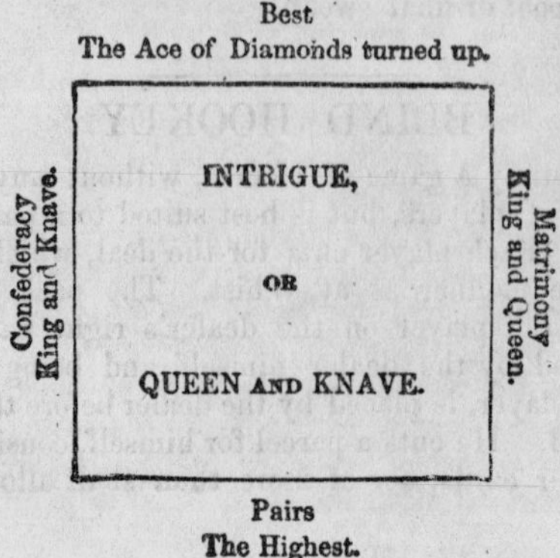

N. B. The ace of diamonds turned up takes the whole pool, but when in hand ranks only as any other ace, and if not turned up, nor any ace in hand, then the king or next superior card, wins the chance styled best.

The game is generally played with counters, and the dealer stakes what he pleases on each or any chance, the other players depositing each the same quantity, except one; that is, when the dealer stakes twelve, the rest of the company lay down eleven each. After this, two cards are dealt round to every one, beginning on the left, then to each one other card turned up, and he who so happens to get the ace of diamonds sweeps all; if it is not turned up, then each player shews his hand, and any of them having matrimony, intrigue, &c., takes the counters on that point; and when two or more people happen to have a similar combination, the eldest hand has the preference, and should any chance not be gained, it stands over to the next deal.

TABLE GAMES.

FARO.

Faro, Pharo, Pharaoh, or Pharaon, is very similar to Basset, a game formerly much in vogue.

RULES OF THE GAME.

The banker turns up the cards from a complete pack, deliberately, one by one, laying them alternately, first to his right for the bank, and then to his left hand for the punter, till the whole are dealt out.

The punter may, at his option, set any number of stakes, agreeable to the sum limited, upon one or more cards chosen out of his liveret, from the ace to the king inclusive, either previous to dealing the cards, or after any quantity of coups are made, or he may masque his bets, or change his cards whenever he pleases, or finally decline punting, except an event is unsettled when not above eight cards are undealt.

The banker wins when the card, equal in points to that on

which the stake is set, turns up on his right hand, but loses when it is dealt to the left.

The punter loses half the stake when his card comes out twice in the same coup.

The last card neither wins nor loses.

The last card but one is called hocly, and forms part of the banker's gain; but now is frequently given up, and generally so in the last deal

When by accident or design the pack happens to contain more or less than 52 cards, or should the last coup be found deficient, owing to any misdeal, however arising, whether discovered at the end or during the game, the bank must then pay every stake depending at the period when the error is detected, which payment must also be made if the cards are thrown up.

The dealer should hold the cards close in his hand, and always be prepared to inform any punter how many cards remain.

The first card is never valid till the second is dealt.

No person but the dealer or croupier should ever meddle with the cards, unless to cut them.

A paroli, &c., may be purchased by paying a sum equivalent to the stake.

METHOD OF PLAY.

The tailleur and croupier sit opposite each other at a large oval table covered with a green cloth, on which is a line marked by coloured tape, or a wooden rim about an inch high, and eight from the edge of the table, for the purpose of separating those cards punted on from the others. Money is placed either loose in a well, or done up in rouleaus. The tailleur is to deal, while the croupier pays and receives, guards against errors, and shuffles another pack of cards.

The game may be played by any number of persons, each punter being furnished with a livret, from which having chosen a card, or cards, and placing the same upon the table, just within the line, putting the stake either thereon, or upon other cards placed face downwards at the head of those betted on. The stakes are answered by the banker, who usually limits the sums according to his capital; and at public tables has generally two or more croupiers Then the dealer having previously counted and shuffled the cards, and had them cut by a punter, should hold the pack tight in his hand, and show the bottom card, as a caution to avoid punting on it near the conclusion of the game, and to prevent mistakes, a similar card, with the corners cut off, is usually laid in the middle of the table; next he says play, and proceeds to deal slowly, first to the right, afterwards to the left, mentioning every one as he goes on, and stopping between each two cards, while the croup settles the event.

When a punter gains, he may either take his money or paroli; if he wins again, he may play sept et le va; should he then prove successful, he can paroli for quinze et le va; afterwards for trente et le va; and, finally, for soixante et le va, which is the highest chance in the game. Should the punter not like to venture so boldly, he may make a paix, or point; afterwards a double or treble paix, &c., or a single double, or treble paix-paroli. When doublets are dealt, the punter may either pay or make a pli.

A reckoning may be kept of the number of times each card is dealt, by properly placing a livret and bending the corners of similar cards one way for the punter, another way for the dealer.

TERMS USED AT FARO.

Banker; the person who keeps the table

Cocking. See Paroli.

Couche or *Enjeu;* the Stake.

Coup; a Stroke or Pull. Any two cards dealt alternately to the right and left.

Croupier; Croup. An assistant to the dealer.

Doublet; is when the punter's card is turned up twice in the same coup, then the bank wins half the stake. A single paroli must be taken down, but if there are several, only one retires.

Hocly; a Certainty; signifies the last card but one, the chance of which the banker claims, and may refuse to let any punter withdraw a card when eight or less remain to be dealt.

Livret; a small Book. A suit of 13 cards, with 4 others, called *Figures*, viz., one named the little figure, has a blue cross on each side, and represents ace, deuce, tray; another yellow on both sides, styled the yellow figure, signifies, 4, 5, 6; a third with a black lozenge in the centre, named the black figure, stands for 7, 8, 9, 10; and a red card, called the great or red figure, for knave, queen, king; these figures are useful for those who punt on several cards at once.

L'une pour l'autre; One for the other; means a drawn game, and is said when two of the punter's cards are dealt in the same coup.

Masque; signifies turning a card, or placing another face downwards, during any number of coups, on that whereon the punter has staked, and which he afterwards may play at pleasure.

Oppose; the Opposite Game; is reversing the game, and having the cards on the right for the punter; and those on the left for the dealer.

Paix; Peace. Equivalent to double or quits; is, when the punter having won, does not choose to paroli and risk his stake, but bends or makes a bridge of his card, signifying that he ventures his gains only. A double paix is, when the punter having won twice, bends two cards one over the other. Treble paix, thrice, &c. A paix may follow a sept, quinze, or trente, &c.

Paix-Paroli; is when a punter has gained a paroli, wishes then to play double or quits, and save his original stake, which he signifies by doubling a card after making his first paroli; double-paix-paroli succeeds to winning a paix-paroli; treble-paix-paroli follows double, &c.

Paroli or *Parolet;* Double. Sometimes called *Cocking*, is when a punter, being fortunate, chooses to venture both his stake and gains, which he intimates by bending a corner of his card upwards.

Pli; Bending; is used when a punter, having lost half his stake by a *doublet*, bends a card in the middle, and setting it up with the points and foot towards the dealer, signifies thereby a desire either of recovering the moiety, or of losing all.

Pont; a Bridge. The same as Paix.

Ponte or *Punt;* a Point. The punter or player.

Quinze et le Va; Fifteen and it goes; is when the punter having won a sept, &c., bends the third corner of the card, and ventures for 15 times his stake.

Sept et le Va; Seven &c.; succeeds the gaining of a paroli, by which the punter being entitled to thrice his stake, risks the whole again, and, bending his card a second time, tries to win seven-fold.

Soixante et le Va; Sixty-three, &c.; is when the player having obtained a trente, ventures all once more, which is signified by making a fifth paroli, either on another card, if he has parolied on one only before, or by breaking the side of that one which contains four, to pursue his luck in the next deal.

Tailleur; the Dealer. Generally the banker.

Trente et le Va; one and thirty; follows a quinze, &c., when the punter again tries his luck, and makes a fourth paroli.

ODDS AT THE GAME OF FARO.

The chances of doublets vary according to the number of similar cards remaining among those undealt.

The odds against the punter increase with every coup that is dealt.

When 20 cards remain in hand, and the punter's card but once in it, the banker's gain is 5 per cent.

When the punter's card is twice in 20, the banker's gain is about the 34th part of the stake.

When the punter's card is thrice in 20, the banker's gain is about 4 per cent.

When the punter's card is 4 times in 20, the banker's gain is nearly the 18th part of the stake.

When only 8 cards remain, it is 5 to 3 in favor of the bank, when but 6 are left, it is 2 to 1; and when no more than 4, it is 3 to 1.

TABLE EXHIBITING THE ODDS AGAINST WINNING ANY NUMBER OF EVENTS SUCCESSIVELY: APPLICABLE TO HAZARD, BILLIARDS, FARO, ROUGE ET NOIR, OR OTHER GAMES OF CHANCE.

That the punter wins or loses the first time is an even bet.

That he does not win twice together, is 3 to 1; three successive times, 7 to 1; four successive times, 15 to one; five successive times, 31 to 1; six successive times, 63 to 1; seven successive times, 127 to 1, eight successive times, 255 to 1; nine successive times, 511 to 1; ten successive times, 1023 to 1; and so on to any number doubling every time the last odds, and adding one for the stake.

N. B. A punter plays on the square by placing a stake, referring to both at the head of two cards that have been dealt thrice each, and neither of which is the bottom one

A TABLE FOR FARO, WHEREBY THE SEVERAL ADVANTAGES OF THE BANKER, IN WHATEVER CIRCUMSTANCES HE MAY HAPPEN TO BE, IS SEEN SUFFICIENTLY NEAR AT THE FIRST VIEW.

Number of Cards in the Stock.	The Number of times the Punter's Card is contained in the Stock.			
	1	2	3	4
52	**	**	**	50
50	**	94	65	48
48	48	90	62	46
46	46	86	60	44
44	44	82	57	42
42	42	78	54	40
40	40	74	52	38
38	38	70	49	36
36	36	66	46	34
34	34	62	44	32
32	32	58	41	30
30	30	54	38	28
28	28	50	36	26
26	26	46	33	24
24	24	42	30	22
22	22	38	28	20
20	20	34	25	18
18	18	30	22	16
16	16	26	20	14
14	14	22	17	12
12	12	18	14	10
10	10	14	12	8
8	8	11	9	6

Example I.—To find the gain of the banker when there are 30 cards remaining in the stock, and the punter's card twice in it.

In the first column seek for the number answering to 30, the number of cards remaining in the stock: over against it, and under 2, at the head of the table, you will find 54, which shows that the banker's gain is the fifty-fourth part of the stake.

Example II.—To find the gain of the banker when but 10 cards are remaining in the stock, and the punter's card thrice in it.

Against 10, the number of cards, in the first column, and under number 3, you will find 12, which denotes that the banker's gain is the twelfth part of the stake.

Example III.—To find the banker's profit when the punter's cards remain twice in 22.

In the first column find 22, the number of cards over against it under figure 2, at the head of the table, you will find 38, which shows that the gain is one 38th part of the stake.

Example IV. To find the banker's gain when eight cards remain, and the punter's card thrice among them.

In the first column seek for 8, on a line with which under the 3 stands the figure of 9, denoting the profits to be 1-9th, or 2*s.* 4*d.* in the guinea.

Corollary 1.—From the table it appears, that the fewer cards there are in the stock, the greater is the gain of the banker.

Corollary 2.—The least gain of the banker under the same circumstances is, when the punter's card is but twice in hand, the next greater when three times, still greater when once, and the greatest of all when four times.

The profit of the banker is three per cent. upon all the sums adventured, supposing the punters to stop when only six cards remain, but with hocly it is full five per cent.

BOSTON.

This game very much resembles Whist, and is somewhat like Quadrille. The players put 8 fish each into a pool, and the dealer 4 more. The cards are distributed as at Whist, except that the last is not to be turned up. During every deal, the player opposite the dealer, should shuffle a pack to be cut by his right hand neighbour, and turn up a card, for the *first Preference;* the suit of the same colour, whether red or black, is styled the *second Preference*, and the other two are common suits. The player who misses deal does not lose his turn; but as a punishment is to put 4 more fish into the pool.

When the eldest hand thinks he can get 5 or more tricks, he is to say '*Boston;*' if otherwise, he says '*Pass,*' unless he plays *Misère*, that is, so as to lose every trick. *Petite Misère* is to put out a card, and lose every remaining trick; *Grande Misère* is to lose them without putting one out; *Petite Misère Ouverte* is to put out a card, and lay the others down, and then lose all; *Grande Misère Ouverte* is the same without laying one out. When the eldest hand has '*Passed*' the second may proceed as the eldest; or if the eldest has said '*Boston,*' the second or after him the third, and the dealer, may also say '*Boston,*' if he will engage to win 5 tricks with either Preference for the trump; or the second and other hands may say '*Petite*' or '*Grand Misère,*' or undertake to get 6 or more tricks, the trump being any suit, for these declarations will supersede that of Boston simply, as appears by the table at page 298; where all are arranged according to the order in which they take place of each other; the highest, called *Grand Slam*, is, undertaking to get 13 tricks. By engaging to *do more*, the elder hand may, as at Quadrille, supersede the younger. If all pass, the cards must be thrown up, and dealt by the person to the left of the former dealer, the new dealer putting 4 fish into the pool; and the new eldest hand, unless he has previously passed, may also supersede the declaration of any other, or say '*Pass;*' and so on, till at length every person, except one, has '*Passed,*' and that person (if he has declared '*Boston*') is to name the trump, always in the choice of the player; and also (unless he has undertaken more than 7 tricks) whether he chooses a partner. In the last case, any person who engages to get the required number of tricks may answer '*Whist:*' the right of answering begins with the next eldest hand to him who has declared. The partner must undertake to get 5 tricks if the player undertakes 7; 4, if the player undertakes 6; and 3 if he undertakes 5, as is in the table. When this is settled the playing begins, as at Whist, except that the partners may be differently placed, and each is to take up his own tricks.

If the player obtains, or the player and partner jointly get the proposed number of tricks, or more, he or they are entitled to the fish in the pool, called the *Bets*, and besides the number of tricks which they have won together, added to the number of honours they both held, is to be multiplied by the number in the table at page 298, over against the tricks they undertook, and under the name of the suit the trump was in; whether in the Preference or common suits; the product must then be divided by 10, and the quotient shows the number of fish to be paid to each of the successful players, by the other two; or in the event of a *Solo* to be paid him by each of the three others: should the product happen to be less than 10, one fish is to be paid nevertheless; if 15 or upwards, and under 20, it is to be considered as 20, and two fish to be paid; if 25 or upwards, and less than 30, as 30, and so on, viz:

Suppose the player and partner have undertaken 5 and 3 tricks, the trump in a common suit; they get 8, their proposed number, this, if they have no honours, is to be multiplied by one, (because in a common suit) the product is only 8, which cannot be divided by 10, but one fish is, however, paid to both player and partner by the other two. If they undertake 5 and 3 tricks, and get 9, the trump in Second Preference, no honours, then 9 multiplied by 2 producing 18, is considered as 20, and divided by 10, making two fish to be paid to each of them. Should they undertake and win 6 and 4 tricks, the trump in a common suit, having two by honours; 2 and 10 are 12, which multiplied by 2, as stated in the table, make 24, that is, two fish to be paid; the remainder not being taken notice of.

But if the player, or player and partner do not get their tricks, then the number they are deficient, added both to what they undertook, and the honours they held, is to be multiplied by the number found in the table, and divided by 10, to show the fish to be paid by them to their antagonists; for instance, when they undertake 5 and 3 tricks, having 2 by honours, the trump in a common suit, suppose they get only 6 tricks, then 6 subtracted from 8 leave 2, which, added to 8, the number they undertook, and 2, the honours they held, make 12; this multiplied by one, and divided by 10, gives one fish. If they undertake 5 and 3 tricks, having 2 by honours, the trump in Second Preference, should they get but 7, then 1 they are deficient, added to 8 they undertook, and 2 honours, make 11; this multiplied by 2, the number in the table, makes 22, which divided by 10, leaves 2, the fish to be paid. Should they undertake 6 and 4 tricks, having 4 honours, the trump in the First Preference; suppose they get but 8 tricks, 8 from 10, leave 2, which added to the 10 they undertook, and 4 honours from 16, that multiplied by 8, as in the table, make 128, then 130 divided by 10, gives 13 fish to be paid by them.

When the player and partner each fail to get their proposed number of tricks, then the fish to be paid by them is to be defrayed in equal proportions between them; exactly the reverse of what would have been done, had they been successful. But if one gets his number of tricks, and the other fails, then the unsuccessful person bears the whole of the loss, and when the player is alone, he pays the allotted number of fish to each of his three opponents.

In all failures, whether the player has a partner or not, he or they pay a *Bast* to the pool, equal to the number of fish they would have taken from it, had they proved successful; this is the invariable rule for assessing the *Basts*, which are not to be directly put into the pool, but laid aside, to be brought into the same at a future period, when some successful person has emptied it of the *Bets*, and all succeeding *Basts* are to be kept separately, to supply the pool at the end of different deals, and till all are exhausted the game cannot end, unless after any round is completed, the parties agree to share the *Basts*.

In respect to playing *Misère*, when a person has any kind of hand that he thinks will enable him to lose all the tricks, the method is as follows: if he thinks it requisite to get rid of any particular card, then the declaration must be only

'Petite Misère;' if this is not superseded by the other players, he puts out a card without showing it, and the game commences, as at Whist, by the eldest hand, but in playing *Misère* of any kind there are no trumps. The parties (still endeavouring to lose their tricks) proceed as at Whist, except that the general rules with regard to playing are reversed at *Misère.*

Whenever the *Misère* player is obliged to win a trick, the deal is at an end, and he is Basted, exactly as in playing Boston; and moreover, is to pay to each of the other persons 4 fish, as appears in the table: on the contrary, if the 12 tricks are played without winning one of them, he is entitled to the contents of the pool, and also to 4 fish from each of his antagonists. After a similar manner, *Grande Misère* is played, with the difference of not putting out a card, and having, of course to lose 13 tricks; which, if effected, entitles him to the pool, and 8 fish from each of his adversaries; if otherwise, he must pay 8 fish to each of them, and a bast to the pool, equal to what he would have taken out, had he gained his point. *Petite Misère Ouverte,* and *Grande Misère Ouverte* differ from the foregoing, merely by laying down the cards to be played on the table, so as to be seen by all parties (except the card put out, in the case of *Petite Misère Ouverte,*) and the playing is nearly the same; the only variation in the reckoning consists in paying or receiving 16 or 32 fish, explained in the Boston table, at the end.

When the deal is concluded and settled according to the afore-given directions, one or two persons will have won and taken the contents of the pool, or some, on the contrary, have been basted. In the former case, all the parties must furnish the pool afresh, as at the beginning: but when either of the players is basted, the new dealer has only to add 4 fish to the old pool, and so on till some one wins, who is entitled to the bets, and then the bast of greatest value (if there are more than one) is brought into the pool The basts may be of different value, because they are to be equal to the contents of the pool at the time of paying each of them, as already mentioned.

If there are several basts, and the players wish to finish the game, it will be necessary to put two or more basts into the pool at once, or else the parties must share the fish on the table

THE BOSTON TABLE.	Tricks to be won by the		Reckoning for the Game.			
	Player.	Partner.	First Preference.	Second Preference.	Common Suits.	Misere.
Boston	5	3	4	2	1	..
Petite Misère.. ..	..	..	..	..	..	4
	6	4	8	4	2	..
	7	5	12	6	3	..
Grande Misère	..	..	..	..	..	8
	8	..	16	8	4	..
	9	..	20	10	5	..
Petite Misère Ouverte	..	..	..	..	..	16
	10	..	24	12	6	.
	11	..	28	14	7	.
Grande Misère Ouverte	..	..	..	..	..	32
	12	..	32	16	8	..
Grand Slam	13	..	36	18	9	..

REVERSIS.

AS PLAYED WITH TWO QUINOLAS.

Reversis is played by four persons, with a box, containing* thirty-six fish, twenty-four counters, and six contracts; likewise with two pools, viz., the great and the little Quinola pools, (the great one to be under the little) they are always to be placed on the dealer's right hand.

For reversis the tens must be taken out from a pack of cards; the deal is to the right, giving three cards to each player the first round, and four to the dealer, afterwards always four, so that each of the three players will have eleven cards, and the dealer twelve, with three cards remaining

* Six fish make one counter, and eight counters one contract, or square

36 fish - - - - - - - -	36
24 counters, each 6 fish - -	144
6 contracts, each 48 fish - -	288
	468

which are to be placed singly in the middle of the table opposite to each player, who will put out a card from his hand, under the pools, and will replace it with the card that is on the table, opposite to him; the dealer likewise puts out a card, but having none to take in, he will find himself with eleven cards, like the rest of the players: these four cards form the party: should, however, there be three remises or stakes in the pools, (as it is convenient to prevent mistakes to have some distinguishing mark for each pool, when there are three remises or stakes in them; *it is not unusual* to have flags for that purpose, a red one to distinguish the great quinola, and a blue one the little quinola:) then it is in the player's option to take a card or not, if he does not, he has on declaring his intention, permission to see the card, and to place it to the discard under the pools.

Before a card is played, the opposite parties exchange a card with each other.

The ace takes the king, the king the queen, and so on.

The points in the tricks are forty, each ace reckoning four, king three, queen two, and knave one.

The most interesting parts in this game, are the quinolas, the party, the reversis, and the espagnolette.

THE QUINOLAS.

The great quinola pool, is to consist of twenty-six fish, which number is to be renewed every time the pool is cleared, or has fewer in it than the twenty-six fish; this stake is attached to the knave of hearts or great quinola, and is one of the most important cards in the game; the great quinola cannot be put to the discard, unless there are three stakes or a hundred fish in the pool.

The little quinola pool consisting of thirteen fish, is attached to the queen of hearts, as little quinola, which is to be renewed in the same manner, in proportion to the stake as the great quinola, and the little quinola cannot be put to the discard, unless there are three stakes, or fifty fish in the pool.

Each time the quinolas are placed, or played on a renounce, they are entitled to the stakes attached to them, except when there are three stakes in the pool, in which case the great quinola is entitled to receive only a hundred fish, and the little quinola fifty; and on the contrary, each time the quinolas are forced, led out, or gorgé, the stakes are paid in the same proportion as they would have been received, except in the single instance of the person who played the quinolas making the reversis; and then in order to derive any benefit from the stakes, the quinola which is to be entitled to such benefit, must be played before the two last tricks.

THE PARTY.

The points in the discard, (to which add four for the party,) reckon as in the tricks, with the exception of the ace of diamonds, and the knave of hearts as great quinola; the former reckoning five, and the latter four.

He who has the fewest points wins the party. It will frequently happen, that two players will have the same number of points; then he who has the fewest tricks, has the preference; if points and tricks are equal, then he who is best placed wins; the best placed is he who dealt last; but he who has no trick, has the preference of him who has no trick without points; in general in cases of equality the best placed has the preference.

When the espagnolette is played, and won, he wins the party in preference to the best placed.

When every trick is made by one person, there is no party; and this is called (by way of excellence) making the reversis.

THE REVERSIS.

Every trick without exception must be made by one person to make the reversis.

The reversis is undertaken when the first nine tricks are made by the same person; there is then an end of the party and of the quinolas; the great quinola being only as the knave of hearts, and the little quinola as the queen of hearts, except the person who wins the reversis, plays his quinolas at any time before the two last tricks, he is then entitled to the stakes; but on the contrary, should the reversis be broken by one of the players winning either of the two last tricks, he then not only pays the reversis broken, but the stakes to the pools, for the quinolas he may have played before the reversis was undertaken.

All consolations paid for aces or quinolas, by the person undertaking the reversis, is to be returned on his winning it.

THE ESPAGNOLETTE, OR THE FOUR ACES.

The espagnolette is either simply four aces, three aces, and one quinola, or two aces and two quinolas.

The player having the espagnolette, has a right to renounce in every suit, during the whole game, and if he can avoid winning any trick, and there is no reversis, he of course wins the party in preference to him who is better placed; but if he is obliged to win a trick, he then pays the party to him who would otherwise have received it, and returns the consolations he may have received for aces or quinolas; and if he has a quinola, he will pay the stake to the pool, instead of receiving it, unless a reversis is made upon him.

The player having the espagnolette, is at liberty to waive his privilege, and to play his game as a common one, but loses that privilege the moment he has renounced playing in suit.

The espagnolette receives consolation in any part of the game, if he forces the quinola, and this can only happen in three instances:—

I.—By playing a heart eldest hand, and the quinola being single in some other hand.

II.—If having through inattention, made a trick during the course of the game, he returns a heart, and forces.

III.—If by being obliged to enter at the tenth trick, or choosing to enter sooner, he should have a heart to play, and by that means forces it.

If any person wins the reversis, the espagnolette pays singly for all the company.

If any person undertakes a reversis, and another breaks it, the espagnolette pays the whole to the person who broke it.

The person holding the four aces or espagnolette, can likewise break the reversis, and is payed as before mentioned, by the person whose reversis he broke; he can likewise undertake the reversis, but then his hand must be played as a common game, for he cannot renounce.

If the espagnolette has placed his quinola, and there is a reversis either made or broken, he is not to receive the stake; according to the general rule, viz., when the reversis takes place, the pools are neither received or paid, except by him who undertakes the reversis.

If another player having the ace or king of hearts, the espagnolette has in any part of the game, either of his quinolas forced, he pays the stake, and his consolation the same as the two other players, which is due to him that forces, except there is a reversis.

PAYMENTS.

The dealer always puts two fish into the great quinola pool, and one into the little, over and above his common stake of six and three, besides which every one puts into the former, for the first stake six fish, and into the latter three; so that the great quinola pool, will consist of twenty-six fish, and the little quinola pool of thirteen fish; each time the stakes are drawn, or when there are fewer fish in the pool than the first original stake, the pool must be replenished as at first.

The person who gives an ace upon a renounce, receives a fish from the person who wins the trick; if the ace of diamonds, he will receive two.

The person who forces an ace, receives the same payments from each of the players, as well as the person forced.

The great quinola placed upon a renounce, receives six fish; the little quinola placed upon a renounce, receives three fish; and if either of them is forced, the person who forces, receives the same payment from each player.

These payments should be made immediately without being asked for.

One or more aces, or either of the quinolas played or gorgé, that is, led out, pay the same as if they had been forced, and are paid to the person who wins the party, but it is for him to recollect and demand them.

When either ace or quinola are placed, played, or gorgé the last card, it is called *à la bonne*, and pays double, and all payments whatever, are double to the person who sits opposite.

The payment for the reversis made or broke, is eighty fish; each player paying twenty, and the opposite party forty, when the reversis is made; but when it is broken, the whole is paid to the person who breaks it, by the person whose reversis is broken; that is, he pays the persons breaking it, exactly the same number of fish he would have received from the whole table, had he won it.

LAWS OF THE GAME OF REVERSIS.

I.—The eldest hand ought to take care that all the players have put their stakes into the pools; if not, he will pay for those whom he has not called upon to pay their stake.

II.—The person who misdeals, loses his deal.

III.—If the player takes his card without having put out to the discard, the deal goes for nothing.

IV.—The discard is not to be changed after it is once put out.

V.—The eldest hand should be attentive not to play a card till the discard is complete; should he have played one, he is permitted, if nobody has played to it, to take it up and play another.

VI.—No person must play before his turn.

VII.—He who flings down his game, thinking he has the rest of the tricks, is to pay for any ace or quinola that has or can be placed or given; but, in case of a reversis, the person who might break it, can oblige him to take up his cards, and play them one after another, as the person who can break it shall direct.

VIII.—When a player thinking he has won the party, or willing to favor the person who has won it, asks for the aces or quinolas led out, before the person who has won the party has demanded them, he is to pay for him who might have been called upon to pay them.

IX.—If at the end of the game, it is perceived there is an error in the discard, either by putting out too many cards or too few, the deal goes for nothing and must be made again; and if it is discovered that a quinola has been put to the discard, without there being three remises in the pool of the quinola so put out; the person from whose hand such quinola was put out to the discard, pays the party, and the stake to the pool, the same as if his quinola had been forced or gorgé.

X.—When the cards are cut, it is too late to ask for the payment of any ace or quinola, which may have been played or gorgé; as likewise for the party or the stake in the pools.

XI.—Before you play your cards, it is always permitted to ask how the cards have been played, but it is not permitted to observe it to others who may not make the inquiry.

XII.—If any player, not having the espagnolette, revokes

he shall pay a counter to each of the pools; and can neither receive the party or any payment.

XIII.—The player is permitted to examine all his own tricks at any time, but not to look at the tricks of any other person, the last trick excepted.

A FEW HINTS TOWARDS PLAYING THE GAME OF REVERSIS

There seem to be four great objects in this game; the first, winning the party; the second, placing the quinolas; the third, making the espagnolette; and the fourth, making the reversis: there is likewise a lesser object, viz., that of placing the different aces on a renounce.

In playing your cards you should endeavour to give your quinolas, your aces, and great cards on a renounce, when the person who sits opposite to you is likely to make the trick, as all the payments are double from him; if you win the party, he may by that means lose it; and if you lose the party, most probably you will not have it to pay to him.

In order to gain the party, you must avoid, if possible, winning a trick, for which purpose keep all the lowest cards in your hand, such as two's and three's.

AN ELDER HAND LIKELY TO WIN THE PARTY.

Suppose the elder hand to be dealt the ace, seven, four, and two of spades; the king, four, and three of clubs; four and two of hearts; and six and five of diamonds.

The ace of spades should be put to the discard, because you hope from your hand to win the party; and by discarding a high card, you increase its value; suppose the card you take up from the table to be the seven of diamonds, you should then given the seven of diamonds to the person who sits opposite to you, in preference to the king of clubs, with which you would have much less chance of winning a trick than with the seven of diamonds, because your lowest card in this suit is only a five, while that in clubs is a three; suppose you receive in exchange for the seven of diamonds, the queen of spades, with this hand you will play your four of hearts to force the quinolas: the person who wins the trick will most probably do the same, to which you must play your two of hearts; if another heart should be played, then part with your six of diamonds, which is a worse card to keep than the king of clubs or the queen of spades; because having the latter with three small spades, and the former with two small clubs, you have very little chance of winning a trick in those suits, and with a five or six of any suit, when hearts have been played three or four times, you have a very good chance to win a trick with one of them, as every player will, of course, fling away their highest cards, unless they suspect a reversis is attempted to be played.

AN ELDER HAND LIKELY TO LOSE THE PARTY.

An elder hand composed of the king, nine, and eight of hearts; queen, seven, and five of diamonds; knave, eight, and seven of spades; ace and nine of clubs; with this hand it is most probable you will lose the party; therefore you should put to the discard a card of no value; for which reason the seven of diamonds would be the best card; suppose in the place of which you take up the seven of clubs, having three high hearts, it would be highly dangerous to part with one of them, as you might receive a quinola from the person who sits opposite to you, as well as take one in from the table. The queen of diamonds should be given to the person who sits opposite to you, which will leave you with only the five of diamonds, and give you the best chance should the person who is opposite to you give you a quinola to get the lead out of your hand. Suppose the person who is opposite to you gives you the nine of spades, with this hand you have nothing to do, but lead out your king of hearts, and to follow with the nine and eight, if not taken, in hopes of forcing the quinolas. If they are not forced by your three hearts, and you have still the lead, you should play the spades, till all those spades lower than your own are out: then you will play your nine of clubs, and then your five of diamonds, which if taken and played again, you should immediately place your ace of clubs upon the renounce. If the diamond was not taken, then play your seven of clubs, and with winning that trick in all probability you will make the reversis, as you will have the ace of clubs, and most probably the best spade remaining.

AN ELDER HAND WITH THE QUINOLAS.

An elder hand composed of the knave, seven, six, five, four, and two of hearts; four and five of diamonds; four, three, and two of spades; with this hand the five of diamonds should be put to the discard; suppose in return you take up the two of clubs, you will then give the four of diamonds to the person who is opposite to you, who in return gives you the queen of hearts; which with your hand, becomes a valuable present, as most probably you will not get a trick, and are sure of placing both your quinolas upon a renounce, and cannot possibly have them forced; with this hand you should lead the seven of hearts, which most probably will be taken; you are then sure of winning no trick, and of placing your quinolas, and which you will take care to do with the great quinola the very last card, which is called *à la bonne*, and for which you are paid double what you would receive if played at any other part of the game.

A quinola should never be kept in your hand, unless accompanied with three other hearts; therefore if you have two quinolas, and only one heart, you must give that quinola which has the greatest remise to the person who is opposite to you. If you have both quinolas, and one or two hearts, and there are three remises in one pool, or in both, the quinola, whose three remises are in the pool, should be put to the discard, and the other to the person who is opposite to you; if both quinolas have three remises, the great quinola should be put to the discard.

AN ELDER HAND WITH THE ESPAGNOLETTE.

An elder hand composed of the ace, king, queen, knave, four, and two of hearts: the ace of diamonds; the queen and knave of spades; the four and three of clubs; this hand having the espagnolette, or four aces, you should put the king of hearts to the discard, to make the party as great as you can; because if you win the espagnolette, you are sure of gaining the party, in preference to the person who is better placed; suppose you take up in return the five of spades, you will then give the five of spades to the person who sits opposite, (as giving him too high a card, might assist him in making a reversis against your espagnolette) and in return receive the seven of clubs; with this hand you should play the four of clubs to get the lead out of your hand: and when hearts are played, you must, if possible, not discover too soon, by renouncing your espagnolette; but play a heart in suit once, preserving, nowever, the two, which may be a card of much more consequence to you; and if more hearts should be played, get rid of your spades, and if a second player wins a trick, (by which means the reversis cannot be made against your espagnolette) give your aces, and if all the hearts have been played, give your great quinola *à la bonne;* but if there are yet hearts remaining, you must give it away, and keep your lowest cards for the two last tricks.

AN ELDER HAND PLAYING FOR THE REVERSIS.

An elder hand composed of the ace, king, queen, knave, nine, seven, and four of hearts; king and two of diamonds; queen and knave of clubs: with this hand in expectation of winning the reversis, you should discard the two of diamonds: suppose in return you take up the eight of spades; you will then give up the eight of spades to the person who sits opposite to you, who in return gives you the king of clubs. You will then begin playing your ace and king of hearts, and then your nine, which will most probably take out all the hearts: but you should still play one more, in hopes the ace of clubs will be thrown away upon a renounce. (if not already discarded,) you will then play your king, queen and knave of clubs; then your queen of hearts, taking care to play the knave of hearts before the two last tricks; because when the reversis is made, that quinola which is played in either of the two last tricks, does not receive the stakes out of the pool, but becomes simply the knave or queen of hearts.

THE YOUNGEST HAND WINNING THE PARTY, AND PLACING THE QUINOLAS.

Suppose the youngest hand or dealer to have the king, knave, eight, six, four, three, and two of hearts; knave, seven, five, three, and two of spades. The dealer having twelve cards has the advantage of putting to the discard, without taking up a card in return; having seven hearts the quinola cannot be forced; therefore put out the king of hearts to the discard, as from your hand and situation in being best placed, you are almost sure of winning the party; except the espagnolette should be played and won. You will then give the knave of spades to the person who sits opposite to you, who in return gives you the little quinola: with this hand your are sure of placing both your quinolas, and of not taking a trick; the only thing therefore (on account of your quinolas) you have to fear, is one of the players making the reversis; which would then prevent your having the remises out of the pool.

MINOR CARD GAMES.

THE catalogue of the Minor Card Games has been far more reduced by those which have become obsolete within these last hundred years than the list of those played and introduced during the nineteenth century will seem to balance. "The Compleat Gamester," published in 1734, contains treatises upon Ombre, Quintille, Basset, Gleck, French Ruff, Five Cards,* Costly Colours, Bone-Ace, Wit and Reason, Art of Memory, Plain Dealing, Queen Nazarene, Peneech, Post and Pair, Bankafalet, Beeste, the famous game of Verquere, the noble and courtly game called Grand Trick Track, Tick Tack, Doublets, Slice Ace, Catch Dolt, Inn and Inn, and Passage; games scarcely known by name in the present day, and never played. Many of the lesser games popular now, are, no doubt, indebted for their existence to the notices of them written by Hoyle, and left by him as a revertive legacy to those who seek relief from *ennui*, and the still graver visitations of life. These "small deer" of the card-player enjoy a roving commission. At a loo table you will find as many versions of the matter for discussion as men to propose and propound them. Commerce is variously conducted in various places,—and Matrimony is constantly a source of difference of opinion...............As the best course in this dilemma, we have chosen that which seems the most apt. A more convenient principle than that which Hoyle has adopted in founding his systems has not been suggested by any who have followed him. For this reason we give most of them from his text, departing from him only in a few instances, where we have been able to improve.

* Five Cards is still played in Ireland under the name of Five Fingers or Spoilt Five.—ED.

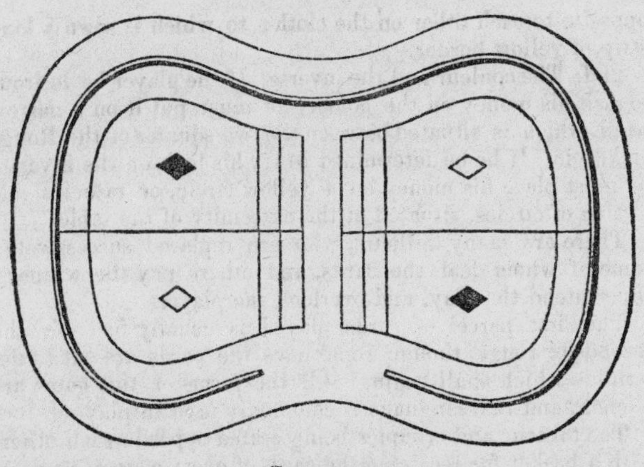

ROUGE ET NOIR.

ROUGE ET NOIR, (Red and Black,) or Trente-un, is a modern game, so styled, not from the cards, but from the colours marked on the tapis or green cloth with which the table is covered.

To form the game, it is necessary that there should be a banker, or *tailleur* (DEALER,) who represents him, and players, the number of whom are unlimited.

The table usually employed for this game is of an oblong form, thirty feet long, and four feet wide, covered with a green cloth; in the middle of which the bank is placed; in other words, the money that belongs to the banker, and which is destined to pay the fortunate players. The company are at liberty to place their money on the right and left of this table, upon the chances that seems to them most likely to win. Those chances are:—

1st. Le Noir (the black) le Rouge (the red) designated by two large spots on the green cloth, marked red and black, something in the shape of the ace of diamonds, and placed opposite to each other on the cloth; to which is sown a long strip of yellow border.

2nd. The couleur and the inverse. If the player be desirous to risk his money on the colour, he must put it on a narrow band, which is situated between the two squares of the Rouge and Noir. If he be determined to try his luck on the inverse, he must place his money on a yellow circle, or rather a collection of circles, situated at the extremity of the table.

There are many tailleurs, who are replaced successively; some of whom deal the cards, and others pay the winners, superintend the play, and overlook the players.

The first parcel of cards played, is usually for noir, the second for rouge, though sometimes the cards are cut to determine which shall begin. All the terms of this game are French, and that language is commonly used in playing.

The tailleur and croupier being seated opposite each other, with a basket for receiving the cards of every coup after dealing, placed on the middle of the table, one of the tailleurs commences the game, by unsealing before the company six packs of cards, which are regularly counted in their presence; and, after being shuffled, he passes them to another sitting opposite to him; who also shuffles them in his turn by a handful at a time, and hands them to the punter who happens to be on the right hand, who has the privilege to shuffle them if he pleases: they are ultimately transmitted to the tailleur, whose duty it is to deal, and who again shuffles them by a handful at a time. He then puts the six packs together, shuffles them once more, and gets them cut.

The cut is made by presenting a blank card to one of the players, who places it in any part of the six packs of cards that he thinks proper: he cannot, however, cut less than three cards.

The tailleur completes the cut, by putting those cut under the top cards.

This ceremony being over, the punters place on the Rouge, the Noir, the Couleur, or the Inverse, the sum they wish to risk. No individual can put down less than five francs, nor more than twelve thousand at the same time, except in the two following cases; viz:—

1st. When the banker agrees to an augmentation of the stake, after a proposition made to him by the player.

2nd. When a player is forced to augment his mass, the consequence of a martingale.

During this interval, the tailleur places before him the cards, of which he takes a handful, and cries out, "Le jeu est fait, rien ne va plus:" that is to say,—the deal having commenced, no more money is to be placed on the table than the sum already staked. After those words are pronounced, should any one put money on the table, it will be taken up by one of the tailleurs, and returned to him; for the player putting money down too late can neither win nor lose.

The tailleur now draws a card, which, after showing to the company, he lays on the table: he draws a second; a third, which he places in the same row, right and left, until the number of points on the cards amount to at least thirty-one; so that if he should happen to count only thirty, he must still draw another.

The cards retain their nominal value. The ace counts as one point; the II, two points; the III, three points; the IV, four points; the V, five points; the VI, six points; the VII, seven points; the VIII, eight points; the IX, nine points; the X, ten points; and the court cards ten points each.

The first row of cards, of which the number of points are at least equal to thirty-one, and cannot consequently pass the number of forty, is for the Noir; that is to say, it determines the chance of those who have placed their money upon that part of the cloth where the black mark is; which we have already described as being in the shape of a diamond.

The tailleur immediately afterwards draws in the same manner another row of cards for the Rouge.

If he has counted thirty-six points in the first row of cards, he calls out, in a loud voice, to the players, six, to avoid the too frequent repetition of the word thirty, which would recur too often, but which is well understood; and thirty-five points in the second row of cards, which he also announces in like manner by saying five. He adds, "Rouge gagne," red wins; because it is always the thirty-one points, or those which more closely approach to them, that win. At that moment, the four tailleurs, who are placed opposite each other, gather by the aid of their rakes all the money which is placed on the Noir, and double all that placed on the Rouge, which is immediately withdrawn by the lucky players.

It now only remains to speak of the money placed on the chances, the Couleur and the Inverse. The first card drawn by the banker determines the couleur. If, then, the first card of the preceding cut drawn by the tailleur is Noir, as it is Rouge which gains, the couleur will lose.

The tailleurs have then a right to draw to the bank all the money which was placed upon the chance of the couleur, and double all the money which was placed upon the chance of the inverse.

To make this better understood, a contrary example may be cited: that is to say, a case in which the Noir and the Couleur win. Let us suppose, that the tailleur turns up for the first row, the king of spades, ten of clubs, seven of diamonds, and four of spades, which count thirty-one, and which he expresses by one, pronounced in a loud voice; and that he next turns up for the second row, the queen of clubs, nine of hearts, nine of spades, and five of diamonds, which count thirty-three, which he expresses by three. Noir wins; since the tailleur has turned up in the first row of cards thirty-one; and, as we have already observed :—

1st. That the first row of cards is for La Noir.

2nd. It is the chance of thirty-one, or the point which approaches the nearest to it, that wins.

The tailleur then cries out, "Roùge perd," red loses, and adds, "et Couleur gagne," and colour wins; because the first card turned up is a king of spades, consequently black; and in that case, the colour being black, the colour wins because black wins. If the first card had been the king of diamonds, the colour would have lost because it is the black which has won; which the dealer would have expressed by saying, "Rouge perd et Couleur," the red and the colour loses

When the dealer has turned up in the second row of cards, which is for the red, the same number he has turned up in the first row for the black, it is what is called un refait; that is to say, that the cut is null, and that the dealer must again turn up other cards. The punter can in this case change his game by playing more, less, or not at all; as he may think proper.

When the points turned up for the black and for the red are thirty-one, half of all the money which may be on the red, or the black, the colour, or the inverse, belongs to the banker, which half, the punters may either pay, or have their stake moved into the middle semicircles of the colour they then choose, called "la première prison," the first prison, to be determined by the next event, whether they lose all or are set at liberty; but if "un refait second trente et un," a second doublet of one-and-thirty, should occur in the next succeeding deal, the punters lose only one-half of their remaining moiety, making three-fourths of their original stakes, and are removed into the smallest semicircle, styled "la seconde prison," the second prison, and the next coup determines whether the punter loses all or is to be removed again into "la première prison."

Thus if a player had at the first coup one hundred francs, by the first thirty-one turned up he would lose fifty; he has no more then in prison than fifty francs, after the first thirty-one; twenty-five francs, after the second; twelve francs and a half, after the third; and six francs and a quarter, after the fourth.

Happily for the player, it seldom happens, that thirty-one is three or four times successively repeated in favor of the banker.

Punters after winning may paroli, &c., and pursue their luck up to a soixante, as at faro; but as no livrets are used at Rouge et Noir, they cannot make either paix or pont.

At this game a banker cannot refuse any stake not exceeding his fund; which the punter declares, by saying, "Je va la Banque, Va la Banque, or Va Banque," I aim at the Bank.

Bankers generally furnish punters with slips of card paper, ruled in columns, each marked N or R at the top, on which accounts are kept by pricking with a pin, and when "un refait" happens, the same is denoted by running the pin through the middle line.

Some banker give up the profit of "le refait" during the first deal.

The odds against "le refait" being dealt, are reckoned 63 to 1, but bankers expect it twice in three deals, and there are generally from 29 to 32 coups in each deal.

For the table exhibiting the odds against winning any number of events successively, vide page 339.

EXPLANATION OF THE TERMS USED AT ROUGE ET NOIR.

Banquier, or Tailleur—The dealer.

Fausse Taille—Occurs when the dealer commits a fault, which subjects him to double all the money staked.

To Martingale—Is to play one coup at least more than the stake previously lost. This is the boldest manner of playing at any of the games of chance.

Paroli—Is doubling the stake you have won at the preceding coup. A plan usually adopted by all players.

Paroli et masse en avant—Is double the sum staked the preceding coup, more than the player has risked. If the gamester has played five shillings the first time and has won the second coup, instead of taking up his money, he must add five shillings to his mass, which makes fifteen shillings, and which he risks the second coup: this is called "Faire Paroli et masse en avant." Perhaps this is the safest and best method of playing, especially for a novice. In pursuing this plan it is possible to win; and it is impossible to lose much, provided the first stake does not exceed a crown.

Refait de Trente et un—A coup by which the banquier wins one-half the money staked. It is effected by dealing thirty-one for each colour.

Refait—Occurs when the banquier deals the same sum for both colours, from thirty-two to forty.

Sept et le va—Seven times the amount first staked.

Taille—Is made every time the dealer has turned up all the cards.

Figure—The name given to the kings, queens, and knaves

Point—The number which results from the sums of the cards dealt by the banquier.

Punter—Those who play against the banquier.

LA ROULETTE.

THE table employed for the Roulette is somewhat in the shape of that used for the game of Rouge et Noir; it is of an oblong square form, covered with green cloth. In the centre is a round cavity usually made of mahogany, and resembling in some degree a punch-bowl. The sides are immovable, and around it are placed at equal distances several bands of copper, which commencing at the top descend to the extremity of the machine. In the centre of it, which is movable, a circular bottom is formed, containing thirty-eight holes, to which the copper bands just mentioned are attached, and upon which are painted, alternately, in black and red, thirty-six numbers, from one to thirty-six, a Zero (0), and a double Zero (00).

In the middle is a moulinet (mill) of copper, surmounted by a cross of the same metal, which serves to impress the movable bottom with the rotary motion that any one would wish to give it.

There is a banker, or rather many tailleurs who represent him: the number of players are not limited.

One of the tailleurs puts the machine in motion, by turning with his fore-finger the cross which surmounts it from right to left, thus impressing the bottom that contains the thirty-eight holes, which produces, as before stated, a rotary motion. At this instant, he throws an ivory ball into the concavity of the Roulette, in a direction opposite to the movement which he has given to the movable bottom. This ball moves in the interior with great velocity, making several revolutions; until at length from the feebleness of its motion, and after many irregular bounds, it falls into one of the thirty-eight holes, formed, as already stated, by the copper bands.

It is the hole into which the ball enters that determines the gain or the loss of the numerous chances which this game presents.

To the right and left of this machine are figured on the green cloth, for the accommodation of the players, the thirty-six numbers, and the Zeros, simple and double, in the following manner.

[See Diagram, page 348.]

The other chances are also designated on the green cloth, divergent from its centre, on one side "l'impair, la manque et le rouge;" on the other "le pair, le passe, et le noir."

The impair wins, when the ball enters a hole numbered impair. The manque wins, when the ball enters a hole numbered eighteen, and all those under that number. The rouge wins, when the ball enters a hole of which the number is red, and *vice versâ.*

This game affords seven chances, comprising that of the

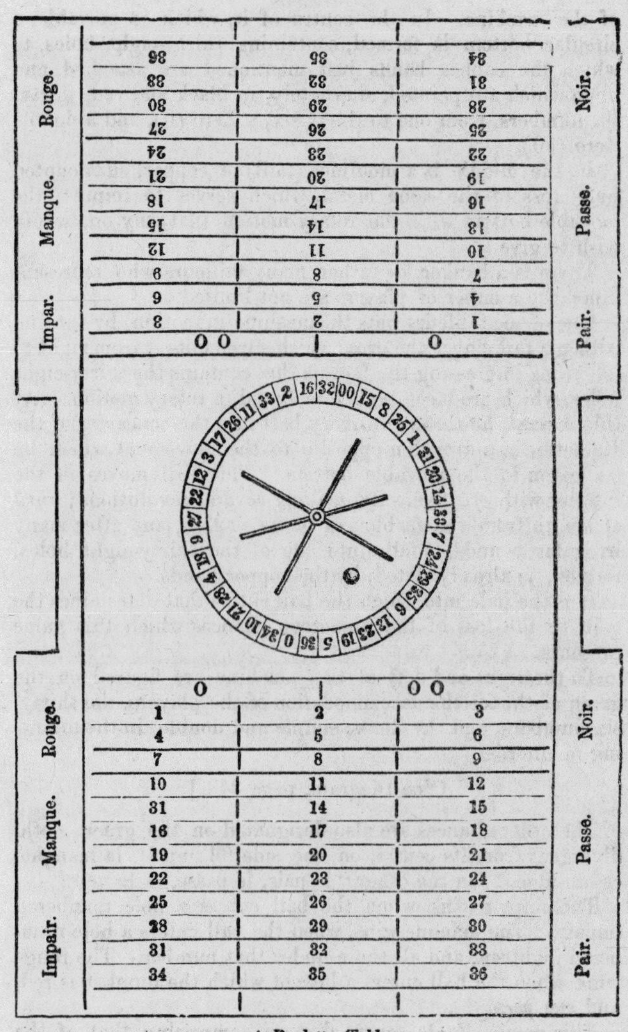

A Roulette Table.

numbers; and this latter chance divides itself into many others, of which we shall presently give a brief detail.

The player puts upon those chances of which he makes choice, any sum he pleases; that is to say, from two francs, the least stake admitted, to 12,000, the highest; unless in the like cases of which we have already spoken respecting the game of Rouge et Noir.

The player who puts his money on one of the numbers, or the Zeros painted on the green cloth (which is called plein), gains thirty-five times the amount of his stake, should the ball fall into the corresponding number, or Zero, marked in the interior of the roulette.

The gamester who plays on the numbers may play the twelve first, the twelve middle, and the last twelve. If the ball enters the hole in the interior, which corresponds with one of those twelve numbers marked on the green cloth, on which the player has put his money, he is paid three times the amount of his stake.

To play the Colonnes, the player places his money in the square, which is at the foot of each column marked on the green cloth. If the ball enters one of the holes corresponding with one of the numbers of the column, the player gains three times the amount of his stake.

He may equally, and at his pleasure, play two, three, four, six numbers, and he wins and loses always in the same proportion; eighteen times the stake for two numbers; twelve times the stake for three numbers; nine times the stake for four numbers; six times the stakes for six numbers; and the rest in the same proportion.

The player who may have put his money on one or the other of the six chances wins double his stake if the chance arrives. If, then, the ball enters a hole of which the number is thirty-six, and rouge, the banker pays double all the money which is placed on the following chances—la passe, le pair, and le rouge, and pays thirty-five times the amount of the sum which was placed on the number thirty-six, and draws to the bank all the money which was placed on the other chances.

If the ball should happen to enter the hole numbered seventeen, noir, the banker pays the player double the amount of the stakes which may have been placed on the following chances, la manque, l'impair, and la noire, and thirty-five times the amount of the stake played on number seventeen, and draws to the bank all the money that may have been placed on the other chances.

When the tailleur perceives that the ball has but a few seconds to roll, he cries out—"Le jeu est fait, rien ne va plus." After this the players cannot put any money on the table; should they do so, their money is taken up by a croupier and returned to them.

E. O.

An E O table is circular in form, but of no exact dimensions, though in general about four feet in diameter. The extreme circumference is a kind of counter, or depôt, for the stakes, marked all round with the letters E and O; on which each adventurer places money according to his inclination. The interior part of the table consists, first, of a kind of gallery, or rolling-place, for the ball, which, with the outward parts above, called depôt, or counter, is stationary or fixed. The most interior part moves upon an axis, or pivot, and is turned about with handles, whilst the ball is set in motion round the gallery. This part is generally divided into forty niches or interstices, twenty of which are marked with the letter E, and the other twenty with the letter O. The lodging of the ball in any of the niches distinguished by those letters, determines the wager. The proprietors of the tables have two bar-holes, and are obliged to take all bets offered, either for E or O; but if the ball falls into either of the bar-holes, they win all the bets upon the opposite letter, and do not pay to that in which it falls; an advantage in the proportion of 2 to 40, or 5 per cent. in their favor.*

* This very gambling game used to be extensively played some fifty or sixty years ago. One of Gillray's early caricatures represents an E O table in the act of being destroyed by the "Westminster Just-asses," as he denominates them.—*See Bohn's Gillray, plate* 9.

BAGATELLE GAMES.

The following games are played on a board, which is usually from six to ten feet in length, and from one foot nine inches to three feet wide, lined with green cloth; a slip of thin wood being placed round the inside of its upper end, to form a semicircle.

There are nine cups let in level with the cloth, numbered one to nine, into which the balls are to be driven in playing the two first mentioned games. (La Bagatelle and Sans Egal.)

There is also a bridge with small arches likewise numbered from 1 to 9, and through which the balls are to be driven in playing the two last mentioned games (Mississippi and Trou Madame) when the cups are not used.

There are likewise two small cushions placed against the sides, to be used in the game of Mississippi; or instead of these the boards are sometimes stuffed round the sides.

LA BAGATELLE.

Any number of players may join in this game, and use either the mace or cue as may be agreed.

Each player strikes a ball up the board, and whoever gets the highest number is entitled to the lead, and takes possession of the nine balls.

The black ball (which counts for double) is placed on the white spot in front of the holes, at the beginning of every round, and must in the first instance be struck by one of the other balls before there can be any score.

The striker's ball must be placed on the white spot nearest the other end of the board, and is to be struck with the mace or cue at the black ball, the object being to put it into one of the holes. The rest of the balls are to be played up in the same manner, either at the outstanding balls, or for the holes.

Any number of rounds may be played for the game, as may be agreed upon at its commencement.

The player who obtains the greatest number—counting the holes into which he puts the balls, according to the figures marked within them—wins the game.

The holes along the edges of the board are for the purpose of marking the game.

Any ball that rebounds beyond the centre, or that is driven off the board, cannot be used again during that round.

SANS EGAL.

THIS is played by two persons.

The player who leads, which is decided as in bagatelle, chooses four balls of either colour, and places the black ball on the mark in front of the holes, and begins by striking one of his balls up the board.

The other player then strikes one of his balls in the same manner, and so on alternately.

He that holes the black ball counts it towards his game, and also all that he may hole of his own colour.

If a player should hole any of his adversary's balls, it counts for the owner of the balls.

The player who makes the greatest number of points in each round, takes the lead in the next. The game is 21, to 31, according to the arrangement between the players.

MISSISSIPPI.

PLACE the bridge close up to the circle, and the small cushions against the sides.

Each player is then to strike one ball through the bridge, and he who gets the highest number, has the lead, and plays the nine balls in succession.

All balls must strike one of the cushions, previous to entering the bridge, otherwise the number reckons for the adversary.

The game to consist of as many points as may be agreed on at its commencement.

TROU MADAME.

THIS is played in the same way as the preceding game, except that the balls are played straight from the end of the board through the bridge.

RUSSIAN BAGATELLE,

OR

COCKAMAROO TABLE.

Elevated end of the board, which is an inclined plane, lowest at the striking end.

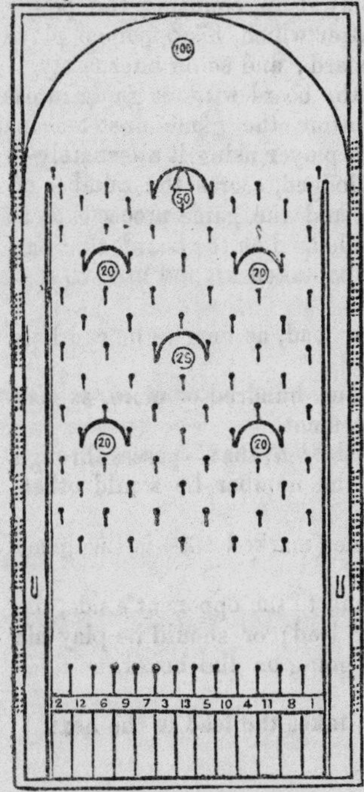

Description of the Board.

A cavity for the red ball to be placed in, at the commencement of the game *only*. It counts double. *i. e.* 100, as marked inside.

An arch with a bell suspended within it, which if rung by any ball in passing through, counts double for whatever that ball may score by the stroke. If it does not pass through, but merely falls into the cup underneath, it counts only as marked, *i. e.* 50.

The remaining arches with cups beneath them, count respectively as marked, viz. 20 on the sides, and 25 in the centre.

The pegs are brass pins standing up, about 1¼ inches in height.

There are slightly indented spots (one on each side of the board) from which the balls are projected.

Cavities into which the balls run, they count according to the numbers placed above.

The board, which is generally four feet six inches in length, and two feet four inches in width, is lined with superfine green cloth. Those of the best description cost about fifteen guineas, and are made, if wished, to shut up so as to have the appearance of a Pembroke table. They are sold by Mr. Thurston of Catherine Street, and other respectable makers

RULES OF THE GAME.

I. Commence the game by stringing for the lead, as well as for choice of balls and side of board; the player who gets the highest number takes the lead.

II. The leader must place his ball in the cavity on the side of the board he selects, and play it up, counting the points he may make by the stroke; after which, his opponent plays from the opposite side of the board; and so on alternately.

III. When a ball lodges on the board without going into a hole or running down to the bottom, the game must be continued with the other ball, each player using it alternately—whoever removes the ball so lodged, scores the number of points made by both the balls, and the game proceeds as at first. Should both the balls be lodged on the board, that ball which was last stopped must be taken up and used to continue the game.

IV. The player continues to lead, as long as he can hole his ball in any of the *cups*.

V. The game to consist of one hundred or more, as may be agreed upon at the commencement.

VI. If the player's ball ring the *bell*, that is passes through the bell arch, he scores double the number he would otherwise gain by the stroke.

VII. Playing into the top hole (marked 100) is the game at once.

VIII. Should the ball go round to the opponent's side, the striker loses five points and the lead; or should he play his ball up, and it returns without going on the board, he loses one point and the lead.

IX. The winner of the game, takes the lead in the next.

AMERICAN BOWLS.

Explanation of the Diagram.

1. Ten pins, something in the shape of large hock bottles, arranged in a triangle, its apex being nearest the player.

2. Platforms, (called alleys,) about sixty feet in length and four feet in width, on which the balls are propelled. The surface must be perfectly smooth and level.

3. The white margins on each side of the platforms are channels into which the balls drop, when not dexterously propelled.

4. The intermediate dark spaces or lines are grooves, elevated on frames about three feet above the level of the platform, with a slight inclination towards the bowler's end. By means of these grooves the balls are returned to the bowlers, boys being placed for that purpose on raised seats beyond the pins.

5 The balls here laid on the marked line at the bowler's end of the platform show whence they are delivered by the player after he has taken his run along five or six feet of the platform.

6. The balls lying in the grooves show how they are delivered to the bowler. They are returned to him at every setting up of the pins.

At the further end of the platform is a recess of a few feet for the pins to fall in, and beyond this (to stop the balls) is a cushion covered with hide, which swings on hinges, and is reverberated by springs.

On one side of the room are sofas for the spectators, and at the bowling end seats for the bowlers; also refreshment tables.

In the American Bowling Saloon, (393, Strand,) whence by the civility of Mr. Thomas Robson, the proprietor, the present particulars have been collected, there are six platforms (running parallel to each other,) and sometimes as many as forty or fifty players engaged on them at one time; especially of an evening, when the saloon is brilliantly lighted, and enlivened by music.

The chief art in playing at this somewhat athletic game seems to consist in hitting the apex or point-pin a half ball, (the larger the ball, the greater the chance of success,) but dexterity is only to be acquired by practice. Some players are so expert as to throw down the whole ten pins at one blow several times in succession, and as they are allowed three balls to each division, or setting up of the pins, those which are spared count in addition; thus if a player at starting should knock down all the ten pins at one blow, this would count ten, and would leave a *double spare* or two spare balls, with which if he threw down eight more, he would add that number to his score and count eighteen in the first division, and then go on to the second division with his next three balls. If by a run of luck or skill the player should knock all ten pins with single balls, six times in the course of his ten *divisions*, he would have twelve balls to spare and would therefore be entitled to add to his score whatever he could make with them. When the ten pins are thrown down with two balls, one ball is spared, and counted after the same manner. The highest number it is possible to make with the balls allotted to the ten divisions, is three hundred, *i. e.* ten for each of thirty balls. The mode of keeping count is on a chequered slate of ten times ten squares, numbered from one to ten down the left or front side, the initials of the different players being placed at the head of the columns. It is usual either for players to follow alternately in single divisions or to play 2, 3, or 5 divisions, at a standing, as may be agreed.

The uninitiated had better not be too fierce in his first onslaught, especially if he play with heavy balls, as the exercise is likely to try the muscles of his arm rather severely, and may leave a reminiscence for some days afterwards.

The balls are usually of four different kinds, varying in size from four to eight inches in diameter, and from four or five to ten or eleven pounds weight.

RULES OF THE GAME.

I. Each player to play sixpence per game, and be allowed three balls for each of the ten divisions; but when spare balls are obtained, then to play on to the extent of them.

II. Any number of players (not exceeding ten) can play together; the lowest half-division paying the game of the highest.

III. Gambling strictly prohibited.

IV. In playing, all pins knocked down considered fair, whether obtained by a front or back (*i. e.* reverberated) ball.

V. No gentleman allowed to stand on the platform in front of the alleys except the players.

VI. All ties to be decided by a single ball.

VII. The marked line on the alleys is the utmost limit allowed to players in advancing to deliver the ball.

VIII. Should any dispute arise between players, the Marker to be called as umpire, and his decision to be final.

IX. The sofas behind the players to be reserved exclusively for their use.

X. Two players cannot retain any alley exclusively to themselves when other parties are waiting to play.

XI. Pitching or lofting the balls is not permitted, and any player doing so (after notice) forfeits his game from that point.

THERE are several varieties of the game played in the United States, among which are the following:

NINE BALL GAME, SOMETIMES CALLED BALTIMORE GAME.

Any number may join in this; each player has nine balls. He may play on until out, or rest on each hand of three balls. Where two are engaged, the one making the least number of pins, pays for the game.

This is, however, often played as a match, in which case if five are rolling, the two highest are clear, the third pays half a game, and the two lowest each pay for a whole game. The same proportion is to be observed when the number of players is increased. Spare balls are counted in this as all others, except the Philadelphia Game.

MATCH GAME

Is played leg and leg, as it is called. Any even number of persons may join, rolling against the same number, three balls only to each. Two semi-circles are drawn on the board, facing outwards, in which the legs of the game are to be marked.

The result of each hand of three balls is put down, until all are out, when the lowest party have one leg marked against them. Thus: party A and party B are playing; the first make on all their balls, 65; the last, 50; party B loses one leg of the game. They roll again, when party B makes 60, and party A 50. A here loses one leg; the third rolling decides the game, by the lowest party paying.

I have here supposed the game to be best out of three rollings, though this is optional with the players. I should prefer five legs to the game, the interest being much greater; and again, many persons who are not constant players require two or three balls to be accustomed to them and the alleys. The price of this is double that of the Baltimore.

PHILADELPHIA GAME.

Nine balls to each player, spare balls not counted; each hand rolls out his nine balls, counting the actual number of pins down, and when all are down they are set up again, continuing until the nine balls are out. An unskilful ball may sometimes, by striking out the head centre pin, make it no easy task to count a large number.

WITHOUT THE CENTRE PIN.

This is played by merely removing the head centre pin. As remarked in the Philadelphia Game, a good player only can make any large number, the ball often passing through the opening thus made, without striking either of the pins.

COCKED HAT

Is played by placing three pins up; the two quarter are outer, and the head centre pins. In many other games, strength and chance may sometimes do much for one, but in this skill only can be successful.

FOUR PIN GAME.

THE two quarter, the head and back centre pins, are placed on the alley the same as "Cocked Hat," with the addition of the back centre pin. As in Cocked Hat, a poor player must always lose.

TO LEAVE CENTRE PIN STANDING

A DIFFICULT game even for a skilful player. The object is to make but nine pins, which counts one; a ten-strike, or where all the pins are down by three balls, counts nothing.

BOSTON GAME.

IN this game the four back pins only are left standing. Three balls to each player. One pin out will count six, but the whole five must be down to count ten.

GAME FOR THE SMALLEST NUMBER.

THIS is a singular, but not less interesting game than any other played.

In all the others the object is to make as *many* pins as possible; in this to make as *few*.

Thus: the balls must all run off the end of the alley, as those rolling off before reaching the end will each count ten. A good player may sometimes get but one pin—a good player only can do this. Three balls allowed each player. In a party of two or three the largest number of pins pays, an increased party the same proportion.

I have seen ordinary players make more pins at this game than when counting by numbers, as the ball must be nicely balanced that will strike but one pin in passing off the end of the alley.

COUNTING OLD AND NEW.

THIS is rarely understood by occasional players, but may be learned by a few moments practice on the board.

The players having each nine balls, should the first ball bring the frame down, in other words be a ten-strike, the player will mark a double check mark above his first compartment; should his second produce the same number, a similar mark above the space to the right; if the third has the same result a double check is marked in the third space

Thus,—the players initial to the left of his game:—

A	‡ 30	‡ 28	‡ 18	—76. This is made with 5 Balls.
B	† 20	‡ 20	† 20	—60. This with 6 Balls.

Explanation.—His fourth ball will count the number of pins made with it, adding the two spares or 20; thus, if he make with his fourth ball 8 pins, he has on his second compartment 28. Should his fifth ball roll off the alley, he will have made 18, the number counted on the previous spares.

The above method is extensively used in the cities, having been adopted from the fact of reducing the time occupied by one game, whilst it is equally interesting with the plan of counting for the three balls, separately, and at the same time gives the player an opportunity of making a heavy game.

HOW TO PLAY DOMINOES.

DOMINOES are pieces of ivory or bone, generally with ebony backs. On the face of each there are two compartments, in each of which there is found either a blank, or black pits, from one to six. These are called, according to the numbers shown, Double-Blank, Blank-Ace, Blank-Deuce, Blank-Trey, Blank-Four, Blank-Five, Blank-Six; Double-Ace, Ace-Deuce, Ace-Trey, Ace-Four, Ace-Five, Ace-Six; Double-Deuce, Deuce-Trey, Deuce-Four, Deuce-Five, Deuce Six; Double-Trey, Trey-Four, Trey Five, Trey-Six; Double-Four, Four-Five, Four-Six; Double-Five, Five-Six; and Double-Six—being twenty.eight in all. They are shuffled on the table with their backs up, and each player draws at random the number that the game requires. There are various games, but those principally played are the Block, Draw, Muggins, Rounce, Euchre, Poker, Bingo, Matador, and Bergen.

BLOCK GAME.

Each player draws seven from the pool. The highest double leads in the first hand, and, after that, each player leads alternately until the end of the game. The pieces are played one at a time, and each piece to be played must match the end of a piece that does not join any other. If a player cannot play, the next plays. If neither can play, the set is blocked, and they count the number of spots on the pieces each still holds. Whoever has the lowest number of spots adds to his count the number held by his opponents. If there are two with the same number of spots, and they are lower than their opponents, there is no count. If any one is able to play his last piece while his opponents holds theirs, he cries "Domino," and wins the hand, and adds to his count the number of spots the rest hold. The number required to win the game is one hundred, but it may be made less by agreement.

DRAW GAME

Each player draws seven, as in the block game, and the game is subject to the same rule as block, except when a player cannot play he is obliged to draw from the pool until he can play, or has exhausted the stock of pieces, even though the game be blocked by his adversary. The player may draw as many pieces as he pleases. He *must* draw until he can match. After a lead has been made, there is no abridgment to this right. Many persons confound the Draw game with Muggins and the Bergen game, and in those games the rule is different, as follows: When a player *can* play, he is obliged to. The object of drawing is to enable him to play. Having drawn the required piece, the rule to play remains imperative as before. The *Draw game* is, however, based upon the unabridged right to draw, and is known as a distinctive game by this privilege only.

MUGGINS.

Each player draws five pieces. The highest Double leads after that they lead alternately. The count is made by fives. If the one who leads can put down any domino containing spots that amount to five or ten, as the Double Five, Six-Four, Five-Blank, Trey-Deuce, etc., he counts that number to his score in the game. In matching, if a piece can be put down so as to make five, ten, fifteen or twenty, by adding the spots contained on both ends of the row, it counts to the score of the one setting it. Thus a Trey being at one end, and a Five being at the other, the next player in order putting down a Deuce-Five would score five; or, if Double-Trey was at one end, and a player was successful in playing so as to get Double-Deuce at the other end, it would score ten for him. A Double-Six being at one end, and Four at the other, if the next player set down a

Double-Four, he counts twenty—Double-Six, *i. e.* 12 + Double-Four, *i. e.* 8 = 20. The player who makes a count must instantly announce it when he plays his piece, and if he fail to do so, or if he announces the count wrongly, and any of his opponents call "Muggins," he is debarred from scoring the count. If a player cannot match he draws from the pool, the same as in the Draw game, until he gets the piece required to match either end, or exhausts the pool. As in the Draw or Block game, the first one who plays his last piece adds to his count the spots his opponents have; and the same if he gains them when the game is blocked, by having the lowest count. But the sum thus added to the score is some multiple of five nearest the actual amount. Thus, if his opponents have twenty spots, and he has nineteen, he adds twenty to his score. If they have twenty-two he adds twenty, because that is the nearest multiple of five; but if they have twenty- three he would add twenty-five, twenty-three being nearer that than to twenty. The number of the game is two hundred, if two play; but one hundred and fifty, if there be three or more players.

BERGEN GAME.

Each player draws six pieces from the pool. The lowest double leads at the beginning, and is called a double-header. After that the parties lead alternately from right to left. If no one has a Double when his turn comes to lead, he plays the lowest piece he has. When a player sets down a piece which makes the extremities of the line the same, it is called a double-header. If one of the extremities be a Double, and the next player can lay a piece that will make the other extremity of the same value, or if a Double can be added to one end of a double-header, it makes a triple-header. If a player is not able to match from his hand, he draws one piece from the pool and plays. If he is still not able to play, the next plays, or draws, and so on alternately. If domino is made, the one who makes it wins the hand. If it be blocked, they count and the lowest wins; but if the lowest holds a Double in his hand, and his opponent none, the opponent wins. Or if there be two with Doubles, and one with none, the last wins. If there be a double in each hand, the lowest double wins. If there be more than one Double in any one's hand, and all have Doubles, the one with the least number of Doubles wins, without reference to the size of the Doubles he holds. Thus: if a player hold two Doubles, though they be the Double-Blank and Double-Ace, and his adversary holds but one Double, though it be the Double-Six, the latter wins. The game is ten when three or four play, and fifteen when two. A hand won by either "domino" or counting, scores one. A double-header, either led or made, counts two. A triple-header counts three. But when either party is within two of being out, a double-header or a triple-header will count him but one; and if he be within three of being out, a triple-header will count him but two. A prudent player will retain the Doubles in his hand as long as possible, in order to make triple-headers.

DOMINO ROUNCE.

This is a pleasant game, and from two to four may participate in it. The pieces of rank are Six to Blank, and the Doubles are the best of each suit, trump being superior to any other suit. The game begins by "turning for trump," and he who turns the highest domino is trump-holder for that hand. The dominos are then shuffled, and each player takes five pieces, when the player at the *right* of the trump-holder turns the trump, and the end of the piece having the greatest number of spots upon it becomes trump for that round. The players to the left of the trump-holder then announces in regular succession whether they will stand, discard their hand and take a dummy, or pass. When two or three play there is only one dummy of seven pieces, and the eldest hand has the privilege of taking it. When all the players pass up to the trump-holder, the last player may elect to give the trump-holder a score of five points instead of standing or playing dummy. The trump-holder may, if he chooses, discard a weak piece and take in the trump turned, or he may discard his hand and take a dummy, provided there is one left; in which case he must abandon the trump turned. The player who takes a dummy must discard so as to leave only five pieces in his hand. After the first hand, the trump passes to the players at the left in succession. The game begins at fifteen, and is counted down until the score is "wiped out," each trick counting one. The player who fails to take a trick with his hand is "Rounced," *i. e.*, sent up five points. It is imperative that suit should be followed, and if in hand, trump led after a trick as in Loo, but a player is not compelled to "head," *i. e.*, take a trick when he cannot follow suit.

DOMINO EUCHRE.

This game is usually played by four persons. The pieces rank as follows: The Double of the trump suit is the Right Bower, and the next lower Double is the Left Bower. There is, however, an exception to this rule, for when Blank is the trump it being impossible to have a lower Double than the Double-Blank, the Double-Six is adopted instead, and becomes the Left Bower. In this instance the lowest Double is Right Bower, and the highest Double is Left Bower. After the Right and Left Bower the value of the Dominoes is governed by the number of spots following the trump. For instance, if Six is trump, the Double-Six is Right Bower, and the Double-Five is Left Bower, followed by Six-Five, Six-Four, Six-Trey, and so on down to Six-Blank. If Ace be the trump, the Double-Ace is Right-Bower, and the Double-Blank is Left Bower, the Ace-Six is next in value, the Ace-Five is next, and so on down to the Ace-Blank But when the Blank is trump, the Double Blank is Right-Bower and the Double-Six becomes Left Bower, the next trump in importance being Blank-Six, the next, Blank-Five, and so on down to Blank-Ace, which is the lowest trump. When a suit is not trump, the value of the pieces take rank from the Double of the suit in regular order, downward.

At the beginning of the game the players usually draw to decide who shall turn up trumps, he who draws the lowest piece is entitled to the privilege, and is termed the dealer. When the dominoes have again been shuffled, each player draws five pieces, beginning with the eldest hand; the dealer then turns up one of the remaining pieces for trump. That portion of the domino which has the highest number of spots upon it determines the suit of the trump. Thus, if Six-Ace be the piece turned, then Six is trump suit. After the first hand the privilege of turning trump passes to each player in succession. The eldest hand does not have the lead unless he exercises the privilege of ordering up, or making the trump. Only the player who takes the responsibility of the trump, that is, the player who takes up, orders up, assists, or makes the trump, has the right to lead. With this exception, Domino Euchre is like the card game of the same name.

DOMINO POKER.

In this game only twenty pieces are employed, the Double-Ace and all the Blanks being discarded. The hands rank in regular order, from one pair up to the Royal Hand, which is the highest hand that can be held, as follows:

One Pair.—Any two Doubles; Double-Six and Double-Deuce will beat Double-Five and Double-Four.

Flush.—Any five of a suit not in consecutive order; as Six-Ace, Six-Trey, Six-Four, Six-Five and Double-Six.

Triplets, or Threes.—Any three Doubles. The Double-Ace and Double-Blank being discarded, it follows that only one hand of triplets can be out in the same deal.

Straight Four.—A sequence, or rotation of Fours; as Four-Six; Four-Five, Double-Four, Four-Trey, and Four-Deuce.

Full Hand.—Three Doubles, and two of any suit; as Double-Six, Double-Trey and Double-Deuce, together with Deuce-Four and Deuce-Ace.

Straight Five.—A sequence, or rotation of Fives.

Fours.—Any four Doubles.

Straight Six.—A sequence, or rotation of Sixes.

Royal Hand, or Invincible.—Five Doubles.

When none of the above hands are out, the best is determined by the rank of the highest leading pieces; thus, a hand led by Double-Six is superior to a hand led by Doubie-Five, but a hand headed by Double-Deuce will beat Six-Five, and Six-Five will outrank Five-Four.

Domino Poker is governed by the same laws as the card game called Straight Poker, and is played in precisely the same manner; one game being played with cards and the other with dominoes. The hands consequently rank differently, but in every other particular they are identical.

BINGO.

This game is played as similarly to the card game of Sixty-Six as the difference between dominoes and cards will permit. The rank of pieces is the same as in other domino games, except that Blanks count as seven spots. The Double-Blank, which is called Bingo, and counts for fourteen spots, is the highest Domino, and will take the Double of trumps.

The game is played by two persons, and is commenced by each drawing for the lead, and he who draws the lowest piece has the lead. Each player then draws seven pieces, after which the eldest hand turns up another piece, the highest spot on which is trumps. The eldest hand then leads, and the play is conducted in the same manner as Sixty-Six at cards.

The game consists of seven points, which are made in the following manner: The player who first counts seventy, scores one point towards game; if he makes seventy before his opponent has counted thirty, he scores two points; if before his adversary has won a trick, three points. If Bingo capture the Double of trumps, it adds at once one point to the winner of the trick.

The pieces count as follows to the winner of the trick containing them: the Double of trumps always twenty-eight; the other Doubles and all the other trumps according to their spots; the Six-Four and Three-Blank are always good for ten each, whether trumps or not; the other pieces have no value.

If a player have, at any time, two Doubles in his hand, he can, when it is his turn to lead, play one, show the other, and announce twenty points, which are added to his count as soon as he has won a trick. If he holds three Doubles, he counts forty for four Doubles, fifty; for five Doubles, sixty; for six Doubles, seventy points. If Bingo be among the Doubles held, it adds ten more to the count.

MATADOR.

This differs from all other games of Dominoes, in this great point, that each player, instead of matching the pieces, must make up the complement of seven. For instance, a Five requires a Two to be played to it, because two added to five make *seven*. On a Six, an Ace must be played; on a Four, a Three, spot, and *vice versa*.

It will be seen that there is no piece capable of making a Seven of a Blank; to obviate this difficulty there are four *Matadors*, the Double-Blank, and three natural Seven-spots, namely-Six-Ace, Five-Two and Four-Three. These four Matadors can be played anywhere, at any time, and are, of course, the only ones which can be played on a Blank.

Each player, at the commencement, draws three pieces; the one who has the highest Doublet commences; or, if neither have a Doublet, then the highest piece.

We will suppose Double-Four to have been led, the player, whose turn it is next, must play a Three to it; or failing to have a Three in his hand, must draw till he gets one. Supposing it to be a Three-Five, the end spots will be a Four and a Five—the next player must then either play a Three on the Four, or a Two on the Five, and so on.

This game may be played by two, three, or four persons. When two play, there must be three pieces left undrawn, to prevent each from knowing exactly his opponents hand. When more than two engage in the game, all the Dominos may be drawn. The player who makes domino first, counts the spots on the other hand, or hands, and scores them toward game, which is one hundred or more, as agreed on before commencing the game.

If domino be not made before the drawing is ended, and a player cannot play in his turn, he must pass and await his next turn to play, but he must play if he can; the failure to do so deprives him of any caunt he may make with that hand.

In playing, a Doublet counts only as a single piece; for instance, Double-Six is a Six, and can only be played on an Ace spot, or on Double-Ace; but if left in hand after domino is called, it counts twelve points to the winner.

If the game be blocked, and neither player can make domino, then the one whose hand contains the least number of spots wins, but his own hand does not count to his score.

The Blanks are very valuable at this game—the Double Blank being the most valuable of all the Matadors. As it is impossible to make a Seven against a Blank, so that if you hold Blanks you may easily block the game and count.

When you have the worst of the game, and indeed, at other times as well, guard against your adversary's Blanks, and prevent him from making them; which you may do by playing only those dominos which fit with the Blanks already down.

Never play a Blank at the lead unless you have a Matador or a corresponding Blank.

Keep back your Double-Blank till your opponent makes it Blanks all; you can then force him to play a Matador, or compel him to draw till he obtains one. It is better to have a mixed hand.

TIDDLE-A-WINK.

This is a very amusing game, and suitable for a round party. If six or more play, each takes three dominos. The Double-Six is then called for, and the person holding it leads with it.

If it is not out the next highest double is called forth, and so on downwards until a start is made.

In this game, he who plays a Double, either at the lead or at any other part of the game, is entitled to play again if he can—thus obtaining two turns instead of one. The game then proceeds in the ordinary way, and he who plays out first cries Tiddle-a-wink, having won. In the event of the game being blocked, he who holds the lowest number of pips wins.

DICE.

DICE are small cubes of ivory or bone, marked on each of their sides by spots, representing one, two, etc., up to six—and arranged in a similar manner to the corresponding spots on dominoes. The sum of the spots on the opposite sides of a die is always seven. Thus Six, Five, and Four are opposite Ace, Two, and Three respectively.

A Dice-box is a cylindrical case, generally about four inches high, and one and a half or two inches in diameter, open at the top, and usually grooved inside, to insure the thorough shaking of the Dice. In all Dice games, unless any different arrangements be previously made, the highest throw wins. Dice games are generally played with three Dice. Vingt-un, however, requires one Dice only; and Draw-Poker is played with five Dice, there being five cards in a hand in the card game of the same name. Backgammon, although played with the aid of two Dice, can hardly be considered a Dice game. The most simple game is that of

THROWING DICE.

Each player throws the three Dice, three times, and the sum of the spots, which are uppermost at each throw, are added together and placed to the score of that player. Ties throw over again, if it be necessary to establish any result.

For instance: A is throwing Dice; at the first throw he makes Ace, Four and Six, which added together count eleven. His second throw is Five, Two and Three, together ten. Third throw two Fives and a Four, making fourteen—the sum of eleven, ten and fourteen, which is thirty-five, is counted to his score. And so with any number of players—the one who scores the highest winning the game.

When articles are Raffled, *i. e.*, put up at lottery, the future possession of them being decided by the use of Dice, the method usually adopted is that of Throwing Dice. and not Raffles, as the term used would seem to imply.

RAFFLES.

Three Dice are used, which are thrown by each player until he succeeds in throwing two alike; the first throw made containing a pair, counts the number of spots to the thrower's score. Triplets, or three alike, take precedence of pairs, so that three Aces (the lowest triplet) will beat two Sixes and a Five.

This is sometimes, by previous arrangement, played differently, triplets counting only as pairs—thus three Fives would be reckoned as fifteen points, and would be beaten by two Fives and a Six.

DRAW POKER.

Is played with five Dice; each player having one throw, with the privilege of a second throw if he desire it. In the first throw all the five Dice must be thrown—the player can leave all, or as many as he pleases, on the table, then gather up such as do not satisfy him, and throw them again, it being understood that a player can throw twice if he pleases, but is not *obliged* to throw more than once if he be content with the result of the first throw.

The throws rank in the same manner as in the card game, beginning with the lowest; one pair, two pairs, triplets, a full hand, four of the same. The highest throw is five alike, ranking in the order of their denomination, from six down to one; so that five Sixes make an invincible hand; this, of course, can only occur in the Dice game, while a flush occurs only in the card game.

It should be understood that Six is the highest and Ace the lowest, the intermediate numbers ranking accordingly.

Suppose A is throwing at Draw Poker, and the first throw consist of 5, 3, 6, 2 and 5. He will naturally leave the two 5's on the table, and throw again with the three remaining Dice—if this second throw is a lucky one, he may throw a a pair of Two's and a Five—this will give him a full hand of Fives.

MULTIPLICATION.

This is played with three Dice, and three throws, as follows: the first throw is with three Dice; the highest one is left on the table, and the other two taken up and thrown again; the higher one is left, and the lower one is taken up and thrown again. The spots on the two left on the table are added together, and the sum multiplied by the spots on the third, or last die thrown; and this total placed to the score of the thrower.

Thus, we will suppose the player to throw as follows:

First throw, say Three, Two, and Five; the Five will be left on the table, and the Three and Two returned into the Dice-box for the

Second throw, say Four and Six; the Six will remain on the table, and the Four replaced in the Dice-box.

Third throw, say Three;

This will count 33; thus, the sum of Five and Six, the Dice remaining on the table after the first and second throws, is eleven; this sum multiplied by three, the result of the third throw, makes 33.

ROUND THE SPOT.

This is played with three Dice, which are thrown three times—the sum of the spot being thus reckoned—those spots only count which lay around a central spot, viz., the Three and Five—the Three spot counting for two, and the Five spot for Four—thus it will be seen that Six, Four, Two, and Ace do not count at all; and therefore a player may throw three times and count nothing.

GOING TO BOSTON.

This is also played with three Dice, which are thrown precisely as in Multiplication. The difference is in the counting: the result of the last throw being added to, instead of serving for a multiplier of, the sum of the two remaining on the table. Thus, making use of the example of the last game, the thrower would count 14, the sum of 5, 6, and 3.

HELP YOUR NEIGHBOR.

This amusing game is played with three Dice, and may be played by six persons as follows:

The players throw in regular rotation. The first player, or number one, throws 2, 4, 6, and as he has not thrown *one*, the number corresponding to his own, he scores nothing; but 6 being the highest number thrown, number six scores 6 points.

The second player now throws, and he throws 2, 3, 5; he therefore counts two, and helps his neighbor five to 5 points.

The third player throws, and he throws *Fours*, so he gets nothing, while his neighbor number four, scores 4 points; the raffles counting 4 instead of 12.

Number four now plays, and throws 1, 3, 3, making nothing for himself, but 3 for number three, or the third player.

Number five being the next player, throws three Fives, which count him 5 points.

Number six throws three Aces, which counts him nothing, but enables number one to score 1 point.

In this way the game proceeds until some one of the players wins the game, by making the number of points previously agreed upon. When the game is played for a pool made up by the joint contributions of the players, the first man out wins; but if for refreshments, the last player out loses.

SWEAT OR CHUCKER LUCK

This game is extensively played on our Western rivers, upon race-fields, and at all large gatherings of men. The percentage of the game, when fairly played, is very strong, but the low gamblers who generally play it, add to its strength by skillful cheating. It is played with Dice upon a cloth numbered thus:

1	2	3	4	5	6

The money bet is deposited upon these numbers, according to the choice or fancy of the player. The bets being made, the "dicer" puts three Dice into a cup, shakes them up, and throws them upon the table; the numbers thrown win for the player, while the bank takes all the money not upon the fortunate numbers.

For example: if a bet be placed upon the 6, and one Six is thrown, the amount bet is paid—if two Sixes have been thrown, the bet is paid double, and triple if three Sixes have been thrown.

This constitutes the well-known game of "*Sweat*," over which many an unlucky player has *sweat* "more than the law allows."

VINGT-UN

Is played with a single die, each player throwing it as many times as is necessary to get the sum of the spots equal to or as near as possible, but not over, twenty-one. Throwing twenty-two or more *bursts* the player, depriving him of further participation in the game for that round. The thrower of twenty-one, or failing that, the nearest to it wins the game; but where a forfeit is played for, the player who fails the most in approaching to twenty-one, loses the game. We will suppose B playing at Vingt-un, and throws as follows, viz.: Six, Four, Ace and Five; he has now sixteen, and should his next three throws be a Five, he will be just twenty-one, but if his last throw, instead of Five, had been Six, it would have *burst* him, as he would be twenty-two.

SHUFFLE-BOARD.

THIS is an old Scotch game, and has also been long in use in some parts of Germany, but it is only occasionally to be found in this country. It bears some resemblance to the game of bowls, only that instead of balls, flat weights, are slid down a board previously sprinkled with fine, dry sand. The board should be thirty feet long, and twenty inches wide, adjusted to a perfect level, and constructed of a material sufficiently strong to prevent warping. All round the outer edges of the board there is a gutter similar to, and serving the same purpose, as the gutter of a Ten-Pin alley. Five inches from each end a line is drawn across and parallel with the ends of the board. The weights, or "pieces," are eight in number, divided into two sets of four each, the pieces of each set having a distinctive mark; they are flat, and should weigh about a pound each.

The game is played by four persons, two on each side—each player having two "pieces." One of each side being at each end of the board. The object of the game is to score twenty-one points, which are made as follows: each piece which lays over, or inside of, the line, at the end of a round is said to be "in," and scores two points for the party to whom it belongs.

Each piece partly projecting over the end of the board at the end of a round, scores three points.

When, at the end of a round, no piece is "in," then that piece which lays nearest to the line counts one point.

A piece lying exactly on the line is considered "in."

Pieces score only as they remain at the end of each round.

Supposing A and B are playing at shuffle-board against C and D; then A and C will occupy one end of the board, and B and D the other end. A commences and "shuffles" one of his pieces, endeavoring to get it "in;" C follows with one of his, and tries either to shuffle his own "in" or drive A's off the board. A then shuffles his remaining pieces, and is followed by C, and the result is scored to either party, as the case may be.

B and D next play in a similar manner from the other end. There are always, therefore, at each end of the board, one of each party to note his partner's and opponent's play, and the party or side that first scores game, wins.

THE RULES OF BRIDGE.

The Rubber.

The Rubber is the best of three games. If the first two games be won by the same players, the third game is not played.

Scoring.

A game consists of thirty points obtained by tricks alone, exclusive of any points counted for Honors, Chicane, or Slam.

Every hand is played out, and any points in excess of the thirty points necessary for the game are counted.

Each trick above six counts two points when spades are trumps, four points when clubs are trumps, six points when diamonds are trumps, eight points when hearts are trumps, and twelve points when there are no trumps.

Honors consist of ace, king, queen, jack, and ten of the trump suit. When there are no trumps they consist of the four aces.

Honors in trumps are thus reckoned:

If a player and his partner jointly hold—

I. The five honors of the trump suit, they score for honors five times the value of the trump suit trick.

II. Any four honors of the trump suit, they score for honors four times the value of the trump suit trick.

III. Any four three honors of the trump suit, they score for honors twice the value of the trump suit trick.

If a player in his own hand holds—

I. The five honors of the trump suit, he and his partner score for honors ten times the value of the trump suit trick.

II. Any four honors of the trump suit, they score for honors eight times the value of the trump suit trick. In this last case, if the player's partner holds the fifth honor, they also score for honors the single value of the trump suit trick.

The value of the trump suit trick referred to in this law is its original value—*e. g.*, two points in spades and six points in diamonds; and the value of honors is in no way affected by any doubling or re-doubling that may take place.

Honors, when there are no trumps, are thus reckoned:

If a player and his partner jointly hold—

I. The four aces, they score for honors forty points.

II. Any three aces, they score for honors thirty points.

If a player in his own hand holds—

The four aces, he and his partner score for honors one hundred points.

Chicane is thus reckoned:

If a player holds no trump, he and his partner score for Chicane twice the value of the trump suit trick. The value of Chicane is in no way affected by any doubling or re-doubling that may take place.

Slam is thus reckoned:

If a player and his partner make, independently of any tricks taken for the revoke penalty—

I. All thirteen tricks, they score for Grand Slam forty points.

II. Twelve tricks, they score for Little Slam twenty points.

Honors, Chicane, and Slam are reckoned in the score at the end of the rubber.

At the end of the rubber, the total scores for tricks, honors, Chicane, and Slam obtained by each player and his partner are added up, one hundred points are added to the score of the winners of the rubber, and the difference between the two scores is the number of points won, or lost, by the winners of the rubber.

If an erroneous score affecting tricks be proved, such mistake may be corrected prior to the conclusion of the game in which it occurred, and such game is not concluded until the last card of the following deal has been dealt, or, in the case of the last game of the rubber, until the score has been made up and agreed.

If an erroneous score affecting honors, Chicane, or Slam be proved, such mistake may be corrected at any time before the score of the rubber has been made up and agreed.

Cutting.

The ace is the lowest card.

In all cases, every player must cut from the same pack.

Should a player expose more than one card, he must cut again.

Formation of Table.

If there are more than four candidates, the players are selected by cutting, those first in the room having the preference. The four who cut the lowest cards play first, and again cut to decide on partners; the two lowest play against the two highest; the lowest is the dealer, who has choice of cards and seats, and, having once made his selection, must abide by it.

When there are more than six candidates, those who cut the two next lowest cards belong to the table, which is complete with six players; on the retirement of one of those six players, the candidate who cut the next lowest card has a prior right to any after-comer to enter the table.

Two players cutting cards of equal value, unless such cards are the two highest, cut again; should they be the two lowest, a fresh cut is necessary to decide which of those two deals.

Three players cutting cards of equal value cut again; should the fourth (or remaining) card be the highest, the two lowest of the new cut are partners, the lower of those two the dealer; should the fourth card be the lowest, the two highest are partners, the original lowest the dealer.

Cutting Out.

At the end of a rubber, should admission be claimed by any one, or by two candidates, he who has, or they who have, played a greater number of consecutive rubbers than the others is, or are, out; but when all have played the same number, they must cut to decide upon the out-goers; the highest are out.

Entry and Re-Entry.

A candidate, *whether he has played or not, can join a table which is not complete by declaring in at any time* prior to any of the players having cut a card, either for the purpose of commencing a fresh rubber or of cutting out.

In the formation of fresh tables, those candidates who have neither belonged to nor played at any other table have the prior right of entry; the others decide their right of admission by cutting.

Any one quitting a table prior to the conclusion of a rubber, may, with consent of the other three players, appoint a substitute in his absence during that rubber.

A player *joining* one table, whilst belonging to another, loses his right of re-entry into the latter, and takes his chance of cutting in, as if he were a fresh candidate.

If any one break up a table, the remaining players have the prior right to him of entry into any other; and should there not be sufficient vacancies at such other table to admit all those candidates, they settle their precedence by cutting.

Dealing.

The pack must neither be shuffled below the table nor so that the face of any card be seen.

The pack must not be shuffled during the play of the hand.

A pack, having been played with, must neither be shuffled by dealing it into packets, nor across the table.

Each player has a right to shuffle once only (except as provided by Law 33) prior to a deal, after a false cut, or when a new deal has occurred.

The dealer's partner must collect the cards for the ensuing deal, and has the first right to shuffle that pack.

Each player, after shuffling, must place the cards, properly collected and face downwards, to the left of the player about to deal.

The dealer has always the right to shuffle last; but should a card or cards be seen during his shuffling, or whilst giving the pack to cut, he may be compelled to re-shuffle.

The Deal.

Each player deals in his turn; the order of dealing goes to the left.

The player on the dealer's right cuts the pack, and, in dividing it, must not leave fewer than four cards in either packet; if in cutting, or in replacing one of the two packets on the other, a card be exposed, or if there be any confusion of the cards, or a doubt as to the exact place in which the pack was divided, there must be a fresh cut.

When a player, whose duty it is to cut, has once separated the pack, he cannot alter his intention; he can neither re-shuffle nor re-cut the cards.

When the pack is cut, should the dealer shuffle the cards, the pack must be cut again.

The fifty-two cards shall be dealt face downwards. The deal is not completed until the last card has been dealt face downwards. *There is no misdeal.*

A New Deal.

There must be a new deal—

I. If, during a deal, or during the play of a hand, the pack be proved to be incorrect or imperfect.

II. If any card be faced in the pack.

III. Unless the cards are dealt into four packets, one at a time and in regular rotation, beginning at the player to the dealer's left.

IV. Should the last card not come in its regular order to the dealer.

V. Should a player have more than thirteen cards, and any one or more of the others less than thirteen cards.

VI. Should the dealer deal two cards at once, or two cards to the same hand, and then deal a third; but if, prior to dealing that card, the dealer can, by altering the position of one card only, rectify such error, he may do so.

VII. Should the dealer omit to have the pack cut to him, and the adversaries discover the error prior to the last card being dealt, and before looking at their cards; but not after having done so.

If, whilst dealing, a card be exposed by either of the dealer's adversaries, the dealer *or his partner* may claim a new deal. A card similarly exposed by the dealer or his partner gives the same claim to each adversary. The claim may not be made by a player who has looked at any of his cards. If a new deal does not take place, the exposed card cannot be called.

If, in dealing, one of the last cards be exposed, and the dealer completes the deal before there is reasonable time to decide as to a fresh deal, *the privilege is not thereby lost.*

If *the dealer*, before he has dealt fifty-one cards, look at any card, his adversaries have a right to see it, and may exact a new deal.

Should three players have their right number of cards—the fourth have less than thirteen, and not discover such deficiency until he has played any of his cards, the deal stands good; should he have played, he is as answerable for any revoke he may have made as if the missing card, or cards, had been in his hand; he may search the other pack for it, or them.

If a pack, during or after a rubber, be proved incorrect or imperfect, such proof does not alter any past score, game, or rubber; that hand in which the imperfection was detected is null and void; the dealer deals again.

Any one dealing out of turn, or with the adversary's cards, may be stopped before the last card is dealt, *otherwise the deal stands good,* and the game must proceed as if no mistake had been made.

A player can neither shuffle, cut, nor deal for his partner without the permission of his opponents.

Declaring Trumps.

The dealer, having examined his hand, has the option of declaring what suit shall be trumps, or whether the hand shall be played without trumps. If he exercise that option, he shall do so by naming the suit, or by saying "No trumps."

If the dealer does not wish to exercise his option, he may pass it to his partner by saying "I bridge it, partner," and his partner must thereupon make the necessary declaration, in the manner provided in the preceding law.

If the dealer's partner make the trump declaration without receiving permission from the dealer, their opponents may demand:

I. That the declaration so made shall stand.

II. That there shall be a new deal.

But if any declaration as to doubling or not doubling shall have been made, or if a new deal is not claimed, the declaration wrongly made shall stand. The eldest hand is the player on the left of the dealer.

If the dealer's partner pass the declaration to the dealer, the eldest hand may demand:

I. That there shall be a new deal.

II. That the dealer's partner shall himself make the declaration.

If either of the dealer's adversaries makes the declaration, the dealer may, after looking at his hand, either claim a fresh deal or proceed as if no such declaration had been made.

A declaration once made cannot be altered, save as provided above.

Doubling and Re-Doubling.

The effect of doubling and re-doubling, and so on, is that the value of each trick above six is doubled, quadrupled, and so on.

After the trump declaration has been made by the dealer or his partner, their adversaries have the right to double. The *eldest hand* has the first right. If he does not wish to double, he shall say to his partner "May I *lead?*" His partner shall answer "Yes," or "I double."

If either of their adversaries elect to double, the dealer and his partner have the right to re-double. The player who has declared the trump shall have the first right. *He may say, "I re-double" or "Satisfied." Should he say the latter, his partner may re-double.*

If the dealer or his partner elect to re-double, their adversaries shall have the right to again double. The original doubler has the first right.

If the right-hand adversary of the dealer double before his partner has asked "May I lead?" the declarer of the trump shall have the right to say whether or not the double shall stand. If he decide that the double shall stand, the process of re-doubling may continue as described in Laws 55, 56, 58.

The process of re-doubling may be continued until the limit of 100 points is reached—the first right to continue the re-doubling on behalf of a partnership belonging to that player who has last re-doubled. *Should he, however, express himself satisfied, the right to continue the re-doubling passes to his partner. Should any player re-double out of turn, the adversary who last doubled shall decide whether or not such double shall stand. If it is decided that the re-double shall stand, the process of re-doubling may continue as described in this and foregoing laws (55 and 56). If any double or re-double out of turn be not accepted there shall be no further doubling in that hand. Any consultation between partners as to doubling or re-doubling will entitle the maker of the trump or the eldest hand, without consultation, to a new deal.*

If the eldest hand lead before the doubling be completed, his partner may re-double only with the consent of the adversary who last doubled; but such lead shall not affect the right of either adversary to double.

When the question, "May I lead?" has been answered in the affirmative, or when the player who has the last right to continue the doubling expresses himself satisfied, the play shall begin.

A declaration once made cannot be altered.

Dummy.

As soon as a card is led, *whether in or out of turn,* the dealer's partner shall place his card face upwards on the table, and the duty of playing the cards from that hand, which is called Dummy, and of claiming and enforcing any penalties arising during the hand, shall devolve upon the dealer, unassisted by his partner.

After exposing Dummy, the dealer's partner has no part whatever in the game, except that he has the right to ask the dealer if he has none of the suit in which he may have renounced. If he call attention to any other incident in the play of the hand, in respect of which any penalty might be exacted, the fact that he has done so shall deprive the dealer of the right of exacting such penalty against his adversaries.

If the dealer's partner, by touching a card, or otherwise, suggest the play of a card from Dummy, either of the adversaries may, but without consulting with his partner, call upon the dealer to play or not to play the card suggested.

When the dealer draws a card, either from his own hand or from Dummy, such card is not considered as played until actually quitted.

A card once played, or named by the dealer as to be played from his own hand or from Dummy, cannot be taken back, except to save a revoke.

The dealer's partner may not look over his adversaries' hands, nor leave his seat for the purpose of watching his partner's play.

Dummy is not liable to any penalty for a revoke, as his adversaries see his cards. Should he revoke, and the error not be discovered until the trick is turned and quitted, the trick stands good.

Dummy being blind and deaf, his partner is not liable to any penalty for an error whence he can gain no advantage. Thus, he may expose some, or all of his cards, without incurring any penalty.

Exposed Cards.

If after the deal has been completed, and before the trump declaration has been made, either the dealer or his partner expose a card from his hand, *the eldest hand* may claim a new deal.

If after the deal has been completed, and before a card is led, any player shall expose a card, his partner shall forfeit any right to double or re-double which he would otherwise have been entitled to exercise; and in the case of a card being so exposed by the leader's partner, the dealer may, instead of calling the card, require the leader not to lead the suit of the exposed card.

Cards Liable to Be Called.

All cards exposed by the dealer's adversaries are liable to be called, and must be left face upwards on the table; but a card is not an exposed card when dropped on the floor, or elsewhere below the table.

The following are exposed cards:

I. Two or more cards played at once.

II. Any card dropped with its face upwards, or in any way exposed on or above the table, even though snatched up so quickly that no one can name it.

If either of the dealer's adversaries play to an imperfect trick the best card on the table, or lead one which is a winning card as against the dealer and his partner, and then lead again, without waiting for his partner to play, or play several such winning cards, one after the other, without waiting for his partner to play, the latter may be called on to win, if he can, the first or any other of those tricks, and the other cards thus improperly played are exposed cards.

Should the dealer indicate that all or any of the remaining tricks are his, he may be required to place his cards face upwards on the table; but they are not liable to be called.

If either of the dealer's adversaries throws his cards on the table face upwards, such cards are exposed, and liable to be called by the dealer.

If all the players throw their cards on the table face upwards, the hands are abandoned, and the score must be left as claimed and admitted. The hands may be examined for the purpose of establishing a revoke, but for no other purpose.

A card detached from the rest of the hand of either of the dealer's adversaries, so as to be named, is liable to be called; but should the dealer name a wrong card, he is liable to have a suit called when first he or his partner have the lead.

If *a player*, who has rendered himself liable to have the highest or lowest of a suit called, or to win or not to win a trick.

fail to play as desired, though able to do so, or if when called on to lead one suit, lead another, having in his hand one or more cards of that suit demanded, he incurs the penalty of a revoke.

If either of the dealer's adversaries lead out of turn, the dealer may call a suit from him or his partner when it is next the turn of either of them to lead, or may call the card erroneously led.

If the dealer lead out of turn either from his own hand or from Dummy, he incurs no penalty; *but he may not rectify the error after the second hand has played.*

If any player lead out of turn and the other three have followed him, the trick is complete, and the error cannot be rectified; but if only the second, or the second and third, have played to the false lead, their cards, on discovery of the mistake, are taken back; and there is no penalty against any one, excepting the original offender, and then only when he is one of the dealer's adversaries.

In no case can a player be compelled to play a card which would oblige him to revoke.

The call of a card may be repeated until such card has been played.

If a player called on to lead a suit have none of it, the penalty is paid.

Cards Played in Error, or Not Played to a Trick.

Should the third hand not have played, and the fourth play before his partner, the latter (not being Dummy or his partner) may be called on to win, or not to win, the trick.

If any one (not being Dummy) omit playing to a former trick, and such error be not discovered until he has played to the next, the adversaries may claim a new deal; should they decide that the deal stand good, or should Dummy have omitted to play to a former trick, and such error be not discovered till he shall have played to the next, the surplus card at the end of the hand is considered to have been played to the imperfect trick, but does not constitute a revoke therein.

If any one play two cards to the same trick, or mix a card with a trick to which it does not properly belong, and the mistake be not discovered until the hand is played out, he (not being Dummy) is answerable for all consequent revokes he may have made. If, during the play of the hand, the error be detected, the tricks may be counted face downwards, in order to ascertain whether there be among them a card too many; should this be the case they may be searched, and the card restored; the player (not being Dummy) is, however, liable for all revokes which he may have meanwhile made.

The Revoke

Is when a player (other than Dummy), holding one or more cards of the suit led, plays a card of a different suit.

The penalty for a revoke:

I. Is at the option of the adversaries, who, at the end of the hand, may, after consultation, either take three tricks from the revoking player and add them to their own—or deduct the value of three tricks from his *existing* score—or add the value of three tricks to their own score;

II. Can be claimed for as many revokes as occur during the hand;

III. Is applicable only to the score of the *game* in which it occurs;

IV. Cannot be divided—*i. e.*, a player cannot add the value of one or two tricks to his own score and deduct the value of one or two from the revoking player.

V. In whatever way the penalty may be enforced, under no circumstances can the side revoking score Game, Grand Slam or Little Slam, that hand. Whatever their previous score may be, the side revoking cannot attain a higher score towards the game than twenty-eight.

A revoke is established, if the trick in which it occur be turned and quitted—*i. e.*, the hand removed from the trick after it has been turned face downwards on the table—or if either the revoking player or his partner, whether in his right turn or otherwise, lead or play to the following trick.

A player may ask his partner whether he has not a card of the suit which he has renounced; should the question be asked before the trick is turned and quitted, subsequent turning and quitting does not establish the revoke, and the error may be corrected, unless the question be answered in the negative, or unless the revoking player or his partner have led or played to the following trick.

At the end of the hand, the claimants of a revoke may search all the tricks.

If a player discover his mistake in time to save a revoke, any player or players who have played after him may withdraw their cards and substitute others, and their cards withdrawn are not liable to be called. If the player in fault be one of the dealer's adversaries, the dealer may call the card thus played in error, or may require him to play his highest or lowest card to that trick in which he has renounced.

If the player in fault be the dealer, the eldest hand may require him to play the highest or lowest card of the suit in which he has renounced, provided both of the dealer's adversaries have played to the current trick; but this penalty cannot be exacted from the dealer when he is fourth in hand, nor can it be enforced at all from Dummy.

If a revoke be claimed, and the accused player or his partner mix the cards before they have been sufficiently examined by the adversaries, the revoke is established. The mixing of the cards only renders the proof of a revoke difficult, but does not prevent the claim, and possible establishment, of the penalty.

A revoke cannot be claimed after the cards have been cut for the following deal.

If a revoke occur, be claimed and proved, bets on the odd trick, or on amount of score, must be decided by the actual state of the score after the penalty is paid.

Should the players on both sides subject themselves to the penalty of one or more revokes, neither can win the game by that hand; each is punished at the discretion of his adversary.

Calling for New Cards.

Any player (on paying for them) before, but not after, the pack be cut for the deal, may call for fresh cards. He must call for two new packs, of which the dealer takes his choice.

General Rules.

Any one during the play of a trick, or after the four cards are played, and before, but not after, they are touched for the purpose of gathering them together, may demand that the cards be placed before their respective players.

If either of the dealer's adversaries, prior to his partner playing, should call attention to the trick—either by saying that it is his, or by naming his card, or, without being required so to do, by drawing it towards him—the dealer may require that opponent's partner to play his highest or lowest of the suit then led, or to win or lose the trick.

Should the partner of the player solely entitled to exact a penalty, suggest or demand the enforcement of it, no penalty can be enforced.

In all cases where a penalty has been incurred, the offender is bound to give reasonable time for the decision of his adversaries.

If a bystander make any remark which calls the attention of a player or players to an oversight affecting the score, he is liable to be called on, by the players only, to pay the stakes and all bets on that game or rubber.

A bystander, by agreement among the players, may decide any question.

A card or cards torn or marked must be either replaced by agreement, or new cards called at the expense of the table.

Once a trick is complete, turned, and quitted, it must not be looked at until the end of the hand.

DUMMY BRIDGE.

Is played by three players.

The player who cuts the lowest card deals first, and has the Dummy throughout the first rubber; the player who cuts the next lowest card has the Dummy for the second rubber.

The dealer can make any of the ordinary Bridge declarations on his own hand, or he can leave it to the Dummy, in which case he must look at the dummy, without exposing it, and must make the declaration as follows:

I. If Dummy holds three or four aces, he must declare "no trumps."

II. If Dummy has not three aces, he must declare his numerically longest suit.

III. If Dummy has two or three suits of equal length, he must declare the strongest, reckoned by addition of the pips, an ace counting eleven, and each of the other honors ten.

IV. If Dummy's equal suits are also of equal strength, reckoned as above, then the most valuable of them must be declared.

The adversaries can double as at ordinary Bridge, and the dealer has the right of re-doubling, although he has seen two hands; but he may not look at his own hand again before deciding whether to re-double. The hand is then played as at ordinary Bridge.

When either of his opponents deals, the player of Dummy must look first at the hand which has to lead, and must double or lead to the first trick before looking at his other hand.

The game can be played in either of the two following ways:

I. As soon as the first card is led, Dummy's hand is exposed on the table, and the game proceeds as at ordinary Bridge.

II. As soon as the first card is led, both the Dummy's hand and the dealer's partner's hand are exposed on the table, and the hand is played Double Dummy.

When it is Dummy's deal, his partner looks at his own hand first, and makes the declaration or passes it precisely as in the case of his own deal, the only difference in the play being that the first lead is by the player on his right, and is consequently through his hand instead of up to it.

In all other cases the Rules of Bridge apply.

Double Dummy.

The rules are the same as in Dummy Bridge, with the following exceptions:

The dealer deals for himself each time, never for his Dummy; and the hand on his left always leads first, and has the first right of doubling.

Neither player may look at more than one of his two hands before the first card is led, excepting in the case of the dealer when the call is passed to Dummy.

Either player is liable to the penalty of a revoke in his own hand, but not in his Dummy.

THREE-HANDED BRIDGE.

Is played by three players, all against all.

The player who cuts the lowest card has the first deal, and plays the Dummy for that hand. The player cutting the next lowest card sits on the dealer's left, and the remaining player on the dealer's right.

When the first hand is finished, the player on the right moves into Dummy's place, and the player on the left (*i. e.*, he who had cut the second lowest card), deals and plays the Dummy for that hand, and so on, until the completion of the rubber; the player on the dealer's right always moving into the vacant seat.

The rules for declaring, leading, and doubling are the same as at Dummy Bridge.

When the dealer wins the odd trick or more, the value of such trick or tricks is scored by him precisely as at ordinary Bridge; but when he loses one or more tricks the value of it or them is scored to each of his opponents above the line, instead of below it.

Under no circumstances do the dealer's opponents score anything below the line. Honors are scored as at ordinary Bridge; and when they are against the dealer they are scored to each opponent equally, however they are held.

The game is 30 scored below the line, as at ordinary Bridge, and the player who first wins two games wins the rubber and adds 100 to his score; but the fact of one player winning his first game does not affect the scores of the other two—they still retain anything that they have scored below the line to count towards the next game.

The rubber consists of four games; but when two games have been won by the same player, the other or others are not played.

At the conclusion of the rubber, the total scores for tricks, honors, Chicane, and Slam obtained by each player are added up, one hundred points are added to the score of the winner, and the difference between his score and that of each of his opponents is the number of points won from or lost to each of them separately by the winner of the rubber. The difference between the scores of the two losers is also paid by the third player to the second.

ETIQUETTE OF BRIDGE.

The following rules belong to the established Etiquette of Bridge. They are not called laws, as it is difficult—in some cases impossible—to apply any penalty to their infraction, and the only remedy is to cease to play with players who habitually disregard them.

It is to be borne in mind that, from the nature of the conditions under which the game is played, acts may be so done, and words so spoken, as to convey a very distinct intimation to a partner. To do so is to offend against the most important of the proprieties of the game.

Declarations ought to be made in a simple manner—*e. g.*, by saying, "I make hearts trumps"; "There are no trumps"; or, "I leave it to you." There ought to be neither intimation of doubt in, or reason for, making this declaration. Nothing ought to be done or said by the declarent which may afford an indication or intimation of the hand which he holds, or draws attention to the state of the score.

A player should avoid any unnecessary hesitation in passing the trump declaration to his partner, or giving any well-marked indication of doubt or perplexity.

Similarly, a player who has the first right of doubling or re-doubling, on behalf of a partnership, ought not to decline to exercise that right, and so pass it to his partner, after any unnecessary hesitation, or after giving any well-marked indication of doubt or perplexity.

Any one, having the lead and one or more winning cards to play, should not draw a second card out of his hand until his partner has played to the first trick, such act being a distinct intimation that the former has played a winning card.

A player who has looked at his cards ought not to give any indication by word or gesture as to the nature of his hand, or call the attention of his partner to the score of the game.

A player who desires the cards to be placed, should do it for his own information only, and not in order to invite the attention of his partner.

No player should object to refer to a bystander, who professes himself uninterested in the game and able to decide, a disputed question of facts; as to who played any particular card—whether honors were claimed though not scored, or *vice versa*—etc., etc.

It is unfair to revoke purposely; having made a revoke, a player is not justified in making a second in order to conceal the first.

HINTS TO BEGINNERS.

The Declaration.

Two kinds of hands are especially adapted for "no trumps"—those with one very strong suit, and those with protection in every suit.

Declare "No Trumps":

With an established black suit of six or more cards, and a king guarded in another suit.

With an established suit, without protection in another suit, if the state of the score is desperate—*e. g.*, with a score of 28 to 0, and a game up in favor of the adversaries.

With three aces or equivalent strength (an ace being considered equal to a king and queen together), with three suits guarded, unless able to make a strong heart declaration or very strong diamond (six with two honors).

With protection in every suit and a king more than one's fair share of honors—*i. e.*, one of each kind.

Always with four aces; but do not sacrifice four honors in hearts to anything less, and seldom sacrifice four honors in diamonds.

Hands containing two long suits are especially strong in a suit declaration.

If the hand is of average strength as regards high cards—*e. g.*, with ace, king, queen, knave, ten, one of each kind, generally declare—

Hearts: With six; with five, including two honors; or four, all honors.

Diamonds: With six; five, including three honors; or four, all honors.

Clubs: With seven, including three honors; or five, with four honors.

Spades: Practically never.

With increased all-round strength the player may declare hearts more readily (with five and one honor), but should be more chary of declaring clubs; diamond declarations are almost independent of the general strength of the hand.

With weak hands, such as with one king only and no other card of value, a defensive declaration of five cards in a black suit can be made.

With nothing of value in the hand, a suit of two spades may be declared; but four clubs, five diamonds, or six hearts would probably prove less expensive.

At advanced states of the score any black suit which gives a good chance of winning the game may be declared.

With one's score at twenty-eight, any suit of five cards may be declared as giving a better chance of the odd trick than a pass.

Passed Declarations.

The dealer's partner should generally declare "no trumps" when he would have done so as dealer, unless there is another good declaration possible; occasionally he may declare with less strength when the only alternative is spades.

Remember that unguarded high cards have little value when they are exposed.

With a hand of nearly "no trump" strength, the best suit can be chosen, even though it consists of four cards only.

With an average hand, the best suit can be chosen if it contains five cards; otherwise a black suit must be declared—spades if both are poor.

With weaker hands, the player may be driven to declare a short suit of spades; but he should nearly always prefer clubs if he can thus obtain two more trumps. With however weak a hand, a suit of six cards should be chosen in preference to a short suit of spades.

Doubling and Re-Doubling.

Compare the strength of your hand with that which would justify an original declaration. If your hand is stronger than this, either by two extra trumps or two extra aces, you may double; or with one extra, if you are to the left of the strong hand.

You may double a spade declaration with five trumps and an otherwise average hand; a spade declaration by the dealer may be doubled with somewhat less strength.

It is safer to double on strength in trumps than on all-round strength.

Double rather more freely when you wish trumps to be led, and also in states of the score when the doubled value will lessen the number of tricks required to give you the game, but will not assist the adversaries.

Doubling by the leader's partner against a "no trump" declaration indicates that the player has a very strong suit which he wishes to be led. In response, the leader will lead his weakest suit as the one most likely to be his partner's strongest.

In some circles a heart is led. The player should ascertain the convention followed before sitting down to play.

In order to re-double, the player should have a very strong hand—nearly two tricks stronger than for doubling.

The Play of the Hand.

Dummy's hand should be carefully examined immediately it is exposed, by all the players, especially the dealer. Many mistakes are made through playing too hurriedly to the first trick, before the position suddenly brought to view is fully realized. The plan of campaign for the hand must be formed at once and adhered to, unless the cards lie more unfavorably than expected.

When the original scheme is seen to be impossible, it is the mark of a good player to change the tactics promptly, and make the best of the situation.

With No Trumps.

The main object of each side is to establish a long suit. Usually the adversaries will endeavor to bring in the suit first opened. The player with the long suit will generally keep every card of it. It is his partner's duty to assist him as much as possible by returning the suit as often as he can, and keeping guards to the dealer's suits. When the suit first opened is abandoned, the object will usually be to bring in the long suit of the original third player, and the positions of the partners will be reversed. The chance of saving the game depends on their coöperation.

Generally lead and return your highest card of a suit which you are endeavoring to establish for your partner; but should you hold five or more cards in the suit opened by your partner, it is likely that you are longer in the suit than he, and you should return your lowest, unless you hold the best card or a sequence of high cards.

The dealer will generally choose the longest suit in the two hands; but he must pay attention to the difficulty of establishing it, which depends on the number and size of the cards held by the adversaries. It is useless to establish a suit in a hand that is too weak in cards of re-entry.

Deep finesses can be made on both sides in the suit to be established. It is not advantageous to win tricks early, but often the reverse. It is often wise to hold up the winning card, both of one's own suit and the adversary's, since being able to win the third round of the suit often determines whether the suit shall be brought in or not. Finesses should seldom be made in suits which neither side is trying to establish.

With a Suit Declared.

The dealer's chief object is to prevent the adversaries making tricks, by discarding his losing cards either to winning high cards in his other hand or to an established suit, the latter course rendering it necessary that trumps should be first led. The dealer should endeavor to make tricks by trumping with the weaker hand, if possible, before leading trumps; it is easier to do this when the weaker hand is unseen. If there is no chance of making worthless trumps by ruffing, it is generally wise to lead trumps even when not holding strong hands.

The two chief objects of the dealer's adversaries are to make tricks before the dealer can discard, and to play the cards to the best advantage by leading through tenaces, and avoiding leading from and up to tenaces. These objects are frequently inconsistent. Early in the hand the greater attention must be paid to tenace play. Avoid leading from a tenace; lead up to Dummy's weak suit, and in a less degree through Dummy's strong suit, if the strength is broken. When the establishment of a suit is threatened, disregard the question of tenaces, and lead suits in which you are strong and Dummy is weak. Do not hold on to a tenace too long. Tricks are frequently lost when one player holds the ace, queen, and his partner the king, knave, and each is afraid of leading into a tenace.

Be cautious of leading a suit in which Dummy is very short, early in the hand. If Dummy is weak, he may make a trick by trumping; if he is strong, he may get a discard. The suit must, however, be led before Dummy has been able to discard from it.

Forcing the dealer involves loss of the lead, and should usually be avoided. It can be done with advantage when the strong hand also has the long suit that is to be feared.

If there is a chance of making tricks by ruffing, try to do so. A singleton lead often gains tricks. A lead from a suit of three cards, not containing a strong sequence, is the worst of all leads.

General Advice.

Do not hesitate in making a declaration, so as to give information as to your hand.

Do not take advantage of such information given by your partner.

Always bear the score in mind. Make certain of saving or winning the game, if possible, by leading out winning cards if you see that there is any danger of losing it.

HOW TO PLAY AUCTION BRIDGE.

The rules governing Auction Bridge are the same as Bridge Whist in all respects, except as to manner of bidding and scoring. After the dealer has made his declaration; i. e., one "spade," or two "no trump," etc., each player in turn on the dealer's left has the right to make a higher declaration, or to double the last bid made, or to redouble a bid which has been doubled. A player cannot double his partner's bid or redouble his partner's double, but he may redouble a bid of his partner which has been doubled by his opponent.

A player in turn may overbid the previous bid any number of times and may also overbid his partner, but he cannot overbid his own declaration which has been passed by the other three players. When the final bid has been made, i. e., when the last declaration has been passed by the other three players, the player who made such bid shall play the Dummy, as in Bridge. A bid of two clubs is higher than oneheart, etc.

After the final bid has been made a player cannot give his partner any information as to a previous bid, whether made by himself or either opponent; but a player is entitled to enquire at any time during the play what was the final bid.

The act of doubling or redoubling reopens the bidding. A player whose bid has been doubled, or whose double has been redoubled, can in his proper turn make a further higher bid.

If a player double out of his turn, the opponent on his left may demand a new deal.

When the final bid has been made the play shall begin, and the player on the left of the bidder shall lead.

The scoring is the same as in Bridge, except when a bidder fails to make good his declaration, his opponents score fifty points for each trick short of the number bid, or if the bid has been doubled or redoubled, one hundred or two hundred, respectively, for each under trick. Neither the bidder nor his opponents score anything toward the game.

When a player whose bid has been doubled makes good by winning at least the declared number of tricks, he scores a bonus of fifty for winning and fifty for each additional trick above his bid. If he or his partner have redoubled, the bonus is doubled.

RULES FOR GAME OF RHUM

(OR RHUMMY)

The Pack.—Full pack of fifty-two cards, which rank from the king down in sequence to the ace; the suits have no rank.

Number of Players.—From two to six—four to six making the best game.

Cutting and Shuffling.—The cards are spread and drawn for choice of seats and the first deal; low wins, and ace is low. Each player has a right to shuffle, the dealer last. Player to the right of the dealer cuts.

Dealing.—When two play, nine cards are given to each; when three play, eight cards to each; when four or more play, seven cards to each. Cards are dealt one at a time, and the next card is turned face up and placed beside the stock, which is left in the center of the table, face down.

Objects of the Game.—To get rid of the cards dealt to the player by laying them out in triplets, or in sequence and suits of three.

The Play.—The player to the left of the dealer must either draw a card from the top of the stock (without showing it), or must take the card that lies face up beside the stock, discarding one in its place after he sees what he gets.

If he holds three of a kind, such as three tens, or three of any suit in sequence, such as 6, 7, 8 of clubs, he lays them face up on the table in front of him. If he has no such combination, he should draw so as to get one together.

The eldest hand having played, each player in turn to his left must draw a card and may lay out any combination he holds, discarding a card in place of the one drawn. Only one combination can be laid down at a time. After a few plays there are usually several cards on the table face up and the player after drawing may play one card at a time on any sequence.

The game is sometimes rendered more difficult by having only one card face up, each discard being placed on the top of the original faced card, so that there are two piles to draw from, one face up and one face down, but only the top card may be taken from either. This makes the game much longer, but adds to the skill demanded, as the cards passed must be remembered. A card once covered cannot be used.

After drawing from the stock and before discarding, any player may get rid of one card in his hand by putting it on some combination already laid down by another player. If he holds the 8 of hearts, for instance, and some one had laid the 5, 6, 7 of hearts on the table, the 8 may be added to those three cards, but only one card at a time may be got rid of in this way.

The first person to get rid of all the cards dealt to him and drawn by him, either by laying six on the table in front of him, or by laying four or five and giving the others to other players' layouts, discarding his last card, wins the game and the others settle with him according to the number of pips on the cards they have left in hand, ace counting one and so on up, the jack 11, queen 12 and king 13.

No player is allowed to lay down any combination or get rid of any combination except in his proper turn, so that if a player wins the game it is too late for any of the others to lay down or get rid of any cards that they could have got rid of.

It is usually better for those who cannot use any of the cards faced on the table to draw from the stock on the chance of getting something to fit their hand, but in case of doubt it is wiser to play for the smaller combinations, such as three treys than for three jacks, because if you do not get the third one before some player wins the game, you will have to pay for the pips on the cards you hold.

The last card drawn from the stock and discarded cannot be taken up for the purpose of reducing a player's pip, but only if it gives a play of threes or by the holding of intervening plays on board.

If all the stock is drawn before any player wins the game, there are two ways to play:

1. All the hands are shown and the lowest pip value wins. In this method the play ends with the person who draws the last card, the next player not being allowed to use his discard.

2. The discards are all gathered up, shuffled and cut, and the top card turned face up, the remaining cards being left face down, and the game proceeds as if the original stock were still there.

HOW TO PLAY HEARTS

This game is played the same as a "No Trump" in Bridge, the object being to take no tricks containing hearts. Each heart scores one against the player taking the trick and the queen of spades scores thirteen against the player taking the trick.

HOW TO PLAY FIVE HUNDRED.

The game of Five Hundred is a game adopted for three players, but is also played by four, two of the players as partners against the other two.

How to Use the Deck.

For the three-handed game, all the cards above the six-spot are used. For the four-handed partner game, all the cards above the three-spot are used, excepting the four of diamonds and hearts. Always use the joker.

How to Deal the Cards.

Choice of seats can be had by cutting cards. The cards are laid out face downwards in the shape of a half circle; each player draws a card; the lowest card drawn wins the deal, the joker lowest of all. If the cards drawn by two players are of the same value, and equally entitled to the deal they draw again; the lowest card thus drawn wins the deal.

The deck is then shuffled and the player to the right of the dealer cuts, and not less than five cards must be left in either packet. The deal is performed by the dealer giving on the first round three cards to each player in rotation, beginning with the player on his left, then two on the second round, three cards on the third, and two on the fourth, making ten cards in all to each player. The three cards for the widow are dealt face down on the table, after the end of the second and before the beginning of the third round. After the first deal the right of dealing passes in regular rotation to the left. A misdeal does not lose the deal.

What Each Card Designates.

The cards in suits, not trumps, rank as in Whist, the ace being the highest and the four being the lowest. When a suit is made trumps, the cards rank as follows: The joker is always the highest trump card; the jack of the suit declared is the next highest trump; the other jack of the same color (black or red, as the case may be) is the third highest trump, and the others follow—ace, king, queen, ten, nine, etc., of the suit declared.

In a "no trump" hand the joker is the only trump card. It can be played in any suit, provided the player has no card of

How to Make a Bid.

the suit led in his hand. If the joker is led, the player leading it has the privilege of naming the suit he wishes played to it, and the players must, if possible, play a card of the suit called for.

After the cards have been dealt, the eldest hand (the player to the left of the dealer) begins the bidding for the privilege of making the trump, or may decline to bid at all if so desired. Each player, in turn continuing to the left, has then the right to bid, but if he bids out of turn he loses the right of bidding for that deal. The highest bidder is entitled to the widow and discards all but ten cards. No bid can be made for less than six nor more than nine tricks. If there is no bid for at least six tricks the cards are bunched and the deal passes to the next player on the left. Each player bids to take a certain number of tricks, calling the suit he is bidding on, thus: Seven in clubs, eight in diamonds, etc. If he is bidding without trumps he must so declare.

A bidder is barred from making any alterations from his bid once made, and if his bid is successful he is compelled to play it out.

The suits rank in value, clubs being the lowest, spades, hearts, diamonds. No trumps being the highest.

The rank of a bid depends upon the score value of the tricks bid. Thus, eight tricks in hearts (240) would outrank eight tricks in spades (180); but nine tricks in clubs (160) would outbid seven tricks in hearts (160), because, although of the same score value, the preference is given to the suit which requires most tricks to make the same score.

Scoring.

The game consists of 500 points. The player whose score first reaches 500 points wins the game. The following table shows the scoring value of the tricks in each suit:

Table of Scoring Values.

If trumps are—	6 Tricks	7 Tricks	8 Tricks	9 Tricks
Spades..........	40	80	120	160
Clubs............	60	120	180	240
Diamonds........	80	160	240	320
Hearts...........	100	200	300	400
No trumps.......	120	240	360	480

After the hand is played out, if the successful bidder makes as many tricks as he has bid, he has the first count; he scores according to the above table. He cannot score for any tricks taken more than he bid; except should he take all ten tricks he is entitled to score 250 in place of any lower amount he has bid. Each player other than the bidder counts ten for every trick he takes, but he cannot score them until after the successful bidder has scored his points. Should the bidder fail to take the required number of tricks bid he is "set back" the number of points his bid calls for. Should the bid successfully made put the bidder out, he may claim the game as soon as the number of tricks he bid are taken. If either of the opponents during the play of the hand should make sufficient points to win the game he cannot score them until after the bidder has scored his points, he having always the right to score first.

How to Play the Hand.

The player who makes the highest bid leads any card he pleases, and each player, beginning with the one to the left of the leader, must play in turn a card to the lead. Each player must follow suit if he can; failure to follow suit when able to do so constitutes a revoke. If he has no card of the suit led he is not compelled to trump, but may play a card of any suit he chooses. When all the players have played to the lead, that constitutes a trick. The winner of the first trick leads to the next, and the playing proceeds in this way until all the cards held by each of the players are played out.

Revoking.

When a revoke is established the cards remaining unplayed, if any, are abandoned. If the bidder has revoked he is set back the amount of his bid, and his opponents score what tricks they have so far made.

If either of the opponents has revoked neither of them can score anything, and the bidder scores the amount of his bid.

Any details relating to the information of the table, shuffling, cards liable to be called, cards played in error or out of turn not covered by the above rules, follow the Rules of Whist.